DEATHS
✦ BIRTHS ✦
MARRIAGES

from
Newspapers Published
in
Hamilton
Madison County
New York

1818-1886

*Abstracted from Newspapers Filed in the
Archives of Colgate University
Hamilton, Madison County
New York*

HERITAGE BOOKS
2008

HERITAGE BOOKS
AN IMPRINT OF HERITAGE BOOKS, INC.

Books, CDs, and more—Worldwide

For our listing of thousands of titles see our website
at
www.HeritageBooks.com

Published 2008 by
HERITAGE BOOKS, INC.
Publishing Division
100 Railroad Ave. #104
Westminster, Maryland 21157

Copied from the original by permission of Mrs. E. P. Smith
by Joyce C. Scott and Mary K. Meyer
1958

Second Edition published by Libra/Pipe Creek Publications
Mt. Airy, Maryland
1996

All rights reserved. No part of this book may be reproduced or transmitted in any form or by any means, electronic or mechanical, including photocopying, recording or by any information storage and retrieval system without written permission from the author, except for the inclusion of brief quotations in a review.

International Standard Book Numbers
Paperbound: 978-0-7884-3296-5
Clothbound: 978-0-7884-7275-6

TABLE OF CONTENTS

Death records.......................1
Birth records....................105
Marriage records.................112
Miscellaneous records............214
Geographical Locator Guide.......221
Index............................231

****

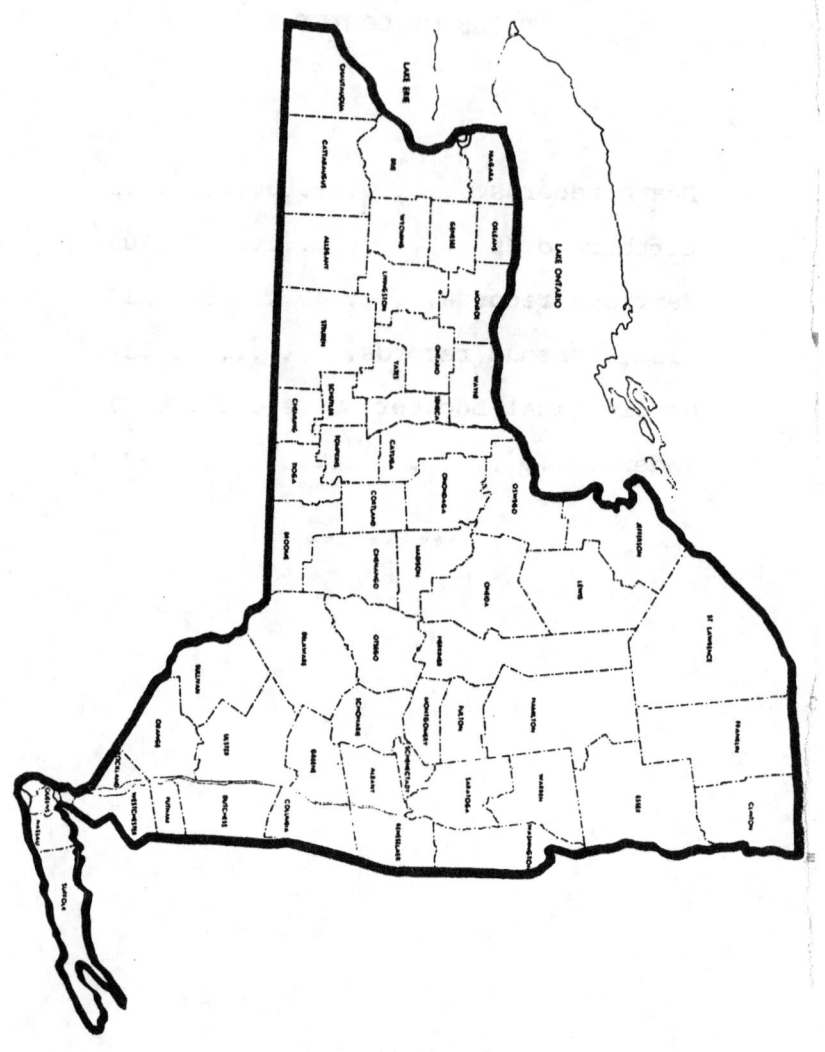

INTRODUCTION

For some time past, Dr. Howard D. Williams, Archivist of Colgate University, Hamilton, New York, has been assembling, as nearly as possible, a complete file of newspapers that have been published in Hamilton, Madison County, New York.

Realizing the value and convenience of having available for easy reference the many names and dates pertaining to residents of the area around Hamilton, Dr. Williams kindly allowed the members of the Sherburne Genealogy Group to have access to the file for the purpose of copying all notices of deaths, births, and marriages for the years 1818-1886, inclusive. These notices are fairly complete for Hamilton and the adjoining towns in Madison County, and include a limited number for towns in northern Chenango County.

In the Index, every name appearing in the notices has been included, with the exception of the ministers who officiated at marriages, who were listed only when their names first appeared.

Representing, as it does, the work of a number of interested persons, and carried on through a period of over three years, there are doubtless errors in copying or typing, for which apologies are hereby made.

The Sherburne Genealogy Group is happy to have had this opportunity to prepare this collection of valuable records relating to our area in Central New York State, and trusts that many searchers will be able to find records herein that would not be available elsewhere. It represents the combined labor of the Group members, but special mention should be made of the assistance rendered by Mrs. Duane Boise, Mrs. A. K. Benedict, and Mrs. John Calman for their work in searching out the items wherever they appeared in each newspaper.

Indexing and typing was done by Mrs. Edwin P. Smith, Sherburne, New York.

DEATH RECORDS

As Published in Newspapers Published in

HAMILTON, MADISON COUNTY, NEW YORK

****

THE HAMILTON RECORDER
Vol. 1, No. 1
For year beginning July 2, 1822

Aug. 16, 1822, at New Woodstock, Mrs. Anna SMITH, wife of Nathan SMITH, at 53 yr.
Aug. 29, 1822, In Hamilton, Mr. Lyman TORRY.
Aug. 29, Mr. Reuben PHILLIPS, long an inhabitant of this town [Hamilton.]
Oct. 2, in Georgetown, Frederick FREVAU, age 115. He fought in the Battle of Bunker Hill and served throughout the Revolutionary War.
Nov. 28, in Hamilton, Mrs. Thirza GREENLY, wife of Dr. Thomas GREENLY, in her 37th year.
Nov. 29, in Lebanon, Charlton CLARKSON, age 29.
Dec. 4, in Hamilton, Mr. John BENEDICT, age 49.
Dec. 2, in Lebanon, Pliny SEXTON, age 33; a suicide. He leaves his wife and two small children.
Dec. 12, in Hamilton, Gurdon KIBBY, at 59.
Dec. 12, in this town [Hamilton], Mr. BEACH, age about 80.
Dec. 12, Lyman HUBBARD, son of Mr. Ira HUBBARD, age 14.
Dec. 12, in Hamilton, Mr. PEASE, age 83.
Dec. 23, in Madison, Job PECKAM, age 65.
Dec. 17, in Hamilton, Abijah POOL Jr.

1823

Jan. 6, in Eaton, Elisha HERRICK, age 43.
Jan. 23, Sally CLEVELAND, age 17.
Jan. 29, Mr. Daniel HARRIS, age 81.
Jan. 28, in Eaton, Eliza, dau. of Stephen FITCH, age 13.
Feb. 17, at Brookfield, Robert GREENE, age 51.
Feb. 18, at Hamilton, Mrs. JUDD, wife of Heman JUDD, age 42.
(No date), in this village [Hamilton], infant son of Mr. Reuben WINCHELL.
Mar. 10, in Hamilton, Mr. Jared PARMELY, age 74.
Mar. 9, infant son of Elisha PAINE, age 3 (?) months.
Mar. 16, in Lebanon, Capt. Allen WOOD, age 37.

HAMILTON RECORDER - 1823

Mar. 26, Mrs. Harriet STOWER, wife of John G. STOWER, Esq., age 27.
Mar. 1, at Truxton, Mrs. Elizabeth BLANCHARD, wife of Dr. Azarial, age 31.
Mar. 13, Calvin, son of Dr. Azarial BLANCHARD, age 11 months.
Apr. 9, Catherine Harriet VAN SICE, age 13.
May 2, in Hamilton, Nancy ELDREDGE, wife of James B. ELDREDGE, age 34.
June 4, in Hamilton, Moses DOTY, age 65. A Revolutionary Pensioner.
July 30, at Ballston, Ralph HASCALL, age 47.
July 29, of consumption, Miss Melissa VALE, daughter of Harry VALE, of Homer.
Aug. 11, in Eaton, Dr. Jason LESTER, age 82.
From Oct. 15th issue: In Steuben, Oneida Co., NY, Samuel SIZER, Esqr., father of Asa B. SIZER, formerly of this County, age 70. He was a Revolutionary soldier.
Last week, in Rome, Miss Ann HUNTINGTON, age 20, second daughter of Henry HUNTINGTON, Esq.
Oct. 13, in Utica, Joseph MOTT, age 42, formerly of Bridgewater, and recently an inhabitant of Hamilton.
Oct. 17, in Hamilton, Samuel HAYWARD, age 72. A Revolutionary Soldier.
Nov. 7, in Hamilton, Mrs. Freedom OLMSTEAD, age 55.
Dec. 18, in Fenner, David MARSH, age 45.
No date: in Litchfield, Conn., Hon. Tapping REEVE, age 75, former Chief Justice of Connecticut.

1824

From Jan. 21st issue: In Brookfield, Elias BUTTON, age 105 years, 7 months & 20 days.
Jan. 23, in Brookfield, Sheffield COLLINS, age 36.
Mar. 16, in Hamilton, Esther CHAPEL, of Montville, Conn., age 73.
Mar. 20, at Lenox, of typhus fever, Hannah PALMER, age 16; also
Mar. 20, at Lenox, Lydia PALMER, age 24, both daughters of Joseph PALMER. There were eight other people in the same family who had the same disease at the same time.
Apr. 13, in Lenox, Joseph PALMER, Esq., age 57.
June 2, in Boston, the Hon. Abraham LINCOLN, of Worcester, age 62.

HAMILTON RECORDER - 1824

June 5, in Lenox, Rebecca MC GREGOR, age 27 years, wife of John, daughter of Joseph PALMER.
July 29, at New Hartford, Mrs. Almeda MONROE, wife of James MUNROE (sic), age 22; late of this town [Hamilton].
Sept. 1, at Smithfield, Henry WELCH, colored man, age 118.
Nov. 16, at Utica, the Hon. Morris S. MILLER, 1st Judge of Oneida County, in his 45th year.
Nov. 24, at Sullivan, William J. HOPKINS, Esq., Counsellor at Law, formerly one of the judges of the Court of Common Pleas of this County.
Nov. 29, at Charleston, SC, Charles PINCKNEY, age 66; a distinguished citizen.

Beginning 1825

Jan. 20, in Eaton, Mrs. Gilbert F. JONES, age 25.
Mar. 15, at Yonkers, [NY], Truman STAFFORD, Esq., of Madison

Vol. IV, No. 1

June 27, in Lebanon, Nahum NILES, age 86.
Sept. 13, at Orleans, Jefferson Co., Mr. Joseph COLWELL, Jr., age 7 years, son of Joseph COLWELL of this place [Hamilton].
Sept. 17, at Natchez, Miss., of yellow fever, Mr. Justin HIGGINS, merchant, formerly of this place [Hamilton].

Beginning 1826

Jan. 10, at Eaton, Charles CRANE, Esq.
Jan. 4, at Erieville, Mr. Sturges PECK, age 22, formerly of this village [Hamilton].
Jan. 3, at Madison, Mr. Lockert BERRY.
Mar. 5, at Eaton, Mr. Benajah DEAN.
Feb. 24, in Hamilton, Mrs. Sophia, age 33, wife of Mr. Matthew COZZENS; and a few hours after her death;
Feb. 24, in Hamilton, William, age 15, son of Mr. COZZENS.
Mar. 1, in Hamilton, Miss Lucinda, age 22, daughter of Mr. Charles SMITH.
June 2, in Hamilton, Daniel SMITH, Esq., age 65.
Sept. 28, Mr. Luke CLARK, of Brookfield, farmer.

HAMILTON RECORDER - 1826

Oct. 24, in Hamilton, Mrs. Sally ELDREDGE, wife of James E. ELDREDGE, Esq., age 40.
Oct. 27, William, son of John FOOTE, Esq., age 3.
Oct. 31, Mrs. Marinda KENT, age 40.
Nov. 13, in Peterboro, Mr. Ira NORTHRUP, age 34.
Nov. 16, in Smyrna, Mrs. Mary K. FOOTE, Consort of the Hon. Isaac FOOTE, Esq., in her 82nd year.
Nov. 29, in Hamilton, Anna Maria, daughter of John P. VAN SICE, age 1 year.

Beginning 1827

Mar. 11, in Hamilton, Mrs. COX, wife of Thomas COX, age 59.
Feb. 23, in Newark, Tioga Co., NY, Mr. Enoch SLOSSON, age 94.
Apr. 20, at Lebanon, Mr. Jonathan BATES, in his 73d year. He was the oldest male settler in the town. He was one of the men who accompanied Cols. Allen and Arnold at the capture of Ticonderoga. He was one of the rear guard that covered the retreat of Gen. Warren when that officer fell at Bunker Hill. He was engaged in several slight skirmishes with marauding parties and was afterwards engaged in the Battle of Newtown when Sullivan defeated the Indians.
Apr. 26, at Lebanon, Mrs. Elizabeth BATES, wife of the late Mr. Jonathan BATES, in her 77th year.
May 2, Mr. Zara SIMMONS, of Madison, age 81. He was one of the first settlers of the town of Madison, and a Revolutionary Soldier.
Apr. 3, in Monson, Mass., Joseph TRUESDELL, son of Perly, age 16.

Vol. VI, No. 1

June 21, in Lebanon, Miss Lois PARKER, age 16.
Nov. 5, in Madison, Mr. Cainan GIFFORD, age 61.

REPUBLICAN REGISTER
Published at Hamilton, Madison County, NY
Vol. 1, No. 1

1828

Aug. 10, Mr. Phillip MATHEWSON, an early settler near the [Hamilton] Center.

1829

Mar. 2, in this town [Hamilton], Mrs. Matilda POOL, wife of Capt. Isaac POOL, age 40 years.
July 5, in Cazenovia, Mrs. Mary LYMAN, wife of Dr. Isaac LYMAN, age 64.
July 8, in Eaton, Hannah DEAN, age 33 years, 1 month.
Aug. 9, in Hamilton, Mrs. Celinda, wife of George ABERT, age 40.
Aug. 7, in Hamilton, John C. PAYNE, age 71.

HAMILTON PALLADIUM
Vol. II, No. 1

July 3, Robert CONICK, age 49.
July 21, at San Augustine, Texas, of typhus fever, Mr. Elisha G. WILLIS, formerly of Eaton, age 21.
Oct. 6, at Leonardsville, Stephen HOXIE, member of the religious Society of Friends, age 101 years, 4 months & 16 days.
Oct. 5, in Jamestown, Mrs. Hannah, wife of Deacon Perez H. BONNEY, age 44.
Oct. 14, in Smyrna, Mrs. Juliaett A., wife of Mr. Vincent SHEPARD, age 22.
Oct. 17, in Hamilton, infant daughter of Prof. John MAGINNIS, age 2 days.
Oct. 22, Mr. Stephen DWINNELL, age 58.

1840

Jan. 31, in Hamilton, Mrs. Lucy W., wife of Wesley LATTIN, age 32.
Feb. 4, in Madison, Miss Maria, daughter of Nathan PECK, in 13th year.
Feb. 29, in Poolville, Mr. James WILLIAMS, age 83; a Revolutionary Pensioner.
Mar. 5, Mr. John STONE, in Hamilton, age 87; a Revolutionary Pensioner.

HAMILTON PALLADIUM - 1840

Apr. 14, at Canastota, in her 20th year, Mary Jane, wife of Israel S. SPENCER, Esq., and daughter of Nathan S. ROBERTS, of Lenox.

1841

July 21, Mr. Hiram GRAY, son of David GRAY, of Hamilton; struck by lightning and instantly killed while working as a carpenter on a barn in West Meredith.

Aug. 20, in Hamilton, Thompson KING, son of Nathaniel KING, age 25.

Aug. 3, at Prarie Du Chien, Wisconsin Territory, John GLEASON, formerly of this village, age 25.

Aug. 28, in Hamilton, Col. George A. WILLIAMS, age 40.

Sept. 19, in Hamilton, Oscar Eugene, youngest son of Alfred WELLS, age 5 months.

Oct. 11, in Eaton, William Henry, only son of Col. William F. BONNEY, age 7 months.

Oct. 14, in Hamilton, George V., oldest son of Mr. John WOODMAN, age 6.

Nov. 1, in Hamilton, Mary C., wife of Rowland R. COLLINS, at 34 years.

Oct. 28, in New Orleans, of yellow fever, Mr. Alfred G. MANNERING, age 35, formerly of this place.

Nov. 30, in Hamilton, J. Rollin ROOT, age 30.

Dec. 13, in Lancaster, WI, Orren DEWEY, age 23, son of Hon. Ebenezer DEWEY, of Laurens, Otsego County, and brother of James DEWEY of Hamilton.

Dec. 30, in Hamilton, Smith PARKS, age 93 years. He was a Revolutionary Soldier.

1842

Feb. 23, at Georgetown, Mrs. Mary G. HEWS, wife of Moses HEWS, in her 44th year.

Feb. 7, at Georgetown, of whooping cough, infant daughter of Samuel and Eleanor BARNETT, age 10 weeks.

Mar. 3, in Eaton, Charles Wesley, son of George W. and Caroline DARROW, age 1 year, 8 months.

Mar. 25, in Hamilton, Mrs. Aner, wife of Pardon MORRIS, age 56.

Apr. 16, in LeRoy, Genesee Co., Joshua Chamberlain, only son of A. S. UPHAM, age 3 years, 2 months, 11 days; also;

Apr. 17, Elizabeth C., daughter of the same, age 4 years, 11 months, 14 days.

HAMILTON PALLADIUM - 1842

May 25, in Lebanon, Francis WHITMORE, age 60. He was one of the early settlers of Lebanon.
June 1, in this village [Hamilton], Helen, daughter of George F. BURGESS, age 9.
June 22, in Eaton, Edward BONNEY, at 77 years.
June 21, in Mayville, Chautauqua Co., NY, Ebenezer P. UPHAM, M.D. in his 51st year, formerly of Hamilton. He read medicine under Dr. GREENLY. Was one of the earliest settlers of Mayville, coming there 24 years ago; was one of the founders of Mayville Academy.
June 10, in Eaton, Mrs. Caroline E. SMITH, age 27, daughter of Mrs. CRAMPHIN.
July 4, in Lebanon, Mary Ann, daughter of Moses and Rosina CAMPBELL, age 9 years, 5 months, 21 days.
Sept. 28, at Columbia, Jackson Co., MI, of consumption, Mrs. Jerusha HAYNES, wife of Hiram HAYNES, daughter of Thomas DIBBLE, Esq. of this town [Hamilton].
Oct. 29, in Hamilton, Isaac WEAVER, son of Zebulon WEAVER, in his 35th year.
Nov. 15, in Madison, Mr. Isaac W. GARDINER, age 58.
Nov. 15, in Hamilton, Mr. James BROWN, age 34.
On Monday morning last, in Eaton, very suddenly, Mr. Joseph SANFORD, age 57.
Nov. 8, in Remsen, Oneida Co., Mr. Alanson MERRIFIELD, age 39.
Nov. 30, in this town [Hamilton], Mr. Oliver HUBBARD, age 82.
Dec. 1, in this town [Hamilton], Mr. Asahel ANDRUS, age 58.

1843

Feb. 4, in this village [Hamilton], Hon. Elisha PAYNE, age 80 years. Mr. Payne was one of the first settlers of this village, having moved here with his brother March 1795. He formerly owned most of the land on which our village is located, after whose name it was called for many years. He has been a converted Christian for 55 years, and a member of the Baptist Church about 45 years. He has had two wives, the second of whom survives. By his first wife he had four children, and by the second sixteen, making twenty in all, who, excepting four who died in infancy, are all living. He was a Soldier of the Revolution, and has been Judge of the Common Pleas for this County.

7

HAMILTON PALLADIUM - 1843

Feb. 11, in this village [Hamilton], Cornelia Ann, only child of Charles MASON, age 2 years, 3 months, 15 days.

Feb. 14, Francis S., son of Hon. L. SHERWOOD, age 2 years, 2 months.

Feb. 22, in Vernon, Mr. Martin TURNER, age 56.

Mar. 1, in New York, Mr. John P. VAN SICE, printer, formerly of this village [Hamilton], age 43.

Mar. 11, in Madison, Mary, consort of J. WICKWIRE, Jr., age 25.

Apr. 18, in Eaton, Mr. Simeon CHUBBUCK, age 86, a Revolutionary Soldier.

Apr. 8, in Binghamton, Sophronia, wife of J. R. ORTON, age 34.

Apr. 13, in Essex Co., NY, after a short illness, Stephen ROWE, in his 34th year.

May 8, in Hamilton, Mrs. C. S., wife of J. EDMUNDS, Jr., age 35.

Apr. 28, in this village [Hamilton], of consumption, Mr. Lyman C. OSGOOD, age 24.

May 3, Mrs. Caroline M. COMPTON, wife of Capt. Henry COMPTON, age 19 years, 5 months.

Feb. 18, in Annsville, Oneida Co., Mahlon, son of James LILLIBRIDGE, in his 15th year, also;

May 15, Ira J., son of James LILLIBRIDGE, age 20 years, 11 months.

May 8, near Baltimore, on his return from a tour in the South for the benefit of his health, Mr. J. O. EDMUNDS, age 32. His remains were brought to this village [Hamilton] and interred beside his wife in the Seminary Burying Ground.

Apr. 24, in this village [Hamilton], Mrs. Martha CHAPELL, age 66.

May 18, in Lenox, Mr. Jacob MONTROSS, age 100 years, 6 months.

May 21, in Watertown, Hon. William RUGER, Senator, age 48.

June 3, in this town [Hamilton], of scarlet fever, Henry G., only child of Daniel P. and Sarah M. HILL, age 1 year, 4 months, 21 days.

June 6, in Sherburne, Doct. Elijah K. WHITE, late from Florida, age about 30. His brother, Dr. Amos K. WHITE, died at the same place less than a year since.

June 25, in this town [Hamilton], Mr. Goodwin BIXBY, age 27.

DEMOCRATIC REFLECTOR
Published Tuesdays, Hamilton NY
Issue of Nov. 1, 1842 being Vol. I, No. 2

Nov. 15, in Hamilton, Mr. James BROWN, age 34.
Nov. 7, in Eaton, Mr. Ashbel MASON, Revolutionary Soldier, age 85 years.
Nov. 6, in Lenox, Miss Fanny M. MONTROSS, in her 24th year.
Nov. 18, in Hamilton, Mr. Cyrus RISLEY, age 18.
Nov. 15, in Madison, Mr. Isaac GARDNER, age 58.
Nov. 13, in Canastota, Mr. David L. SANFORD, son of Beardsley SANFORD, of Harpersfield, age 27.
Nov. 8, in Remsen, Mr. Alanson MERRIFIELD, age 39, formerly of this town [Hamilton].
Nov. 30, in Hamilton, Mr. PEASE, age 82.
Nov. 30, in Hamilton, Mr. Oliver HUBBARD, age 82.
Dec. 1, in Hamilton, Asahel ANDRUS, age 58.
Dec. 31, in East Hamilton, Mrs. Sophia FOOTE, consort of Dr. Noah B. FOOTE, age 66 years, 5 months.

1843

Feb. 5, in Hamilton, Elisha PAYNE, Esq., age 80, one of the first settlers of the town.
Feb. 15, in Hamilton, Cornelia Ann, only child of Charles MASON, Esq., age 2 years, 3 months, 15 days.
Feb. 14, in Hamilton, Francis S., son of the Hon. L. SHERWOOD, age 26 months.
Feb. 17, in Hamilton, Mary, oldest daughter of Zepheniah SHORES, age 6 years, 6 months.
Feb. 23, in Vernon, Mr. Martin TURNER, age 56.
Mar. 18, in Hamilton, Sanford Orsino, son of Col. S. BOON, age 17.
Mar. 17, in Lebanon, Hepzibah, consort of Alanson BISHOP, age 38.
Apr. 8, in Binghamton, Sophronia, wife of J. R. ORTON, and daughter of the late Cyrus HOTCHKISS, of Windsor, age 34.
Apr. 28, in Hamilton, Mr. Lyman C. OSGOOD, age 24.
May 3, in Hamilton, Mrs. Caroline M., wife of Capt. Henry COMPTON, age 19 years, 5 months.
May 7, in Hamilton, Cordelia S., wife of J. EDMONDS, Jr., age 35.
June 3, in Hamilton, Henry G., only child of Daniel P. and Sarah M. HILL, age 1 year, 4 months, 21 days.
May 25, in Hamilton, Mr. Goodwin BIXBY, age 27.
July 14, in Hamilton, Eliza, youngest daughter of Hon. James B. ELDREDGE, age 5.

DEMOCRATIC REFLECTOR - 1843

Aug. 13, in Morrisville, Andrew S. Sloan, formerly Clerk of the County, age 55.
Sept. 26, Mr. Amasa LELAND, in Madison, age 56.
Oct. 10, in Hamilton, Mr. Abel SANFORD, age 45.
[Note: Beginning with Vol. II, No. 1 issue of Nov. 22, 1843, this newspaper was published on Wednesdays.]
Oct. 23, in Brookfield, Harriet JOHNSON, daughter of Samuel HILL, and wife of Moses JOHNSON, age 32 years, 6 months.
Nov. 23, in Hamilton, Mr. Joel LOVELAND, age 40.
Dec. 28, in Hamilton, Mortimer W. PERCIVAL, age 16.

1844

Jan. 10, in Eaton, at the residence of his son, Mr. Jabez BURCHARD, age 78.
Jan. 10, in Hamilton, Deacon White OSBORN, age 85.
Jan. 11, in Lebanon, Mary S. RUSSELL, age 10 months.
Jan. 18, in DeRuyter, Thankful, wife of James NYE, Esq., in her 64th year.
Jan. 25, in Oxford, Robert A. LEAL, Editor and Prop. of the *Oxford Republican*, in his 23d year.
Jan. 28, in Hamilton, David CRAWE, in his 88th year. He was a Revolutionary Pensioner.
Jan. 7, in Eaton, Mr. Constant Avery, a Revolutionary Soldier, age 88.
Jan. 17, in Eaton, Mr. John WHITE, age 46.
Feb. 28, in Earlville, Sophronia CARRIER, wife of J. N. CARRIER, age 42.
Mar. 11, in Hamilton, Mrs. Lydia, wife of Mr. Alanson NILES, and daughter of Elijah BROWN, of Georgetown, age 32.
Mar. 11, in Hamilton, Eli T., youngest son of Dr. Sherman and Phebe KIMBERLY, age 16 months, 12 days.
Mar. 6, in Eaton, Riley, only child of Morris W. WILLIS, age 6.
Mar. 17, in Madison, Roxanny WEBBER, widow of Samuel WEBBER, age 52.
Mar. 8, in West Winfield, Mary, consort of Dr. Joel CARRIER, and daughter of Dr. Asa BISHOP, of Lebanon.
Mar. 25, in Hamilton, Alanson Eugene, son of Alanson NILES, age 3.
Mar. 15, in DeRuyter, Mr. Jasper CRANDALL, age 83 years, 6 months.
Mar. 14, in Sullivan, Thomas CLARK, Esq., age 69.

DEMOCRATIC REFLECTOR - 1844

Mar. 13, in Morrisville, Flavilla Cornelia, daughter of the Rev. Moses and Caroline ADAMS, age 4 years, 6 months.
Apr. 16, in Hamilton, Charles B., son of John J. EVANS, age 2.
Last week in Hamilton, Thomas DIBBLE, age 67.
Apr. 22, in Hamilton, widow Fanny STANLEY, age 41.
Apr. 14, in Eaton, Mr. Rufus ROGERS, age 33.
Apr. 8, in Madison, John EDGARTON, age 69.
Apr. 11, in MADISON, James D. COOLIDGE, age 84.
Apr. 18, in Cazenovia, Hon. Barak BECKWITH, age 62.
Apr. 26, in Hamilton, Mrs. Elsie SHERWOOD, wife of Lorenzo SHERWOOD, age 30.
Feb. 20, in Napoli, Miss Lydia Lurancy HATCH, age 16 years, 3 months, daughter of Stephen and Mary HATCH.
May 1, at Oneida Depot, Mary Chaney, daughter of Mr. Socrates W. SQUIER, age 6.
May 15, in this village [Hamilton], on the 11th inst., Benjamin Wait, son of Dr. W. B. and Hannah BABCOCK, age 6 years, 4 months.
Apr. 24, in Perry, Wyoming Co., Rev. D. ACKLEY, formerly of this village [Hamilton].
No date, in Chittenango, Peter LANSING, Esq., age about 60.
May 21, in this village [Hamilton], John Marshall, son of Col. John and Clarissa ATWOOD, age 9 years, 2 months, 17 days.
May 10, in Madison, Mrs. Mary TOMPKINS, age 73.
July 2, in Jeffersonton, Culpepper (sic) Co., VA, Mr. Thomas W. DIBBLE late of this village [Hamilton], age 25.
Aug. 31, in Lebanon, Mrs. Polly EDDY, age 92.
Sept. 19, in Earlville, Chester CHAPIN, age 39.
Sept. 22, in Hamilton, Elmer H. OSGOOD, age 22.

Vol. III, No. 1

Nov. 1, in Richmond, VA, Mr. Lyman O. DANIELS, formerly of this place [Hamilton], age 28.
Nov. 25, in Hamilton, Mr. Henry COMPTON, age 27.
Sept. 17, in Smithfield, Franklin Merselon, son of Charles and Cornelia LEWIS, age 3.
Dec. 21, in Hamilton, Mr. Samuel THOMPSON, age 33.

DEMOCRATIC REFLECTOR - 1845

1845

Jan. 16, in East Hamilton, Noah B. FOOTE, M.D., age 67.
Jan. 24, in Eaton, Gelusia BONNEY, age 27.
Jan. 17, in Hamilton, Mrs. Susan WILLARD, age 57.
Jan. 31, in Fort Plain, at the home of her son-in-law, Levi S. BACKUS, Publisher and Propr. of the *Radii and Phoenix*, Mrs. Hannah ORMSBY, widow of the late Daniel ORMSBY, of Lebanon, age 75 years, 5 months, 2 days.
Feb. 14, in Eaton, Mr. Samuel SHERMAN, age 75.
Feb. 22, in Hamilton, William, son of Alsbro and Elizabeth BARBER, age 1 year, 11 months.
Feb. 23, in Hamilton, Miss Nancy WILLIAMS, age 37.
Feb. 21, in DeRuyter, James NEY, Esq., in his 67th year.
Mar. 23, in Brooklyn, Frances Melvina, eldest daughter of Ferdinand and Almira WALKER, late of this village [Hamilton], aged 11 years, 10 months.
Mar. 27, in Lebanon, Mr. Charles HAMILTON, age 84, a Revolutionary Soldier.
Mar. 24, in Lebanon, Thomas Jefferson Simon Bolivar STEBBINS, in his 19th year.
Apr. 13, in Hamilton, Susannah, wife of Jedediah WOODARD, Esq., and daughter of Jedediah POPE, Esq., formerly of Burlington, in her 47th year.
Apr. 8, in Gaines, Orleans Co., Mrs. Laura BABCOCK, wife of Hon. Alfred BABCOCK, late member of Congress.
May 4, in Hamilton, Martha A. SANFORD, age 18.
May 12, in Hamilton, Mrs. Ruth WICKWIRE, age about 60.
May 5, in Lebanon, Mrs. Beulah LONT, daughter of Stephen OSTROM, and wife of Capt. John F. LONT, age 46 years, 8 months.
Mar. 24, in Hamilton, Martha, wife of Jonathan O. PIERCE, age 45.
May 16, in Nelson, Sophina B. WEBBER, infant daughter of Henry and Mary WEBBER, of Eaton, age 10 months, 15 days.
May 4, in Berlinville, Erie Co., OH, Eliza, wife of William H. NOBLE, formerly of Hamilton.
June 21, at Madison, Mr. Henry HULL, age 33 years, 3 months.
June 21, at Madison, Pheba, wife of Lyman M. ROOT, age 41.
June 22, at Madison, Deacon Prince SPOONER, age 77.
June 22, at Madison, Susanna, wife of Mr. Solomon ROOT Sr., age 76.
June 21, in Eaton, Mr. John ALBE, age 52.

DEMOCRATIC REFLECTOR - 1845

July 12, in East Hamilton, Clarissa K., wife of James H. GLEASON, and youngest daughter of Mr. and Mrs. BOYCE, age 38.

July 15, in Madison, at the residence of Daniel BARKER, Mr. Amos BURTON, of Cazenovia, age 77.

Aug. 5, in Lebanon, Mr. Charles CAMPBELL, age 76.

Aug. 15, in Handy, Mr. Harlow NORTH, late of Madison Co., age 23.

No date, in East Hamilton, Mrs. Ruth BOYCE, age 73.

Sept. 6, in Munnsville, Mrs. Lucinda H. SIMMONS, age 22, wife of Br. Walter SIMMONS, of Madison Tent, No. 25, L. O. of R.

Sept. 2, in Eaton, Mary E. PAYSON, age 40.

Sept. 23, in Eaton, Lydia H., consort of Brother E. W. MANCHESTER, of Eaton Tent C.R. of Empire Dist. I.O. of R., age 27.

Sept. 29, at Irving, Barry Co., MI, Mrs. Mary M., wife of George B. MANCHESTER, Esq., formerly of this County.

Oct. 13, in Madison, Mr. Philip CRAIN, age 66.

Oct. 31, in Madison, Charlotte A., daughter of Lyman and Malissa SWAN, age 14.

Dec. 2, Dr. Samuel COLLESTER, age 54.

Nov. 10, in Hamilton, Miss Sally, daughter of Thomas E. and Electa DORMAN, in her 18th year.

Nov. 14, in Lebanon, Henry F., son of Ezra and Meroa CAMPBELL, age 6 years.

Nov. 15, in Eaton, Lucian Mason, son of Ellis and Sophronia COMAN, age 6.

1846

Jan. 9, in Eaton, Mrs. Catherine CHUBBUCK, widow of the late Samuel CHUBBUCK, Esq., age 81.

Jan. 10, in Eaton, Mrs. Beulah ORTON, relect of the late Thomas ORTON, Esq., of Hamilton, age 69.

Jan. 21, in East Hamilton, Merville H., only son of Benjamin and Evaline PARLIN, age 3 years, 10 months, 12 days.

Feb. 3, in Hamilton, Amelia J., youngest daughter of John and Jane WOODMAN, age 18 months.

Feb. 24, in Eaton, Elsie Jane, only daughter of Emilius J. and Lucy Ann ENOS, age 1 year, 3 months, 6 days.

Mar. 27, in Eaton, Deacon Duty LAPHAM, age 74.

Apr. 11, in Hamilton, Mr. Ezekiel TREADWAY, age 84, a Revolutionary Soldier.

Apr. 20, in Hamilton, Mrs. Marsia L., wife of Dr. V. H. VAN VLECK, in her 42nd year.

DEMOCRATIC REFLECTOR - 1846

Apr. 26, in Hamilton, Charles Perrin, youngest son of George and Celinda ABERT, age 1 year, 5 months, 26 days.

Apr. 22, in Hamilton, Mrs. Sarah C., wife of Jared WARREN, age 28.

June 6, in Hamilton, Mr. Esek STEERE, age 62.

May 30, in Lebanon, Cordelia P., youngest daughter of Isaac and Antrace HITCHCOCK, age 1 year, 6 months.

May --, in Lebanon, Mr. Henry SQUIRES, age 23.

June 5, in Eaton, Mrs. Harriet F., wife of Col. William F. BONNEY, age 30.

June 25, in Hamilton, Mr. Sanford WILCOX, age 44.

June 22, in Eaton, Mrs. Vashti MOSELEY, wife of Mr. Ambrose MOSELY, age 59.

June 6, in Hamilton, Mr. Esek STEERE, Esq., age 61. [sic, see above]

July 5, in Cazenovia, Mrs. Mary LYMAN, wife of Dr. Isaac LYMAN, in her 64th year.

June 8, in Janeville, WI, Isaac DAVIS, formerly of Eaton, age 24.

July 8, in Eaton, Miss Hannah DEAN, age 33 years, 1 month.

Aug. 9, in Hamilton, Mrs. Celinda, wife of Mr. George ABERT, age 40.

Aug. 7, in Hamilton, John C. PAYNE, age 71. His son-in-law was Rev. Jacob KNAPP, pastor of a Church in Albany. He left several children.

Aug. 15, in Hamilton, Mary Otis, daughter of Henry L. and Anna E. WEBB, age 10 months, 5 days.

Aug. 20, at Erieville, Mr. Jerry AYER, formerly of Eaton, age 23.

Sept. 2, in Morrisville, Mr. Conway LEWIS, age 55.

Sept. 2, in residence of his brother, John DELANCEY, in Brookfield, Henry DELANCEY, age 47.

Aug. 25, in Hamilton, Josiah ROGERS, eldest son of Dr. Timothy ROGERS, age 68.

Sept. 1, in Napolean, Jackson Co., MI, Benjamin R., son of Mr. Charles CHUBBUCK, of Hamilton, age 37.

Sept. 24, in Madison, Mary Avaline, daughter of Sheppard and Mary WEBBER, age 5 months.

Sept. 26, in Earlville, Lyman B. SWEET, age 33.

Oct. 5, in Morrisville, Mr. William HAUGHTON, age 56.

Sept. 22, in Fenner, Mr. Isaac P. DOOLITTLE, age 68.

Oct. 15, in Fenner, Mr. Jacob BARRETT, in his 86th year. He was a Revolutionary Soldier.

Oct. 3, in Dresden, Muskingum Co., OH, Mr. Arah LEONARD.

Oct. 12, in Dresden, OH, Alfred W., son of Arah LEONARD, age 26, formerly of Hamilton; of typhus fever.

DEMOCRATIC REFLECTOR - 1846

Oct. 28, in Hamilton, George D., oldest son of Joshua and Catherine PIERCE, age 6 years.
Nov. 4, in Hamilton, Charles A., son of Samuel and Flavia WHITE, age 21.
Nov. 5, in Hamilton, Emalissa, wife of Mr. Oliver HARTSHORN, age 44.

1848

Aug. 23, Bro. Charles T. CURTIS of Stockbridge Lodge I.O.O.F., and Madison Tent, I.O.R., age 42.
Aug. 25, in this village, Ann Eliza, daughter of David LAWRENCE, age 1 year, 4 months.
Aug. 26, in Sherburne, Thomas STEWART, in his 44th year.
Aug. 25, in this village, Mrs. Sally ALLEN, widow of the late Francis ALLEN, age 51.
Aug. 12, in Earlville, Mr. Erskin BLAIR, son-in-law of William MORRIS, of Lebanon, Madison Co., age 30.
Aug. 16, Gertrude, only daughter of Erskin and Catharine BLAIR, age 3.
Aug. 18, DeAlton, only son of Erskin and Catharine BLAIR, age 7.

1852

Oct. 23, in Eaton, Jay Leroy, youngest child of Augustus and Maribee C. HAUGHTON, age 4 years, 9 months.
Nov. --, at Pratt's Hollow, Edward MANCHESTER, Esq., age 38.
Nov. 7, in Oberlin, OH, Mrs. Harriet M. BOWEN, age 19.
Nov. 30, in New York, of consumption, Mr. James COLE, age about 40.

1853

Dec. 26, (1852), in Stockbridge, of measles, Bethiah MATTHEWSON, daughter of Sylvenus MATTHEWSON, age 13 years, 11 months.
Jan. 29, in this village [Hamilton], Phebe LOCKMAN, age 22.
Feb. 28, After a protracted illness, Daniel Smith COLWELL, Esq., a native of this village [Hamilton], but for the last 30 years a resident of New York; in his 48th year.

DEMOCRATIC REFLECTOR - 1853

Mar. 4, at Eaton, Mary Elizabeth, only child of Henry and Elizabeth KEITH of Clarkville, age 1 year.

Mar. 9, in this village [Hamilton], at the residence of her son-in-law, Dr. B. LEWIS, Mrs. Rachel PRATT, mother of Milo PRATT, Esq., of Utica, age 73.

Mar. 8, at Eaton, at the residence of her uncle, M. W. SMITH and wife, (her foster parents), Cornelia Adelaide, youngest daughter of F. W. and Amarilla STILLMAN, of Hamilton, age 10.

Mar. 24, at Lebanon, the youngest son of Alfred and Rhoda SEYMOUR, age 9 months.

April 1, at East Hamilton, after a short and painfull illness, Mr. Samuel BRIGHAM, age 63.

Apr. 3, in Madison, Miss Mathilda M. HOWES, age 18.

Apr. 1, in Morrisville, Miss Julia TILLINGHAST, daughter of Mr. and Mrs. Bradley TILLINGHAST, age 18.

Apr. 10 (about), in this village [Hamilton], of consumption, Edward N. OSGOOD, age 32.

No date, in this town, at the residence of her son, T. J. HUBBARD, Mrs. Wealthy HUBBARD, age 89.

Apr. 12, in Madison, Mrs. Hopey GARDINER, age 65.

No date, in Lebanon, Mrs. Catharine STERNBERGH, age 78.

Apr. 10 (about), in Eaton, Betsey E. ISBELL, age 23.

Mar. 19, in Fenner, Deacon Amos COREY, age 73.

Apr. 11, in Hamilton, Marverick C., infant son of Chauncey and Julia Ann WILSON, age 1 year, 5 months, 19 days.

May 10, in Vernon Center, Mr. Charles T. ARMSTRONG, of the above place, age 17.

May 5, in Brookfield, Mrs. Betsey W., wife of Charles B. LANGWORTHY, Esq., age 34.

May 27, at Bouckville, Moses MAYNARD, Esq., age 77.

June 1, at Pecksport, Mr. Josiah PECK, age 80.

June 18, in Utica, Betsy, wife of John T. HOOKER, formerly of this village [Hamilton], age 39.

July 16, at his residence near Earlville, Horace NASH, age 59.

July 10, in Syracuse, Col. George EHLE, formerly of Cazenovia, age 61.

July 15 (about), in Morrisville, Mrs. Mary BURCHARD, wife of Mr. P. H. BURCHARD, age 26. (Correct date of death July 14.)

June 17, in town of Nelson, Mr. William YEOMANS, age 72.

June 24, in Greenville, IN, Mrs. T. C. BLOSSOM, age 60.

July 20, in Norwich, Chenango Co., Mrs. M. Emeline BARNETT, wife of Capt. Ezra BARNETT, formerly of Morrisville, age 35.

Aug. 21, in this village [Hamilton], Mr. George BRIGHT, age 65.

DEMOCRATIC REFLECTOR - 1853

Aug. 18 (about), in this village [Hamilton], Charles Henry, son of William and Helen CURTIS, age 2 years, 6 months.
Aug. 31, in this village [Hamilton], Mr. Jonas BROWN, age 24.
Aug. 31, in Munnsville, Mr. Charles JOSLIN, age 35.
Sept. 3, in Waterville, Mr. William HALL, age 88.
Sept. 6, in Morrisville, Mr. Roswell P. THOMPSON, age 57.
Sept. 6, in Clarksville, Cynthia L., youngest daughter of Eli and Mary GATES, age 2.
Sept. 8, in Lebanon, Jabez MORSE, age 25.
Sept. 9, in Lebanon, Bathsheba CONKEY, age 63.
Sept. 12, in this village [Hamilton], Mrs. Esther PAYNE, age 75.
Sept. 27, in this place [Hamilton], Mr. I. A. SHAPLEY, age 38.
Oct. 2, in Pratt's Hollow, Isaac F. CHAMBERLAIN, age 45.
Aug. 30, in Sacramento, CA, John W. HALL, formerly of Hamilton, age 88.
Oct. 6, in DeRuyter, Madison Co., at the residence of his father, Hon. Benjamin ENOS, Samuel Dotty ENOS, late a clerk in the office of the Comptroller, age 88 years, 1 month, 4 days.
Sept. 30, in Fenner, Nathaniel KEELER, age 96. A Soldier of the Revolution.
Oct. 7, in Smyrna, Harriet CARD, age 20.
Oct. 11, near Morrisville, Miss Eliza A. KNIGHT, in her 19th year.
Sept. 26, in Warrington, MS, Melville K. CALKINS, age 30.
Nov. 7 (about), in this village [Hamilton], Mrs. Sophia BURCHARD, wife of Theodore BURCHARD, age 59.
Nov. 23, in Lebanon, Catharine THAYER, age 76.
Nov. 9, in Smyrna, John DIX, age 75.
Oct. 24, in Hamilton, Keturah, wife of Hyleman SMITH, age 51.
Dec. 5, in Eaton, Helen Cornelia, eldest daughter of Sheldon and Sarah B. FITCH, age 12.

1854

Jan. 1, in Clarksville, Mrs. Fanny, wife of Asah FRINK Jr., age 49.
Jan. 11, in this village [Hamilton], Frances Josephine, youngest daughter of J. P. and Frances A. RHODES, age 1 year, 3 months.
Jan. 2, in this village, Harriet, daughter of Mrs. Judson SANFORD, age 3 years, 9 months.

DEMOCRATIC REFLECTOR - 1854

[No date], at his residence in Bloomington, IL, Mr. Giles LAWTON, formerly of this town [Hamilton], age 47.

Dec. 3, (1853), in Eaton village, Mrs. Sophronia E. WHITE, age 30.

Jan. 21, in Lebanon, Capt. Truman BILLINGS, age 75.

Jan. 24, in Lebanon, Polly, wife of Capt. Truman BILLINGS, age 74.

Jan. 21, in Bouckville, Andrew BRIGGS, age 63.

Jan. 20, in Waterville, of consumption, John BABBOT, age 25.

Feb. 1, in Eaton, C. A. BOOTH, age 2 years, 8 months.

Feb. 1, in Hamilton, Eugene MOSHER, age 3 years, 7 months.

Jan. 22, in Marion, Linn Co., IA, of consumption, Lucy A., wife of John C. WARD, in her 31st year; buried in Earlville.

Feb. 4, in Madison, Cornelius SIMMONS, age 70.

Feb. 4, in Eaton, John L. VAN WINKLE, age 36.

Feb. 3, in this village [Hamilton], Henry A. COMPTON, age 4 years, 14 days.

Feb. 5, in Lebanon, Henry F. HOTCHKIN, age 2 years, 16 days.

Feb. 4, in East Hamilton, Olive, wife of Stephen BRAINARD, age 74.

Feb. 5, in Madison, infant son of James G. PARMALEE.

Feb. 8, in Madison, infant son of E. T. HATCH.

Feb. 10, in Philadelphia, Mrs. Avaline Amelia, wife of William KRAMER, daughter of Mr. Asa CHAPIN, formerly of this village [Hamilton], in her 44th year.

Jan. 17, in Chicago, of consumption, in her 23rd year, Mrs. Mary C. GRIGGS, daughter of Charles WALKER of Chicago.

Feb. 5, in this village [Hamilton], Henry A., son of John R. and Sarah A. COMPTON, age 4 years, 14 days, also;

Feb. 14, Armena Mary COMPTON, daughter of the above, age 19 months.

Feb. 12, in Poolville, Julia A., wife of Damon RICHMOND, age 29.

Feb. 13, in Eaton, Charles A. PEARCE, age 18.

Feb. 10, in Madison, Mary A., daughter of Otis LEWIS, age 9 months.

Feb. 15, in Eaton, Clarissa CLARK, age 73.

Feb. 21, in Clarkville, Amy, wife of Maxson CLARK Jr., age 46.

Feb. 16, in Scotia, NY, Rev. John D. GREEN, formerly of Madison University, age 35.

Feb. 25, in this village [Hamilton], Albert Burdette, only child of Elisha and Harriet STEDMAN, age 7 months.

DEMOCRATIC REFLECTOR - 1854

Feb. 24, in Eaton, Mary M., daughter of Jarit WICKWIRE, age 2.
Mar. 4, in Lebanon, of malignant erysipelas, Eva Amelia, daughter of S. B. and L. A. BENEDICT, age 3 months, 2 days.
Mar. 10, in Eaton, Mrs. Lucina BIRCHARD, age 86.
Mar. 11, in Eaton, Samuel SHERMAN, age 64.
Mar. 14, in Lebanon, Lucy M., daughter of Avery KINGSLEY, age 12.
Mar. 16, in Madison, William PETLEY, age 16.
Mar. 20, in Earlville, Lucy MILLER, age 52.
Mar. 22, in Madison, Asa MORSE, age 82.
Apr. 4, in Hamilton, Alice Aletta, daughter of David H. and Caroline E. SHERRILL, age 3.
Apr. 1, in Hamilton, Margaret MACOMBER, wife of Joseph MACOMBER, age 78.
Apr. 10, in Madison, Joseph BROWN, age 91.
Apr. 17, in Madison, Ebenezer GRAY, age 77.
Apr. 17, in Rochester, Miss Mary GREEN, of Brookfield, age 18.
Apr. 22, in Lebanon, Desire, wife of Zar BENEDICT, age 72.
May 6, in Hamilton, little DeAlton, son of G. R. and Mary E. WALDRON, age 6.
No date, in Madison, at home of Seth BLAIR 2d, Miss Kezia RICHMOND, age 54.
No date, in Unadilla, Mr. Benson H. WEBBER, son of Rev. S. S. WEBBER, formerly of Madison, age 20.
May 12, in Hamilton, at residence of her son, Mrs. Hannah CURREY, age 77 years, 1 month. Rowley, Essex Co., MA papers please copy; Baltimore papers may also.
May 17, in this town [Hamilton], Mr. Heman BONNEY, age 65.
May 18, in Hamilton, Clara E., daughter of Nelson and Abigail WILLCOX, age 4 years, 2 months, 13 days.
May 16, in Hamilton, Deacon Elijah BUELL, age 61 years, 8 months. He was born in the town of Newport, then Chester, now Sullivan Co., NH. His father and family moved to Lebanon, NY in 1796; was member of Lebanon Baptist Church; moved to Hamilton in 1846.
May 23, of consumption, Sophia NASH, wife of Daniel P. NASH, of Oneida Community, and daughter of Uriah CHURCH of this town [Hamilton], age 41.
May 27, in Madison, Mrs. Eliza DICK, age 34.
July 20, in Hamilton, Elisha L., son of Samuel and Sarah THOMAS, age 5 years, 5 months, 5 days.
No date, in Cortlandville, Cortland Co., James F., only son of James W. and Sarah STURTEVANT, age 4 years, 3 months.
Aug. 9, at Fenner, Solomon COVEY, age 35.

DEMOCRATIC REFLECTOR - 1854

Sept. 11, at Morrisville, Mrs. E., wife of Hiram LEWIS, Esq., age 29.

Sept. 5, at Madison, Ann Janette, only daughter of Samuel and Sarah THOMAS, age 4 years, 1 month, 5 days.

Sept. 28, in Madison, Capt. Samuel WHITE, Soldier of the Revolution, age 91. He was born in Petersham, Worcester Co., MA 22d of June, 1763. He enlisted at 16 years. He was at West Point in 1779 and 1780. Was body-guard of Andre when he was executed. Was wounded at an attack near New York and was in the hospital when his term of enlistment expired. He married, Mar. 1796, and in 1798, moved to Madison.

Sept. 16, in Earlville, George HALL, age 25.

Sept. 12, in Madison, Bulah, wife of Capt. Samuel WHITE, age 87.

Oct. 7, in Earlville, Emiline M., wife of B. N. GUSTIN.

Oct. 4, in Baltimore, MI, Ransom H. HARMON, age 41. He was brother-in-law of Adon SMITH. He was a resident of Hamilton, and visiting friends in Michigan when he died.

Oct. 13, in this village, Peter MC QUADE, age 56. He was buried in Pratt's Hollow.

Oct. 15, in Madison, Jennie I., daughter of Horace and Susan MOSHER, age 3 years, 6 months.

Oct. 31, in Eaton, of consumption, Martha EVERETS, wife of Edwin D. SMITH, age 25.

Nov. 19, in Eaton, Henry DE LONG, age 41.

Nov. 25, in East Hamilton, Mrs. Syril BONNEY, age 47.

Nov. 9, at Baton Rouge, LA, of yellow fever, Mr. Charles G. TERRY, son of Leonard TERRY, of Sangerfield, age 22. He was recently a student of Madison University and, for some time, Principal of Nelson Academy, OH; lately a teacher in Baton Rouge.

Nov. 16, in Madison, John COLLISTER, age 20.

Dec. 21, in Waukegan, IL, Thomas PLIMBLEY, recently of this village [Hamilton], age 21.

Dec. 20, in Galesburg, Knox Co., IL, Mrs. Esther Jane, wife of Frederick W. FOOTE, Esq., formerly of Hamilton, in her 21st year.

Oct. 15, at Salem X Roads, NY, Clinton E., only son of Clinton S. and Almira A. FAY, age 20 months.

1855

Jan. 3, in Hamilton, Alonzo MOSHER, age 22.

Jan. 23, in Petersburg, VA, John W. ALLEN, recently of Lebanon.

DEMOCRATIC REFLECTOR - 1855

Feb. 19, in Earlville, Cynthia A., wife of Warren FELT, age 43.
Feb. 21, in Eaton, William DELINE, age 23.
Feb. 22, in Hamilton, John JONES Jr., age 52.
Mar. 16, Sarah E., eldest daughter of Richard L. STANFORD, of Munnsville, age 24.
Mar. 16, in Earlville, Mrs. R. M. RANSOM, wife of Dr. David RANSOM, age 30.
Mar. 19, in Madison, Mary HOWARD, age 59.
Feb. 26, in Hamilton, Mr. Pardon MORRIS, age 78.
Mar. 26, in Peterboro, Nehemiah HUNTINGTON, age 79.
Feb. 23, in Welshfield, Geauga Co., OH, Mr. Lysander PACKARD, formerly of this town [Hamilton].
Mar. 26, at North Brookfield, Alexander M. COVEY, Esq., age 39.
Apr. 18, in Hamilton, George Murray MOSELEY, age 22.
Apr. 18, in Erieville, Harvey B. RICH, age 32.
May 6, in Lebanon, Jane A. BRIGGS, daughter of J. M. and Ann BRIGGS, age 21.
June 8, in Smyrna, Thomas WILCOX, age 76.
June 8, in Hamilton, David COMPTON, age 39.
May 31, in Pine Woods, Miss Jemima KNAPP, age 35.
Apr. 14, in Hamilton, Mrs. Marinda CRANSTON, wife of Phineas CRANSTON, age 48.
May 31, in Lebanon, Adon MORRIS, son of William and Sarah MORRIS, age 9 years, 2 months, 26 days.
Apr. 30, in Lebanon, Mrs. Rachel ALBE, age 55.
May 2, in Hamilton, Mrs. Mary B. LATHROP, age 63.
Apr. 23, in Alderbrook, Mr. Simeon CHUBBUCK, brother of Charles CHUBBUCK, of this village [Hamilton], age 62.
Apr. 28, in Fabius, at the house of her father, J. DOUBLEDAY, Esq., Eliza S., wife of Chauncey STEVENS, formerly of this village [Hamilton], age 62.
Apr. 28, in Twin Grove, IL, Deacon James TOMPKINS, formerly of this village [Hamilton], in his 56th year.
June 6, in Hamilton, at the residence of her son-in-law, E. CURREY, Lois DARLING, widow of Capt. Alpheus DARLING, age 77.
June 1, in Hebron, Tolland Co., CT, Mr. Jabez BACKUS, father of the publisher of the *Radii*, age 78.
June 6, in Hamilton, Mary, daughter of Abram and --- SANFORD, age 19.
Apr. 30, in CA, Abram DE LONG, formerly of Lebanon, age 40.
July 2, in Hamilton, Mrs. Levina R. CHUBBUCK, wife of Mr. Charles CHUBBUCK, and mother of the late Mrs. E. C. JUDSON, age 70.

DEMOCRATIC REFLECTOR - 1855

July 1, in Brookfield, Mr. Joshua BREED, age 26.
July 23, in Solsville, Mr. Corydon TUCKER, age 28.
July 19, in Earlville, Helen F., oldest daughter of L. L. NICHOLS, late of Sault Ste. Marie, MI.
July 15, at Oneida, at the residence of John M. MESSENGER, Miss Martha M. STOWER, age 28. She was the daughter of the late Dennis P. STOWER, formerly of this village [Hamilton], but had lived as an adopted daughter, in Gen. MESSENGER's family for 17 years.
Aug. 4, in Madison, Mr. John GRIMSHAW, age 65.
No date, at the residence of his father, Solomon BACON, near Hubbard's Corners, Charles BACON, age 19.
July 30, in Cazenovia, Samuel HITCHCOCK, father of the Hon. Simon C. HITCHCOCK, age 80.
Aug. 5, in Seneca, McHenry Co., IL, Caroline E., wife of David H. SHERRILL, recently of Lebanon, and daughter of Charles and Deborah HUNT, of Hamilton, age 27.
No date, in Iowa City, IA, Rev. A. Russel BELDEN, son-in-law of Ira ALLEN, of Eaton, age 36.
Aug. 24, in Burlington, IL, Deacon Jonathan THURSTON, recently of Hamilton, age 70.
Aug. 29, in Madison, Mrs. Phebe PUTNAM, widow of the late Dr. Elijah PUTNAM, and mother of Dr. John PUTNAM, age 80.
Aug. 30, in Madison, Mrs. Lucinda CURTIS, age 81.
Aug. 30, in Madison, Mr. Aruna GILMORE, age 62.
Sept. 4, in Lebanon, Mrs. Mary P. SQUIRES, age 95.
No date, in Hamilton, Charles PARKER, age 63.
Sept. 11, at the Hartford Retreat, Hartford, CT, Justus S. MASTERS, Esq., formerly of Hamilton.
No date, at the residence of the late E. C. PEARL, in Clinton, Joshua UPHAM, age 86.
Aug. 24, in Elmira, Mrs. Betsey Hills, wife of W. H. MOORE; a deaf mute.
Sept. 26, in Nelson, Delos WEAVER, age 30.
Oct. 8, in Xpsilanti, MI, Mr. Albert G. HALL, of Solsville, age 44.
Oct. 28, in Brooklyn, Charles H. ARNOLD, age 24; a deaf mute.
Nov. 6, in Poolville, William LORD, Esq., age 71.
Nov. 16, in Hamilton, Daniel YOUNGLOVE, Esq., age 58. He was many years a citizen of Lebanon.
Nov. 25, in Hamilton, Mrs. Melissa E., wife of Mr. David SQUIRES, age 31.

****
INCOMPLETE FILES
OF
VARIOUS NEWSPAPERS
****

ALBANY GAZETTE

In issue of Jan. 18, 1829: DIED--In New York, on Sunday morning, Mr. Philip ALLEN, in the 40th year of his age; eldest son of Stephen ALLEN, late mayor of that city.

DEMOCRATIC UNION
Hamilton

In issue of Dec. 10, 1857: DIED--at Utica, on the morning of the 9th inst., Richard LALOR, age 33 years, 3 months.

In issue of Sept. 4, 1862: DIED--in the town of Cazenovia, July 25, of diptheria, Mary Emma, age 12 years; Aug. 4, Ann Elizabeth, age 15; Aug. 6, Edger Pope, age 13 years, children of Runyon R. and Mary CHURCH WARD. Also;

DIED--in Sherburne, on the 21st, Captain John CORBIN, age 80 years, 24 days.

1872, Oneida, NY Deaths

In Fenner, Feb. 29, Emma W. DEMMON, age about 20. She was the daughter of Rev. O. Ads TAYNTOR.

Mar. 17, Mary Lydia BURTON, age 19 years, 7 months.

Mar. 20, in Richland, C. CLARK, formerly of Verona, age 68.

Mar. 25, in Verona, Thomas J. BARBER, age 41 years, 6 months, 9 days.

Mar. 18, in Canastota, Amos ATKINS, age 24 years.

Mar. 12, in Canastota, Araminta, wife of Hiram A. PETRIE, age 52.

Mar. 25, in Hamilton, Mulford ROGERS, age 60.

Mar. 23, in Morrisville, Sarah ELMER, age 26.

Mar. 27, in Morrisville, Patience SANFORD, age 87 years, 11 months.

Apr. 1, in Deansville, Stewart J. MILLER, age 16 months, 17 days.

Dec. 20, (1871), in West Hoboken, NJ, Hon. James CLARK, of South Otselic, age 75.

Mar. 25, in Stockbridge, Mrs. Fidelia, wife of J. C. DUNHAM, age 48.

Mar. 30, in Morrisville, Augustus LUMBARD, age 73.

MADISON COUNTY JOURNAL
1851

Aug. 20, at Frankford, Herkimer Co., Miss M. A., eldest daughter of R. G. W. FERGUSON, age 19.
Aug. 5, at Boston, MA, Miss Miranda, daughter of Nathan EATON, of Poolville, age 26.

1852
No deaths recorded.

DEMOCRATIC REPUBLICAN
Hamilton
(scattered issues)
1856

Oct. 8, in Oneida, Samuel F. BOYDEN, age 46 years, 20 days.
Oct. 6, in Stockbridge, NY, Thomas H. BETSINGER, age 19 years, 1 month, 9 days.

1857

Mar. 12, in Erieville, Phineas HAMBLET, in 74th year.
Apr. 3, in Cazenovia, of consumption, Mrs. Phebe WESTCOTT, age 57.
Apr. 2, in Cazenovia, of spotted fever, John NICHOLS, in 62nd year.
Apr. 8, in Fenner, Herman BROWNSON, age 17.
Mar. 30, in Marshall, Mary, wife of Jesse PARKER, age 35 years, 18 days.
[No date], in Lebanon, at home of her son-in-law, William LEWIS, Widow Lucretia WYLIE, age 77.

1858

Oct. 6, in Madison, Harriet S. HEAD, age 29 years, 2 months.
Oct. 6, Amos CROCKER, age 74; funeral at Congregational Church.

1859

June 30, Samuel F. STONE, of Anderson Co., KS, whither he moved from this town [Hamilton] in the spring of 1857. He leaves a widow and two children.

DEMOCRATIC REPUBLICAN - 1859

July 17, in Canastota, Per Lee, son of Samuel and Elsie JARVIS, age nearly 4.

1861

July 30, in Hamilton, Harriet Roselthia, daughter of James W. and Angeline SHORES, age 19.
July 26, in Hamilton, of scarlet fever, Hattie Eliza CLARK, age 1 year.
July 17, in Earlville, of scarlet fever, Charles Morton, age 8; and July 22, Henry Onslow, age 3, children of Linus H. and Maria D. MILLER.
July 23, in town of Madison, of diptheria, Albert COLLINS, age 11.
July 27, in Lebanon, Margaret, wife of A. G. MOREY, age 45.

1862

Feb. 13, in Madison, DeWitt WHITE, age 33.
Feb. 18, at Eaton, Richard JEFF, age 46.
Mar. 17, in Madison, Addie Julia, daughter of Theodore L. and Sarah E. SPENCER, age 6 years, 8 months; the last one of three victims of scarlet fever and diptheria.
Mar. 16, in Manchester, VT, Ambrose MOSELEY, late of Eaton, age about 87.
On Aug. 11, drowned, a son of Elder BRONSON, of Georgetown, in pond in Smyrna.
Aug. 16, at York, PA, Lewis F., son of Lewis F. and Janette ALLEN, only grandchild of E. D. WHEELER, of Hamilton, age 4.
Aug. 19, in Hamilton, Charles MORE, age 67.

1863

On Jan. 6, of diptheria, Emille B., age 4 months; and on 31st, Ward W., age 8 years 3 months, children of Benjamin N. and Maricon C. WHITE, of Morrisville.
No date, in Georgetown, Zadoc HAWKS, age 92 years, 4 months, 15 days, at the home of his son Horace HAWKS.
Jan. 29, in Madison, Adin HOWARD, age 56.
Feb. 8, in Peterboro, John HOLLINGSWORTH, age 40.

DEMOCRATIC REPUBLICAN - 1863

In issue of Feb. 19, Notice of Memorial Service for Corp. David C. KERN, 97th Reg. NY Vol., Killed in Battle of Fredericksburg.

Jan. 28, at Underhill Cottage on Alder Brook, Miss O. Anna STEWART, age 27.

Jan. 6, in New Orleans, of typhoid fever, Norman G., son of Willis HUMPHREY, of Nelson, age 23.

Feb. 16, in Lebanon, of strangulation, Floyd, only son of Enos and Nancy GREEN, age 8 years, 9 months, 15 days.

Mar. 1, in Hamilton, Mrs. Anna, wife of Theophilus ROBINSON, age 77.

Feb. 16, in Georgetown, of diphtheria, Oscar A. WEDGE, age 19 years, 10 months.

Mar. 8, in Eaton, Aurelia ALLEN, age 73, at home of C. A. EDWARDS.

[No date], at Elk Creek, Erie Co., PA, George Washington PECKHAM, infant son of Arowit and Sarah J. PECKHAM, age 2 weeks.

Mar. 17, at Preble, Capt. DUNBAR.

Feb. 21, in Norwalk, OH, Amanda CORNELL, wife of Rev. Alfred CORNELL, formerly of Eaton.

Mar. 23, at Oriskany Falls, Jerome BACON, age 6.

In issue of Apr. 2, Frederick WALTON, soldier, died near Falmouth, VA.

Mar. 27, Janette, daughter of Nelson FAIRCHILD, age 21, at Hamilton.

Feb. 23, at Marathon Hospital, New Orleans, F. G. WILLIAMS, Co. A, 176th Reg. NY Vol., formerly of East Hamilton, age 25.

Apr. 12, at her residence near Earlville, Marila FAY, wife of James R. FAY, deceased, age 63.

Apr. 1, in Earlville, of consumption, William BRESEE, age 21.

May 3, in Georgetown, Mr. Alfred BROWN, age 75.

About May 1, in Madison, Mrs. Charlotte COE, age 81.

May 4, in Madison, George LANE, of Westmoreland, age 35.

Buried at Hubbard's Corners, May 2, Mrs. Emily C. HART, wife of Elias K. HART, age 55.

May 3, in Morrisville, Mrs. Maria CROSS, wife of Dwight CROSS, Esq., age 30; only daughter of A. WAGER, Esq., of Sullivan.

Apr. 16, in the hospital at Bayou Beouf, LA, of typhoid fever, Curtis HOLT, Co. A, 176th Reg. NY Vol., age 38, of East Hamilton.

Apr. 6, in Overton Hospital, Memphis, TN, of chronic diarrhea, Mr. L. W. LADD of Co. B, 31st Iowa Reg., age 39 years, 7 months, formerly of Lebanon.

DEMOCRATIC REPUBLICAN - 1863

June 9, in this village [Hamilton), of consumption, Mr. Horace W. CAMPBELL, age 27.

May 31, in Rapid City, IL, of consumption, Mr. H. Philander BROWN, eldest son of Rev. P. P. BROWN, of Madison, in his 53d year.

June 9, in Georgetown, Jennie N., youngest daughter of Hanford and Clarissa A. NICHOLS, age 11.

[No date], at residence of his brother-in-law, H. W. WOODRUFF, Esq., in St. Louis, MO, John Pierce OSGOOD, age 35.

Jan. 21, in Hospital at Nashville, TN, in the Battle of Murfreesboro, Silas Seymour SLATER, son of Amos and Fannie SLATER, of Cherry Valley, Ashtabula Co., OH, late of Lebanon, NY, and grandson of Silas SEYMOUR, in his 23d year.

June 16, in Eaton, Mr. Alansing MILES, age 87.

June 19, in Earlville, Ruth A. YOUNG, age 35.

June 23, in Eaton, Mrs. Ruth PAYSON, age 87.

June 24, in Earlville, Frank W., only child of John and Caroline E. HOUGHTON, age 3 years, 5 months.

Funeral in Hamilton, June 19, for Lieut. E. L. DUNHAM, 44th Reg., NY Vol., killed at Battle of Gettysburg.

Funeral at Norwich, Sunday, July 13, for Col. SMITH, 114th Reg. NY Vol.

July 22, in New Haven, CT, Mr. J. W. KING, brother of Mrs. Alex WELTON, of this village [Hamilton], age 50.

June 1 7, at her residence near Earlville, Mrs. Louisa C. CUSHMAN, age 27.

July 3, in Memphis, TN, Mr. Horace PIERCE, formerly of Hamilton, age 50.

July 8, in Hospital at Newbern, NC, of brain fever, Henry N. BLAIR, Batt. H, 3d Artillery, NY Vol., only child of Harvey BLAIR of Madison, age 20 years, 9 months, 1 day. Buried in Hospital Cemetery at Newbern.

Andrew J. SAWDEY, non-commissioned officer of 114th Reg., wounded in battle before Port Hudson June 14; died at Baton Rouge July 12; funeral at Poolville Aug. 9.

Aug. 8, Erastus D. WHEELER, age nearly 68. He was born in New Caanan, Columbia Co., NY, Nov. 28, 1795, and came to Hamilton at 18 months of age. Learned cabinet-maker trade of Mr. HIGGINS, father of Mrs. T. H. GREENLEY, and worked for undertaker establishment for many years.

Aug. 10, in this village [Hamilton], Lelia A., daughter of C. F. and Angela E. EDGERTON, age 22 years, 4 days.

Aug. 20, Mary S. Welton, youngest daughter of Edward E. and Emma N. WELTON, age 1 year, 4 months, 16 days.

DEMOCRATIC REPUBLICAN - 1863

Aug. 22, in South Otstlic, Miss Francella A., dau. of Homer and Mary SCHERMERHORN, age 16 years, 1 month.

Sept. 17, at Siloam, Town of Smithfield, William FOSTER, age 36. He leaves a wife and three children.

Sept. 8, in Whitewater, WI, Samuel WHITE, formerly of this place [Hamilton], age 73.

Sept. 30, at Pratt's Hollow, Mr. Almon TEMPLE, age 35.

Sept. 29, at Peterboro, of diphtheria, Herbert, son of Theo. ANDREWS, age 4.

Oct. 6, in Hamilton, Mr. Archibald CAMPBELL, age 68.

Oct. 2, in Hamilton, Mrs. Malinda WILBER, age 60.

Oct. 9, in Morrisville, Josiah CLOYES, age 60.

Oct. 1, in Nelson, Deacon Eli WHITE, age 59.

Sept. 28, near Bouckville, Georgie S., 2d son of Mr. Frank COOLIDGE, of Madison, and foster son of Mr. David Z. and Mrs. Elizabeth BROCKETT, age 4 years, 6 months.

Oct. 1, near Bouckville, Hattie B., youngest daughter of W. W. and Alvira LAWRENCE, age 4 years, 2 months.

Sept. 11, in CA, Freddie H., son of Nelson and Abigail WILCOX, age 18 months.

Nov. 5, in Galesburg, IL, Dr. John BABCOCK, age 68, formerly of Hamilton.

Nov. 12, in Lebanon, of typhoid fever, Louisa, wife of Samuel B. BENEDICT, age 36.

Sept. 25, in Lebanon, Mr. Dunham SHAPLEY, age 84 years, 7 months, 26 days. He was born Jan. 30, 1779 in MA. His parents soon moved to New Lebanon, NY, and united with the Shakers. At age 21 he left the Shakers, finally persuaded his parents to leave, and they moved to Lebanon in 1800, becoming a pioneer family in that town. He married Sally BELDEN Dec. 4, 1800 at Lebanon; they had 8 children who lived to grow up.

Dec. 9, in Rome, of congestional fever, Sarah M., wife of John J. PARRY Jr., and daughter of Benjamin WILBER, of this place [Hamilton], aged 30 years, 3 months.

Dec. 13, in Norwich, Mr. George L. RIDER, age 71 years, 3 months.

Dec. 13, at Hubbardsville, Mrs. Susan HUBBARD, wife of Calvin HUBBARD, age 77.

Dec. 15, in Hamilton, Widow Mercy SMITH, age 83.

Dec. 29, Betsey, wife of the late William RHODES, age 75 years, 9 months, 9 days.

Dec. 7, at Ada, MI, Cornelia J., wife of Frank WASHBURN, and daughter of Nelson E. MURDOCK, formerly of Hubbardsville, age 29.

Dec. 25, in Smyrna, Benjamin B. HAYWARD, age 72 years, 9 months.

1864

Nov. 15, (1863), at US General Hospital, New Orleans, Sgt. Joel C. RICHMOND, Co. D, 114th Reg., NY Vol., age 28, formerly of Lebanon; member of Baptist Church of West Eaton.

Dec. 12, (1863), in US Hospital at New Iberia, LA, George W. DUNHAM, Co. G, 114th Reg., NY Vol., age 21.

Jan. 21, at his home near this village [Hamilton], Oscar MOSELEY, age 45.

Oct. 21, (1863), at Yorktown, VA, of fever, Kelsey, son of Nelson BROOKS, of Earlville, age 19.

Jan. 30 or 31, in St. Louis, Mrs. BIRGE, wife of Dr. J. W. BIRGE, late of this village [Hamilton.]

Jan. 21, at his residence near this village [Hamilton], of pneumonia, Mr. Eli ROWELL, age 74.

Jan. 23, at Fairville, Wayne Co., NY, Lucy Tompkins, formerly of Madison, wife of Rev. Chester HOLCOMB, age 57.

1864

Feb. 8, in this village [Hamilton], Adeline, wife of E. W. FOOTE, in her 37th year.

Jan. 27, in Nelson, Joshua WELLS, age 91 years, 6 months, 10 days. He was born in RI, and one of the first settlers in the town of Nelson. He had 10 children, 28 grandchildren, and 24 great-grandchildren.

Feb. 3, Mr. Leonard L. RISLEY, age 20 years, 9 months.

[No date], at New York City, Miss Lola P. ABBOTT, only daughter of Samuel S. and Mary C. ABBOTT, age 20 years, 1 month, 25 days.

Feb. 2, of diphtheria, Alice L., aged 8; on Feb. 3, Nellie L., aged 3; on Feb. 10, Aaron F., aged 5; only children of Merton and Adelia BEACH, of Poolville.

Feb. 20, in Cazenovia, of palsy, Mr. Eleazer SEYMOUR, formerly of Lebanon, in his 60th year.

[No date], in Port Byron, IL, of consumption, A. Judson BROWN, son of Rev. P. P. BROWN, of Madison, age 38.

Feb. 19, in Augusta, Almon STEWART, age 75.

Feb. 26, in Hamilton, Mr. Henry A. BAKER, of consumption, aged 23 years, 7 months.

Jan. 17, in Franklin Hospital, LA, Truman Z. WEDGE, Musician in Co. D, 114th Reg., NY Vol., son of Merrit and Mary WEDGE, of South Lebanon, in his 23d year.

DEMOCRATIC REPUBLICAN
1864
(File complete)

Dec. 12, (1863), at Kingsbury Ferry, CA, Mr. George HUBBARD, of consumption, age 40; formerly of Hamilton, NY.

Mar. 1, 1864, in Centralia, IL, Mrs. Sarah WILLARD, age 85.

Mar. 17, in Lebanon, Mr. J. M. BRIGGS, age 64. He leaves a widow and 2 sons--Lieut. Morris BRIGGS, of the army, and Walter BRIGGS.

Feb. 17, 1864, of putrid canker rash, Annette SQUIRES, age 5. [Also;]

On Feb. 26, of the same disease, Herlbert SQUIRES, age 3, both children of William SQUIRES.

Mar. 22, in Sherburne, Mrs. Sarah ROBINSON, of inflamatory rheumatism, age 23 years, 9 months, 9 days; daughter of C. R. POTTER.

Feb. 14, in Big Flats, Chemung Co., Mr. William R. HUBBARD, husband of Sophia Abbe.

Mar. 10, Mrs. Mariar (?, Marian) HARTSHORN, age 64 years, 5 months, 22 days. She was born in Becket, Berkshire Co., MA.

In issue of Apr. 14: We learn by telegraph, that Hon. Alfred NICHOLS, Special Co. Judge of Chenango Co., died at his residence in Sherburne on Sunday night last, of diphtheria.

Apr. 16, in South Hamilton, Mr. Daniel WELLS, age 61.

Apr. 23, in Lebanon, Phoebe, widow of Charles CAMPBELL, age 88.

Apr. 13, in Galesburg, IL, of consumption, Mrs. Sarah A. BABCOCK, wife of Charles; age 33 years, 6 months, formerly of Hamilton.

May 6, at Hamilton, of consumption, Chloe A., wife of H. S. HAYWARD, age 23.

Apr. 26, in Fultonville, Coralinn E. FOX, age 10 months 11 days, and;

Apr. 28, Ida Minette FOX, age 3 years, 3 months, both children of Wilson and Carrie FOX. Mrs. FOX is a daughter of G. R. WALDRON of this place.

May 21, Kitty NUZUM, age 2 years, 1 month, 12 days, adopted daughter of William and Eliza NUZUM, of Hamilton.

May 9, in Lebanon, Mr. James K. BENEDICT, of congestion of the lung, age 74. He was born in Danby, CT.

May 15, in Hamilton, James WICKWIRE, age 88.

June 28, in Hamilton, Charlie R. BACON, age 6 years, 10 months.

DEMOCRATIC REPUBLICAN - 1864

May 11, at the hospital in Washington, Sgt. Warren BAKER, one of the original members of Capt. BROOKS Co., of the 61st Reg., NY Vol.; buried at Munnsville; age 26.

June 27, in Hamilton, Mr. John TRACY, age 71 years, 4 months.

June 17, in Hamilton, Willie H., son of T. and B. HOBBS, of croup; age 2 years, 8 months.

June 27, in Eaton, Angie L. CADY, wife of Israel BONNEY, (son of J. M. BONNEY of this village), of consumption, age 21.

June 27, in Eaton, Levell, son of Israel and Angie L. BONNEY, of inflammation of the brain, age 6 months.

[No date], at the Battle of White Oak Swamp, Charles Downing GORMAN, son of Rev. S. GORMAN; of Canton, OH, age 17 years, 9 months, 19 days.

July 10, at Eaton, Cordelia, daughter of E. W. and C. M. LANCKTON, age 19.

July 18, in Lebanon, Mrs. Hannah LIVINGSTON, age 88 years, 7 months.

July 17, in Hamilton, of consumption, James ONDERDONK, age 23 years, 11 months.

June 6, in Pierceville, of diphtheria, Andrew N., age 6 years, 16 days, son of Amos and Luna HAMMOND.

[No date], in Pierceville, Alfarettie Alzina, age 19 days, daughter of Amos and Luna HAMMOND.

[No date], in Hamilton, Alvah, infant son of Leonard A. and Lydia BROCKETT, age 6 months, 21 days.

July 11, in Hamilton, Willie Pearl, son of James L. and Maria O. FAYE, age 8 years, 7 months.

Aug. 8, in Hamilton, of enlargement of the heart, George WILCOX, age 17 years, 11 months.

Aug. 6, in Lebanon, Mrs. Amanda, wife of E. G. OATMAN, age 27.

Aug. 22, in Earlville, Fannie, wife of Ebenezer CRAIN, age 57.

Aug. 12, in Brooklyn, Thomas WYLIE, Esq., age 80.

Aug. 14, in Eaton, Samuel Warren, son of Warren J. and Esther BUELL, age 3 years, 5 months, 4 days.

Col. Carter VAN VLECK, son of Dr. V. H. VAN VLECK, of this village, died while serving his country, near Atlanta, GA, Aug. 23. Was a member of the 78th IL Vol. Buried at Macomb, IL.

Sept. 8, in Hamilton, George ALBERT, age 58.

Sept. 19, Mrs. Lydia BUELL, wife of Ira W. BUELL, age 32 years; at Steuben, Oneida Co.

Sept. 17, in Lebanon, of dysentery, Carrie, daughter of John Jr. and Nettie A. FISK, age 13 months, 16 days.

DEMOCRATIC REPUBLICAN - 1864

Sept. 14, at Post Hospital, Ft. Slocum, Washington, DC, of typhoid fever, Cpl. Edgar L. WARNER, age 35.

Sept. 29, in Hamilton, of typhoid fever, Mrs. Lydia P., wife of L. A. BROCKET, age 35.

Sept. 17, in Quincy, IL, Cornelia A., wife of D. A. KELSEY, formerly of Smyrna, age 26.

Sept. 25, in Madison, Benjamin ALVERSON, age 77.

[No date given], at the Tyler House, Ft. Monroe, VA, of typhoid fever, Jerusha D. DAY, of Lebanon.

Sept. 18, at Winchester, Stephen WEAVER, 1st Sgt. Co. "F", 114th Reg. Vols., age 21 years, son of Jehial WEAVER, of Smyrna.

Oct. 6, in Lebanon, Asa B. GEER, age 38.

Oct. 16, in Brookfield, Albert G., son of Samuel and Mercy CLARK, age 25.

Oct. 18, in Lebanon, Betsey, wife of Amos GEER, age 78

Oct. 2, in Hospital at Winchester, VA, Albert J. HOLMES, of the 114th Reg. NY Vols., son of Jabez HOLMES, Esq. of Poolville.

Oct. 18, at Lebanon, Jennie, daughter of M. L. and S. M. RUSSELL, age 4 years, 3 months.

Oct. 18, in South Hamilton, Simeon B. CLARK, age 70 years, 9 months, 15 days.

Oct. 16, in Lebanon, of diphtheria, Sarah Ann, daughter of J. and W. A. OSTROM, age 1 year, 10 months, 14 days.

Oct. 19, in Stockbridge, J. M. LIVERMORE, Jr. of Madison, age 27.

Sept. 19, in Hampton Hospital, Ft. Monroe, VA, age 19, Truman SMITH, son of Lucius SMITH, of Brookfield.

Nov. 14, in Lebanon, of diphtheria, John OSTROM, age 49 years, 9 months, 9 days.

Dec. 23, in Cooperstown, of pulmonary consumption, Dr. W. WEBER, formerly of Plymouth, ME, age 30.

Oct. 7, in Lebanon, Chauncey BUELL, age 61.

Nov. 16, at Hamilton, Mrs. Susan N. CAMPBELL, age 66 years, 10 months.

Nov. 29, in Quincy, IL, Dr. N. B. MEAD, of Smyrna, age 74.

Dec. 22, in Hamilton, Frances Ann, wife of J. P. RHODES, age 43.

[No date], in Brookfield, Deacon Bell LEWIS, age 58.

Dec. 27, in Rochester, Araunah MOSELEY, age 93.

1865

Jan. 6, in Smyrna, Julius KELSEY, age 61.

Dec. 22, (1864), Mrs. Frances W., wife of J. P. RHODES, age 43.

DEMOCRATIC REPUBLICAN - 1865

Jan. 14, in Peterboro, Silas MARSH, age 70.
Feb. 1, in Madison, Samuel BURNHAM, age 88.
Jan. 2, in Oriskany Falls, wife of Charles S. MACUMBER, age 25 years, 11 days.
Feb. 20, at Eaton, Benjamin T. CAMPBELL, age 64.
Feb. 16, in Brookfield, May F., only daughter of E. R. and Jennie S. BARDINE, age 2 years, 3 months, 2 days.
Mar. 2, in Hamilton, Mrs. Mary STEERE, relict of Capt. Esek STEERE, deceased, age 79. She was born in Woodstock, CT.
Mar. 14, in Hamilton, Charles SMITH, age 16.
Mar. 17, Miss Nancy WEIR, age 83.
Mar. 17, in Hamilton, Mrs. Sarah CARDER, age 79.
Mar. 26, in East Hamilton, of inflamation of the lung, Samuel A. BRAINARD, age 57.
Mar. 23, in Madison, Mrs. Mariette DICK, age 52 years, 6 months, 10 days.
Mar. 28, in Eaton, Abigail MILES, age 35.
Mar. 29, in Hamilton, Tryphenia TITUS, age 38.
Apr. 4, in Earlville, Joseph LONG, age 83 years, 11 months, 20 days.
Apr. 8, in Richfield, of consumption, Sarah L. BURGESS, wife of O. E. WILCOX, M.D., age 27 years, 10 days.
[No date], at Canton, NY, of malignant scarletina, Willie R., son of Lisle and Fannie C. HOLMES, age 4 years, 9 months.
Apr. 24, in Lebanon, Nancy R., wife of Bryant WYNN, age 24.
May 1, in Madison, of typhoid fever, Miss Frankie L. RICHMOND, age 22 years, 10 months.
Apr. 27, in Eaton, Mrs. M. WHITNEY, age 72.
Apr. 26, in Earlville, of brain fever, Myrtie I., son of Myron and Eugenia HENRY, age 10 years, 6 months.
May 12, in Earlville, Othnial SLOCUM, age 87.
May 12, at his grandfather's in Eaton, John Landon, 2d son of William Henry and Kate L. DAVIS, age 5 years, 5 months.
Apr. 26, in Lebanon, Mrs. BAKER, wife of Samuel BAKER, age 70.
May 2, in Earlville, Harry FELT, age 56.
June 8, at the home of Mr. LETCHWORTH, Buffalo, Miss Hattie PEARL, daughter of Erastus and Clara PEARL, of Hamilton, age 17 years, 7 months.
June 24, in Lebanon, Chauncey S. HALL, son of Reuben S. and Finetta HALL, age 5 years, 6 months.
July 15, in Lebanon, Silas N. GATES, age 67.
July 18, in Madison, Miss Carrie Jane HENDERSON, age 3 years, 8 months.

DEMOCRATIC REPUBLICAN - 1865

July 23, in Lebanon, Mrs. Sally GREEN, age 69 years, 6 months.

July 21, in Lebanon, Josiah LASELLE, age 92 years, 10 months.

July 21, in Georgetown, Mr. Albert STILES, eldest son of Whitford and Sarah STILES, age 21.

June 15, at Boonsboro, IA, Joseph A. NORTON, Esq., age 59. He was a native of Lebanon. His brother-in-law, F. B. HOPPIN, died recently.

July 29, in Earlville, NY, Emma A., daughter of Andrew B. and Fannie M. NASH, age 17 years, 11 months, 6 days.

July 22, in Sempronius, NY, Philip VAN SLYCK, in his 72d year.

Aug. 10, in Hamilton, Deacon Westel BRONSON, age 70.

Aug. 21, in Lebanon, Freddie Lincoln, youngest son of Alfred and Rhoda SEYMOUR, age 6 months.

Aug. 21, in Hamilton, John B. SIMPSON, age 62.

Aug. 19, in Earlville, Charles WATERS, age 19.

[No date], in Hamilton, Mrs. Marcella W. PARKER, age 36.

Aug. 27, in Hamilton, Rosie May, infant daughter of Lyman and Eliza FRISBIE, age 4 months.

Aug. 23, in Lebanon, Cornelia POWELL, age 51.

Aug. 25, in Hamilton, James BROGAN, age 54.

Aug. 28, in Hamilton, Bridget BROGAN, age 86.

Aug. 25, in Madison, Minnie A. BROWN, age 5 mos., 20 days.

Aug. 30, in Hamilton, Mr. Albinus HUNT, age 36.

Sept. 11, in Hamilton, Mrs. Mary H. OLMSTED, age 80.

Sept. 8, in Hamilton, Mrs. Huldah A. SPURR, age 48.

Sept. 4, in Hamilton, Mrs. Lucinda PIERCE, age 80.

Sept. 4, in Hamilton, Linus M. CAMPBELL, age 10 months.

Sept. 10, in Eaton, Richard WATERS, age 78.

Sept. 6, in Vineland, NJ, Alanson P. POND, son of Eli POND, of Hamilton, age 22.

Sept. 7, in Madison, Charles BROWN, son of James BROWN, age 7 months, 9 days.

Sept. 16, in Brookfield, Sylvester RISLEY, age 68 years, 3 months.

Sept. 17, in Hamilton, James PUTNAM, age 64 years, 3 months.

Sept. 16, in Madison, Rebecca PEEBLES, age 86.

Sept. 13, in Pine Woods, William EVANS, age 73.

Sept. 16, in Hamilton, Mary GLEASON, age 77.

Sept. 13, in Lebanon, George CHAMPLIN, age 77 years, 3 months.

Sept. 13, in Lebanon, Reuben BISBEE, age 89.

Sept. 16, Richie, only child of Albert and Lucinda PIERCE, age 4 months.

Sept. 28, in Baldwinsville, Robert A. CAMPBELL, age 40.

DEMOCRATIC REPUBLICAN - 1865

Oct. 2, in Eaton, Nancy, wife of S. R. SHERRILL, age 69.
Sept. 28, in Lebanon, Nettie J., daughter of Philander C. and Ann C. BUELL, age 9 years, 8 months.
Oct. 5, in Eaton, Edward LEWIS, age 59.
Oct. 1, in Willet, Adam F., son of Henry and Julia A. WILES, age 35 years, 3 months.
Oct. 6, in Hamilton, Amy Y. GRIMSHAW, age 60 years, 6 months.
Oct. 14, in Madison, Margaret EVANS, age 47.
Oct. 16, in Eaton, Rhoda CHAPMAN, age 60.
Oct. 17, in Lebanon, Esther LEWIS, age 88.
Oct. 19, in Lebanon, Clarissa E. ARMSTRONG, age 77.
Oct. 22, in Hamilton, Charles H., son of Rev. W. R. BROOKS, age 20 years, 5 months, 9 days.
Oct. 30, in Hamilton, Zenas NASH, age 67.
Sept. 19, in Franklin, Delaware Co., from injuries received in the Army, Hobart E. SHARTS, age 28 years, 7 months, 12 days.
Nov. 12, in Hamilton, Susan, relict of Joseph MOTT, age 80.
Nov. 4, in Earlville, John M. HOWARD, age 49.
Nov. 5, in East Hamilton, Louisa RAY, age 43.
Nov. 9, in Eaton, Clarissa ABBOTT, age 6 7.
Nov. 13, in Eaton, Augustus HOUGHTON, age 59.
Nov. 20, in Hamilton, Asa HARTSHORN, age 69.
Nov. 20, in Hamilton, Catherine, wife of Amasa ROWELL.
Nov. 23, in Hamilton, Harriet, relict of Zenas NASH, age 60.
Nov. 29, in Morrisville, Mary YOAR, age 73.
Nov. 26, in Morrisville, Adeline M., wife of E. C. TOPLIFF, age 53.
Dec. 5, in Earlville, Clara E. ROBINSON, age 4 years, 5 months, 14 days.
Nov. 30, in Norwich, Deacon Williams AVERY, age 67, of Georgetown, formerly of Sherburne.
Oct. 8, in Brighton, Sacramento Co., CA, Corda Violet, daughter of Nelson and Abby WILCOX, age 9 months, 24 days.
Dec. 24, in Eaton, Sylvester FINNEY, age 78.
Dec. 27, in Hamilton, Lucy, wife of Ebenezer DEWEY, age 74.

1866

Jan. 10, at Hamilton, Miss A. Jane DEWEY, daughter of Ebenezer DEWEY, age 28 years (?).
Jan. 7, at East Hamilton, Ellen R., daughter of Hiram R. and Julia ACKLEY, age 18 years, 8 months.

DEMOCRATIC REPUBLICAN - 1866

Jan. 9, in Lebanon, Mrs. Frances CUPPERNULL, age 21.
Jan. 2, in Smyrna, Mr. John W. REYNOLDS, age 40.
Jan. 2, in Eaton, Willie JONES, age 4.
Jan. 8, in Morrisville, of lung fever, Caroline MORSE, age 63.
Jan. 29, in Jeffersonville, IN, of typhoid fever, Miss Hattie M. EVERTS, age 20. She was a native of Eaton; taught music.
Feb. 2, in Hamilton, Mrs. Mary Ann SMITH, age 52 years, 10 months.
Feb. 3, in Hamilton, Polly RUSSELL, age 78.
Feb. 6, in Hamilton, Carrie, daughter of Seneca B. and Irene BURCHARD, age 11 years, 8 months.
Feb. 4, in Eaton, Betsey Lovina HAMMOND, age 53.
Jan. 25, in Madison, Ella VAN HOESEN, age 11.
Feb. 5, in Madison, John BIDWELL, age 10.
Feb. 1, in Georgetown, at residence of her son-in-law, Mrs. Mary CONANT, age 85.
Feb. 7, in Lebanon, of diphtheria, Philander C. BUELL, age 36 years, 6 months.
Feb. 7, at the residence of O. B. LORD, of croup, Lulu, only daughter of DeForest and Hannah LORD, age 1 year, 7 months.
Feb. 19, in Washington, DC, Rev. Rufus F. BUELL, late missionary to Greece, and eldest son of Eli BUELL, of this place [Hamilton]. He was buried in Evergreen Cemetery, Washington.
Mar. 2, in this village [Hamilton], of consumption, Sidney D. FAIRCHILDS, age 29.
Feb. 25, in Hamilton, Sophia BEACH, age 78.
Feb. 25, in Eaton, Jacob TUCKERMAN, age 64.
Feb. 27, in Madison, Mrs. Harriet PALMER, age 69.
Feb. 3, in Lebanon, of diphtheria, Mary E. BUELL, dau. of P. C. BUELL, age 4 years, 6 months.
Feb. 25 (?), in Lebanon, Orson T. LADD, age 56.
Mar. 2, in Hamilton, Leroy SMITH, age 24.
Mar. 1, in Eaton, Solomon HAMMOND, age 59.
Mar. 6, in Madison, John E. BURTON, age 79.
Mar. 11, in Morrisville, Byron O. NICHOLS, age 21.
Mar. 13, in Hamilton, Clarissa B., wife of John SMITH, age 74.
Mar. 11, in Morrisville, Calvin THOMPSON, age 88.
Mar. 14, in Hamilton, Mary F., daughter of Alonzo H. and Helen F. WEST, age 1 year, 9 months, 27 days.
Mar. 17, in Eaton, Blendena MATHEWS, age 25, of Fabius.
Mar. 20, in Lebanon, Dorcas LASELL, age 55 years, 9 months, 10 days.
Mar. 21, in Lebanon, John FISK, age 69.

DEMOCRATIC REPUBLICAN - 1866

Mar. 28, in Solsville, Mrs. Nancy JACOBY, age 27 years, 9 months.
Mar. 30, in Madison, Nancy LIVERMORE, age 51.
Apr. 3, in Poolville, Harriet WEBSTER, age 52.
Apr. 5, in Eaton, Louis L. CLARK, age 33.
Apr. 5, in Hamilton, Henry RUSSELL, age 26, of disease contracted in the Army.
Apr. 6, in Hamilton, Barbary FLAHERTY, age 45.
Apr. 7, in West Eaton, Frances A. MORGAN, age 19 years, 3 months.
Apr. 6, in Madison, Mrs. A. E. MATHEWSON, age 37 years, 7 months, 9 days.
Apr. 8, in Hamilton, Cora G. RICE, daughter of Warren RICE, age 4.
[No date], in Newark, Wayne Co., Mrs. Caroline LORD, formerly of Hamilton, age 82 years, 3 months.
Apr. 18, in Vineland, Mr. James GOVE, formerly of this village [Hamilton], age 64.
Apr. 11, at Buffalo, Mr. Sherman RISLEY, of Rolland, Ionia Co., MI. He was a brother of Charles and Allen RISLEY, of Hamilton; buried at Cole Hill, Madison.
Apr. 28, in Eaton, Leroy BONNEY, age 30.
Apr. 23, in Eaton, Mr. Asa CHASE, age 69 years, 9 months.
Apr. 11, in Eaton, Ervin MONTENA, age 3 months, 9 days.
Apr. 11, in Eaton, Mrs. Elmina BROWN, age 60.
Apr. 28, in Hamilton, Mrs. Laura WILLARD, age 66.
Apr. ??, in Eaton, Mrs. Ann TAINTER, age 63.
May 11, in Georgetown, Mr. Joel ANDREWS, age 72. He moved here from Westmoreland just four weeks before his death.
May 5, in Hubbardsville, Christina RHODES, age 36.
May 11, in Hamilton, Mary L., daughter of H. T. and Louise FRISBIE, age 2 years, 7 months.
May 22, in Hamilton, Miranda, wife of E. CURREY, age 58.
May 18, in Georgetown, Mrs. E. CURTIS, age 67.
May 17, in Hamilton, Mr. James Fenner SANFORD, age 18 years, 3 days.
May 3, in Canastota, Melissa, wife of Franklin BACON, age 23.
May 22, in Hubbardsville, Nathan BROWNELL, age 77.
May 29, in Earlville, Philura, wife of Allen HAYWARD, age 60.
May 26, in Earlville, Ann C., widow of the late Philander C. BUELL, age 34.
May 29, in Hamilton, Lewis CHAPPELL, age 78.
June 5, in Eaton, while on a visit, James T. HEWES, age 69.

DEMOCRATIC REPUBLICAN - 1866

June 7, in Hamilton, Lillian Eva, daughter of F. S. and Aurelia BONNEY, age 13 years, 6 months.
June 8, in Georgetown, Deacon Benjamin HURD, age 79. He was one of the first settlers of the town, and served in the War of 1812.
June 13, in Earlville, Chester C. RISLEY, age 30.
June 18, in Earlville, William FELT, age 66.
July 5, in Hamilton, Joshua WILLARD, age 71.
July 4, in Hamilton, H. Louise, youngest daughter of Rev. H. A. and Mrs. E. L. SMITH, age 13 years, 9 months.
July 9, in Morrisville, Mary LA MUNION, age 27.
July 8, in Madison, Silas E. GROSE, age 21.
June 25, in Eaton, Louisa B. COMAN, age 51.
April 26, in Brookfield, Emily A., wife of George E. PALMITER, daughter of Samuel and Mercy CLARK, age 22. (Note: the date--April--is as printed.)
July 4, in Hubbardsville, Celinda, wife of Lambert FULLER, age 75 years, 9 months. she was the youngest of 12 children.
July 19, in Hamilton, Henry F., youngest son of O. S. and --- CAMPBELL, age 4 years, 9 months, 13 days.
Aug. 4, in Poolville, Mrs. Abbie, wife of Charles AVERY, and daughter of Alpha DUNHAM, age 29.
Aug. 1, in Erieville, Ann, wife of Franklin W. SALISBURY, and daughter of Alfred MEDBURY, Esq., age 35.
Aug. 4, in Hamilton, Mr. Willard WELTON, age 84 years, 6 months.
July 27, in Brookfield, Willie H. BROWNELL, age 3 years, 2 months, 7 days.
July 25, in Madison, C. R. TYLER, age 29 years, 6 months.
July 22, in Madison, Lydia COMSTOCK, age 83.
Sept. 6, in Lawrence, MI, Mrs. Artimecia STURTEVANT, wife of Oran STURTEVANT, formerly of Madison, age 60.
Aug. 30, at Quincy, IL, Sidney S. BABCOCK, age 24.
Sept. 9, at Salem, (IL) Arthur M. BAKER, age 52. He was many years a resident of Hamilton, and Editor of the *Democratic Reflector*. He died at the residence of W. W. WILLARD, and leaves a wife and two sons.
Sept. 21, in Georgetown, a daughter of the late Barnard ANDREWS, age 7.
Sept. 18, in Hubbardsville, Ella, only daughter of Columbus F. and Ellen RHODES, age 9.
Sept. 20, in Hubbardsville, Ellen RHODES, wife of Columbus F. RHODES.
Oct. 15, in Hamilton, at residence of his son, A. V. BARDEEN, Cyrus BARDEEN, age 78.
Sept. 14, in Earlville, Mehitable CURTIS, age 86. She was the oldest member of the Methodist Church.

DEMOCRATIC REPUBLICAN - 1866

Oct. 28, in Poolville, Mrs. Rhoda DUNBAR, widow of David DUNBAR, age 77.

Nov. 10, in Cortland village, Jethro BONNEY, age 96. Was a Soldier of the War of 1812.

Nov. 10, in Lebanon, Mrs. Polly Campbell GATES, widow of Ezra GATES, in her 78th year. She was a native of CT.

Nov. 27, in Oriskany Falls, at residence of her son-in-law, F. N. BUSHNELL, Mrs. Harmony Wight RICE, wife of Baxter RICE, in her 76th year.

Dec. 18, in Hamilton, Medad ROGERS, in his 83d year. He was son of Dr. Timothy ROGERS, and born in Cornwall, Litchfield Co., CT, Oct. 28, 1784. He came to Hamilton in March 1800.

Dec. 5, in Hamilton, Freddie Lester, son of Sylvester BURCHARD, age 8 years, 8 days.

1867

[No date, but was early Jan. 1867], in Hamilton, Orlando Lavell, son of George M. and C. A. RHODES.

Jan. 6, in Hamilton, Mrs. Tryphosa SWEET, age 75, formerly wife of A. T. MURDOCK.

Dec. 29, (1866), in North Brookfield, Deacon Zadoc BEEBE, in his 95th year. He was the oldest but one (Mrs. JOHNSON) in the town. Has resided in Brookfield (North) for 70 years.

Jan. 16, in Poolville, Nehemiah SMITH, age 85.

Jan. 5, in Hamilton, Mrs. Olive BRAINARD, age 88, wife of Ezra BRAINARD, deceased.

Jan. 21, at South Brookfield, Ira B. CRANDALL, Esq., in his 56th year. He leaves a widow and six children.

[No date], in Madison, Gertrude, only child of Alonzo CURTIS, in her 6th year.

Jan. 18, in Georgetown, Mrs. MORSON, mother of Reuben MORSON, in her 85th year.

Feb. 11, in Albany, Mary Loree, eldest daughter of Rev. Andrew B. and Mary C. MORSE, of Eaton, in her 10th year.

Feb. 15, in Oil City, PA, Belinda S., wife of Andrew CONE, and oldest daughter of Calvin MORSE, of Eaton, age 43.

July 21, (1866), at Northeast, Erie Co., PA, David Y. FOOTE, M.D., only son of the late Noah B. FOOTE, M.D., of East Hamilton, age 64.

Feb. 27, in Georgetown, at residence of her son, Mr. John KNAPP, Mrs. Sally KNAPP, age about 70.

DEMOCRATIC REPUBLICAN - 1867

Mar. 4, in Otselic, Vincent GOODSELL, age 27 years, 3 months.

Feb. 14, in Smyrna, Miss Avis CAMPBELL, only daughter of Daniel and Theodocia CAMPBELL, age 27.

Mar. 3, in Penn Yan, Mary A., wife of Rev. E. P. BRIGHAM, age 34 years, 1 month. Funeral held at residence of her father, Alvah HOPKINS, Esq., of Hamilton.

Mar. 6, in Georgetown, Mr. Horace PERRY, age 51.

Mar. 9, in Georgetown, Mrs. Betsey CROSS, age 76.

[No date], in Madison, Willie, only son of George and Rose BAKER, age 4.

Mar. 16, in Masonville, Delaware Co., Mr. Daniel NEFF, in his 86th year. He was born in Amsterdam, Montgomery Co., NY and was father of eleven children, ten now living; the youngest is over 40 years old.

Mar. 19, in Eaton, Frank S., youngest child of Sylvester and Allie BURCHARD, age 10 months, 17 days.

Feb. 21, in Hamilton, Mr. John ROWELL, age 71.

Mar. 22, in Hamilton, Mrs. Prudence O. MOTT, wife of Smith MOTT, and daughter of the late John D. BLISH, age 53.

Apr. 1, in Madison, Mrs. Elizabeth ABBERT, age 88 years, 11 months.

Apr. 7, in Hamilton, Horace WELCH, age 49 years, 11 months.

Apr. 2, in Cazenovia, Mrs. Phila LAWRENCE, age 94. She was born in Bennington, VT, in 1773. Her father, Mr. FILLMORE, held a commission in the American Army in the Revolutionary War and took an active part in the Battle of Bennington in 1777. She married a Mr. DIXON at Bennington, who died within a few years. Later she married Mr. Pitt LAWRENCE, also of Bennington, and they emigrated to Georgetown about 60 years ago, some of the first settlers of the town. They were among the 21 who joined in forming the Baptist Church there. Mr. LAWRENCE died 25 years ago, after which she resided with her son-in-law, Mr. Elijah ATKYNS, in Georgetown, and later, in Cazenovia.

Apr. 21, in Pine Woods, Linn, only son of George R. and Calista SETON, age 2 years, 1 month, 18 days.

Apr. 29, in Morrisville, Mrs. Betsey CRANDALL, age 75.

Apr. 20, in Earlville, Eliza WILBUR, age 41.

May 5, in Hamilton, Albinus HUNT, age 74.

Mar. 20, in Georgetown, Maria, wife of Amasa JACKSON, age 63.

April 13th, in Seneca Falls, NY, Theresa, wife of Charles D. V. CARTER, age 24 years, 4 months, 19 days.

May 7, in Hamilton, J. Thomas RUSSELL, age 26 years.

DEMOCRATIC REPUBLICAN - 1867

May 12, in East Hamilton, Asa CROCKER, age 83 years.
May 12, in East Hamilton, Grace MORGAN, relict of A. Daniel MORGEN (sic), age 82 years.
May 11, in Nelson, George C. IRISH, age 62 years.
May 9, in Nelson, Philip SHAFFER, age 44 years.
[No date], in Nelson, Mrs. Ruhama, wife of Grandly CASE, age 76 years.

****

The Genealogy "The BONNEY FAMILY," by Chas. L. Bonney; 1898 states on page 103(8?):
"RUHAMA BONNEY, born June 12, 1791, d. May 13, 1867; age 76 years. She married Grandly CASE of Hamilton, NY, a farmer. They had: Dwight, Isaac Newton, Lafayette, Hyman P., Byron and Burns, twins, John Quincy Adams, Benjamin Franklin, Caroline and Francis."
"Ruhama was daughter of Edward BONNEY, born in Conn. in 1765, died 1846; moved to Washington Co., NY, where he married Hannah FINCH, Dec. 13, 1787, dau. of Joshua FINCH. Her grandfather was an officer in the French and Indian War, and was shot from his horse by Tories at Greenbush (now East Albany). She had five brothers in the War of 1812. Edward moved to Madison Co., NY in 1801, and purchased a large farm." "Had Neman, Ruhama, Perez, Harwood, Lucretia, Levi, Levi Bisbee, Lucinda, Jethro May, and William Finch."
Edward BONNEY was a son of Levi BONNEY, born 1743, who married Mary MAY. He was a carpenter, served in the French and Indian War and in the Revolutionary War, at the close of which he became a farmer in New York State. He died May 24, 1824.
Levi BONNEY was a son of Job BONNEY, bap. Apr. 26, 1713; married Ruth BISBEE on May 9, 1733.
Job BONNEY was son of James "of Duxbury," married in 1695, Abigail BISHOP, Dau. of James BISHOP of New Haven who was first Secretary of the colony in 1651; representative; Deputy Gov., etc.

****

June 7, in Hamilton, Mr. James L. FAY, age 44 years, formerly of Earlville.
June 9, at Oriskany Falls, NY, by drowning, Peter S. QUICK, age 4 years, 6 months.
May 28, at Georgetown, Lizzie, only child of Frank and Adelia STEWART, age 1 year, 9 months.

DEMOCRATIC REPUBLICAN - 1867

June 7, at Madison, Anna Lewis, daughter of William E. and Lizzie M. MERCER, age 8 months, 7 days.

June 16th, in Hamilton, at the home of her son, Mr. A. J. CADY, Mrs. Susannah CADY, age 93 years. She was one of the first settlers of the Valley, coming here when the country was almost a trackless forest. She attended the first funeral of a white person held in the settlement, that of the wife of the late Elisha PAYNE, who was buried on the spot now occupied by the old burying ground near Hamilton House, then in its primeval state, covered with heavy timber.

July 9, in Madison, Amelia M., wife of Ezra B. CAMPBELL, aged 36 years.

[No date], in East Hamilton, Anna Louisa, daughter of Albert and Juliaette BEEBE, aged 9 months. Mrs. BEEBE came to her native place for the health of herself and child, but the climate proved too severe for little Anna, who died after 2 days. Mrs. BEEBE has gone back to the city.

On the 22nd, in Bouckville, Eugene, son of Joseph and Elizabeth W. FORWARD, aged 4 months.

Aug. 29, in West Troy, John WARNER, aged 28 years.

Sept. 1, in Georgetown, Mrs. TUE, wife of John TUE, aged 50 years.

Sept. 9, in Otselic, Dora, only daughter of Berdett and Lydia CROSS, aged 3 years.

Sept. 17, in Morrisville, Mary, wife of Jonathan WELLS, aged 50 years.

Also, on the morning of the 19th at the same place, of the same disease, typhoid fever, Jonathan WELLS, aged 49 years.

Aug. 27, at Providence, RI, Fidella Valmette, wife of Harry E. MILLARD, formerly of Hartford, CT, and daughter of William O. SUMNER, of Munnsville, Madison Co., NY, aged 30 years.

Sept. 25, in Earlville, Ebenezer CRAIN, aged 80 years.

Sept. 16, at Apulia, Onondaga Co., NY, Henry, youngest child of Nelson and Mary J. TAYLOR, aged 3 years.

Nov. 4, in Sherburne, Charles HUNT, aged 68 years.

Nov. 9, in Morrisville, Miss Hattie FRY, aged 20 years.

Nov. 18, in Madison, Mrs. C. A., wife of L. W. CURTIS, aged 58 years.

Nov. 15, in Hamilton, Charles P. THOMPSON, aged 29 years.

Nov. 18, in Hamilton, Jake JOHNSON, aged 40 years.

Dec. 15, in Eaton, Miss Sarah BONNEY, age 60 years.

Dec. 3, in Eaton, Mrs. William T. EATON, aged 43 years.

Dec. 24, at the residence of her son, A. PECK, Mrs. Elizabeth PECK, aged 93 years.

DEMOCRATIC REPUBLICAN - 1867

Dec. 30, in Hamilton, Philip C. SLOCUM, aged 48 years.
Dec. 12, in Framingham, MA, Joseph Cyril ADAMS, aged 83 years.

1868

Jan. 6, in Morrisville, Rynaldo BURDWIN, aged 72 years.
Jan. 1, in Georgetown, Mr. William P. HARS, aged 69 years.
Jan. 25, in Hamilton, William SHERMAN, aged 27 years.
Jan. 14, in Georgetown, Mrs. Susan STEWART, aged 82 years.
Jan. 29, in Georgetown, Benjamin BONNEY, aged 86 years.
Jan. 29, in Georgetown, Claude W., infant son of William C. and Electa UTTER, aged 24 days.
Feb. 16, in Hamilton, Lizzie WILLIAMS, aged 3 years.
Jan. 30, in East Hamilton, Willie CLARK, aged 15 years.
Feb. 19, in Earlville, Polly, wife of John R. WOODWORTH, aged 70 years.
Feb. 20, in Bouckville, Maria, wife of Major William W. EDGARTON (no age given).
Feb. 19, in Eaton village, Ella May, daughter of Orrin and Jane HAMMOND, age 1 year.
Feb. 23, in town of Eaton, Mr. Calvin CROSS, aged 87 years. He was born in Bennington, VT, from which place he emigrated at 14 years of age, to what is now Hamilton village. Then there was only one house where the village is now located. He remained there a few years, then removed to Georgetown, where he remained until a few months ago. He enlisted in the army in the War of 1812. His march to Sackett Harbor and its attempted capture by the British he often described. He helped build the Baptist Church in Georgetown, and was an active member for 36 years.
Feb. 22, in Georgetown, Mrs. Maria PERRY, wife of Lyman PERRY, aged 52 years.
Feb. 25, in Georgetown, infant child of Charle and Mary J. WILCOX, age 4 months.
Mar. 4, in South Otselic, Mrs. Amanda TURNER, wife of Rev. H. TURNER, aged 64 years.
Mar. 8, near South Hamilton, Stephen B. JENKS, aged 74 years.
Mar. 17, in Madison, Mrs. Amelia RISLEY, widow of Elizur RISLEY, late of Madison, age 87 years.
Mar. 9, in Georgetown, Mrs. Esther DRYER, wife of John DRYER, age 31 years.
Mar. 24, in Solsville, Nathaniel PIERCE, age 81 years.

DEMOCRATIC REPUBLICAN - 1868

April 11, Mary Pauline, daughter of Prof. GOODENOUGH, of the Hamilton Female Seminary, aged 1 year, 5 months.
On the 18th, in Nelson, Susan SWEET, relict of Jonathan SWEET, aged 70 years.
On the 5th, in Nelson, Col. Jacob SCHAFFER, aged 71 years.
April 10, in this village [Hamilton], Clarence J. RHODES, aged 19 years.
Apr. 27, in this village [Hamilton], Mr. Lewis WICKWIRE, aged 66 years.
Apr. 10, in this village [Hamilton], Mr. Levi SHEPARD, father of William SHEPARD and Mrs. PERRIOR, formerly of Hamilton, aged 89 years. This notice from the *Iowa Daily State Register* of April 12th.
May 5, in Eaton, Mrs. Emeline GILBERT, wife of Robert GILBERT, aged 27 years.
May 2, in Hamilton, Bethsheba KEYES, aged 80 years.
May 26, in Hamilton, Lucretia BRONSON, daughter of John BRONSON, Esq., aged 25 years.
[No date], at the residence of her father in Solsville, Calista D. MANCHESTER, wife of Fluvius J. MANCHESTER, aged 34 years.
June 24, in Orange, NJ, at the residence of his father, Rev. R. V. W. SNOW, of the class of '63, of Madison University, aged 27 years.
July 26, in Madison, Melissa N., daughter of E.B. and Ruth H. WOODMAN, aged 18 years.
July 24, in Earlville, Bertha, only daughter of David E. and Chloe NASH, aged 21 years, 4 months.
July 24, in Hamilton, Eugene L. CORWIN, aged 21 years.
July 25, in Eaton, John P. HATCH, aged 47 years.
July 6, in Madison, Isaac CHADWICK, aged 80 years, 9 months, 13 days. Wisconsin and Ohio papers please copy.
Aug. 9, in this village [Hamilton], Mrs. Elizabeth A. WHEELER, age 60 years. She was born Elizabeth UPHAM in Hamilton in 1808. She married Erastus WHEELER in 1832, and survived him by just 5 years. She spent most of her life in Hamilton.
Aug. 10, in Waterville, Miss Amanda BANTON, aged 44 years. She was the daughter of Jonas BANTON, Esq.
Aug. 31, in Hamilton, Harry, infant son of R. H. and Mary HOWE, aged 4 months.
Sept. 22, in Smithfield, Mary, wife of V. M. ARNOLD, aged 50 years.
Sept. 22, in Hamilton, Nettie, daughter of Daniel READ, aged 13 years, 10 months.
Sept. 21, in Eaton, Alita LAMPHERE, aged 25 years.
Oct. 6, in Lebanon, Charlotte E. KINGSLEY, aged 29 years.

DEMOCRATIC REPUBLICAN - 1868

Oct. 5, in Hamilton, Josephine ROGERS, aged 26 years.
Sept. 29, in Morrisville, Ebenezer G. TIDD, aged 76 years.
Sept. 28, in Bouckville, Mrs. A. E. COOK, aged 29 years.
Oct. 20, in Melmore, OH, Jessie T. LADD, aged 49 years, formerly of Lebanon.
Nov. 2, in Hamilton, Edward WILLEY, aged 49 years.
Nov. 15, in Bouckville, Darius MARTIN, age 76 years.
Nov. 9, at his residence in Lebanon, Curtis HOPPIN, age 84 years. He was one of the earliest settlers of Madison Co. He was born at Guilford, CT, July 12, 1785. His parents moved to Berkshire Co., MA, and died there, leaving him an orphan at an early age. He inherited a robust constitution and an empty purse. He commenced life with 2 sheep, a copy of Morse's School Geography, a suit of linsey woolsey, and an energetic self-reliant disposition. During winter evenings and early mornings, he acquired an education, which enabled him to teach, which he did for several years in MA, and during the winters, several years in Lebanon. In the spring of 1810, he started on foot for what was thought to be the far west in search of cheap lands, and bought on what is known by old settlers, as Hoppin's Hill. Later that season he moved his family to his new home, at the same time driving with him his flock of 230 merino sheep, first flock ever to be brought into this country, which, under his care, increased in a few years to 4,000 making him the largest wool grower in Madison County. He served as an Officer of the NY Militia, which was called to Sackett's Harbor in 1814, and served his town as supervisor and in other capacities, and his County as Member of Assembly in 1827. He was a deacon in the Congregational Church at Eaton for many years.
Dec. 4, in Cape May, Erial C. WHEELER, in his 56th year. He was a former resident of Madison Co.
Dec. 3, in Hamilton, at residence of her niece, Sarah J. COON, occurred the death of Mrs. Mary Ann HOXIE, in her 77th year.
Dec. 22, in Hamilton, Thomas GARDINER, aged 22 years.
Dec. 28, in Madison, Cornelia J., wife of Lyman BLAKEMAN, and daughter of Isaac COLLISTER, Esq.

1869

Jan. 28, in Hamilton, Mary, wife of Benjamin BATEMAN, aged 61 years, 10 months.

DEMOCRATIC REPUBLICAN - 1869

Feb. 3, in Hamilton, in the triumphs of a Christian faith, after a long and painful sickness, Caroline, wife of Lyman ROGERS, in her 31st year.

Jan. 29, in Otselic, James R. BROWN, aged 69 years.

Feb. 9, at the residence of her brother-in-law, Rev. T. R. TOWNSEND, Meridian, NY, Emiline SHAPLEY, wife of Rev. H. S. REDFIELD, pastor of the First Congregational Church, Lebanon.

In Clyde, NY, at the residence of his son, H. P. RANGER, Esq., after a short illness, John T. RANGER, aged 68 years. [In issue of Feb. 18, 1869.]

On Stratford St., Madison, NY, Mr. William LEWIS, aged 84 years.

At Madison, Mrs. Mary RICHARDS, wife of Daniel J. RICHARDS, aged 28 years.

At his residence in the village, Feb. 20th, Eli BUEL, 80 years, 6 days.

Feb. 23, in Hamilton, Gertie C., daughter of Hiram T. and Ellen WILCOX, in her 15th year.

Mar. 15, in Lebanon, Caroline, wife of David B. BARBER, aged 63 years, 7 months.

Mar. 20, in Hamilton, Mr. Nelson BAKER, very suddenly, aged 55 years.

In Eaton, Mrs. Laura BOOTH, aged 45 years. [Issue of March 25, 1869.]

Mar. 21, in Lebanon, Mrs. Martha E. BROWN, aged 49 years, wife of A. L. BROWN.

Mar. 21, in Lebanon, J. Milton MEDBURY, age 6 years, 6 months.

Mar. 20, in Poolville, Mr. Mamoris (?) WILLIAMS, age 50 years.

Mar. 31, in Lebanon, Norton NASH, age 58 years.

Mar. 20, in Rockford, IL, Jeremiah GREEN, age 68. He formerly practiced medicine in this village.

Apr. 1, in Lebanon, Mary, wife of Heman HOTCHKIN, age 50 years.

Mar. 26, near Poolville, Miss Hannah GREEN, age 67 years.

Mar. 19, at Poolville, the wife of Burr WICKWIRE, age 65 years. (Her name was not given.)

Apr. 2, at Poolville, Miss Eldora E. SAWDEY, daughter of Calvin W. and Betsey SAWDEY, age 18 years.

Apr. 5, in Bouckville, Miss Elizabeth B. PIERCE, age 64 years.

Apr. 9, in Smyrna, Mrs. Isabelle BARBER, wife of Joshua BARBER, age 83 years. She was the oldest member of the Baptist Church in Smyrna.

Apr. 13, in this village [Hamilton], Mrs. David OSGOOD, age 63 years.

DEMOCRATIC REPUBLICAN - 1869

Apr. 1, in Morrisville, Mrs. Allen (sic) L. GAGE, widow of the late Vine W. GAGE, age 60 years.
Mar. 29, in Earlville, Mrs. Eli W. SAWDY.
Mar. 29, in Sherburne, Helen, wife of Elias FOSTER, age 28 years, 10 months.
Mar. 21, in Sherburne, Miss Sybil SAGER, age 82 years.
Apr. 21, in Madison, Annie M., wife of L. Walker CURTIS, age 23 years.
Apr. 19, in this village [Hamilton], Mrs. Betsey STARR, age 70 years.
Apr. 22, in Eaton village, Amanda LAPHAM, age 92 years.
Mrs. Edith Ballou ROLLER was born in Fenner, Madison Co., NY, Sept. 30, 1849, and died Ottawa City, KS, Mar. 23, 1869, of lung fever. "Edie," as she was called, was a fair and beautiful child, a favorite wherever she went. She married the last day of Sept., it being her 19th birthday, to Prof. W. ROLLER, of Oneida Seminary, and left for KS. In less than 6 months, the happy, beautiful bride was brought back a corpse.
In Brookfield, Amy, wife of Abram COON, age 81 years [in issue of May 6, 1869.]
May 2, in Monmouth, IL, Charles M. CLARK, son of Davil CLARK, of Earlville.
[No date], at DeRuyter, Miss Celia E., only daughter and child of H. C. MINER, age 17 years, 4 months, 5 days.
May 10, in Caneada, NY, Mr. VAN DOZEN, age 78 years. Deceased will be remembered as a colored resident of this village many years.
June 5, in Eaton, Nathaniel WEST, of Oneida, age 67 years.
June 27, in Eaton, Jennie, wife of Major Leonard BRIGGS.
June 8, in Oneida Community, Mrs. Almira W. BURNHAM, age 75 years.
June 1, in Cazenovia, Thomas BURKE, age 19 years.
June 7, in Lebanon, Matilda, wife of Elijah WARNER, age 63 years.
Apr. 20 (sic), in Earlville, Emogene, daughter of Samuel W. and Louisa CURTIS, age 26 years.
June 20, in Hamilton, Mary, wife of Henry COAN, age 52 years.
June 15, in Canastota, Emma I., second daughter of Sumner and Emma J. SMITH, age 9 years, 6 months.
July 5, in Lebanon, Miss Salina E. GILBERT, age 60 years.
Aug. 12, at Onondaga Valley, Abbie, eldest daughter of D. DICK, age 23 years.

DEMOCRATIC REPUBLICAN - 1869

Aug. 25, in Hamilton, Julia DeG., only child of Charles J. and Abbie DeG. JOHNSON, age 1 year, 5 months, 5 days.

Sept. 5, in Hamilton, Georgie K., son of J. Dixon and Fannie O. AVERY, age 2 months, 26 days.

Sept. 8, in Hamilton, Polly, wife of Thaxter POOL, age 71 years.

Sept. 20, at Huntley's Grove, IL, John C. TERREY, age 41 years. Less than a year ago he removed to IL from Earlville, for his health.

Aug. 27 (sic), near Hamilton, Rosagene, eldest daughter of Elisha and Emogene JONES, age 13 years.

Sept. 8, in Madison, Amelia, wife of Alvin BROWNELL, age 59 years.

Sept. 22, in Homer, Elizabeth, wife of Charles WEAVER, age 30 years.

Aug. 30, in Homer, Joshua WEAVER, age 81 years.

Sept. 30, in Madison, Hattie, youngest daughter of William and Mary FISHER, age 2 years.

Oct. 12, in this village [Hamilton], Mr. Warren EDDY, age 69 years.

Oct. 24, in Sacramento, CA, David KENDALL. He was a brother of Mrs. M. A. SMITH, of Hamilton village.

Nov. 16, in Hamilton, Mr. Ebenezer DEWEY, age 81 years.

Nov. 17, Cornelia Eleanor HYDE, age 37 years.

Oct. 30, in Hamilton, Deacon Amasa FOOTE, age 92 years. He was a native of Stafford, CT. He married Miss Sarah KELLOGG, of Colchester, CT, Aug. 1805, having already been a resident of Central New York for several years, whither he emigrated from CT at about 17 years, taking up his residence with his father, Hon. Isaac FOOTE, of Smyrna, Chenango Co., NY. Thence he removed to Hamilton, Madison Co., in 1848, where for 21 years he lived a noble Christian life, conscientious almost to a fault, he illustrated both in public and private life, the principles of the Gospel, endearing him to his friends and neighbors.

Dec. 24, in Poolville, Mrs. Dr. GRISWOLD, aged 18 years, 11 months, daughter of Mr. and Mrs. Andrew J. FORBES.

Nov. 17 (sic), in Addison, Steuben Co., NY, Elizabeth B. EATON, wife of N. P. EATON, age 89 years.

1870

Jan. 10, in Hamilton, Joseph MACUMBER, age 97 years.

DEMOCRATIC REPUBLICAN - 1870

Jan. 6, in Earlville, Helen A., wife of Norman W. TERREY, age 29 years.
Jan. 16, in Buffalo, Mary Jane, wife of Samuel BROWN, formerly of this place [Hamilton], age 41 years.
Jan. 21, at the residence of his son-in-law, William F. WARREN, in Augusta, Capt. Levi DICK, age 84 years.
Jan. 28, in Solsville, Mrs. Emily SMITH, wife of David M. SMITH, age 44 years.
Feb. 13, in Poolville, Walton BLANCHARD, age 81 years.
Feb. 15, in Hamilton, Joseph FOSTER, age 86 years.
Mar. 5, in Hamilton, Thomas HOBBS, age 41 years.
Mar. 1, in Hamilton, Calvin EATON, (no age given).
Feb. 16, in Poolville, George G. NEWTON, age 34.
May 1, at his residence in Madison, Mr. Smith BURTON, age 72 years.
May 12, in Solsville, Mrs. Jerusha CURTIS, wife of Abel CURTIS, age 40 years.
May 12, in Solsville, Mrs. Sarah TYLER, wife of Noah TYLER, age 60 years.
May 18, in Hamilton, W. Frankie, only son of James and Nancy DERRICK, age 1 year, 11 months, 6 days.
May 30, in Solsville, Julius TUTTLE, age 59 years.
May 15, in Lebanon, Mrs. Sophia M. HOPPIN, age 64 years.
May 20, in Madison, Miss Comfort S. COE, age 75 years.
May 23, in Earlville, Deacon James M. CASSELL, age 83 years.
May 23, in Madison, Miss Ellen D. LEWIS, age 19 years.
June 11, in this village [Hamilton], little Frankie, only child of George G. and Minnie A. WILDRON, age 3 years, 2 months.
July 6, in Milo, Delaware Co., IA, Harriet, infant daughter of C. B. and Harriet LONT, aged 7 weeks.
Aug. 8, at the residence of her son-in-law, B. F. CASE, of this village [Hamilton], Mrs. Anna WOODMAN, widow of the late Brownell WOODMAN, of Madison, aged 70 years, 3 months, 29 days.
Aug. 9, in Cazenovia, Henry A. JOHNSON, age 71 years.
Aug. 16, in Hamilton, Lena M., infant daughter of C. S. and Ellen HALL, age 7 months.
Aug. 14, in Madison, Sarah M. BROWNELL, age 24 years.
Aug. 16, in Hamilton, Almon JAMES, age 33 years.
Aug. 29, in East Hamilton, James H. DUNBAR, age 59 years, 6 months.
Sept. 17, in Hamilton, Alice, only daughter of Lorenzo A. and Cornelia M. BARBER, age 18 years.
Oct. 6, in Lebanon, Betsey, wife of Champlin WILCOX, age 75 years. [NOTE: Her tombstone says she was 81 years, 11 months, 23 days of age.]

DEMOCRATIC REPUBLICAN - 1870

Oct. 2, in Jewett, Greene Co., NY, William W. WEST, age 53 years. He was formerly a resident of this village [Hamilton], having left here 16 or more years ago. He was a brother of A. H. WEST.
Oct. 23, in Hamilton, R. Howard HARMON, age 15 years.
Oct. 22, in Hamilton, Mrs. Prudence L. RUSSELL, age 50 years.
Oct. 15, in Eaton, Elder Daniel PUTNAM, age 81 years.
Oct. 27, in Hamilton, Hawley OSGOOD, age 81 years.
Oct. 15, in Lebanon, Sarah F. GILBERT, age 36 years.
Oct. 22, in Lebanon, Ellen C., wife of Lewis BAKER, age 30 years.
Oct. 22, in Lebanon, John H. HEWES, age 15 years.
Oct. 17, in Eaton, Dr. J. W. FRENCH, age 30 years, 10 months.
Oct. 30, in Hamilton, Calista RUSSELL, age 23 years.
Nov. 12, in Hamilton, Experience M., wife of David CLARK, age 64 years.
Dec. 1, in Morrisville, Hiram D. CLOYES, age 65 years.
Dec. 5, in Madison, Allie L. BROCKETT, age 9 years.
Dec. 8(9?), in Sherburne, Cornelia S. CALKINS, age 44 years.
Dec. 19, in Hamilton, Mrs. Wealthy, wife of John M. HOLDREDGE, age 37 years.
Dec. 19, in West Eaton, Roxanna HAMILTON, age 64 years.

1871

Jan. 25, at the residence of her daughter, Mrs. G. F. BURN, of this village [Hamilton], Mrs. Polly GROSS, age 78 years.
Nov. 21 (1870), in Hamilton, Mrs. Mary, wife of Artimas NEWTON, age 69 years.
Feb. 1, in Madison, Roxanna E. WOODS, wife of Wallace WOODS, age 87 years.
Feb. 6, in Madison, Electa MILLEN, age 77 years.
Feb. 11, in Bouckville, Mrs. Rosie, wife of E. PEET, age 32 years.
Feb. 17, in Lebanon, Olive TORREY, age 92 years.
Feb. 18, in Hamilton, Mrs. Sarah, wife of Andrew CLARK, age 29 years.
Feb. 22, in Hamilton, Mrs. Polly, wife of A. Z. KINGSLEY, age 58 years.
Jan. (date not given, but is in issue of Mar. 2d), in Smyrna, Mrs. Elizabeth FERRIS, wife of I. B. FERRIS, age 64 years.

DEMOCRATIC REPUBLICAN - 1871

Mar. 12, Miss Josephine A. COBB, age 22 years, at residence of J. D. AVERY, Esq., one of her friends. She recently came from Syracuse.

Mar. 13, in Madison, Mr. George WHITE, age 83 years.

Mar. 16, at Pine Woods, Jeddie, son of Mr. Thomas APPLETON, age 2 1/2 years.

Mar. 9, in Vernon, Oneida Co., NY, William D. CUMMINGS, age 67 years.

Mar. 30, in North Norwich, NY, Henry J. FRENCH, age 31 years. He formerly lived at Eaton.

Apr. 9, in Lebanon, near Earlville, Clara E. MORGAN, age 10 years.

Apr. 27, in Hamilton, Mrs. E. A. SCOTT, wife of G. D. SCOTT, age 48 years.

Apr. 28, in Lebanon, Dwight BLAIR, age 2 years.

May 27, in Hamilton, Philo SACKETT, only son of S. W. SACKETT, of Watkins, NY, a member of the Senior Class in Madison University, age 21 years. "He stood first in his class, and was exemplary." Buried at Watkins.

May 17, in Hamilton, Mrs. Anna BURCHARD, widow of Sylvester BURCHARD, age 64 years. Her husband died over 20 years ago; she had lived in this vicinity over 30 years, and is survived by 6 children.

May 29, in Madison, Mrs. Abby Ann CLARK, age 30 years.

May 29, in Hamilton, Orrin H. SMITH, age 5 years.

May 30, in North Otselic, Thomas E. DORMAN, age 73 years.

June 7, at West Eaton, Wilmer F. GREENE, age 8 years, 9 months.

June 21, Margaret M. WALLACE, eldest daughter of Rev. William WALLACE, of this city, age 38 years. . . Wheeling WV *Register*, June 25, 1871.

June 13, in Lebanon, Hattie E., daughter of Erastus D. and Mary CLARK, age 9 years, 3 months.

July 8, in Hamilton, Capt. John SMITH, age 81 years. He left his native state, MA, when about 22 years old, going to Delaware Co., NY. He resided there 18 or 20 years, coming to Hamilton about 40 years ago. He was a carpenter and joiner for 30 years here and assisted in building two of the "Buildings on the Hill." He has been retired the past 10 years. He is survived by eight children, the eldest of whom is 50 years old. Three sons live in this village [Hamilton], one at Waterville, and one at Canastota, and one at Painted Post; one daughter resides in MI, and one in OH. He was a member of the village Baptist Church for many years.

DEMOCRATIC REPUBLICAN - 1871

July 6, in Hamilton, Daniel R., son of Mr. and Mrs. A. M. TIBBETS, age 4 years, 6 months, 17 days.
July 23, in Madison, Noah TYLER, age 65 years.
Aug. 8, in Brookfield, MO, Mrs. Elizabeth THURSTON, age 71 years. She went from here, west, about two months ago. The hot weather proved too much for her, and she soon fell victim to dysentyery. She was the mother of Mrs. C. F. RISLEY.
Sept. 8, in Sangerfield, Jonas BANTON, age 90 years.
Sept. 24, in Hamilton, David P. BENTLEY, age 63 years.
Sept. 21, in Skaneateles, Mrs. Adeline M. LORD, wife of Amasa LORD, formerly a resident of Hamilton.
Oct. 8, in Hamilton, Lida BUTLER, age 64 years.
[No date given, but probably in early Nov.], in Hamilton, Joseph TAYNTOR, age 68 years.
Nov. 9, in Hamilton, Freddie SMITH, age 6 years.
Nov. 14, in Lebanon, Mrs. Sarah A. WELTON, wife of M. SHARTS, age 66 years.
Nov. 26, in Augusta, NY, Newton SPOONER, age 15 years.
Dec. 6, at Spuyten Duyvill, NY, Anna Norris, wife of W. F. BISHOP, and daughter of Adon SMITH, age 25 years, 5 months. The funeral was attended from the residence of George G. BISHOP of Newark, CT, on Dec. 9th.
Dec. 23, in Madison, Seth BLAIR, age 66 years.
Dec. 29, in Rochester, Henry S. DEAN, son of Dr. Henry DEAN, age 28 years.

1872

Jan. 25, in East Hamilton, Miss Charlotta ARMSTRONG, age 79 years.
Jan. 28, in Madison, Col. Heman HOWES, age 77 years.
FEb. 5, in East Hamilton, William USHER, age 72 years.
Feb. 4, in West Eaton, Ezekiel WESTCOTT, age 47 years.
Feb. 2, in Madison, Genevieve BROWNELL, age 3 years.
Jan. 30, in Lebanon, Addison BRIGGS, age 4 months, 16 days.
Jan. 28, in Earlville, Warren FELT, age 63 years.
Jan. 27, in Madison, Laura BACON, age 86 years.
Feb. 11, in Eaton, Benjamin TURNER, (no age given).
Feb. 14, in Eaton, Esther SHEPARD, age 80 years.
Feb. 7, at Mr. Lippitt's in Madison, Mr. Julius D. PALMER, age 35 years.
Feb. 12, in Brooklyn, Long Island, Col. Thomas C. NYE, age 70 years. He ran the Park House in Hamilton for some years.
Feb. 20, in Earlville, Jamesie Gates OMENS, age 1 year, 14 days.

DEMOCRATIC REPUBLICAN - 1872

Feb. 21, in Hamilton, Margaret ONDERDONK, age 45 years, daughter of Andrew ONDERDONK.

Mar. 11, in Hamilton village, J. Foster BENEDICT, only child of Frank S. and Della F. BENEDICT, age 6 months, 3 weeks.

Mar. 5, in Cazenovia, Achsah WELLINGTON, relict of Elizur SEYMOUR, age 68 years.

Feb. 28, in South Hamilton, Rev. Bela PALMER, pastor of the 2d Baptist Church of Hamilton, age 60 years.

Mar. 3, in South Hamilton, Samuel TUTTLE, age 54 years.

Mar. 10, in Hubbardsville, NY, William COLSON, age 65 years.

Mar. 9, in Lebanon, Henry L. SHERMAN, age 31 years, 10 months, 17 days.

Mar. 10, in Madison, Sarah COE, age 79 years.

Mar. 8, in Hamilton, Benjamin H. FITCH, age 71 years.

Mar. 7, in Morrisville, Fannie FRINK, age 83 years, 8 months.

Mar. 12, in Smyrna, Zephaniah DIX, age 42 years, 11 months.

Mar. 7, in Madison, D. LEACH, age 73 years.

Feb. 28, in Hubbardsville, Charles COLSON, age 14 years, 5 months, 5 days.

Feb. 26, in Lebanon, Fred L. CARD, age 9 months, 24 days.

Feb. 28, in Darien, Genesee, Co., NY, John BANTON, formerly of Madison, age 63 years, 9 months. Buried in Hubbardsville.

Mar. 15, in Smyrna, William KNOWLES, age 23 years, 4 months, 8 days.

Mar. 12, in Smyrna, Mrs. WINN (no age given).

Mar. 14, in Madison, Mary COE, age 60 years.

Mar. 14, in Morrisville, Miranda M. SMITH, age 42 years.

Mar. 15, in North Brookfield, Nora H. RISLEY, daughter of the late Chester C. and Sarah RISLEY, age 13 years, 1 month, 7 days.

Mar. 25, in Morrisville, Miss Abigail BELLOW, wife (sic) of Alfred D. BELLOWS (sic), age 56 years, 2 months, 11 days.

Mar. 17, Mary Lydia BURTON, youngest daughter of Delia S. and the late Thomas L. BURTON, age 19 years, 7 months, of consumption.

Mar. 26, in Morrisville, of pneumonia, Mr. Elbridge G. TIDD, age 69 years.

Mar. 15, in Nelson, Mr. Charles H. KNOX, formerly supervisor of the town, age 54 years.

Mar. 25, in Hamilton, Mulford ROGERS, age 60 years.

Mar. 23, in Morrisville, Sarah ELMER, age 26 years.

Mar. 27, in Morrisville, Patience SANFORD, age 87 years, 11 months.

DEMOCRATIC REPUBLICAN - 1872

Mar. 26, in Hamilton, Miss Helen Ada COLBORN, age 35 years, 2 months, 13 days.
Mar. 30, in Lebanon, Dr. T. H. RICHMOND, age 67 years.
Mar. 30, in Morrisville, Mr. Augustus LUMBARD, age 73 years.
Mar. 30, in Madison, Mrs. Lydia ANDRUS, age 84 years.
Apr. 4, in Hamilton, Ebenezer KILMER, age 64 years.
Apr. 14, in New Woodstock, Mr. Alfred DRAKE, age 55 years.
Apr. 13, in East Hamilton, Zelotus ACKLEY, age 42 years.
Apr. 10, in Morrisville, Isaac WHITE, age 66 years.
Apr. 27, in Madison, Samuel HITCHCOCK, (no age given).
Apr. 22, in Hamilton, Rebecca L., wife of Hiram WHEELER, age 53 years, 4 months.
Apr. 18, in West Eaton, Amey E. WILCOX, age 2 years, 9 months, 14 days.
Apr. 19, in Canastota, Hiram H. TUCKER, age 17 years.
Apr. 25, in Georgetown, M. Josie, daughter of Russell and Jane M. WHITMORE, age 19 years, 4 months.
May 1, in Madison, Miss Hattie LOOMIS, age about 21 years.
May 10, in Richford, Tioga Co., NY, Amellia, wife of Elder Elbro L. GREEN, age 30 years.
May 11, in Earlville, of typhoid pneumonia, Leroy PORTER, only son of Orlando and Leafy(?) PORTER, age 16 years.
May 10, in Hamilton, George W. BLOOM, age 94 years, 6 months, 2 days.
May 14, in Solsville, James B. ARITY, age 15 years.
May 16, in Friendship, Alleghany Co., NY, Clarissa, wife of John FISHER, age 77 years, 1 month, 6 days.
May 23, in Garwood Station, Alleghany Co., NY, Claud S., son of Sidney and Eliza PECKAM, age 13 months, 8 days.
June 2, in Hamilton, Ruie A. ALBE, age 17 years, 2 months.
June 3, in Lebanon, Herbert HARTSHORN, age 18 years.
May 24, in Brookfield, Ann Eliza CRUMB, age 32 years, 1 month, 20 days.
June 1, in Hamilton, Caroline LAY, age 77 years.
June 23, in this town [Hamilton], Wilmina, daughter of Nelson S. PRESTON, age 3 years, 2 months.
June 26, in Madison, James HOWARD, age 73 years.
June 9, in Lebanon, Emma MERRIFIELD, age 1 year, 4 months, 9 days.
June 25, in Hamilton, Ama M. BEEBE, wife of Darius BEEBE, age 62 years, 5 months.
July 13, in Hamilton, Miss Artelissa M. ACKLEY, age 51 years.
July 6, in Eaton, infant daughter of Rev. A. J. and Phebe WILCOX, age 3 months.

DEMOCRATIC REPUBLICAN - 1872

July 23, in Hamilton, Howard SMITH, age 58 years (see below).
July 24, in Hamilton, infant child of David SQUIRES, age 4 months.
July 12, in this village [Hamilton], Philo A. ORTON Sr., age 68 years, 3 months, 27 days.
July 23, in Hamilton, Harvey SMITH, age 58 years (see above).
Aug. 1, in Lebanon, Hugh STUART, age 69 years, member of Congregational Church.
Aug. 2, in Peterboro, Mrs. Lydia DORN, age 68 years.
Aug. 3, in Hamilton, George W. EATON, D.D., LL.D., in his 69th year.
Aug. 2, in Lebanon, at Smith's Valley, William MONTGOMERY, age 69 years, 8 months.
Aug. 1, in Eaton, Miss Deette L. DE WITT, age 19 years.
Aug. 14, in Morrisville, Hannah HILL, age 39 years.
Aug. 8, in Eaton, Rebecca WESTCOTT, age 77 years, 4 months, 18 days.
Aug. 12, in Madison, Mary RICHMOND, age 87 years, 9 months.
Aug. 13, in Madison, Daniel STOWELL, age 72 years, 7 months.
Aug. 28, in Hamilton, Miss Celinda TYLER, age 62 years.
Aug. 28, in Hamilton, Martha BALL, age 68 years.
Sept. 6, in Winfield, Herkimer Co., NY, Anthony THOMAS, age 76 years.
Sept. 18, at East Hamilton, at residence of her son, Miller YOUNG, Mrs. Deborah YOUNG, age 92 years.
Sept. 28, in Hamilton, Lansing SWIFT, age 49 years.
Oct. 1, in Morrisville, Mrs. Delia D. ALLEN, age 53 years, 8 months.
Oct. 2, in Morrisville, Mrs. Ruth BROWN, widow of the late Duane BROWN, Esq., age 63 years, 8 months.
Sept. 21, in Madison, Asahel SKINNER, age 79 years, 7 months.
Sept. 4, in Morrisville, Mrs. Rebecca FRY, wife of Asa FRY, age 70 years.
Oct. 6, in Earlville, Mrs. Anna BAILEY, age 81 years, 5 months, 3 days.
Oct. 6, in Truxton, at residence of his son, F. M. BUELL, Mr. Thomas BUELL, age 88 years. He was one of the first settlers of the town of Truxton, and one of the organizers of the first Baptist Church in that town.
Oct. 19, in Hamilton, Rhoda SQUIRES, age 80 years.
Oct. 20, in Hamilton, Philena LANPHERE, age 19 years.
Oct. 6, in Hamilton, Mary P. READ, age 81 years.

DEMOCRATIC REPUBLICAN - 1872

Oct. 9, in Lebanon, Susan L. ETSON, age 43 years.
Sept. 30, in Hamilton, Lucy GREENLEY, wife of T. H. GREENLEY, age 78 years.
Oct. 30, in Sherburne, Mrs. Hannah HOWARD, age 75 years.
Nov. 14, in Hamilton, Artemas L. NEWTON, age 83 years.
Oct. 28, in Hamilton, Jeremiah T. GREEN, age 61 years, 10 days.
[No date], in Brooklyn, NY, John G. COLEY, age 33 years. Deceased was son-in-law of William FAIRCHILD of this place, and the body was brought here for burial.
Nov. 17, at Little Falls, Clark D. ANDERSON, age 32 years. He was an adopted son of E. CURRY, formerly of this village [Hamilton]. The body was brought here for burial.
Nov. 18, in Eaton, Mr. GRAHAM, age 19 years.
Nov. 17, in Hamilton, Mrs. Abbie J. COAN, wife of Julius COAN, age 49 years.
Nov. 19, in Madison, Emma Belle HENDERSON, age 5 years, 5 months, 9 days.
Nov. 5, in Madison, William ADAMS, age 54 years.
Nov. 14, near Charlestown (sic??), SC, Levi P. WAGNER, M.D., late surgeon in the 114th Regiment, NY Vols. during the late war, age 41 years. He was a native of Georgetown, Madison Co., NY.
Nov. 11, in Hamilton, Ara BLAKEMAN, age 70 years.
Nov. 22, in Madison, Iantha TOMPKINS, age 25 years, 8 months.
Dec. 8, in DeRuyter, Mr. Oliver MITCHELL, age 76 years.
Dec. 11, in Eaton, Mrs. Edwin STORRS, age 29 years.
Dec. 31, in Washington, IA, Mrs. Julia T. SIMMONS, wife of Isaac SIMMONS, formerly of this place [Hamilton], age 56 years.
Nov. 21, in MI, Mrs. Jacob S. HOWES, formerly of Hamilton, age 54 years. (in issue of Jan. 16, 1873).

1873

Jan. 22, in Hamilton, Mrs. A. Minerva HARTSHORN, wife of Horace P. HARTSHORN, age 48 years, 9 months, 15 days.
Jan. 21, in Hamilton, Miss Adelia F. EDDY, age 23 years, 5 months, 9 days.
Jan. 37, in Richmond, Ede Maria, widow of the late Woodworth ELDREDGE, of Hamilton, youngest daughter of the late Deacon Charles RANDALL, of Norwich, NY. The body of Mrs. ELDREDGE reached this place yester-

DEMOCRATIC REPUBLICAN - 1873

day and funeral held at Mr. H. E. SLOCUM's. (From Richmond, VA, *State Journal*).

Jan. 20, in Sacramento City, CA, Allen W. HUNT, formerly of this village [Hamilton], age 35 years.

Feb. 5, in Hamilton, Lucius D. THROOP, eldest son of W. H. and C. D. THROOP, age 36 years.

Feb. 3, in Hamilton, Margaret Louisa, daughter of James and Bridget HOPKINS, age 10 months.

Feb. 7, in the town of Hamilton, Mrs. Elizabeth DUTCHER, age 39 years.

Feb. 16, in Hamilton, Philo ACKLEY, age 41 years.

Feb. 16, in East Hamilton, Henry C. BUSH, age 3 years, 3 months.

Feb. 21, in Hamilton, George Eaton LASHER, age 11 years, 9 months.

Mar. 4, in Madison, Joshua H. LINCOLN, age 87 years.

Feb. 27, in Nelson, Grandley CASE, age 83 years.

Mar. 11, at her home near East Hamilton, Mrs. Alice V. PALMER, age 60.

Mar. 31, in this village [Hamilton], Mr. Samuel E. WARNER, age 73 years.

Mar. 25, in Eaton, Mrs. Catherine FRYOVER, age 50 years.

Apr. 17, in Hamilton, Mrs. Charlotte L. BARBER, wife of C. B. BARBER, age 38 years, 9 months, 23 days.

Apr. 23, in this village [Hamilton], at the residence of her nephew, R. F. RANDOLPH, Mrs. Sabrina PRATT, widow of Seva PRATT, age 64 years. Burial in Georgetown.

Apr. 27, in Hamilton, at residence of his son-in-law, L. B. FOSTER, Mr. Benjamin BAKER, age 88 years, 22 days.

May 9, in Eaton, Addie LEACH, age 22 years.

May 15, in Hamilton, James E. BRIGGS, age 55 years, 2 months, 12 days.

June 2, in Lebanon, Lyman P. WEDGE, age 48 years.

June 2, in Eaton, Russell AVERY, age 64 years.

June 24, in Lebanon, Batharick STOWER, age 63 years, 9 months, 23 days.

July 15, in Hamilton, Honora LUDDEN, age 70 years. She died suddenly at the home of her son in this village, Father A. P. LUDDE (sic). Her four sons all occupy positions of trust, viz., John, James, and Anthony are all Priests of the Church, and the fourth is a member of the Bar in Binghamton.

Aug. 13, in Hamilton, Dwight SMITH, age 55 years.

Aug. 19, in Bouckville, Aug. 19, Mrs. Harriet LATTINA, age 52 years, 10 months, 10 days.

Aug. 24, in Lebanon, Johnnie CARL, age 2 years, 4 months.

DEMOCRATIC REPUBLICAN - 1873

Aug. 25, in Madison, a son of Charles TAYLOR, age 8 years.
Sept. 3, in Benton Harbor, MI, Miss Abigail STURTEVANT, age 65 years, formerly of Madison.
Aug. 25, in Macon, IL, Ella E. THOMAS, age 17 years, 4 months, 17 days, formerly of Madison.
Sept. 9, in Hamilton, Ida, daughter of Ebenezer and Saville EDDY, age 1 year, 2 weeks.
Sept. 30, in Georgetown, Lewis DURFEE, age 42 years, 6 months.
Sept. 24, in Madison, Calvin B. LEWIS, age 10 years, 6 months.
Oct. 4, in Hamilton, Leonard HOWE, age 73 years.
Oct. 7, in Hamilton, John W. SMITH, age 29 years, 6 months.
Oct. 16, in Smith's Valley, Miss Serepta GROVES, age 41 years.
Oct. 11, in Bouckville, Mrs. Polly RICHARDSON, age 71 years.
Oct. 13, in Bouckville, Milo CLARK, age 65 years.
From the *Chicago Times*:--Died in this city, Oct. 7, at her residence on West Washington St., Frances HOLMES, wife of Hon. Charles H. CURTIS. She was born in Sangerfield, Oneida Co., NY, Apr. 9, 1814, and moved with Mr. CURTIS in 1842; has resided there since.
Nov. 26, in Madison, Frank D., son of A. S. and Mary E. MACOMBER, age 18 years, 7 months, 21 days.
Nov. 24, in Hamilton, ---nder FIELD, age 79 years, 8 months, 23 days.
Dec. 4, in Pecksport, Charles J., son of Amos and Ann TITCHNER, (no age given).
Dec. 28, in Pierceville, Kezia JOSLIN, age 87 years, 8 months, 28 days.

1874

Jan. 28, in Utica, Ada Fitch, only child of Henry C. and Sarah C. WELTON, age 2 years, 11 months, 4 days.
Jan. 24, in Eaton, Mattie L. MOSELEY, youngest daughter of Harvey and Mary MOSELY (sic), age 10 years, 25 days.
Feb. 14, in Hamilton, Emma G. BOWERS, age 27 years, 4 months.
Feb. 12, in Bridgewater, Melissa TOMPKINS, age 33 years, 11 months.
Mar. 9, in Hamilton, Elsie JONES, age 15 years.
Mar. 9, in Hamilton, Charlotte HARTSHORN, age 76 years, 4 months, 9 days.
Mar. 12, in Solsville, widow Lucy GILBERT, age 73 years, 7 months, 8 days.

DEMOCRATIC REPUBLICAN - 1874

Mar. 23, in New York City, Adon SMITH, in his 70th year. Funeral from his residence, 412 Madison Avenue, corner of 48th St.

Mar. 24, in Madison, near this village, George H. STONE, age 39 years, 3 months.

Mar. 21, in Lebanon, Pardon CLARK, age 54 years.

Apr. 19, in Hamilton, Mrs. Jane ABBERT, relict of George ABBERT, age 64 years.

Apr. 19, in Hamilton, S. W. BARNETT, age 74 years, 3 months.

Apr. 11, in North Brookfield, Samuel TALCOTT, age 56 years.

Apr. 20, at his residence near Oriskany, Oneida Co., NY, Capt. Albertis L. HUBBARD, age 78 years.

Apr. 26, in Madison, Mrs. Josephine ALBE, age 24 years. "She leaves two small children, the oldest about two years old, with no father or mother to care for them. She did not long survive the suicide of her husband a few weeks ago."

May 5, in Hamilton, of brain fever, Lena B., infant daughter of Addison J. and Eliza WEST, age 4 years, 1 month, 22 days.

May 18, in Madison, Abbey PECKAM, relict of the late Samuel PECKAM, age 78 years.

In this city, May 11, Eliza A., wife of H. R. TORREY, age 34 years, 5 months, 11 days. (From Aurora, IL *Beacon*.)

May 10, in Lebanon, Morris BRIGGS, age 39 years, 2 days.

May 25, in Ripon, WI, Richard CATLIN, age 65 years. He was an uncle of Mr. H. P. HARTSHORN, of this place [Hamilton].

May 24, in Hamilton, Mrs. Margaret WILBUR, age 36 years.

May 23, in Eaton, John DUNIGAN, age 36 years.

June 4, in Sherburne, Rollen C. BENTON, infant son of Jason M. and Amelia R. BENTON, age 8 months, 13 days.

June 7, in Sherburne, Amelia R., wife of Jason M. BENTON, aged 24 years, 8 months, 3 days.

June 7, at residence of Mr. LEWIS, in Madison village, Corydon TAYLOR, Esq., of Binghamton, age 68 years.

June 14, in Georgetown, Celia MOREY, aged 22 years.

June 24, in Hamilton, at residence of E. JONES, Edward J. EVANS, of Newark, NJ, a member of the Sophomore class of Madison University, age 24 years, 3 months.

June 12, in Eaton, Mrs. S. R. SHERRILL, widow of the late S. R. SHERILL (sic), and step-mother of H. J. SHERRILL, formerly Principal of Hamilton Union School, now of Belvedere, IL, in her 67th year.

DEMOCRATIC REPUBLICAN - 1874

June 20, in Eaton, Henry Bagg MORSE, age 38 years. He was formerly Colonel of the 114th Reg't. of Volunteers, and lately a Judge of the Circuit Court of Arkansas.

July 16, in Hamilton, of inflammation of the brain, Roxie L., daughter of John W. and Mary A. INGALLS, aged 2 years.

July 10, in Hamilton, Freelove, wife of Alpha DUNHAM, age 71 years.

July 10, in Eaton, John LANDON, age 76 years. He had always been a healthy man, had never called a doctor until the day before his death. M.D. LANDON, known as Eli Perkins, is his son.

July 25, in Norwich, after a brief illness, Mrs. Sarah York PRENTICE, mother of Rev. R. R. PRENTICE, of North Parma, NY, formerly of this village [Hamilton], in her 87th year.

Aug. 1, in Hamilton, James W. BROOKS, age 67 years, 4 months.

July 30, in Morrisville, Charles Barclay, infant son of J. Dixon and Fannie O. AVERY, age 5 months, 18 days.

Aug. 4, in Eaton, Deacon Lester JOSLIN, in his 65th year. He was born in the town of Hamilton Oct. 21, 1809, and has spent his entire life in the towns of Hamilton and Eaton. The past 6 years he had had charge of the County Poor House, the condition of which has been very greatly improved under his administration. He was married to Mary LAPHAM, Sept. 10, 1834, and leaved her and two daughters to mourn his loss. He was a member of the Baptist Church since 1830, and for about 20 years has served the Church of Eaton as its Deacon. He was a singularly good and true man . . .

Apr. 21, in Madison, Mr. Nathan FISHER, age 77 years. (This was written April, as above.)

Aug. 19, in this village, at residence of her son-in-law, M. C. WAIT, Esq., Mrs. Elizabeth LEWORTHY, lately a resident of Sangerfield, in her 88th year.

Aug. 22, in Poolville, Henry PARKS, age 67 years.

Sept. 11, in Rome, Betsey, wife of Joel BARBER, age 53 years.

Sept. 15, in Madison, Harriet S., wife of Sidney TOMPKINS, age 55 years.

Sept. 22, in Clifton Springs, David J. MITCHELL, of Syracuse, age 47 years.

Sept. 20, in Cazenovia, Alice C., wife of Charles H. PERKINS, and daughter of A. Z. KINGSLEY, of this village [Hamilton], age 24 years.

DEMOCRATIC REPUBLICAN - 1874

Sept. 21, in Earlville, Arthur Leon, son of M. L. and Emma J. SALEY, aged 10 months, 23 days.
Oct. 15, in Hamilton, Thomas H. KELLY, age 26 years.
Oct. 14, in Chicago, IL, of paralysis, John MC DONALD, age 31 years.
Oct. 9, Mr. James ROWAN, age 60 years, fell dead while assisting with threshing in the western part of the town of Fenner at Keeler's Corners.
Oct. 16, in Hamilton, Richard SMATHEREST, age about 40 years.
Oct. 12, in East Hamilton, Harriet, relict of Loomis FULLER, age 71 years.
Aug. 6, in Hamilton, Mrs. ISHAM, widow of Chancy ISHAM, deceased, age 85 years. She was a respected and highly esteemed by all who knew her in life, and in death she is sadly lamented.
Dec. 21, in Eaton, near Woodman's Pond, Ransom LANPHERE, age 87 years, 7 months.
On Thanksgiving Day, at his residence, near Solsville, Mr. Simeon WYNN, age about 48 years.
Dec. 14, in Hamilton, Mary JOHNSON, age 80 years, 5 months, 14 days. Mary's has been the most familiar face in Hamilton for a score of years. Old residents, coming back after a long absence, failed to fully realize where they were until Mary's appeared to them, in her fantastic habiliments . . . Father LUDDEN of the Catholic Church provided the casker (sic) for her, and others contributed towards the funeral charges . . . For these acts of kindness, and many favors, her children and friends express their heartfelt thanks.
Dec. 8, in Poolville, Mrs. Harriet PRESTON, wife of William PRESTON, age 66 years, 4 months. She was a great sufferer. She had been an affectionate mother and faithful wife.
[No date], at the residence of her father in Madison, Miss Elizabeth HOLLAND, age about 26 years.
Nov. 30, in East Hamilton, John WOODARD, age 72 years.
Dec. 18, in Lebanon, Clarissa R., wife of Deacon PARTRIDGE, age 65 years.
Dec. 18, in Hamilton, Beaulah A., wife of C. P. BONNEY, age 27 years, 8 months, 3 days. She leaves her husband and two small children.
Quotation: A poem which was read at the funeral of Miss Ella BLANDING of Hubbardsville, on Dec. 12.
Dec. 27, in Madison, Frances W., wife of Ranson BACON, age 40 years.

DEMOCRATIC REFLECTOR - 1875

1875

In the issue of Jan. 14, 1875: Mrs. S.B. BURCHARD died at Denver, CO, a few days ago. She was the wife of Seneca B. BURCHARD, of Kankakee, IL, and formerly of this place [Hamilton]. She was a daughter of Deacon Rufus DUNHAM, of Truxton, Cortland Co., NY, where she grew up. Her given name was Irene, and she was about 42 years of age. After her marriage to Mr. BURCHARD, they lived in this community for twelve years, first at the Deacon BURCHARD farm which her husband conducted, and later in this village, where he carried on the forwarding business. In 1866 they removed to Kankakee, where they have since resided. Last November, a pulmonary trouble, resulting from measles, let them to go to Colorado hoping to improve her condition, but to no avail. Two young daughters and a little son mourn her loss, and they had buried two young children here in our cemetery.

Jan. 6, in Smyrna, Eunice H., wife of William R. GEER, age 66 years, 7 months, 26 days.

Jan. 8, in this city, Mrs. Sarah WELTON, wife of Henry C. WELTON, and daughter of James H. and Catherine FITCH, age 30 years, 6 months, 21 days. (Taken from *Utica Herald*.)

Jan. 20, in Hamilton, Mrs. Laura SHORES, age 58 years.

Jan. 19, in Rochester, of consumption, Joseph Edgar MEDBURY, age 23 years. He was buried at Erieville, NY.

Jan. 5, in Earlville, Mattie E. HENRY, age 10 years.

Feb. 21, in Hamilton, Rev. David WESTON, DD, Prof. of Ecclesiastical History in Hamilton Theological Seminary, age 39 years. Survived by his wife.

Mar. 3, in Madison, Ransom RAMSDELL, age 60 years, 11 months.

Feb. 19, in Smyrna, Isaac PHELPS, age 78 years.

Mar. 12, in Hamilton, Mrs. Luna LEACH, age 56 years, 7 months.

Mar. 14, in Brookfield, John PENDOCK, age 72 years.

Mar. 11, in Hamilton, Mr. M. W. SAWDEY, age 46 years.

Mar. 8, in Blissfield, MI, Orin W. JIPSON, age 61 years. He was born in Madison; was a brother of S. R. JIPSON, Esq., of this village [Hamilton], and formerly known to many of our readers.

Mar. 18, in Lebanon, of pneumonia, Mason LASELLE, age 68 years.

Mar. 30, in Hamilton, Ebenezer EDDY, age 73 years, 7 months. He was the father of Mrs. C. P. BONNEY, who died last December.

Mar. 21, at the residence of her son, William F. BUELL, Esq., of East Hamilton, Permelia, relict of Joseph BUELL, age 75 years. Her husband died in 1837. They had 8 children, all living, William being the youngest. Another son, Warren, resides north of this village [Hamilton], others reside in Earlville and Lebanon, and some in the West.

Mar. 24, in Brookfield, Mrs. Lena CRUMB, wife of David CRUMB, age 25 years, 10 months.

Mar. 18, in Earlville, Fannie, wife of S. L. COMSTOCK, (age not given).

Mar. 30, in Morrisville, Mrs. Emily J. GORTON, age 56 years.

Mar. 27, in Hubbardsville, Jennie BROWN, age 8 years.

Mar. 14, in East Hamilton, of penumonia, Justin BEEBE, age 89 years, 8 months.

Apr. 5, in Hamilton, Clara ROLLINS, age 7 years.

Apr. 1, in Pine Woods, Sarah MC QUIEN, age 21 years.

Apr. 1, in Bouckville, Mrs. Bessie LEVI, age 60 years.

Mar. 23, in Stockbridge, NY, at residence of her son-in-law, D. A. NEFF, Mrs. Phebe BUTLER, in her 87th year. She was formerly a resident of Madison.

Apr. 19, in Earlville, Eunice V. BAILEY, age 58 years.

Jan. 20, in North Plains, Ionia Co., MI, Mrs. Roxana LASELLE, age 67 years. She leaves her husband and a large circle of friends. She had formerly resided in Earlville, Madison Co., for over 20 years.

Apr. 5, in Madison, of consumption, Mrs. Bell F. GOODELL, wife of William L. GOODELL, of Springfield, age 31 years, 6 months, 6 days.

May 10, in Hamilton, Mary B. CARSWELL, age 54 years.

May 7, in Lebanon, A. L. WELCH, age 51 years.

May 17, in Lebanon, Babcy R., wife of Ephraim FISK, age 46 years.

May 15, In Hamilton, Linn R., age 3 months, 6 days, and ...

May 19, Leonard O., age 3 months, 10 days, infant twin children of A. M. TIBBITTS.

May 19, in Hamilton, Mrs. Mary E., wife of Deacon Charles C. PAYNE, age 62 years.

May 22, in Hamilton, Ezra CAMPBELL, age 73 years, 8 months.

May 24, in Earlville, J. H., son of W. H. and Ida A. JONES, age 2 years, 1 month, 22 days.

June 25, in Hamilton, Col. William F. BONNEY, age 64 years. He was sheriff for fifteen years, and well and favorably known.

June 19, in Ovid, John G. MOTT, age 11 years, 10 months.

June 26, in Lebanon, Ziba F. BASTIAN, age 62 years.

DEMOCRATIC REFLECTOR - 1875

June 22, in Hamilton, Ann W. BARNARD, age 77 years, 6 months.

July 8 or 9, in Hamilton, Osmond W. GREER, age 75 years. He was baptised in Litchfield, MI, 35 years ago, and was a worthy member of the Baptist Church in Hamilton until his death.

July 24, in Plymouth, Chenango Co., NY, James B., son of Byron J. and Mary L. ORMSBY, age 1 year, 10 months, 22 days.

July 30, in Hamilton, Smith MOTT, in his 71st year. He had been a resident of this village, and in business many years. He returned 27 years ago. All his family, three boys and two girls, were present at his funeral.

July 8, in Newport, KY, Clara VAN SLYCK, eldest daughter of DeWitt C. VAN SLYCK, and wife, Eleanor; age 26.

Aug. 6, in Oneida, Mrs. Sarah BURRITT, wife of C. W. BURRITT of Eaton, age 37 years.

Aug. 13, in Hamilton, Frank H. SMITH, age 20 years, 4 months.

Aug. 26, in Troy, at residence of her grandson, William Lee CHURCH, Phoebe Freeman BUEL, widow of the late Eli BUEL, of Hamilton, in her 81st year.

Sept. 6, in Solsville, Mary Lucina WATSON, daughter of DeWitt C. and Jennie P. WATSON, of Utica, age 10 years, 1 month, 29 days.

Sept. 9, Rev. John SMITSER, an aged minister, well known in central NY, died at his home in Oneida, the day following his 76th birthday. Burial at Eaton.

In issue of Sept. 9, 1875: "Removing Remains." "Tuesday, Deacon C. C. PAYNE commenced the removal of the remains of his friends buried in the old Lebanon St. Cemetery, to the Madison Street Grounds, first opening the grave of his father's first wife who died about 30 years of age, and who was buried some eighty years ago, and it is understood to be the grave of the first white person ever buried in Hamilton. Two other graves were opened, and the remains of the first one buried were found in the most perfect condition. New coffins had to be procured for them all."

Sept. 22, in Eaton, Ebenezer CHILDS, age 66 years.

Oct. 2, in Sherburne, Anna R. BACON, aged 102 years, 2 months, 18 days. Mrs. BACON was the head of what is known in this section as the REESE family, and at their annual picnic gatherings for several years past she has been able to number her descendents by the hundred. Mr. Otto REESE, of Sherburne, is her

DEMOCRATIC REFLECTOR - 1875

son. Miss Anna REESE, who is now winning some fame as a concert singer, is a great-granddaughter. There has been considerable musical talent in the family. Very few live to the good old age this lady reached, and few who do retain their faculties as she did.

Sept. 29, in Hamilton, Sally BARDEEN, age 80 years, 4 months.
Oct. 2, in Earlville, Marsha C. PEARL, age 49 years.
Oct. 6, in North Parma, of pleura pneumonia, Harriet A., wife of Rev. R. R. PRENTICE, age 58 years.
Oct. 8, in Morrisville, Fannie D. Keith AVERY, wife of J. Dixon AVERY, (no age given).
Oct. 16, in Earlville, Mrs. Nancy BOWDISH, age 62 years.
Nov. 13, in Madison, John CARTER, age about 70 years.
Nov. 6, in Eaton, Mrs. Lyman EVARTS, in her 66th year.
Nov. 4, in Pratts Hollow, NY, Georgie, only son of Bryon WILBUR, age 2 years, 8 months.
Nov. 30, in Madison, Mrs. Jerusha IVES, age 21 years.
Dec. 8, in Hamilton, very suddenly, John GREGGS, age about 55 years.
Dec. 12, in this village [Hamilton], Calphurnia Dunbar, wife of William THROOP, age 62 years.
Dec. 13, in Brooklyn, George H. STEELE, age 29 years.
Nov. 19, at Peterboro, of paralysis, Ottillia KING, age 70 years. She was the eldest daughter of Gen. Nathaniel KING, long a resident of Hamilton village. This was her birthplace and here at 13 years she joined the Methodist Episcopal Church. Although laboring under peculiar infirmities and personal disabilities, she always possessed a cheerful temper . . .
Dec. 17, in Hamilton, Lizzie H. TAYLOR, eldest daughter of Prof. Alfred and Eliza A. TAYLOR, age 13 years.
Dec. 22, in North Brookfield, Mrs. Georgia Dunbar, wife of A. T. NASH, age 33 years.
Dec. 25, in Eaton, John, infant of Thomas and Margaret BRANAGAN, age 5 months.
Dec. 15, in Hamilton, William COWAN, in his 88th year.

1876

Jan. 1, in Hamilton, Hannah STOWELL, relict of Enoch STOWELL, late of the town of Eaton, age 90 years, 2 months.
Jan. 25, in Madison, Philip D. WEEDEN, age 85 years.
Feb. 3, in Hamilton, Theodore Bridgeman CROSS, of membranous croup, age 3 years, 29 days.

DEMOCRATIC REPUBLICAN - 1876

[No date], in Hamilton, very suddenly, Rev. E. P. SMITH, Rector of St. Thomas's Episcopal Church. He was the eldest son of the late Hon. Samuel A. SMITH, of Guilford, where he had resided until about ten years ago, carrying on a farming operation. At that time, he decided to study for Holy Orders. His first Rectorship was at Sodus Point, where he remained for three years, thence he removed to White Water, MI, where he spent three. Then he came to Hamilton, where he officiated very acceptably until his death. He was 69 years of age and leaves a family of children, among whom are Homer L. SMITH, Esq., of Sherburne, Dr. W. A. SMITH, of Newark, NJ, formerly of this village, was a brother of Rev. SMITH.

Feb. 11, Mr. Anson BACON, resident of Bacon Hill in the town of Madison. He was unmarried. He leaves three brothers. His only sister, deceased, left a family of children. He was probably in his 79th year.

Mar. 5, in Brookfield, after a distressing illness of 5 days, Sophia BROWN, wife of Lucas BROWN, in her 70th year.

Mar. 20, in Madison, Jay WOODMAN, youngest son of William WOODMAN, age 2 years.

Mar. 18, at the residence of her son, H. G. SHOLES, near Earlville, Mrs. Mary SHOLES, in her 86th year.

Apr. 1, in Eaton, Daniel LANPHERE, age 60 years, 7 months. He had lived over 20 years in the place where he died at the foot of Woodman's Pond. He died from cancer in the throat, leaving his wife and four children, all of whom are married.

Apr. 4, in North Brookfield, Fanny W., wife of David KEITH, age 69 years. She went with her husband to visit her son in North Brookfield, where she died after only a few days illness.

Apr. 12, in Hamilton, Mrs. BRIGHAM, mother of Mrs. L. HOWES, age 84 years.

Apr. 12, in Sherburne, Deacon Ira CRAIN, age 71 years.

Apr. 9, in Hamilton, Harvey OSBORNE, age 54 years.

Apr. 15, in Smyrna, Frank W. FOWLER, age 19 years, 27 days. He was a student in Colgate Academy.

Apr. 15, in Eaton, of consumption, Libbie M. TITCHENER, age 24 years.

Apr. 15, in Hamilton, Melissa L. BRIGHT, wife of James BRIGHT, age 34.

Apr. 27 issue: "Recent deaths in Bouckville: 1. A 7-month old child of Mr. and Mrs. Walter EMMS, also
2. A child, still younger, of Mr. and Mrs. George PARKER, were both buried on Mar. 26."

DEMOCRATIC REPUBLICAN - 1876

3. Miss Minnie ENSON, age 16 years, died a few days ago. Her parents reside at Camden, NY, and she had been residing of late at H. I. PEET's.

4. Mr. John MC CLENTHAN died Mar. 31, age 75 years, one of the early settlers of the community. He leaves his wife, a daughter, and three sons.

May 4, in Hamilton, Rena, infant daughter of Newton R. and Phoebe WICKWIRE, age 9 months, 4 days.

From the *Sherburne News*: Stephen H. WARNER, a farmer living about 3 miles north of Sherburne, committed suicide by hanging himself on Apr. 26. He had been somewhat deranged since the death of his wife in Feb. Mr. WARNER used the same rope (in hanging himself) that his father used for a similar purpose about two years ago. He leaves a child, the adopted daughter of Mr. EASTMAN, of Smyrna. He was about 27 years ald.

May 8, in Hamilton, of Typho-Malarial fever, Dr. F. W. ROOT, age 56.

May 5, in Hamilton, Carrie O. STEARNS, age 8 years, 4 months.

May 23, in Hamilton, Mrs. Mary E. WICKWIRE, wife of Frank WICKWIRE, age 30 years.

May 29, in Little Falls, of typhoid fever, Genevieve W., wife of Rev. A. M. PRENTICE, of Brockport, NY, age 27 years.

May 31, in Hamilton, Anna, daughter of Edward and Catherine HORSTKOTTER, age 1 year, 23 days.

June 9, in Rio, at the residence of her son-in-law, Mr. Jesse MELTON, Mrs. Roxa S. WOODMAN, age 77 years, 2 months, 13 days. She was one of the earliest settlers of the County, having come with her husband from Chenango Co. in the Galesburg colony, nearly 40 years ago. A few years after they moved into this region her husband built the first schoolhouse within the township of Rio. She was left a widow more than 22 years ago, since which time she has made her home with her children, of whom four are deceased, and eight are still living, viz, five sons and three daughters. While in Galesburg she was connected with the First Church, and at her death was probably the eldest person in the Township.

Aug. 8, in Madison, Caroline COLLESTER, age 74 years.

July 27, in Hamilton, Helen M., wife of Arnold THOMPSON, age 39 years.

Aug. 31, Mr. Abijah BENNETT, of Lebanon, residing on the hill above the BOYD farm, hung himself; age about 60 years.

DEMOCRATIC REPUBLICAN - 1876

Sept. 3, in Hamilton, Ruth, wife of Frank SMITH, age 49 years.

Sept. 12, in Hamilton, Mrs. Mary M. THROOP, wife of J. B. BROWNELL, and daughter of W. H. THROOP, age 31 years.

Sept. 14, on the cars, near Sioux City, IA, Charles Finney, son of Rev. and Mrs. R. T. CROSS, age 3 months, 13 days.

Sept. 21, in Hamilton, Mrs. Charlotte BEVINS, age 68 years.

Sept. 19, Lewis GRAVES, highly respected farmer of New Berlin; committed suicide by cutting his throat from ear to ear.

Oct. 3, in Lebanon, at residence of David STONE, Esqr., Mrs. Eliza HAMILTON, relict of Charles HAMILTON, late of Westfield, NY, age 71 years. Some 25 years, or more, ago, Mr. Charles HAMILTON resided on the farm now owned by J. D. F. SMITH at Smith's Valley. He was there 5 years, and then went to Westfield, Chautauqua Co., NY, where he died 6 or 7 years ago. His widow then lived with her son. He died about 4 years ago, leaving her all alone. She came back to Smith's Valley a few days ago, expecting to make her home for the winter at Mr. David STONE's. She had been in usual health, and died very suddenly, undoubtedly from heart disease.

Oct. 14, in Hamilton, Louise Burchard PIERCE, wife of Frank T. PIERCE, age 39 years. She was daughter of the late Sylvester BURCHARD, and grew up on the old homestead north of Hamilton village in the edge of the town of Eaton. She was born on Aug. 28, 1837; married in 1863.

Oct. 18, in Kirkland, NY, Mary J. Wilcox, wife of T. J. ELLENWOOD, age 26 years, 11 months, 13 days.

Oct. 23, in this village [Hamilton], Mrs. Mehala STRADLING, age 59 years.

Oct. 18, in Hamilton, Palmyra A. LORD, wife of O. B. LORD, age 61 years.

Oct. 30, at Lehigh Summit, PA, David R. PIERCE, of Hamilton, age 41 years, victim of D.L.& W. R.R. accident.

Sept. 20, in Madison, Miss Sophia BOND, age 77 years. She was a daughter of Israel BOND, a Revolutionary Soldier who entered the Continental Army at 15 years of age. He served to the close of the War, and when the country began to settle, he was one of the first to make his home in Madison.

Nov. 13, in Hamilton, at the residence of her son, E. H. GREENE, of Lebanon St., Mrs. Chloe GREENE, age 78 years, 10 months.

DEMOCRATIC REPUBLICAN - 1876

Nov. 11, in Madison, Minnie BACON, youngest daughter of Clark BACON, age 7 years.
Nov. 13, in Hamilton, Eliza C. SIMPSON, wife of Sorannius SIMPSON, age 28 years, 6 months, 7 days.
Nov. 20, in Lebanon, Sarah, wife of Corydon CASH, age 29 years, 5 months, 8 days.
Nov. 24, at Sumner, Bremer Co., IA, Timothy B. ORVIS, Sr., age 86 years, 9 months, 20 days. The deceased was father of S. M. ORVIS, of this village [Hamilton], and resided in this County many years. He was a member of the Congregational Church, and went West about 25 years ago.
Dec. 6, in Georgetown, Hiram HAWKS, age 81 years.
Dec. 9, in Georgetown, Charles MACK, age 20 years.
[No date], in Smith's Valley, very suddenly, of congestion of the brain, Charles O. BIERCE, age 57 years.
Nov. 11, in Madison, Minnie BACON, youngest daughter of Clark BACON, age 7 years, 9 months.
Dec. 8, Enoch L. SAVAGE, of Georgetown, senior member of the firm of Savage & Hare, of that village, shot himself. He was about 58 years old, and had been melancholy at times.
Dec. 10, at South Hamilton, Albert J. COLE, age 31 years, 2 months.
Dec. 11, in Manchester, IA, Gerry L., son of H. L. and F. V. HOPKINS, age 8 years, 7 months, 6 days. Mr. H. L. HOPKINS formerly resided at Morrisville.
Nov. 27, Mrs. Julia Ann, wife of David RICHMOND, Esq. died of paralysis at her home in Poolville, in her 63rd year. She had been a helpless invalid for the past 27 years, kindly cared for by her husband.
Dec. 28, in Norway, Herkimer Co., Col. Jefferson TILLINGHAST, aged 73 years.

1877

From the Bridgeport, CT *Daily Standard* of Jan. 3, 1877: Miss Lucy M. WINSTON, niece of Rev. Dr. HARPER, of Hamilton. Her father was Rev. Meriwether WINSTON and her mother a daughter of Birdsey LEWIS, M.D., of Hamilton.
Jan. 1, in Cincinnati, OH, Cornelia Smith, daughter of Russell WHITMORE, of Georgetown, NY.
Jan. 28, at Madison Center, Hannah H. BARKER, age 79 years, 10 months, 6 days.
Jan. 26, in Lebanon, James CLOSE, age 61 years, 11 months.
Jan. 19, in Earlville, Harriet SHAW, (no age given).

DEMOCRATIC REPUBLICAN - 1877

Jan. 19, in East Hamilton, Joshua FIELD, age 69 years, 9 months.
Jan. 30, in Scriba, Oswego Co., NY, Mrs. Della PECKHAM, wife of Orson PECKHAM, age 74 years.
Jan. 29, in East Hamilton, Miss Eleanor PHILLIPS, age 68 years.
Feb. 15, in Hamilton village, Mrs. Theodosia POWER, widow of the late Medad ROGERS, age 82 years.
Feb. 15, in Hamilton, Lynn Julian HARTSHORN, youngest son of William M. HARTSAHORN, age 6 years.
Feb. 26, in Pratt's Hollow, town of Eaton, Malvina S., wife of John KERN, age 39 years.
Mar. 10, at Liberty, MO, Lewright Boardman EATON, only child of Prof. J. R. and M. L. EATON, age 7 years, 6 days.
Mar. 16, Thomas MARSHALL, aged about 70 years.
Mar. 21, in Brookfield, George L. SEABURY, age 19 years.
Mar. 10, in Hamilton, David LOOMIS, of North Brookfield, age 74 years.
Mar. 12, in Hamilton, Ada O. PETERSON, age 21 years.
Mar. 16, in Hamilton, Mrs. Ellen P. Barnett, age 70 years. She was daughter of Deacon PAINE, of Georgetown, and widow of the late S. W. BERRY.
Apr. 3, at her home in Solsville, Mrs. Elizabeth BRIDGE, wife of Benjamin BRIDGE, age 59 years, 5 months.
Apr. 6, at her home in South Augusta, Martha BYRNS, wife of George BYRNS, age 70 years.
Apr. 11, in Hamilton, Mrs. Sally THOMPSON, relict of John THOMPSON, age 80 years.
Apr. 5, in Madison Center, Eliza P., wife of Charles H. WHEAT, age 22 years.
Apr. 11, in Rockford, IL, Mrs. E. S. SALEY, wife of M. L. SALEY, (no age given).
Apr. 10, at Hamilton, William B. HARTSHORN, a son of William M. and Orvilla HARTSHORN, age 9 years, 11 months.
May 3, in Nelson, NY, Sarah JONES, age 53 years.
May 1, in Morrisville, George W. WEST, age 57 years.
May 4, in Hamilton, Maria COLLINS, age 67 years.
May 7, in Friendship, NY, Johnny FISHER, age 10 years.
May 11, in Bouckville, Mary A. COOLIDGE, age 74 years.
May 25, in Lebanon, Miss Roxana V. ALLEN, age 42 years.
May 25, in Lebanon, Jonathan GREENE, age 68 years.
May 27, in Hubbardsville, Lucinda, wife of Elijah NASH, age 61 years.
June 7, in Lebanon, Jonathan GREEN, age 68 years. (See above.)

DEMOCRATIC REPUBLICAN - 1877

June 16, in Earlville, A. S. DOUGLASS, age 45 years, 10 months, 17 days.
June 19, in Earlville, Lena SOUTHWORTH, age 4 years, 7 months.
June 21, in East Hamilton, Hannah, relict of Edwin SMITH, age 62 years.
June 24, in Earlville, Wilmer E. JONES, age 8 years, 8 months, 22 days.
July 7, in Solsville, Alethan Curtis, widow of Charles LEWIS, age 87 years, 3 months.
July 9, in Hamilton, Mary A., wife of Harleigh I. FOSTER, age 52 years.
July 21, in Lebanon, Charles L. SWIFT, age 27 years.
July 14, in Hamilton, Mrs. Cynthia D. MACOMBER, age 42 years.
Aug. 5, in Hamilton, Elihu THOMPSON, age 62 years.
Aug. 4, in Nunda, Livingston Co., NY, Mrs. Hannah B., wife of William P. BONNEY, age 63 years.
July 30, near Groveport, OH, Miss Julia MORSE, formerly of this village [Hamilton]. (No age given.)
July 8, in West Eaton, Mrs. Sarah TOWNSEND, age 95 years.
Aug. 8, in Pecksport, town of Eaton, Middleton TACKABERRY, age 70 years.
Aug. 5, in Yates, NY, Henry O. WHEELER, age 46 years.
Aug. 21, in Lebanon, Fannie O. WEDGE, age 46 years, 3 days.
Aug. 18, in Peterboro, Mrs. Lucy KLINCH, age 85 years, widow of George KLINCK (sic), of Peterboro.
Aug. 24, in Earlville, Samuel P. HANSON, age 66 years.
Sept. 8, in town of Madison, James RUSSELL, age 93 years.
Sept. 16, in Hamilton, John T. ANDRUS, age 37 years.
Oct. 2, in Lebanon, Richard PRICE, age 31 years.
Oct. 2, in Lisbon, NY, Sanford WHITMORE, age 64 years.
Oct. 2, in Hamilton, Daniel BALL, age 78 years.
Oct. 4, Charles B. KINNEY, of Madison, age 76 years.
Sept. 27, in East Hamilton, Almira ARMSTRONG, age 51 years.
Oct. 4, in Bouckville, Sophia A. WASHBURN, age 56 years, 8 months, 5 days.
Oct. 25, in Hamilton, Mary E., infant daughter of James A. and Nancy A. DERRICK, age 1 year, 7 months, 12 days.
Oct. 13, in Greensboro, NC, of diphtheria, Harry ROBIE, age 50 years.
Oct. 30, in Hamilton, Calvin B. BARBER, (no age given).
Oct. 28, at West Eaton, D. C. ENOS, age 86 years.
Nov. 6, at Madison, Fallie PECKHAM, age 28 years.
[No date], in DeRuyter village, Henry T. NIFF, age 67 years.

DEMOCRATIC REPUBLICAN - 1877

Nov. 25, in Galesburg, IL, Mrs. J. M. INGERSOLL, sister of E. F. HANSHAW and Mrs. J. L. SHORT of this city. From *Chicago Tribune*.

Dec. 6, in Kansas City, MO, Frank G. CALKINS, age 39 years.

Nov. 12, in Perrysburg, NY, Clara E. BENTON, age 16 years, eldest daughter of David and Anna BENTON.

1878

Jan. 4, in Jersey City, Adelaide S., wife of George W. FIRTH, and daughter of the late Ira H. POST.

Jan. 3, in Hubbardsville, Benjamin F. RHODES, age 51 years.

Jan. 12, in Earlville, Hortense H. HANSON, age 30 years.

Jan. 12, near Hamilton, Anna E. DUNBAR, age 21 years, 11 months.

Jan. 31, in Hamilton, Anna M. TAYLOR, daughter of Nelson and Mary TAYLOR, age 18 years, 10 months, 24 days.

Jan. 29, at Asbury Park, NJ, William F. BUELL, of East Hamilton, age 42 years.

Feb. 10, in Earlville, Henry, only son of Charles E. PIERSON, age 10 years.

Feb. 15, in Hamilton, Mrs. Emerilla Hopkins CHASE, wife of S. S. CHASE, age 37 years.

Feb. 6, in Hamilton, Palmer SHERMAN, age 68 years.

Mar. 2, in Brookfield, Peleg STANTON, Sr., age 87 years.

Mar. 1, in Brookfield, George W. DABOLL, age 61 years.

Mar. 2, in Jamestown, at the residence of her daughter, Mrs. GOULDING, Sarah W. MORSE, wife of Dennis MORSE, in her 78th year. She was formerly a resident of Madison.

Apr. 8, in Hamilton, Mary, wife of Henry C. SMITH, age 37 years.

Apr. 15, in Hamilton, Anna CASE, wife of B. F. CASE, age 35 years.

Apr. 7, at New Haven, CT, Ira B. ALLEN, of Geneva, WI, age 26 years, 2 months, 27 days. He was son of George ALLEN, formerly a resident of Smith's Valley in this county. He was pursuing theological studies at Harvard, and would have graduated in June.

Apr. 23, in Hamilton, Henry LEACH, (no age given).

Apr. 15, in Earlville, A. B. SWIFT, age 56 years.

May 16, in Hamilton, Mary, wife of John TRACY, age 53 years.

[No date given], in Madison, Mrs. Lucinda THOMPSON, age 74 years.

DEMOCRATIC REPUBLICAN - 1878

May 26, in Madison, David B. BARBER, age 71 years.

May 15, Elias WEAVER died in Logansport, IN. He married Lucy, a daughter of Harmon SHORT, of Homer, NY.

June 21, in Winfield, Jennie A. JONES, daughter of Rev. E. W. JONES, age 24.

June 26, in Earlville, J. A. P. STUART, age 69 years.

June 22, in Hamilton, Mary E. TAYLOR, age 4 years.

June 30, in Earlville, Lena DOWELL, age 13 years, 6 months, 7 days.

July 15, in Hamilton, Charles, only child of George and Lizzie BEAL, age 1 year, 1 day.

July 23, in McComb City, MS, Dr. J. S. DOUGLASS, of Milwaukee, formerly of this place.

July 17, in Sherburne, Mrs. E. E. NELSON, of Hamilton, (no age given).

July 23, at Pratt's Hollow, George KERN, age 77 years.

Sept. 24, in Hamilton, John SHERMAN, age 30 years; of typhoid fever.

Sept. 21, in Hamilton, Alida, daughter of John and Hattie SHERMAN, age 4 years, 11 months; of typhoid fever.

Sept. 20, at Preston, Canada, Mr. Alsbrow BARBER, father of Eli BARBER, of this village [Hamilton], age 86 years. He was residing with his daughter in Preston. His body was brought here for burial in the Madison St. Cemetery.

Oct. 4, at West Troy, Ada L. BOYD, eldest daughter of Roger D. and Adell BOYD, age 21 years.

Oct. 16, at East Longmeadow, MA, Mrs. Flora Lillian, wife of T. B. MARKHAM, and daughter of J. S. WHITEMORE, of this place [Hamilton], age 25 years.

Oct. 20, Mr. Otis B. HOWE, merchant on the central wharf, at his residence in Buffalo. He was born in Hamilton Aug. 15, 1809; removed to Elmira, then to Buffalo in 1858 where he established himself upon the dock as a grain merchant.

Dec. 1, in Bouckville, Mrs. Phebe BRIGGS, daughter of Otis SIMONS, age 57 years.

Dec. 22, in Hamilton, Mrs. Adaline LOOMIS, wife of Calvin LOOMIS, age 70 years.

Dec. 31, in Hamilton, Mrs. Elizabeth YORK, age 45 years.

1879

Jan. 2, at Michigan Bluff, CA, Charles S. RUSSELL, age 69 years. Deceased was born in Madison County in Feb. 1809, and was the father of G. W. RUSSELL and Mrs. W. B. FISHER.

DEMOCRATIC REPUBLICAN - 1879

Jan. 25, at Hamilton, Denas PARKER, age 81 years, 6 months.
Feb. 2, in Lebanon, Sanford HEAD, age 90 years.
Jan. 30, in Hamilton, J. HAYWARD, age 58 years.
Feb. 18, in Lebanon, Anna, wife of the late Sanford HEAD, age 74 years.
Feb. 25, in Hamilton, Meck V., son of C. R. and D. S. PALMITER, age 4 years.
Feb. 25, in Solsville, Benjamin S. BRIDGE, age 58 years, 7 months.
Jan. 25 (26), in Aurora, TX, Frank D. TYLER, age 24 years.
Mar. 4, at Truxton, James W. FREEMAN, age 90 years.
Mar. 15, at Knoxboro, NY, Lavina C., wife of Andrew LA MUNION, and daughter of the late Perez BONNEY of Hamilton, age 36 years.
Mar. 25, at Saginaw, MI, Mrs. Matilda DANFORTH, wife of Erastus WELLINGTON, formerly of Madison County, age 43 years.
Mar. 30, in Madison, Anthony HOPKINS, age 76 years, formerly of Eaton.
Apr. 18, Luther BACON, age 72 years. He was born in this village [Hamilton] Feb. 8, 1807.
[Issue of May 1st], A Miss CHESEBRO, of North Brookfield, daughter of David D. CHESEBORO, died mysteriously (from convulsions) recently.
May 3, in Hamilton, Juline PIERCE, age 70 years.
May 3, in Hamilton, Rev. Allen R. BEACH, in his 83rd year.
May 17, in Hamilton, Thomas GREEN, age 58 years.
May 25, in Eaton, Charles WALKER, age 26 years.
May 22, in Lebanon, Arthur G., son of Charles A. and Mary E. BARBER, age 2 years, 4 months.
June 4, in Hamilton, William STEVENS, age 84 years.
June 8, in Hamilton, Miss Sarah K. FOOTE, age 68 years.
June 5, in Hamilton, Benjamin WILBER, age 81 years.
June 12, in Chicago, IL, Rev. William RONNEY, age 65 years. Deceased was formerly of Hamilton.
June 17, in Madison, John S. LUCAS, age 61 years.
July 1, in Madison, Mary E., wife of A. S. MACOMBER, age 62 years.
July 4, in Morrisville, Joseph Sterling SMITH, age 46 years.
July 15, in East Hamilton, Edward BROWN, age 88 years.
July 15, in Eaton, William APPLEFORD, age 58 years.
July 13, in Madison Center, James DeForest, infant son of D. E. and Jennie Wickwire WEBSTER, age 4 months.
Aug. 16, in Hamilton, Amos LAMB, age 73 years.
Aug. 15, in Hamilton, Bessie Louisa, daughter of J. I. and D. E. BAKER, age 11 months, 3 days.

DEMOCRATIC REPUBLICAN - 1879

Aug. 7, in Macon, IL, Samuel K. THOMAS, age 59 years, formerly of Cazenovia.
Sept. 2, in Madison, James WICKWIRE, age 60 years.
Sept. 2, in Hamilton, Taylor GARNER, age 36 years.
Sept. 5, in Hamilton, the infant son of A. C. RICE, age 3 days.
Sept. 8, in Hamilton, Jethro M. BONNEY, age 78 years.
Sept. 14, in Columbus, Ida E., wife of Rev. W. J. QUINCEY, age 21 years, 4 months.
Sept. 3, in Hamilton, the infant son of Charles and Malinda MACOMBER, age 4 weeks.
Aug. 10, in Hubbardsville, Mrs. Anna GIFFORD, daughter of the late Arisstarchus and Betty WILLIAMS, age 51 years.
Aug. 21, in Hubbardsville, at the residence of her daughter, Mrs. J. S. DART, Betsy, wife of Arisstarchus WILLIAMS, age 77 years.
Oct. 1, in Madison, Mr. Ellis Smith PHILLIPS, age 77 years.
Oct. 3, in Madison, Daniel BUTCHERS, age 77 years.
Sept. 28, in Hamilton, LeRoy H., a son of John Y. and Mattie A. BONNEY, age 2 years.
Oct. 21, in Hamilton, Wells C. RUSSELL, age 62 years. He was one of the directors of the National Hamilton Bank, and a member of the Board of Madison University.
Oct. 10, in Brookfield, MO, Mrs. Emma L. GATES, daughter of the late Thomas and Elizabeth THURSTON, age 38 years.
Rev. Horace BURCHARD was born in Remsen, Oneida Co., NY, April 5, 1833, and died at Brattleboro, VT, Oct. 25, 1879, age 46 years. He spent his boyhood in Hamilton with his parents, where in 1853 he graduated from Madison University, at the age of 20 years, with highest honors of his class. He united with the Baptist Church at Hamilton . . . For an account of his life of teaching and as a minister, see *Democratic Republican*, issue of Nov. 6th.
Nov. 8, in Hamilton, Miss Lillian E. LEWIS, age 19 years.
Dec. 9, in Madison, Mrs. Margaret SHANNON, wife of William SHANNON, age 51 years.
Dec. 31, in Earlville, Frankie BROWN, son of Nicanor and Phebe BROWN, age 23 years.

DEMOCRATIC REPUBLICAN - 1880

1880

Jan. 3, in Oxford, Mrs. Elizabeth GALLAGHER, age 59 years. She came to this village [Hamilton] from Ireland.
Jan. 6, in Lebanon, Samuel T. SHARP, age 78 years.
Feb. 13, in Eaton, Rebecca Shapley SHERRILL, age 77 years.
Feb. 10, in Bouckville, Ambrose PHILLIPS, age 76 years.
Feb. 9, in Hamilton, Merrit D. WEDGE, age 62 years.
Feb. 4, in New Haven, CT, Isaac PARDEE, age 62 years.
Feb. 24, in Norwich, Mrs. Esther, wife of Denos FISHER, age 60 years.
Mar. 8, in West Eaton, Stillman PAYNE, age 61 years.
Mar. 17, in Elizabeth, NJ, Mrs. Julia J., wife of Rev. J. C. ALLEN, age 34 years.
Apr. 6, at Smith's Valley, Mrs. Myra M. MAYDOLE, age 70 years, 10 months.
Apr. 4, in West Eaton, Edwin L. HOPKINS, age 34 years.
Apr. 11, in Pierceville, Dwight TOWNSEND, age 40 years.
Apr. 10, died suddenly, at the residence of her son-in-law, Luzon TUCKER, in Solsville, Mrs. Diana WARD, age 87 years, 7 months.
Apr. 3, in Ninevah, Miss Mary A. SWIFT, age 75 years.
Feb. 23, in New Sharon, IA, Rev. O. L. CRITTENDEN, a student in Madison University, having graduated in 1844.
Apr. 10, in Utica, Clara, only daughter of Charles and Emma SIMMONS, age 3 years, 9 months, 5 days.
Apr. 15, in Nelson, Hiram WESTCOTT, age 52 years.
Apr. 27, in Sangerfield, Mr. Daniel WELLS, age 81 years.
Apr. 28, in Hamilton village, at the residence of her daughter, Mrs. Addison WEST, Mrs. Samuel BROWN, age 75 years.
May 4, in Wyoming, NY, Mrs. Mary Selina MORSE, wife of Prof. MORSE, in her 77th year.
In issue of May 27th: Judge O. S. WILLIAMS, of Clinton, died last Thursday, age 65 years.
June 2, in Madison, Millie A. PECKHAM, age 21 years, 9 months.
[No date], at the home of his father in Nelson, David BLAIR, age 19 years.
June 3, in St. Clair, MI, Mrs. Sarah SANFORD, age 81 years.
June 11, in East Hamilton, Caroline Howe WEAVER, age 69 years.
June 23, at Bouckville, Clarence, youngest son of Michael and Sedate TOOKE, age 9 years, 3 months, 6 days.
July 1, in West Eaton, Mrs. Lyman CAMPBELL, age 30 years.
July 12, in Madison, Mathew K. BURNHAM, age 89 years.

DEMOCRATIC REPUBLICAN - 1880

July 6, in Oriskany Falls, Mrs. Eliza BUTTON, widow of Luther BUTTON, age 55 years.

July 9, in Hamilton, at the residence of her only daughter, Mrs. Alfred TAYLOR, Mary POWELL, widow of the late Thomas WHITE, Esq. of Philadelphia, in her 79th year. She was born in Gloucestershire, England, and was married there to Mr. WHITE in 1826. They came to the US in 1831.

July 15, in Garett, KS, Mrs. Mary M. PAGE, age 55 years. Mrs. PAGE was formerly of this village [Hamilton], and was the sister of Mrs. W. C. JOSLIN.

Aug. 3, in Hamilton, Mr. Eli POND, age 68 years. He was born in Cortland in 1812.

July 19, in Rollin, MI, Rufus HOLBROOK, age 73 years, 4 months, 12 days.

Aug. 29, in Pierceville, Miss Sarah GRIFFIN, age 26 years, daughter of Richard and Sophronia GRIFFIN.

Sept. 3, in Oneonta, NY, Susie C. PARKE. She formerly lived with the Charles R. PAYNE family, of Hamilton. [No age given.]

Sept. 17, in Albany, William A. BOYD, age 78 years.

Oct. 5, in Hamilton, Clara, wife of Deacon A. SANFORD, age 82 years.

Oct. 3, in Hamilton, Catherine, wife of Leroy CLARK, age 62 years.

Oct. 13, in Hamilton, at the residence of Mr. Austin TIBBETS, Miss Leunetta HARRINGTON, age 12 years, 7 months, 26 days.

Oct. 11, in Solsville, Abel RUNDELL, age 77 years.

Oct. 27, at the residence of C. W. UNDERHILL in Hamilton, Louisa D. ROOT, widow of Dr. F. W. ROOT, in her 60th year.

Oct. 11, in West Eaton, Isaac G. HOPKINS, age 39 years.

Nov. 9, in West Eaton, James R. COMES. [No age given; in issue of Nov. 25th.]

Nov. 22, in Poolville, Everett BRAINARD. [No age given; in issue of Nov. 25th.]

Nov. 20, in West Eaton, Marcia V., wife of John J. DARROW, age 43 years, 23 days.

Nov. 3, at Stockwell, Mrs. Betsey Anne LIVERMORE, age 64 years.

Oct. 27, Mrs. Polly P. RANDALL, at Stockwell, age 89 years.

News has been received here that Will LEONARD was murdered near Eureka, NM, on the 10th of last June. He has brothers here.

DEMOCRATIC REPUBLICAN - 1881

1881

Jan. 29, in Exeter, Otsego Co., Sally MOREY, age 77 years, 1 month, 6 days. Mrs. MOREY was sister of Mrs. Abi VAN SLYCK, of this village [Hamilton].
Feb. 19, in Hamilton, I. A. MILLER, age 71 years.
June 27, in Hamilton, David KEITH, age 85 years.
[NOTE: This year's file lacks issues from 24th of February 1881 to the 16th of June, 1881, except for the issue of April 14th.]
July 9, in Hamilton, Lucy F., widow of Stillman EATON, in her 71st year.
July 22, in Hamilton, Lucy, wife of Jacob ALLSTON, age 38 years.
June 21, Hilda BEECHER, wife of Chancey MUNSON, of South Hamilton, age 77 years, 1 month, 13 days.
Aug. 4, in Hamilton, Mary, wife of Charles JOHNSON, age 45 years.
Aug. 8, in Hamilton, M. Lavel, infant son of George and Minnie WAIT, age 10 months.
Sept. 4, in Hamilton, Hettie, daughter of Allen and Mary E. ENOS, age 4 months.
Aug. 29, in Hamilton, Frank Eugene, only child of Rev. E. F. and Hannah ATWOOD, age 9 months. Mr. and Mrs. ATWOOD came from the mission field, near Deadwood, where they have been engaged for some time, to stop with Mrs. ATWOOD's mother, Mrs. Mulford ROGERS.
Sept. 17, in Anamosa, IA, Lyman NILES, in his 70th year. He was born in Lebanon Feb. 13, 1812.
Nov. 2, at Nelson Flats, Mrs. Ruth WHITNEY, wife of Isaac WHITNEY, age 67 years.
Nov. 11, in Hamilton, Abi VAN SLYCK, age 83 years.
Dec. 25, in Hubbardsville, Charles A. PARTRIDGE, age 27 years.
Dec. 30, in Syracuse, Mary Caroline, eldest daughter of Col. William F. WARREN, of Augusta, age 27 years.

1882

Jan. 10, in Madison, Mrs. Matilda ROWLANDS, age 46 years.
Jan. 9, in Hamilton, John J. VAN HOSEN, age 59 years, 5 months.
Jan. 10, in New Lebanon, Columbia Co., Henry WOOD, age 67 years.
[No date], at Meredith, NY, Mr. Byron F. QUIVEY, age 24 years.

DEMOCRATIC REPUBLICAN - 1882

Feb. 3, Mr. Morris W. WILLARD, of North Vineland, NJ, formerly of Hamilton and Eaton. He came to Hamilton 18 years ago and purchased a small farm. His brother-in-law was Mr. W. C. JOSLIN.
Jan. 24, in Hamilton village, Mr. John WOODMAN, age 65 years.
Jan. 31, in Eaton, Mrs. Emily MEDBURY, age 79 years.
Feb. 5, in Pierceville, Mr. William L. PARKER, age 69 years.
Feb. 3, in Nelson, Mrs. Thomas BRADY, age 60 years.
Feb. 19, in West Eaton, Mrs. Polly ENOS, widow of David ENOS, age 89 years.
Feb. 17, in Hamilton, Phebe WICKWIRE, wife of Newton WICKWIRE, age 37 years.
[No date], in Clarksville, Butler Co., IA, Byron H. REYNOLDS, age 37 years.
Feb. 26, in Oneida Co., Mrs. Sophia, wife of Levi B. BONNEY. She died at her home in Cherry St., Oneida. She was 80 years, 6 months old, and was Miss Sophia JUDD before her marriage to Mr. BONNEY.
Mar. 13, at Hamilton Center, Mrs. Susan E. DUNHAM, age 69 years.
Mar. 8, in Saratoga, NY, Mrs. M. A. HOWARD, wife of V. R. HOWARD, age 58 years.
Mar. 12, in Lincoln, NE, Mattie S., wife of Ernest SEELEY, of Rose, Wayne Co., NY, and daughter of S. S. CHASE of Lincoln, age 18 years. She was formerly of Hamilton.
Mar. 14, in Lebanon, Deacon Cooley C. GRAY, age 82 years, 4 months.
Mar. 27, in North Brookfield, Elizabeth BEEBE, age 81 years, 1 month, 4 days.
Mar. 27, in Eaton, Hugh JONES, age 78 years.
Apr. 23, in Hamilton, Mrs. Cora ROOT, widow of Solomon ROOT, age 80 years.
Apr. 22, at Westmoreland, Emanuel VAN SLYCK, of Hamilton, age 68 years.
May 15, in Rose Hill, Columbia Co., VA, at the residence of her aunt Eliza Dielle BLANCON, Miss Addie ARMISTEAD, of Richmond, VA. Miss Addie has visited in Hamilton.
May 14, in Geneva, OH, Charles E. BRETT. He came to make his home in Hamilton a year ago.
June 23, in town of Eaton, Freddie CHASE, age 14 years, 11 months, 14 days.
June 24, in Hamilton, William MORGAN, age 81 years.
June 30, in Hamilton, Mrs. Lucina R. BONNEY, widow of M. BONNEY, age 75 years.

DEMOCRATIC REPUBLICAN - 1882

July 5, in Hamilton, Mrs. Malinda A. SWAN, wife of Lyman SWAN, age 76 years.

[No date], in Troy, NY, David Stewart, infant son of Mr. and Mrs. O. H. STRADLING, age 4 months.

July 5, Harvey POWERS, nephew of Henry POWERS of this village [Hamilton], died at York, Atchinson Co., MO. He was son of Silas and Diana POWERS, born at Scriba, Oswego Co., NY in 1843. Mr. N. S. POWERS, a brother of Harvey, died at the same place less than a year ago.

May 4, Mrs. Marcus C. ALLEN, at Madison. She was a daughter of Alonzo PECK, and had been married about eleven months ago.

Mar. 24, in West Eaton, Mrs. A. W. SMITH, age 71 years.

Aug. 10, at West Eaton, at the residence of her son, J. J. DARROW, Mrs. Thankful DARROW, age 89 years.

Aug. 29, in Madison, Delos COLLISTER, age 57 years.

Sept. 2, Winnie, youngest child of Edwin and Eliza COREY, age 3 years, 11 months, 22 days. [No location given.]

Sept. 14, in Hamilton, the infant daughter of Frank J. and Clara ROOT, age 3 days.

Sept. 6, in Madison Center, Harvey J. PERKINS, age 76 years.

Sept. 11, in Madison, Alice, wife of Charles WOODMAN, age 22 years.

Aug. 31, at Millardston, NC, Jay Morgan FELT, only child of Major E. and Rosa FELT, age 10 months.

Oct. 1, at West Eaton, Dr. J. E. CROSS, age 43 years.

Oct. 9, in Hamilton, Mrs. N. TAYLOR. [No age given, issue of Oct. 12.]

Oct. 5, in Lebanon, Emmet O. ETSON, age 21 years.

Nov. 2, in Hamilton, Miss Emily THOMPSON, age 54 years.

Nov. 1, in Lebanon, Mrs. Mary MULONEY, age 76 years, 1 month.

Nov. 23, in Hamilton, Louise S. UNDERHILL, age 10 years, 2 months, 15 days.

Dec. 28, in Hamilton, Samuel WICKWIRE, age 75 years. (See below.)

Dec. 28, in Lebanon, Allen NILES, age 81 years.

Dec. 27 (sic), in Hamilton, Samuel WICKWIRE, age 76 years (sic).

1883

Jan. 7, in Hamilton, Gertrude MAYNARD, daughter of Rev. MAYNARD. [No age given.]

DEMOCRATIC REPUBLICAN - 1883

Jan. 12, in Lima, NY, Willie L. STEARNS, son of T. O. and E. P. STEARNS, of Lima, age 7 years, 7 months.
Jan. 15, in Augusta, NY, Mrs. Robert SMITH, age 67 years, 7 months.
Jan. 11, in Hamilton, Isaac KELLOWAY, age 79 years.
Jan. 12, in Madison, Capt. Benjamin SIMONS, age 88 years.
Feb. 5, in Hamilton, James A. DERRICK, age 49 years.
Feb. 17, in Madison, Jane CHADWICK, widow of the late Isaac CHADWICK, age 91 years, 8 months.
[No date], in Detroit, MI, Mrs. Harriet ESSLESTYN, age 70 years.
Feb. 26, in Hamilton, Albert F. BONNEY, of Canaseraga, Alleghany Co., NY, age 29 years, 2 months, 20 days.
Mar. 2, at Smith's Valley, at the home of his daughter, Mrs. BIXBY, Chancellor L. BIERCE, age 69 years.
A suicide, by hanging, in Lebanon, last Saturday, Mrs. Carrie SOLES, age 23 years. She was daughter of Solomon GATES, and wife of Elmer SOLES. (In issue of Mar. 8th.)
Mar. 14, in Poolville, Joseph A. SMITH, age 64 years.
Mar. 14, in Georgetown, Mrs. Betsey MARVIN, age 81 years.
Apr. 5, in Utica, Mrs. Lizzie WALLACE, wife of Rev. Robert WALLACE, of Princeton, IL, daughter of W. O. and Mary ROWLANDS, of Madison; age 33 years.
Apr. 21, in Hubbardsville, Herbie W. COLSON, age 19 years.
Apr. 24, in Cazenovia, Mrs. Z. M. JOHNSON, widow of the late Henry A. JOHNSON, age 70 years.
Apr. 24, in Pratts Hollow, Anna J. FIELD, daughter of E. B. and Laura FIELD, age 22 years.
[No date given], in Hamilton, Patrick B. KELLEY, age 20 years. (In issue of May 24.)
May 6, Mrs. Louise M. KENDALL, age 40 years; daughter of D. REED.
May 23, in Hamilton, Joseph Addison MOTT, age 73 years, 9 months, 18 days.
May 17, in Hamilton, Mrs. Eliza C. BALL, wife of J. H. BALL, age 40 years.
May 17, in Madison, May L. CURTIS, daughter of Anson CURTIS, age 18 years.
June 1, in Hamilton, Abram CUSHMAN, age 81 years.
May 20, in Augusta, GA, Emma C. TUTTLE, (no age given).
July 18, in Hamilton, Daniel READ, age 75 years.
June 27, at West Eaton, Hattie BARNES, age 22 years.
July 22, in Hamilton, Albert A. PIERCE, age 50 years.
Dated July 9, 1883 at Hamilton, a citation to appear in connection with settling the estate of Goodwin DURFEE: "The people of the State of New York, to

DEMOCRATIC REPUBLICAN - 1883

Elizabeth B. DURFEE, the widow, of Madison, Madison Co., NY, and Hannah C. MANCHESTER, of Madison: also Sarah K. TALCOTT, of Hamilton
Lucius S. HALL, of Hermitage, Wyoming Co., NY
Marian BRONSON, of Sherburne
Delia LOTTRIDGE, of Sherburne
George SCOTT, of Hubbardsville
Oriana ROLLINS, of Hubbardsville
Thomas CHURCH, of Madison
Lewis COE, of Bouckville
William COE, of Norwich
Ruth COE, of Madison
Melissa COE, of Madison
Frank TOMPKINS, of Auburn, NY
Huldah COE, of Madison
Cyrus THOMPSON, of York, Delaware Co., IA
Harriet GRANGER, of Armanda, MI
Myra DICKERSON, of Freedom, IL
James MADISON, of Canandaigua, Lenawee Co., MI
Martha A. GUILFORD, of Grand Rapids, MI
Mary J. SAMPSON, of Chillicothe, MO
Earl HALL, of Fort Scott, KS
Timothy HALL, of Westfield, IN
Martha A. BOTSFORD, of Vinton, IA
Electa J. COLLINS, of Great Barrington, MA
Jeremand D. HALL, of Tehama, CA
Anson B. HALL, of Sheridan, AR
Harriet C. HUBBARD, of Carbon Run, PA
Thomas E. COLLINS, of Livermore, IA
Hannah R. PALMER, of Mound City, KS
Mary I. WILLIAMS, Fred H. WILLIAMS, Albon C. WILLIAMS, Anna B. WILLIAMS, and Sara A. COVINGTON, all of Darlington, Indian Territory
Mahlon J. WILLIAMS, of Mobetie, TX
Mehlon D. COLLINS, of Corning, IA
Samuel G. HALL, of Providence, RI
Mary D. HALL, of Portsmouth, RI
Francis MOUNT and Arthur S. MOUNT, all of Red Bluff, CA
Hannah M. POLLARD, Youngs A. GALLOP, Everett E. GALLOP, all of Dunnigan, CA
Amanda DURFEE, of Davenport, IA
Alfred SIMMONS, of Detroit, MI
Gideon D. SIMMONS, of Cedar Rapids, IA
Deborah BLACKMAN, Harriet BONNER, of Kalamazoo, MI
Mary STEWART and Stephen DURFEE, of Millville, NJ
Susan SIMMONS, of Philadelphia, PA
Roxana BUMP, of Newfield, NJ

DEMOCRATIC REPUBLICAN - 1883

 Willis B. DURFEE, Cornelius S. DURFEE, of Davenport, IA
 Nina THOMPSON, of Oriskany Falls, NY
 William HALL, of Warsaw, NY
 Clarkson A. HALL, of Gainesville, Wyoming Co., NY, and
  Benjamin DURFEE, Harriet DURFEE, John DURFEE, Samuel DURFEE, James E. C. HALL, Burrington DURFEE, Stephen DURFEE, Judith DURFEE, and Malissa DURFEE, whose residences are unknown and cannot, after diligent inquiry, can not be ascertained; the Society of Friends, of the State of New York.

Devisees, heirs at law, and next of kin, of GOODWIN DURFEE, late of Madison, NY, deceased, and to all persons interested in the estate of the said GOODWIN DURFEE.

June 29, in Hamilton, William H. THROOP, age 76 years.

[No date given], in West Eaton, Minnie, daughter of Mr. and Mrs. George W. JOHNSON, age 14 years. [Issue of Aug. 9th.]

Aug. 5, in East Hamilton, Amos LAMB, age 87 years, 10 months.

Aug. 5, at the residence of Horatio G. SHOLES, near Earlville, Mrs. Betsey SHOLES, age 64 years, 2 months.

Aug. 6, near Earlville, Ida May, youngest daughter of Mr. and Mrs. Nelson F. SHOLES, age 2 years, 10 months.

Aug. 9, in Utica, Mrs. Mary Jane MEYER, age 35 years. She was daughter of O. W. and Mary ROWLANDS, of Hamilton. "For the third time within the past three months her parents have followed a daughter to the grave." Her husband was Van Cortland MEYER.

Aug. 10, in West Eaton, Mrs. Florence S. LONT, age 39 years.

[No date], near Earlville, Mrs. Ann HOLMES, age 80 years, 1 month (In issue of Aug. 23d.)

Aug. 21, in this village [Hamilton], Abigail STEVENS, age 91 years.

Aug. 20, in Earlville, Mary J. TORREY, wife of N. W. TORREY, age 31 years, 11 months.

Aug. 29, in Hamilton, Matilda N. TRACY, age 60 years.

Aug. 20, in McLeansboro, IL, Harry BAKER, age 33 years. He was son of John BAKER, of this village [Hamilton].

Aug. 30, in Poolville, Calvin W. SAWDY, age 74 years.

Sept. 8, at Randallsville, Lewis SHAPLEY, age 76 years.

Oct. 30, in Madison Township, Mrs. Abigail HOWES, widow of Heman HOWES, age 86 years.

DEMOCRATIC REPUBLICAN - 1883

[No date], Miss Nettie NASH, daughter of George E. NASH, of Poolville, age 19 years. (In issue of Oct. 18th.)

Oct. 10, in Madison, Susie, wife of Harry MORGAN, age 22 years.

Oct. 24, in Hamilton, Kate M. MC GLEW, age 23 years.

In the issue of Nov. 8th, a clipping had been cut away; perhaps it contained deaths or marriages.

Nov. 13, at the residence of B. C. ACKLEY, East Hamilton, Perlina, wife of the late Amos LAMB, age 82 years.

Nov. 22, at Solsville, Leverett PERKINS, age 70 years, 8 months, 12 days.

Nov. 17, at Jackson, MI, George H. GILMORE, age 31 years.

Nov. 19, in Brisbane, Malachi SHARTS, formerly of Madison and Lebanon, age 84 years, 7 months, 10 days.

Nov. 27, at Otselic, Mary PIERCE, age 49 years, 11 months.

Nov. 30, in Madison, Mrs. Andalusia KIMBERLY, wife of Henry KIMBERLEY (sic), age 52 years.

Dec. 3, in Lebanon, John GAVIN, age 55 years.

Nov. 8, in Lebanon, Champlin WILCOX, age 91 years, 1 month, 26 days. Mr. WILCOX was one of the pioneers in the settlement of Lebanon, having moved to that town from RI 65 years ago. He lived to see his fifth generation.

Nov. 22, in Madison village, Isaac R. COE, age 55 years, 5 months.

Dec. 15, in Hamilton, Seth BASS, age 87 years.

Nov. 25, in Smith's Valley, Nathaniel BARR, age 87 years.

Dec. 23, near Randallsville, Alfred M. WILCOX, age 31 years, 6 months.

Dec. 14, in Lincklaen, Horace POOL, age 74 years.

Dec. 24, in Munnsville, Mrs. Mary D. COON, age 42 years.

1884

Jan. 7, in Hamilton, Frances Elizabeth, wife of Hon. A. N. SHELDON, and 2d daughter of John B. LADD and Lydia, his wife, in her 59th year. She was born Apr. 28, 1824 about a mile south of Earlville in the town of Sherburne. She was married at the age of twenty, and lived more than forty years of wedded life. She had three children, one of whom died as a child in 1849. The LADD family were among the early settlers of Chenango Valley, their farm bordering the Chenango River for more than a mile.

[No date], George VAN NORMEN, a man of 61 years, who resided in the same house with Emory TIBBETTS on the

DEMOCRATIC REPUBLICAN - 1884

George BACON farm in Madison, dropped dead recently. He was a sailor on the *Flying Dutchman* in the Civil War, and was an Englishman by birth. He came to Cortland last fall. (In Jan. 17 issue.)

Jan. 9, in Eaton, Mr. Brackley COLSON, age 92 years.
Jan. 3, in Munnsville, Miss Minerva HULL, age 75 years.
Jan. 6, in Morrisville, Mrs. Polly NORTON, age 88 years, 10 months.
Jan. 6, in DeRuyter, Timothy G. BROWN, age 58 years, 4 months, 16 days.
Jan. 4, in DeRuyter, Mr. Harmon C. MAXSON, age 56 years.
Jan. 6, at Quality Hill, Nancy A. CLARK, relict of the late Henry CLARK, and sister of Gen. B. F. BRUCE, age 70 years.
Jan. 24, in Hamilton, George Morris ALBERT, age 47 years.
Jan. 23, in Hamilton, Mrs. Amanda SIMMONS, wife of Otis SIMMONS, (no age given).
Jan. 19, in Hamilton, H. P. CASE, age 57 years.
Jan. 22, in Hamilton, Dr. Sherman KIMBERLY, age 78 years, 7 months, 7 days. He was born in Goshen, CT, June 18, 1805. When a year old, his family removed to Berkshire Co., MA. He married Phebe THOMPSON, with whom he lived nearly 58 years. He removed to this place in 1836 and had practiced medicine since 1839. Mr. and Mrs. KIMBERLEY (sic) had five children; but only two sons lived,--Henry and Frank.
Jan. 23, in Madison, Mrs. Isaac TERRY, age 62 years, 1 month, 4 days.
Feb. 9, in Lebanon, Fred E. BROWN, age 22 years, 4 months.
Feb. 10, in Truxton, Rufus DUNHAM, age 92 years.
Feb. 22, in Eaton, John H. BROWN, age 82 years.
Jan. 28, at Pine Woods, NY, Ella E. BOWEN, age 35 years, 10 months.
In issue of March 6th: Rev. Norman HARRIS died very suddenly at his residence on Mill St., age 71 years.
In issue of March 20th: Dwight C. GROVE, many years the publisher of the *Utica Observer*, died in New York City last Monday. He was born in Dec. 1825, and leaves a wife, a son and a daughter.
Mar. 26, in Madison, L. Beach MANCHESTER, age 52 years, 10 months, 21 days.
Mar. 24, in Hubbardsville, Charles W. BRASSE, in his 29th year.
Mar. 30, in Hamilton, Mrs. Norman BROWER, age 44 years.
Mar. 31, in Hamilton, Charles T. WOOD, age 17 years.
From Grand Rapids, MI, paper: In this city, Mar. 24, J. C. REMINGTON, age 84 years, 8 months, 24 days.

DEMOCRATIC REPUBLICAN - 1884

Apr. 10, in West Eaton, Mrs. Emily DICCINSON, wife of Frederick DARROW, age 66 years.
Apr. 14, in West Eaton, Mrs. Caroline M. CHAPHE, age 80 years.
Apr. 22, in Madison, Emeline MACKEY, age 79 years.
Apr. 24, in Hubbardsville, Martha FULLER, age 77 years.
Apr. 24, in Hamilton, Maryett P. NEWKIRK, age 85 years.
Apr. 24, in Hamilton, Arthur L. FULLER, age 27 years, 1 month, 2 days.
May 8, in Hamilton, Lewis F. ALLEN, age 65 years, 8 months, 22 days.
May 9, in Hamilton, Nora, wife of James COOPER, age 23 years.
June 9, in Hamilton, Hiram WHEELER, age 74 years.
June 14, in Hamilton, Alfred G. SLOCUM, age 75 years.
June 14, in Sherburne, H. Q. POWERS, age 81 years, 8 months, 18 days. He was a brother of Henry POWERS, of this village [Hamilton]. His wife died seven months ago.
June 14, in Utica, Huldah, widow of J. and mother of C. R. HAYWOOD, age 75 years. She was interred at North Norwich, Chenango Co., NY.
July 6, in Hamilton, Mrs. Gertrude A. ANDREWS, widow of Rev. James H. ANDREWS, age 35 years, 6 months.
July 15, in this city, Sanford J., only child of O. H. and Agnes STRADLING, age 1 year. (From Troy, NY, *Daily Telegram*.)
July 20, in Madison, Mae E. COLLISTER, age 17 years.
July 21, in Bouckville, Minnie S. TAYLOR, age 12 years, 1 month.
John FOOTE, the oldest person in our village [Hamilton], died Wednesday evening, age 98 years, 2 months, 23 days. (In issue of July 24.) He had partly lost his memory some time ago. His last public appearance as a speaker was on his 90th birthday, Apr. 30, 1876. He belonged to the Temperance Society. He read Law with Mr. HUBBARD as a young man, and practised here through out his life.
Aug. 3, in Hamilton, Rev. George G. DAINS, age 56 years. Mr. DAINS was in his second year as pastor of the Hamilton M.E. Church. He leaves his widow and two sons, one just having graduated from College; the other a young man of 18 years. His remains were interred in Governeur, St. Lawrence Co.
Aug. 9, in Hamilton, Mrs. C. M. ROOT, widow of James W. ROOT, age 61 years, 10 months.
Aug. 19, in Hamilton, Mrs. Louise B. KEITH, wife of Charles A. KEITH. (No age given.)

DEMOCRATIC REPUBLICAN - 1884

Aug. 19, in Hamilton, LaFayette L. WEED, age 49 years.

Sept. 4, at his residence in Madison township, after a long illness, Julius RISLEY, in his 64th year. He was born, as were all his father's large family, near the line between Madison and Brookfield townships, and has lived in or near Madison all his life. He was a very good farmer.

Sept. 21, at Geneva, NY, Mrs. Nellie L. KEITH, age 42 years. She was sister to C. A. KEITH. She practised medicine in Geneva, and for several years in Cuba.

Oct. 8, in Hamilton, Mrs. Mary BAKER, wife of John BAKER, Sr., age 70 years.

Oct. 6, near Waterville, Amanda E. CHAMBERS, wife of Moses EARL, age 38 years, 2 months.

Oct. 8, in DeLand, FL, Louisa C. SLAUGHT, sister of Dr. SLAUGHT of this village [Hamilton]. She died of typhoid malaria. (No age given.)

Oct. 21, in Bouckville, George S. MOTT, infant son of S. R. and Nettie C. MOTT, age 5 months.

Oct. 24, in Madison, Isaac COLLISTER, age 75 years. He was interred in Madison Center Cemetery.

Nov. 6, in Hamilton, Hamistont (?) PECKHAM, age 34 years, of consumption. (See below.)

Nov. 9, in Hamilton, Hamilton PECKHAM, age 34 years.

Nov. 22, in the town of Madison, Mrs. Curtis BACON, age 81 years.

Nov. 19, in Augusta Center, at the residence of Edward CHASE, Mrs. Roseanna COTTRELL, age 81 years. She was a daughter of Daniel and Hannah NEFF.

Dec. 5, in Hamilton, Mrs. Slymena WILCOX, age 82 years.

Dec. 6, at the residence of the late Prof. LEWIS, of this village [Hamilton], Miss Mary LLOYD, age 64 years.

Dec. 11, in Pierceville, Mrs. Clara H. DE LONG, age 31 years.

The remains of Mr. C. P. BONNEY were brought here for burial from Zembrota, MN. He was born in Madison Co., NY, in 1836, thus was 48 years old. He went to MN in 1856, where he was the first man of American birth to locate on the bank of the Zumbro. He is survived by his wife.

1885

Jan. 8, in Hamilton, Oliver WILCOX, age 85 years.
Jan. 28, in Hamilton, Adoniram J. CADY, age 74.

DEMOCRATIC REPUBLICAN - 1885

Feb. 3, in Chenango Forks, NY, Idella SHUFFER, age 28 years.
Feb. 2, in Rome, Mrs. Nettie NICHOLSON, age 27 years.
Feb. 3, in Hamilton, J. Smith PIERCE, (no age given).
Feb. 6, in Hamilton, Julis RYAN, age 10 years.
Feb. 9, in Randallsville, Joseph POOLE, age 78 years.
Jan. 20, in Horton, Bremer Co., IA, J. Harvey ELDRIDGE, (no age given).
Feb. 12, in Hamilton, Gurdon HYDE, M.D., age 84 years.
Feb. 15, in Hamilton, Thaxter POOLE, age 85 years, 10 months.
Feb. 16, in Earlville, Nelson BROOKS, age 68 years.
Mar. 9, in Hamilton, two miles south of Poolville, Mrs. Miles YOUNG, age 54 years. She was a sister of W. E. BROWN, of this village [Hamilton].
Mar. 11, at the residence of his daughter, Mrs. Sidney TOMPKINS, in Madison, Otis SIMMONS, age 89 years.
Feb. 4, in Hamilton, Mrs. C. D. HARTSHORN, age 68 years.
Mar. 5, in Hamilton, James RYAN, age 13 years.
Mar. 18, in Hamilton, Jennie E. MEAD, age 32 years.
James MC QUADE, former resident of this town, was brought here for interrment last Wednesday. He lived in New Haven, CT. His death was caused by the kick of a horse. [In issue of Apr. 16.]
Mar. 26, in Manlius, Elva M., wife of W. N. SCOVILLE. She was the youngest sister of James SEVERANCE. She leaves her husband and three sons.
Apr. 8, in Hamilton, Horace S. BURCHARD, in his 84th year.
June 19, in this city, Frank L. WELLS, age 63 years. His last residence was at 109 Church St. (Taken from New Brunswick, NJ, *Home News*.)
July 1, in Hamilton, Mary A. SISSON, age 31 years.
John A. WILLIAMS, farmer and stone mason, of the town of Nelson, aged 52 years, was killed when his team ran away with him. He was father of Mrs. John BURDEN of Morrisville. (From the *Morrisville Observer* of July 23.)
Aug. 3, in Poolville, DeEtte O. COLE, age 39 years.
July 31, in Huntley, IL, Mr. Dura TORREY, in his 88th year. He was formerly a resident of Hamilton, and removed to Huntley about 18 years ago. He leaves an aged wife and five children.
Oct. 9, in Earlville, Alonzo HOLMES, age 66 years.
Oct. 12, at Fort Robinson, Dawes Co., NE, Florence Ella, only child of Merritt and Mary E. WINTER, age 2 years.
Oct. 30, in Bridgewater, Mrs. Melissa TOMPKINS, age 80 years.

DEMOCRATIC REPUBLICAN - 1885

Oct. 27, in Hamilton, Lucy PYNE, age 41 years.
Nov. 13, in Smyrna, Esther BILLINGS, widow of Truman BILLINGS, age 77 years, 10 months, 24 days.
Nov. 13, in Hamilton, George C. LAY, age 73 years, 6 months.
Nov. 13, in Brookfield, Amasa HILLS, age 73 years, 9 months.
Nov. 14, in Solsville, Mrs. Rebecca KERSHAW, wife of Marsden KERSHAW, age 67 years.
Nov. 27, in Hubbardsville, Lewis RHODES, son of Columbus RHODES, age 20 years.
Nov. 26, in Madison, Elizabeth, wife of D. Z. CROCKETT, (no age given).
Nov. 25, at East Hamilton, David AMES, age 57 years.
Nov. 25, in Hamilton, Mrs. Nancy POWERS, wife of Henry POWERS, age 78 years, 9 months, 21 days.
Dec. 25, in Hamilton, Helen M., wife of O. S. HALL, age 43 years.
Dec. 19, in East Hamilton, Mrs. Lida FIELD, age 68 years.

1886

Jan. 4, near South Hamilton, Mary, wife of Wilson LUCAS, age 65 years.
Jan. 7, at South Hamilton, Rhoda, wife of Zara SIMMONS, age 73 years, 10 months.
Feb. 1, in Hamilton village, John M. BENNING, age 45 years.
Feb. 3, in Hamilton, Miss Clarinda BRIGHAM, age 73 years.
Jan. 28, in Hamilton, Charles Beebe CULVER, son of Frank and Mina CULVER, of Bay City, MI, age 2 years.
Jan. 17, in Waverly, MI, Olivia West ROWELL, in her 86th year.
Feb. 17, at Covington, KY, DeWitt C. VAN SLYCK, age 67 years.
Feb. 17, at West Eaton, Franklin DARROW, age 83 years.
Feb. 28, at Pine Woods, Mary FIELDS, age 24 years.
Feb. 28, on Bonney Hill, Mrs. Kate LAWLOR, age 32 years.
Feb. 18, in Lake City, FL, Rev. L. W. DAVIS, age 68 years.
Feb. 7, in Augusta, Solomon WELLS, age 72 years.
Feb. 12, in Oneida Valley, John N. FOSTER, age 32 years.
Feb. 21, in Oneida, Daniel, son of James O'CONNELL, age 18 years.
In Lima, NY, Mrs. J. B. PARMELE, age 78 years. [No date given; in issue of March 4th.]
Feb. 25, in Poolville, Bertrand HUBBARD, age 31 years.
Feb. 20, in Earlville, Almira PALMER, age 62 years.
Feb. 21, in South Hamilton, Lavilla DENNISON, age 64 years.

DEMOCRATIC REPUBLICAN - 1886

Mar. 10, in Oneida, Levi B. BONNEY, age 85 years.

Mar. 4, in Waterville, Sarah, widow of Elijah CONGER, age 80 years.

Feb. 23, in Canastota, Sarah A. VAN VALKENBURGH, age 82 years.

Feb. 20, in Brookfield, Betsey, wife of Lewis KEITH, age 63 years.

Feb. 27, in Oneida Castle, Margaret, wife of Alvin SMITH, and mother of Dr. C. A. SMITH, of Oneida, age 75 years.

Mar. 2, at Lamsons, Peter M. S. THOMPSON, a native of Morrisville, age 74 years.

Mar. 6, in Smithfield, Solomon TEMPLE, age 86 years.

Mar. 15, in Poolville, Michael FITZGERALD, age 38 years.

Mar. 10, on Preston Hill, Susan G. BONNEY, age 46 years.

Mar. 11, in Poolville, Sarah L. JOHNSON, age 21 years.

Mar. 9, in Bouckville, Mrs. Mary BRENNAN, age 48 years, 8 months.

Mar. 11, in Lyons, NY, Owen KLINCK, age 50 years.

Mar. 22, in Hamilton, Cyrus RUNDELL, age 47 years.

Mar. 22, in Hamilton, Mrs. Ida FLETCHER, age 29 years.

Mar. 19, in Hamilton, David WHITE, age 77 years. (See hereafter.)

Mar. 19, in Bouckville, Laura Zoe, only daughter of Eugene and Sarah GOWDY, age 15 months.

Mar. 12, in Pratts Hollow, Mrs. Polly HALBERT, age 87 years, 5 months.

Mar. 14, in Vernon, Joshua CASE, age 64 years.

Mar. 10, on Quality Hill, George TABOR, age 57 years.

Mar. 8, in Chittenango, J. Albert DE WITT, age 46 years, 6 months, 5 days.

Mar. 13, at Fish Creek, James H. FREAR, age 66 years.

Mar. 13, in Peterboro, Miss Louisa DORRANCE, age 69 years, 6 months.

Mar. 7, in Morris, Ann, widow of the late Solomon CRESSON, age 69 years.

Feb. 28, in Greenwood, Steuben Co., Bradshaw WHITE, formerly of Eaton, age 79 years.

Mar. 8, in Brookfield, Hannah, wife of Otis GRIFFIN, age 80 years.

Mar. 3, at Mt. Morris, NJ, Miss Janette C. WILBUR, daughter of the late Jeremiah WILBUR, of Hamilton, (no age given).

Mar. 19, near Hubbardsville, David WHITE, formerly of Madison, age 77 years. (See above, Mar. 19.)

Mar. 6, in Waterville, Julia, wife of Edward MASON, age 73 years.

Mar. 9, in Cazenovia, David P. GRIFFITH, age 70 years.

DEMOCRATIC REPUBLICAN - 1886

Mar. 20, in Augusta, Sarah E., wife of Benjamin F. HICKS, age 30 years.
Feb. 15, Norton J. REED, formerly of Nelson, age 69 years.
Mar. 18, in Oneida, John B. JONES, age 27 years.
Mar. 18, in Morrisville, Ella T., wife of David A. BOYCE, age 26 years.
Mar. 26, at Chittenango Falls, Mrs. Naomi, wife of Joel NOURSE, age 75 years.
Mar. 23, in Syracuse, Franklin W. WALRATH, formerly of Chittenango, age 64 years.
Mar. 28, at Morrisville, Mrs. Bethia KNOX, age 67 years.
Mar. 28, at Eaton, George W. CURTIS, age 64 years.
Mar. 19, in Eaton, Mrs. Louisa GIFFORD, formerly of New Woodstock, age 72 years.
Mar. 9, in Georgetown, Huldah, widow of the late Darius TAYLOR, age 79 years.
Mar. 21, in Canastota, Ellen PHILLIPS, age 74 years.
Mar. 20, at Pulaski, Altie M. GREENWOOD, age 23 years.
April --, at Poolville, Esther HILL, age 52 years, 10 months.
Apr. 3, in Hubbardsville, Lydia SAUNDERS, age 70 years. (See below.)
Apr. 2, in Morrisville, Appleton TUCKER, age 85 years.
Mar. 30, in Bancroft, MI, Mrs. Emily M. DOUGLASS, formerly of Peterboro, age 69 years.
Apr. 1, in Canastota, Frank JONES, age 52 years.
Mar. 27, in Klockville, Samuel SNYDER, age 61 years.
Mar. 30, in Canastota, Richard FERRY, age 63 years.
Mar. 12, in Randallsville, Mrs. Abigail W. BABCOCK, age 76 years.
Mar. 20, in Auburn, Daniel WOODWORTH, formerly of Lenox, age 85 years.
Apr. 3, in Hamilton, Mrs. Lydia SAUNDERS, age 71 years. (See above.)
Mar. 15, in Norwich, George PECKHAM, age 73 years.
Mar. 24, at Cedar Lake, NY, Emory MILLS, age 70 years. He resided near Hamilton Center for many years.
Mar. 27, at Hubbardsville, Harvey R. PALMER, age 83 years.
Apr. 10, in this village [Hamilton], John BEAL, age 78 years.
Apr. 9, at South Hamilton, Miss Phebe FRENCH, age 77 years.
Apr. 10, at Madison, Mrs. Lillie BACON, age 32 years.
Mar. 28, at Waterville, Rollin COLSON, age 79 years.
Apr. 20, in Hamilton, Adon, son of Ella J. and Adon N. SMITH, age 9 years.
Apr. 14, in this village [Hamilton], Sarah M., wife of D. P. HILL, age 66 years.

DEMOCRATIC REPUBLICAN - 1886

Apr. 15, in Hamilton, Eunice K. PADDOCK, wife of Hiram C. PADDOCK, age 76 years.
Apr. 17, in this village [Hamilton], Lyman SWAN, age 83 years.
Apr. 16, at Randallsville, Aaron C. WHEELER, age 83 years.
Apr. 10, at Utica, James CLARK, age 82 years.
Apr. 1, in Oneida, Mrs. Rebecca HUBBARD, age 81 years on April 11.
Arp. 14, in Oneida, Christopher KILTS, born May 23, 1806.
Apr. 8, in North Brookfield, Thomas R. GORTON, age 81 years.
Apr. --, in Poolville, Esther HILL, age 52 years.
Apr. 6, in DeRuyter, Lucinda, wife of David PERRY, age 66 years.
Apr. 15, in this village [Hamilton], Mrs. L. SHIPMAN, age 38 years.
Apr. 13, in New Berlin, Thomas MILLER, aged about 65 years.
Apr. 15, in South Hamilton, Alvin JONES, age 91 years.
Apr. 24, in town of Lebanon, Emily A. LOOMIS, age 55 years.
Apr. 24, in this village [Hamilton], Hattie TORREY, age 25 years.
Apr. 27, in this village [Hamilton], James LYONS, age 21 years.
Apr. 19, in Oneida, Mrs. Lucretia PEBBLES, age 47 years.
Apr. 16, in Higginsville, James BIRD, age 61 years.
Apr. 13, in Vernon, Belle PARDEE, age 83 years.
Apr. 10, in Fenner, Rufus MAY, age 85 years.
Apr. 22, in Oneida, Allen TURNER, age 50 years.
Apr. 12, in Cazenovia, Ellen J. NICHOLS, age 42 years.
May 3, in this village [Hamilton], Cynthia B. ANDREWS, wife of Dr. F. L. ANDREWS, age 41 years.
Apr. 30, in West Eaton, Mrs. Phebe, wife of Joseph E. DARROW, age 77 years.
May 3, in Poolville, Eliza Ann HUNT, age 65 years.
Apr. 27, in Oneida, Mrs. Ida May, wife of Sands H. RANDALL, age 21 years.
Apr. 12, near Klockville, William WILCOX, age 66 years.
Apr. 16, in DeRuyter, Sedanna, wife of Lorenzo VAN HORN, age 55 years.
Apr. 16, in DeRuyter, Mary, wife of Deloss MAINE, age 45 years.
May 3, in Burlington, WI, Miss Sophrona BEEBE, age 58 years.
May 9, in this village [Hamilton], Miss Sophia WILCOX, age 87 years.
May 6, in Hamilton, Samuel BROWNELL, age 67 years.
May 5, in Pratts Hollow, Amzi S. HUNGERFORD, formerly of Morrisville, age 80 years.

DEMOCRATIC REPUBLICAN - 1886

May 16, in this village [Hamilton], William F. COOK, age 30 years.
May 16, in this village [Hamilton], Deacon Nathaniel ANDREWS, age 85 years.
May 17, in Madison, Malissa WHEELER, age 81 years.
May 11, in Madison, Miss Ada HENDERSON, age 29 years.
May 12, in Lebanon, Polly CLOSE, age 88 years.
May 12, in Oneida, Florence Estella BAKER, age 6 months.
May 25, in Madison, Henry W. BOND, age 56 years.
May 20, near Morrisville, Mrs. John MARSTON, age 48 years.
May 19, in Springfield, MA, Bertie, son of J. H. BROWN, of Oneida, age 14 years.
May 2, in Shedd's Corners, Jennie, wife of Madison ELMORE, age 25 years.
May 10, in Oneida, M. Rose, wife of David DIVER, age 43 years.
May 22, in Sangerfield, James YOUNG, age 84 years. (See below.)
June 3, in Oneida, George C. MOTT, age 59 years.
June 7, at Madison, Deborah S. BABCOCK, age 61 years, 2 months, 3 days.
June 13, in Morrisville, Harry S. PHILLIPS, age 26 years, 7 months, 6 days.
June 17, at Hamilton, Mary RICHARDS, age 67 years.
June 20, in Hamilton, Joel SOUTHWORTH, age 68 years.
June 23, in Hamilton, Myra CLARK, age 53 years.
June 16, in Morrisville, Frank HOVEY, age 33 years.
June 6, in Klockville, Elmer CHAMPNEY, age 83 years.
May 22, near Sangerfield, James YOUNG, age 83 years. (See above.)
June 14, in Georgetown, Leonard ALLEN, age 79 years.
June 15, in Brookfield, Warren J. TALCOTT, age 37 years.
June 16, in Munnsville, Ann, wife of John POTTER, age 75 years, 3 months.
June 22, in Oneida, George B. PHILLIPS, in his 81st year. He was father of John H. PHILLIPS.
June 18, in Brookfield, George PHELPS, age about 55 years.
June 21, in Munnsville, Mrs. Susan CHILDS, age 86 years.
June 18, in Pierceville, Amos HAMMOND, age 59 years. He died near Alderbrook, of pneumonia. He was born in Delhi, Delaware Co., NY; spent his boyhood in Montrose, PA, and came to this place in 1849 where he married Miss Luna CHASE in 1852. Since then, with the exception of a few years in Cortland Co., he has resided here. He was a man of high moral character and strictly temperate. . . He had a remarkable love for children and was especially kind to the aged and helpless . . . He leaves a son, Dr. W. A. HAMMOND,

of Paris, NY, and his wife, Mrs. L. M. HAMMOND, well known in Central NY as a historical author. He was the second son of Nathan HAMMOND, and of the twelve children of Nathan, Amos is the first to die. Both his parents died in this place. His funeral was held from the M.E. Church in West Eaton, and he was buried beside his two children who died in 1864.

June 25, in Smyrna, Ruth RACE, age 81 years.

June 26, in Morrisville, George CROSS, age 59 years.

June 18, near Poolville, Benjamin BRATLEY, age 46 years.

Joab STAFFORD, of Canajoharie, brother-in-law of Dr. PRESTON, died in Sangerfield a few days ago. He married Miss Elizabeth PRESTON eleven years ago. (In issue of July 1.)

June 30, in Unionville, CT, Mrs. Elizabeth WILCOX, aged about 54 years, formerly of Hamilton.

June 29, in Brookfield, Rudolphus PAUL, age 46 years, 2 months.

June 30, in the town of Madison, Eliza, wife of Daniel MANCHESTER, age 68 years.

June 30, in DeRuyter, of consumption, Elder Thomas FISHER, age 70 years.

July 1, in Nelson, Norman WESCOTT, aged 64 years, 2 months.

July 1, in this village [Hamilton], Mrs. Lydia BUTLER, age 63 years, 3 months.

June 21, at Ripton, WI, Charles N. MC LEAN, formerly of Morrisville, aged 68 years.

June 25, in Cazenovia, David M. JONES, aged 55 years.

June 21, in Fenner, Mrs. J. J. FITCHER, age 58 years.

July 6, in Sullivan, Mrs. Rachel R. MASON, age 78 years.

July 3, in Morrisville, Mrs. Laura L. BELLOWS, wife of Alfred BELLOWS, age 57 years.

June 30, in West Eaton, Daniel BENNETT, age 80 years.

July 6, in DeRuyter, Frank E., son of H. Jerome and Mary E. CRANDALL, age 25 years, 5 months, 14 days.

July 12, near Pratts Hollow, Nicholas MOON, age 35 years.

July 23, in this village [Hamilton], Rev. Stephen Henry STACKPOLE, age 43 years. He was born in Boston, July 24, 1843, and lived there until he took his first pastorate at Westborough in 1871. He joined the Dudley St. Church in 1857; in 1862 he entered Harvard College and graduated with distinguished rank in 1866. Thence he went on to theological seminary at Newton Centre, MA, where his studies were interrupted one year which he spent in German universities. He graduated at Newton in 1870. His pastorates have been at Westborough, MA, Saxton's

DEMOCRATIC REPUBLICAN - 1886

River, VT, and Hamilton, NY. His record here seems to be an almost unspeakable loss . . . Burial was at Woodlawn Cemetery. His pastorates were all in Baptist churches.

July 22, in Brookfield, Annie, daughter of the late Deloss and Helen M. BEEBE, aged about 17 years.

July 22, in Vernon, Jennie M., wife of Ard. JUDSON, Jr., (no age given).

July 16, at Quality Hill, Sally, relict of Stephen CHAPMAN, age 79 years.

July 17, in Fenner, Peleg SLOCUM, in his 84th year.

July 18, in Syracuse, Mrs. Maria BROWN, formerly of Morrisville, age 80 years, 6 months.

July 12, in Shed's Corners, Mrs. Ervilla HUNT, wife of Mordecai HUNT, age 65 years, 5 months, 12 days.

July 15, in Brookfield, Sophronia F., wife of James L. GORTON, age 42 years, 7 months.

July 19, in the town of Madison, Mrs. George HAMLIN, age about 45 years.

July 18, in the town of Eaton, Mrs. Harriet SQUIRES, in her 86th year.

July 10, in PA, Fanny L., daughter of Sterry S. and Sarah THROOP, of Hubbardsville, age 13 years.

July 15, near Solsville, William BOND, age 72 years.

July 31, in Morrisville, Miss Emma KIMBALL, age 26 years, 4 months.

July 28, near Morrisville, Mary J., wife of Deacon Lyman G. DEAN, age 68 years.

Aug. 3, in Morrisville, Maudie, daughter of Mr. Charles COON, age 4 years, 1 month.

July 30, in the town of Eaton, Mr. Morris WILLIAMS, age 79 years.

July 22, in Peterboro, Mrs. Jane A. HARDY, age 76 years.

July 29, in Earlville, Libbie LOGAN, age 38 years.

July 27, near Morrisville, Jay, son of John HART, age 9 years.

July 25, Fannie M. Lincoln, widow of the late Daniel A. REXFORD, of Sherburne, (no age given).

July 25, in the town of Sherburne, David N. WILLEY, age 74 years.

July 30, in Clockville, Nelson FOWLER, age 84 years.

July 28, in Erieville, Mrs. Benjamin RICHARDSON, age 76 years.

Aug. 5, in Hamilton, Eunice Melvina, wife of George KELLOWAY, age 45 years. She was born in Madison Nov. 26, 1840 and married on June 11, 1862. She had resided in this village [Hamilton] the past 23 years, and is survived by her husband and two children.

DEMOCRATIC REPUBLICAN - 1886

Aug. 4, in Sherburne, Mrs. Larinza ADAMS, age 80 years.
Aug. 2, in Sherburne, Alice TOMLINSON, age 17 years, 28 days.
July 31, in DeRuyter, of typhoid fever, Harriet, wife of Casper HOLLENBECK, age 74 years, 6 months.
July 31, in Vernon Center, J. K. PERCIVAL, age 76 years.
Aug. 4, in Madison Township, Lewie J. TAYLOR, age 2 years, 5 months.
Aug. 2, in Lebanon, Samuel, son of the late Philip and Mary SWANCOTT, formerly of Brookfield, age 46 years, 28 days.
Aug. 7, in Madison, Mrs. Clarissa CURTISS, age 89 years, 4 months, 28 days.
Aug. 9, in Elmira, William H. STRINGER, of Munnsville, age 46 years, 10 months, 13 days.
Aug. 7, at the residence of her daughter, Mrs. John EDGERLY, of 263 West Madison St., Chicago, Mrs. Sophronia PAYNE, of Hamilton, age 75 years, 11 months, 23 days. For obituary, see below.
Eddie HASWELL, aged 13 years, 10 months, was drowned at Woodman's Pond on Wednesday. (In issue of Aug. 12.) He had injured a knee about 6 years ago, and had since been a cripple. He was the youngest of three sons of his parents. His mother is a widow residing on Hamilton Street, and his father was a missionary to Burmah.
Aug. 11, in Bouckville, Daniel FAIRCHILD, age 67 years.
Aug. 12, in Poolville, at the home of his sister, Mrs. Millard BEACH, A. M. STICKER, age 22 years. He was buried in Rome.
Aug. 13, in Hubbardsville, Cynthia COLSON, age 77 years.
Aug. 12, in Oneida, Mrs. Julia A., wife of Jacob SPEISS, age 40 years, 4 months.
Aug. 11, in the town of Sullivan, Mrs. Nancy R., wife of John O. FRENCH, age 57 years, 7 months, 9 days.
Aug. 7, at Chittenango Falls, Merwin B. WOODWORTH, age 21 years, 26 days.
Aug. 7, in Georgetown, Jane, wife of Erastus MARVIN, age 53 years.
[No date], Mrs. Nancy PARKS, mother of Barney PARKS, of Munnsville, dropped dead in the road last Tuesday. She resided midway between Peterboro and Munnsville. She was over 70 years old.
Aug. 24, in Oneida, Orville L. KNOX, age 76 years.
Aug. 20, in Madison, Anna TAYLOR, age 14 years.
Aug. 14, in Munnsville, Mr. D. Jerome MERRILL, age 68 years.

DEMOCRATIC REPUBLICAN - 1886

Aug. 17, near Hamilton, Mrs. William ROTH, age 37 years, 10 months.
Aug. 15, in Morrisville, Mrs. Melissa S. BICKNELL, age 86 years, 9 months.
Aug. 23, in this village [Hamilton], Mary E., daughter of Mr. and Mrs. John ALLEN, age 9 months.
Aug. 25, in Poolville, Melvin WILD, (no age given, see below).
Aug. 22, in Poolville, Richard FLEMING, age 84 years.
Aug. 27, in Morrisville, Mary Jane, wife of John TILLINGHAST, of Chicago, age 66 years.
Aug. 27, in Haton township, Miss Harriet N. STOWELL, age 65 years.
Aug. 27, in Earlville, Miss Caroline DANIELS, age 78 years.
Aug. 24, in Poolville, Melvin F. WILD, age 57 years.
Aug. 29, in Fenner, Mrs. Cornelia BARBER, age 49 years.
Sept. 3, in Munnsville, Mrs. Samuel BARR, age 46 years.
Sept. 1, at Bouckville, Chauncey CRAIN, age 81 years.
Aug. 31, at Lebanon, Mary N. NILES, age 79 years.
Sept. 7, in town of Eaton, Mrs. Mary FRANKLIN, (no age given).
Sept. 6, at Brookfield, Deacon Chauncey R. (or V.) HIBBARD, age 62 years, 10 months, 21 days. He is survived by his wife, two daughters and three sons. The funeral was held from the Baptist Church.
Sept. 1, at the home of his sister, Mrs. MARTIN in Utica, occurred the death of Mr. BEDELL, age 47 years. He is survived by his wife, mother, and three sisters. Deceased was a resident of West Eaton. He died of consumption, said to have been contracted while serving in the army.
Sept. 10, in Oneida, of cholera infantum, Willie, infant son of Albert and Frances TILLOTSON, deceased, aged about 11 months.
Through the courtesy of R. L. HENRY, of St. Louis, MO, we have word of the death of L. L. RICHMOND, formerly of Lebanon, which occurred recently at Jennings' Station, a small place just outside St. Louis. He was born 46 years ago in this county, and was favorably known in Lebanon and vicinity. He served in the late War and received a severe wound through the lungs at the Battle of Bull Run. After the War, he went West, making his home in St. Louis, where he became identified with the Knights of Labor and various temperance and Christian movements. He leaves his wife and four children.
Sept. 10, in Sherburne, Caroline Powers JENKS, age 70 years.

DEMOCRATIC REPUBLICAN - 1886

Sept. 13, in Hamilton, Michael FLAHERTY, age 62 years. He fell from a wagon, receiving injuries from which he died, in 3/4 of an hour. He was a farmer, and about 62 years old.

Last Friday morning, Newton R. STEVENS, son of Postmaster Judson T. STEVENS, was accidently killed by his own gun while hunting, about 3 miles from Utica. Newton graduated from Utica Free Academy last June, and expected to enter Cornell this fall. He was 18 years old.

Sept. 14, in DeRuyter, Carrie E., wife of Simeon DYE, age 47 years, 7 months, 2 days.

Sept. 14, in DeRuyter, of cancer, Charlotte, relict of Amasa BARBER, age 89 years.

Sept. 6, in Earlville, Josephine B., infant daughter of Mr. and Mrs. Jay D. HOPKINS, (no age given).

Sept. 12, in St. Randolph, WI, Mary Ann W., wife of J. R. OWEN, and mother of Mrs. J. J. LOOMIS, of Oneida, age 62 years, 8 months. Deceased was formerly of Oneida.

Sept. 9, in Brookfield, Mary A. DOLAN, age 11 months, 19 days.

Sept. 7, in North Brookfield, Elijah FRISBIE, age 78 years, 2 months.

Sept. 12, in Brookfield, Alice M. HOSTLER, wife of Charles H. BROWN, age 25 years, 5 days.

Sept. 20, in Hubbardsville, N. B. WOOD, age 76 years.

Sept. 18, in this village [Hamilton], Mrs. Achsa M. SHERRILL, age 64 years.

Sept. 17, in this village [Hamilton], Mrs. Cynthia M. BALDWIN, age 68 years. She was the wife of Rev. G. C. BALDWIN, prominent Baptist clergyman, of Troy. She died very suddenly at the residence of her son-in-law, Prof. Benjamin S. TERRY. Burial in Troy.

Sept. 18, in this village, infant son of Mr. and Mrs. B. F. RISLEY, age about 9 months.

Sept. 10, in Sherburne, Mrs. Caroline Powers JENKS, formerly of Hamilton, in her 70th year.

Sept. 21, in town of Stockbridge, Samuel C. BLACK, age 77 years.

Sept. 20, in Oriskany Falls, Mrs. Mary BROWN, age 61 years.

Sept. 23, at Oneida Castle, Rev. A. COCHRAN, age 68 years.

Sept. 17, in Bradford, PA, Frankie, son of Frank CARMAN, formerly of Canastota, (no age given).

Sept. 22, in Vernon, Miss Mary BRENAN, age 73 years.

Sept. 28, in Madison township, Mrs. Margaret WHALEN, age 60 years.

DEMOCRATIC REPUBLICAN - 1886

Sept. 24, in Hamilton township, Abbey Odessa, daughter of Mr. and Mrs. M. G. YOUNG, age 6 weeks.

Sept. 18, in Seneca, Lenawee Co., MI, James D. MANCHESTER, age 80 years, 4 months. He was a former resident of Madison township, but had resided in MI the past 20 years.

Oct. 2, in Oneida, Frederick Washington ALLEN, age 41 years.

Oct. 2, in Oneida, William GAUT, age 56 years.

Oct. 2, in Hamilton, Mrs. Lois S. BEEBE, age 82 years, 10 months, 16 days. She died at the residence of her daughter. Mrs. A. C. KING, in this village. She was born Nov. 14, 1803 at Becket, MA, removing to this County early in life. She has resided most of her life in Brookfield. About 63 years ago she married Eleazer BEEBE who died 4 years ago. They had 8 children, two sons and six daughters: LeRoy and Dr. F. D. BEEBE, and the daughters: Mrs. Daniel MARSH, Mrs. B. F. CONE, Mrs. C. F. RHODES, Mrs. H. R. BABCOCK, Mrs. M. F. RISLEY, and Mrs. A. C. KING.

Sept. 18, in Bangor, MI, Cynthia HUNT, wife of Alonzo SHEPPARD, age 58 years. She was formerly of this village [Hamilton].

Oct. 4, in Madison township, Mrs. Clarissa BRAINARD, age 78 years.

Oct. 3, in Lebanon, Rev. H. G. ALLABEN, age 35 years.

Oct. 4, Mrs. James REYNOLDS, died at her home in this village. She leaves her husband and three small children. Burial in Hamilton. (Taken from *Sherburne News*.)

Oct. 10, in Hamilton, Gertrude E. HUNT, age 26 years.

Oct. 9, in Morrisville, Mrs. Melona SEYMOUR, widow of Miranda (sic) SEYMOUR, deceased, aged 78 years.

Oct. 5, in the town of Nelson, Mr. Landon MILES, age 71 years.

Oct. 7, in the town of Hamilton, Alexander CROWELL, age 77 years, 6 months.

Oct. 8, in Madison, Alpha LIVERMORE, age 73 years.

Oct. 6, in Earlville, Eben HITCHCOCK, age 85 years.

Oct. 12, near Oriskany Falls, Henry OLIVER, age 63 years.

Oct. 10, in Brookfield, Mrs. Polly YAW, age 82 years, 4 months.

Oct. 12, in Oneida, Mrs. Emily, widow of Nathaniel WEST, age 70 years.

Oct. 13, in Munnsville, Calvin BUSH, aged about 68 years.

Oct. 18, in Oneida, Ambrose LYPE, in his 60th year.

Oct. 16, in Canastota, William VAN DYKE, age 10 years.

DEMOCRATIC REPUBLICAN - 1886

Oct. 14, in Canastota, Mrs. Harriet L. HARRISON, age 49 years.

Oct. 17, in Madison township, Helena A. TAYLOR, age 31 years, 4 months.

Oct. 20, Rev. Frederick A. POTTER, pastor of the Whitesboro Baptist Church. He was born in Carthage, Jefferson Co., NY, and was 33 years of age. He graduated from Madison University Theological Seminary, 1884. That July he took up his duties as pastor of the Baptist Church in Whitesboro. He was a member of Delta Upsilon, and was married. His remains were brought to Hamilton for interment.

Oct. 19, in Cazenovia, Miss Eliza WHITE, age 38 years.

Oct. 22, in Canastota, Ella, daughter of Mr. and Mrs. Edward HOPKINS, age 7 years.

Sept. 28, in the town of Cazenovia, Harrington MARSHALL, father of Rev. A. H. MARSHALL, of Madison, age 88 years.

Oct. 23, in Oneida, of consumption, Mrs. Louisa A., wife of James BALDWIN, age 38 years, 6 months.

Oct. 22, in Durhamville, Claude, son of Mr. and Mrs. Mott MILLER, age 7 months.

Oct. 21, near Siloam, Mrs. Wealthy A., wife of George F. PARKHURST, age 73 years, 21 days.

Oct. 23, in Madison, Mrs. Mary ROWE, age 81 years.

Oct. 17, in Marathon, Cortland Co., NY, Mary, wife of Joseph BURT, age 63 years. Deceased was a sister of E. D. VAN SLYKE, of this village [Hamilton].

Oct. 29, at Utica, Sidney SMITH, age 81 years. The remains were brought to Hamilton for interment.

Oct. 27, at Oneida Castle, Leander BUDLONG, age 78 years.

Oct. 27, at Vernon Mills, Lois A. P. WILLIAMS, age 72 years.

Oct. 25, in Cortland, Merrill OMANS, formerly of West Eaton, age 42 years.

Oct. 26, in Nelson, Ray, son of Mr. and Mrs. Henry BENNETT, age 11 months.

Oct. 22, in Cazenovia, Orlando LOOMIS, age 69 years.

Oct. 23, near Knoxboro, Ephraim WOOSTER, age 84 years.

Oct. 22, in Eaton, Levi WYMAN, of Brookfield, age about 82 years.

[No date], in Galesburg, IL, Mrs. Hannah BABCOCK, aged 86 years. Her remains were brought to Hamilton and interred at the Madison St. Cemetery, with services at the M.E. Church.

Oct. 28, Alexander MURDOCK was found dead in bed at his rooms in Elmira. He was once pastor of the Congregational Church here. While living in Hamilton he

DEMOCRATIC REPUBLICAN - 1886

married the widow of Lyman N. ROOT, and lived in Madison for many years. He removed to Elmira several years ago, and engaged in the practice of law in the office of his brother, John MURDOCK. He was buried in the family grounds in Elmira.

Mrs. Margaret DUNN, an old lady residing on the corner of Eaton and Canal Sts., was found dead on Nov. 3d.

From the *Waukegan Weekly Gazette*: On Oct. 16, Mrs. Alathea BLODGETT, beloved wife of Judge H. W. BLODGETT, died at the family home in Waukegan. She was the daughter of Amos CROCKER, Esq., of Hamilton, NY, and was born at that place Nov. 11, 1822. In 1848, she came to Waukegan as a teacher of languages and music in the then new Waukegan Academy. It was while here that Judge BLODGETT made her adcquaintance. She returned to her home in Hamilton, and about a year thereafter, on Apr. 29, 1850, she and Judge BLODGETT were married. She was the mother of five children, only two of whom survive: Warren, and Miss Carrie., Two of her children died in early childhood, and the other, the eldest daughter, died three years ago. Services were held from the Episcopal Church, with interment in Oakwood Cemetery.

Oct. 29, in Ontario, IL, Mrs. Hannah, relict of Dr. Benjamin BABCOCK, formerly of Hamilton, in her 87th year.

Mrs. Charles CLARK died in Eaton last Sat., Nov. 6, age 62.

Oct. 29, in Morrisville, Henry C. SMITH, age 46 years. The deceased was the son of Charles H. SMITH, of Hamilton, and resided here until about 10 years ago. In 1861 he enlisted as a member of Co. A., 157th NY Vol. Three years after the close of the War he accepted a clerkship in the St. Charles Hotel in Syracuse, which position he held 7 or 8 years. He then removed to Sandy Creek and ran the Clarke Hotel for a year, then returned to Hamilton where he resided a year and a half. After that he was clerk at the Lincklaen House in Cazenovia two years; then went to the Stanton Hotel of Cazenovia for a time. Later he became proprietor of the Lake View House at the head of Cazenovia Lake, after which he went to Morrisville, where he lived until his death. He was a member of the Cazenovia Post G.A.R., and was twice married. His widow and 14-year-old son survive, also a daughter 12 years old. He was buried in the Madison St. Cemetery in this place.

DEMOCRATIC REPUBLICAN - 1886

Nov. 9, in Morrisville, at the residence of A. P. TILLINGHAST, Mrs. Elizabeth H. WOOD, widow of the late Danforth WOOD, in her 80th year.

Nov. 8, near Morrisville, infant daughter of Mr. and Mrs. Sidney COLE, age 5 months.

Oct. 30, in Canastota, Daniel S. PECKHAM, age 73 years.

Nov. 14, in Sherburne, Alonzo D. GORHAM, age 69 years. (see below)

Nov. 15, in Madison, Ruth, wife of Seth HITCHCOCK, age 78 years, 8 months.

Nov. 15, in Madison, Hiram N. WAITE, age 70 years.

Nov. 15, at Pine Woods, Timothy COLLINS, age 52 years, formerly of Rome, NY. He was born in Ireland. For many years he resided in Florence, Oneida, Co., and later in CA and NV. About 1873 he returned from the west and settled in Rome. A few years ago he conducted a hotel in Pine Woods which was burned down a year ago. He leaves, besides his wife, a son, Patrick COLLINS, Jr., of NV, and two daughters, Mrs. Lawrence CARET and Mrs. Edward HOLLAND, also a brother Patrick COLLINS, of Rome. His funeral was held from St. Mary's Church, Hamilton, and burial was in Rome.

Oct. 16, Ira F. WARNER, son of S. J. and Ella L. (FELT) WARNER, aged 5 years, 41 days. Mr. and Mrs. WERNER were old residents of Hamilton, having left in the spring of 1876 for a home in NE, together with their eldest child, Brettie, then 3 years old. Since going west, two sons have been born to them, both of whom died. Burial was made in the Leland Cemetery, beside his little brother, Irwin.

Nov. 15, at South Brookfield, Lydia, beloved wife of Gideon P. BABCOCK, age 48 years, 10 months.

Nov. 13, in Brookfield, Ashael INGRAHAM, age 81 years, 7 months.

Nov. 14, in Oriskany Falls, Charles C. SMITH, age 69 years, 11 months.

Nov. 14, in Earlville, Alonzo GORHAM, age 59 years, (see above).

Nov. 15, in Nelson, Mrs. Elizabeth, widow of Evan D. HUGHES, age 66 years.

Nov. 15, in Oriskany Falls, Frank TAYLOR, of Jordan, NY, age 23 years.

Nov. 21, near Morrisville, Giles SKINNER, age 32 years.

Nov. 17, in Nelson, Mrs. Mary A. WRIGHT, wife of John WRIGHT, age 65 years.

DEMOCRATIC REPUBLICAN - 1886

Nov. 23, at Oneida, Mrs. Eunice HURLBURT, an inmate of the Old Ladies' Home, formerly of Earlville, age 68 years.

Mr. Eneas E. ENOS, for the past ten years one of our prominent merchants, died Nov. 24 from severe injuries received when the carriage in which he was riding was struck by a train at Randallsville. He was about 45 years old, and is survived by his wife, an aged father and mother, and a brother. The funeral was conducted by Rev. John R. LEWIS, of Boonville, and Rev. J. H. DE MILLS, rector of St. Thomas' Church, Hamilton. Interment was at Morrisville. He was a member of the Supreme Order of the United Workingman.

Nov. 29, at Bouckville, Mrs. Orinda P. NEWCOMB, age 46 years. She was born Orinda P. MANCHESTER, in the town of Madison, July 30, 1840. On May 6, 1875, she married Mr. E. NEWCOMB, and for about two years they resided at Deposit, NY, then removing to Bouckville where they continued to reside. He died Dec. 27, 1878, and since then she has lived with her sister, Miss Emogene MANCHESTER, at the same place. Before she was married, she was a teacher. She was a member of the M.E. Church. She is survived by a brother, J. E. MANCHESTER, of West Winfield, and two sisters, Mrs. John LAMB, of Hamilton, and Miss Emogene. Six nephews acted as bearers at her funeral, the burial being at Madison.

Nov. 24, in East Hamilton, Mary A., wife of Milo B. FENTON, aged 51 years. She died at the home of her sister, Mrs. Dr. PALMER. She was buried at West Winfield, and is survived by her husband, a daughter, and a brother, and two sisters.

Nov. 23, in Canastota, Anna YOUMANS, age 6 years, 6 months.

Nov. 19, in Nelson, Archibald BATES, age 86 years.

Nov. 17, in Nelson, of consumption, Martha, wife of Humphrey WILLIAMS, age 34 years.

Nov. --, in Sherburne, Mrs. Jane E. BORDEN, formerly of Stockbridge, age 69 years.

Nov. 25, in Oriskany Falls, of consumption, Maude, daughter of the late H. M. HINDS, age 30 years, 11 months.

Nov. 26, in the town of Cazenovia, David WELLINGTON, age 80 years.

Nov. 26, in Grant, Herkimer Co., of consumption, Ray Randall HILLS, age 23 years, 7 months, 22 days.

Nov. 24, in Sherburne, Miss Nellie D. PUDNEY, age 31 years.

DEMOCRATIC REPUBLICAN - 1886

Nov. 30, in Hamilton, James, son of Nancy DERRICK, age 16 years.
Dec. 5, in Peterboro, Avery FORT, age about 65 years.
Dec. 1, in Middleport, George W. WELCH, age 19 years.
Dec. 3, in Madison, Esther BURTON, age 59 years.
Dec. 4, in Hamilton Township, Lee MAXSON, age 19 years, 9 months.
Dec. 8, in Eaton, Duane, son of William STANBRO, age 28 years, 9 months.
Dec. 10, in Hamilton, Marlitta, wife of Joel WHITMORE, age 67 years, of consumption. Her maiden name was Marlitta NEWTON, and she traced her ancestry in an unbroken line to Sir Isaac NEWTON. She was born in Marshall, Oneida Co., Oct. 16, 1819, and when three years of age, her family removed to Sandy Creek, Oswego Co., NY, where she was educated. She taught several terms of school. On Sept. 9, 1844, she married Joel WHITMORE, and they came to live on his farm in Lebanon, remaining until 1867 when they removed to this place where they have since resided. They had three children: Mrs. Flora MARKHAM, who died in 1878; Frances Y. WHITMORE, of West Union, IA; and Newton H. WHITMORE, of this place. Besides her children, she is survived by her father, now in his 91st year, her husband, six sisters and a brother.
Dec. 11, near Hamilton, Miles R. MACOMBER, age 49 years.
Dec. 9, in Randallsville, Thomas FLEMING, age 68 years.
Dec. 10, in Lebanon, Louisa WILCOX, age 78 years.
Dec. 9, in Madison, Greenly BACON, age 55 years.
Dec. 9, in Canastota, Catherine, wife of George HALE, age 60 years.
Dec. 3, in Peterboro, Mrs. Bridget HAYES, mother of Mrs. Thomas HANLEY, age 71 years.
Dec. 20, in town of Hamilton, William ELLIS, age 74 years.
Dec. 13, at the home of her nephew, A. J. LA MUNION, near Munnsville, Miss Sibyl LA MUNION, age 91 years, 11 months, 13 days.
At his home in Smyrna, Mr. George LEETS, died last week. He was well known in Lebanon where he had a number of relatives, including his sister, Mrs. R. H. GEER, and cousins, J. H. WAGONER, M. STUART, and others.
Dec. 25, at Hamilton, Frank G. WICKWIRE, age 40 years, 9 months, 8 days.
Dec. 17, James HORTON, old and respected citizen of Pine Woods, aged 85 years. He is survived by two daughters: Mrs. CORNICE, of Eaton, and Mrs. MONTENA, of

DEMOCRATIC REPUBLICAN - 1886

Pine Woods. He had been in poor health for many years.
The funeral of the late Dr. Theodore MEAD was held at Perryville Dec. 15th.
Dec. 21, in Morrisville, John CASEY, Jr., age 21 years.
Dec. 23, at Oneida Castle, Harriet L., widow of Hon. Timothy JENKINS, age 83 years.
Dec. 26, in Brookfield, Esther A., wife of Gilbert POWERS, age 61 years, 7 months.
Dec. 28, in Earlville, Miss Amelia WHITE, in her 57th year.
Dec. 30, in Morrisville, Mr. J. P. CLARK, age 77 years.

******

BIRTHS

DEMOCRATIC REPUBLICAN

1877

Mar. 26	A son to William and Anna RAY.
Apr. 3	A daughter to Mr. and Mrs. F. L. KNAPP.
Mar. 31	A son to Mr. and Mrs. John KENNEDY.
Apr. 9	A son to Mr. and Mrs. Michael MOONEY, in Hamilton.
Apr. 5	A son to Mr. and Mrs. Walter BRIGGS, of Lebanon.
Apr. 15	A daughter to Prof. and Mrs. J. W. FORD, of Hamilton.
Apr. 18	A daughter to Mr. and Mrs. H. H. HILL, of Hamilton.
May 8	A daughter to Mr. and Mrs. W. H. EBBERT, of Hamilton.
May 10	A daughter to Mr. and Mrs. George WHITE, of Hamilton.
Apr. 28	A son to Rev. D. C. and Mrs. Mary POTTER, of New York.
May 29	A daughter to Mr. N. R. and Mrs. Phebe WICKWIRE, of Hamilton.
July 23	A son to Mr. and Mrs. Myron TOMPKINS, of Hamilton.
Aug. 15	A daughter to Mr. and Mrs. Charles WICKWIRE, of Hamilton.
Aug. 22	A daughter to Mr. and Mrs. William MINER, of Madison.
Aug. 31	A daughter to Mr. and Mrs. H. S. GARDNER, of Hamilton.

DEMOCRATIC REPUBLICAN - 1877

Sept. 22	Twin daughters to Mr. and Mrs. J. HOLCOMB, of Hamilton.
Oct. 29	A daughter to Mr. and Mrs. Richard SAVAGE, of Madison.
Nov. 10	A son to Dr. and Mrs. A. R. ROOT, of Hamilton.
Nov. 12	A daughter to Mr. and Mrs. H. B. HICOK, of Lebanon.
Nov. --	A son to Mr. and Mrs. John BROWN, of Hamilton.
Nov. 11	A daughter to Mr. and Mrs. Byron RISLEY, of Madison.
Dec. 3,	A son to Mr. and Mrs. A. C. RICE, of Hamilton.
Dec. 30	A son to Dr. and Mrs. J. F. BANTON, of Hamilton.

1878

Feb. 19	A daughter to Prof. and Mrs. S. BURNHAM.
Mar. 5	Twin daughters to Mr. and Mrs. John HARMON, of Lebanon.
Mar. 24	A son to Mr. and Mrs. J. W. HURN, of Madison.
Mar. 1	A son to Mr. and Mrs. Daniel T. STOWELL, of Madison.
Mar. 5	A son to Mr. and Mrs. Michael J. CASEY, of Hamilton.
Apr. 5	A son to Mr. and Mrs. B. G. BOARDMAN, of Hamilton.
Apr. 8	A son to Mr. and Mrs. D. Marcello MINER, of Eaton.
Apr. 10	A son to Mr. and Mrs. Charles J. JOHNSON, of Hamilton.
Apr. 13	A daughter to Mr. and Mrs. Adelbert SQUIRES, of Hamilton.
May 2	A daughter to Mr. and Mrs. James DERRICK, of Hamilton.
May 30	A daughter ot Mr. and Mrs. Frank NEGUS, of Jay, NY.
June 8	A daughter to Mr. and Mrs. H. H. HILL, of Hamilton.
June 10	A son to Rev. and Mrs. G. R. SIMONS, of Hamilton.
Aug. 5	A son to Mr. and Mrs. Adon N. SMITH, of Hamilton.
June 15	A son to Prof. and Mrs. F. W. TOWLE, of Hamilton.
Aug. 8	A daughter to Dr. and Mrs. D. S. GARDNER, of Hamilton.

DEMOCRATIC REPUBLICAN - 1878

Aug. 27	A daughter to Mr. and Mrs. Henry COAN, of Hamilton.
Sept. 1	A daughter to Mr. and Mrs. Cyrenus BISBEE, of Lebanon.
Sept. 19	A son to Mr. and Mrs. William RALPH, of Hamilton.
Nov. 23	A daughter to Mr. and Mrs. J. C. BARBER, of Hamilton.
Dec. 3	A son to Rev. and Mrs. James COOTE, of Hamilton.
Nov. 25	A son to Mr. and Mrs. Bartley HOPKINS, of Hamilton.
Dec. 14	A daughter to Mr. and Mrs. George SCOTT, of Hamilton.

1879

Jan. 4	A son to Mr. and Mrs. Charles R. POWERS, of Hamilton.
Feb. 15	A daughter to Mr. and Mrs. George KERN, of Hamilton.
Feb. 24	A daughter to Mr. and Mrs. Clark D. WILCOX, of Lebanon.
Mar. 14	A son to Mr. and Mrs. D. E. WEBSTER, of Madison, weight, three and one-fourths pounds.
Apr. 1	A son to Mr. and Mrs. Pliny APPLEGATE, in Madison.
May 5	A son to Mr. and Mrs. Will LOGAN, of Hamilton.
May 9	A daughter to Mr. and Mrs. E. C. BUTLER, of Hamilton.
May 24	A daughter to Mr. and Mrs. William MOORE, of Hamilton.
Aug. 10	A daughter to Prof. and Mrs. E. S. GARDNER, of Hamilton.
Aug. 7	A daughter to Mr. and Mrs. Myron CASE, in Eaton.
Aug. 14	A daughter to Mr. and Mrs. Will EATON, in Hamilton.
Sept. 2	A son to Mr. and Mrs. A. C. RICE, of Hamilton.
Sept. 21	A son to Rev. and Mrs. D. C. POTTER, of New York.
Sept. 15	A son to Rev. and Mrs. C. Winton PATTERSON, of Edmeston, NY
Aug. 28	A daughter to Mr. and Mrs. Alfred W. SLOCUM, of Penn Yan, NY
Nov. 25	A son to Rev. and Mrs. S. T. FORD, of Hamilton, "the first fruits of the triple wedding."

DEMOCRATIC REPUBLICAN - 1879

Dec. 23   A son to Mr. and Mrs. Pat KELLEY.

1880

Jan. 27   Twin sons to Mr. and Mrs. Charles ALDERMAN, of So. Hamilton
Mar. 2   A son to Prof. and Mrs. TOWLE, in Hamilton.
Feb. 28   A son to Mr. and Mrs. James COLLISTER, in Madison Center.
Apr. 7   A daughter to Mr. and Mrs. Will BOONE, of Hamilton.
Apr. 23   A daughter to Mr. and Mrs. Cola DEPRAY, of Hamilton.
Apr. 21   A son to Mr. and Mrs. FITZPATRICK, of Hamilton.
May 9   A daughter to Mr. and Mrs. Ernest BUTLER, in Hamilton.
May 15   A son to Prof. and Mrs. TAYLOR, in Hamilton.
June 29   A son to Mr. and Mrs. A. M. TIBBETS, of Hamilton.
July 24   A daughter to Rev. and Mrs. James COOTE, of Waterville.
July 29   A daughter to Mr. and Mrs. John BROWN, of Hamilton.
Aug. 30   A son to Mr. and Mrs. Adelbert GOODRICH, of Madison.
Sept. 14   A daughter to Mr. and Mrs. J. I. BAKER, of Hamilton.
Sept. 17   A daughter to Prof. and Mrs. J. W. FORD, of Hamilton.
Oct. 4   A daughter to Rev. and Mrs. A. J. WILCOX, of Boston.

1881

Feb. 16   A daughter to Mr. and Mrs. Henry B. LEONARD, of Hamilton.
July 6   A daughter to Dr. and Mrs. S. P. BARCHET, of Hamilton.
Sept. 22   A daughter to Prof. and Mrs. W. R. ROWLANDS, of Hamilton.
Sept. 27   A son to Mr. and Mrs. George CASTIDY, of Binghamton.
Oct. 10   A daughter to Mr. and Mrs. Mabbett J. ENOS, of Hamilton.

DEMOCRATIC REPUBLICAN - 1881

Oct. 19   A son to Mr. and Mrs. James DERRICK, of Hamilton.
Dec. 8   A daughter to Prof. and Mrs. George A. WILLIAMS, of Hamilton.
Dec. 20   A daughter to Mr. and Mrs. Cyrus BISBY, of Sherburne.
Dec. 20   A son to Mr. and Mrs. Elmer ROOT, of Hamilton.

1882

June 7   A son to Mr. and Mrs. C. H. SIMMONS, of North Bend, Dodge County, NE
June 23   A son to Mr. and Mrs. O. E. TUTTLE, of Hamilton.
Aug. 7   A daughter to Mr. and Mrs. Milo RUSSELL, of Hamilton.
Aug. 29   A daughter to Mr. and Mrs. A. J. SMITH, of Hamilton.
Nov. 18   A son to Mr. and Mrs. J. M. WOODMAN, in Madison.
Dec. 15   A daughter to Mr. and Mrs. F. A. FARGO, in Eaton.

1883

Jan. 2   A daughter to Mr. and Mrs. C. S. BILLS, of South Lebanon.
Feb. 2   A daughter to Mr. and Mrs. John BROWN, of Hamilton.
Feb. 13   A son to Prof. and Mrs. E. P. SISSON, of Hamilton.
Feb. 19   "Friends of Rev. N. HARRIS, returned missionary from Burmah, helped celebrate his 70th birthday at his home in Hamilton."
Mar. 27   A son to Rev. C. A. and Mrs. Jennie NICHOLS, of Basein, British Burmah.
May 14   A son to Mr. and Mrs. F. E. BONNEY, of Hamilton.
May 17   A son to Mr. and Mrs. Niles LEACH, of Hamilton.
May 18   A daughter to Mr. and Mrs. Henry LILLIE, of Pine Woods.
June 16   A son to Mr. and Mrs. Frank CULVER, of Bay City, MI.
July 17   A daughter to Mr. and Mrs. Frank STODDARD, of Hamilton.

DEMOCRATIC REPUBLICAN - 1883

July 20	A daughter to Mr. and Mrs. John SMITH, of Hamilton.
Aug. 28	A son to Mr. and Mrs. Elbert FAGAN, of Madison.
Sept. 21	A daughter to Dr. and Mrs. J. E. SLAUGHT, in this village [Hamilton].
Sept. 22	A son to Mr. and Mrs. HOSTKOTTER.
Nov. 19	A son to Mr. and Mrs. Nathan TOOKE, of Eaton.
Nov. 22	A son to Mr. and Mrs. Milo RUSSELL, of Hamilton.

1884

Jan. 19	A son to Mr. and Mrs. George CASTIDAY, of Binghamton.
Feb. 7	A daughter to Mr. and Mrs. Peter HAND.
Feb. 19	A daughter to Mr. and Mrs. J. C. SAWDY, of Hamilton.
Feb. 25	A daughter to Mr. and Mrs. Alvah COLE, of Eaton.
Apr. 27	A son to Mr. and Mrs. M. A. AUSTIN, of Madison.
May 1	A son to Mr. and Mrs. William BURGESS, of Madison.
May 11	A daughter to Mr. and Mrs. F. A. FARGO, of Pine Woods.
May 15	A son to Mr. and Mrs. Willey LUCAS, of Hamilton.
May 22	A son to Mr. and Mrs. Richard HALEY, of Hamilton.
May 6	A daughter to Mr. and Mrs. W. H. MATHISON, of Hamilton.
June 14	A son to Mr. and Mrs. Edwin FLEMING, of Lebanon.
June 14	A daughter to Mr. and Mrs. C. M. WICKWIRE, of Hamilton.
July 6	A daughter to Mr. and Mrs. Henry RISLEY, of Madison.
July 15	A son to Mr. and Mrs. W. F. EATON, of Hamilton.
Sept. 24	A son to Mr. and Mrs. D. M. MINER, of Eaton.
Aug. 30	A daughter to Mr. and Mrs. E. C. BUTLER, of Hamilton.
Sept. 26	A daughter to Mr. and Mrs. Emory TIBBETTS.
Nov. 8	A son to Mr. and Mrs. Frank CASH, of Hamilton.
Nov. 18	A son to Mr. and Mrs. G. I. WILCOX, in Lebanon.
Dec. 8	A son to Mr. and Mrs. E. J. FARLEY, of Hamilton.

DEMOCRATIC REPUBLICAN - 1884

Dec. 15   A son to Mr. and Mrs. William L. JOHNSON, of Hamilton

1885

Jan. 11   A son to Mr. and Mrs. F. J. ROOT, of Hamilton.
Nov. 27   A son to Rev. and Mrs. C. A. NICHOLS, of Bassein, Burmah. (1884)
Apr. 13   A son to Prof. and Mrs. E. P. SISSON, of Hamilton.
May 22   A daughter to Mr. and Mrs. George ROSS, of Madison.
Aug. 18   A son to Mr. and Mrs. Emmett TOOKE, of Pratts Hollow. "You can't touch Grandpa, George KELLOWAY, now, with a 40 ft. pole."
Oct. 9   A daughter to Prof. and Mrs. B. S. TERRY, of Hamilton.
Oct. 14   A son to Rev. and Mrs. S. H. STACKPOLE, of Hamilton.
Oct. 16   A daughter to Dr. and Mrs. A. F. ROOT, of Hamilton.
Nov. 3   A daughter to Mr. and Mrs. William BURGESS, of Madison.
Nov. 8   A daughter to Rev. and Mrs. C. V. PATTERSON, of Rochester; weight 8 1/2 lbs.
Nov. 27   A daughter to Mr. and Mrs. Frank BEST, of Hamilton.
Dec. 28   A daughter to Mr. and Mrs. Jay F. AUSTIN, of Lebanon.

1886

Jan. 22   A son to Mr. and Mrs. J. E. WILKINSON, of Hamilton.
Jan. 22   A daughter to Prof. and Mrs. J. W. FORD, of Hamilton.
Feb. 11   A daughter to Mr. and Mrs. George CASTIDY, of Grand Island, NE.
In issue of Feb. 25: A daughter to Mr. and Mrs. E. C. PHILPOT, of Pratts Hollow.
Apr. 29   A son to Mr. and Mrs. Z. S. WOODMAN, in Madison.
May 4   A daughter to Mr. and Mrs. William WENTWORTH, in Hamilton.
July 16   A son to Mr. and Mrs. Charle B. VAN HOUSEN.
Aug. 8   A daughter to Mr. and Mrs. Ed. LAMB.

DEMOCRATIC REPUBLICAN - 1886

Aug. 7	A daughter to Mr. and Mrs. H. S. LILLIE, of Pine Woods.
Aug. 11	A daughter to Mr. and Mrs. Soren AUSS, of Hamilton.
Aug. 29	A daughter to Mr. and Mrs. S. D. DAVIS, near Hamilton.
Oct. 10	A son to Mr. and Mrs. Stephen BENEDICT.
Oct. 28	A daughter to Mr. and Mrs. Bert SPERRY.
Nov. 1	A son to Mr. and Mrs. William BARTLE.
Nov. 8	A daughter, weight 9 lb., to Prof. and Mrs. HARKNESS.
Nov. 8	A son, weight 9 1/2 lb., to Prof. and Mrs. HARKNESS (sic).
Nov. 25	A son to Mr. and Mrs. H. L. (or H.I.) HILLS.
Dec. 7	In Hubbardsville, a son to Mr. and Mrs. A. J. PARTRIDGE.
Dec. 25	In Hamilton, a son to Mr. and Mrs. E. KINSBURY.

****

MARRIAGE RECORDS

As Published in Newspapers Printed in

HAMILTON, MADISON COUNTY, NY

****

THE HAMILTON RECORDER

Vol. I, No. 1
For year beginning July 2, 1822

July 27, in Eaton, by Rev. ACKLEY, Mr. Chauncey STOCKING to Miss Harriet PRATT.

Aug. 18, at New Woodstock, by J. WHIPPLE, Isaac BUMPUS, of Nelson, to Matilda OSGOOD, of Otselic.

Sept. 1, at Paris, by Rev. ROBINSON, Capt. Lewis PIERCE, of Lebanon, to Nancy BARTON, of Paris.

Nov. 21, in Verona, Palatiah BARD to Hannah LAINING.

Dec. 4, in Hamilton, Mr. Justus BEACH to D. TYLER.

Dec. 5, in Hamilton, Loomis FULLER to Harriet ACKLEY, by Mr. STACY.

Dec. 5, in Hamilton by Rev. POTTER, Marvin GAGER to Clarissa HUNT.

1823

Feb. 2, by Rev. POTTER, Ira WILLOUGHBY to Minerva COLSON.
Feb. 9, in Hamilton, by John G. STOWER, F. H. LOOMIS, of Verona, to Olive LAINING, of Hamilton.
Feb. 25, at Hamilton, Rev. Jonathan WADE, to Deborah LAPHAM, daughter of Deacon LAPHAM, of Hamilton.
Mar. 13, in Lebanon, Stephen OSTROM Jr. to Miss Lydia PADDLEFORD, by Elder KINDRICK.
Mar. 18, in Eaton, William MORSE to Sally SHAW.
Mar. 27, in Hamilton, by Rev. LATHAM, William BARKER to Electa WEST, of Hamilton.
Mar. 26, in Hamilton, by Rev. ACKLEY, Pierce KINGSBURY to Lydia GOODELL.
Apr. --, in Madison, Isaac KNAPP to Mary NORTON.
Apr. 10, in Brookfield, by Rev. D. COON, Sheffield PALMER to Margaret GREEN.
May 15, in Sherburne, by Rev. REXFORD, Chauncey BARNES to Amanda PALMER.
In issue of May 28th, but date of marriage not given, Dr. Hiram HAVENS, age 26, to Mrs. Esther C. CARVER, age 69.
> "If Cupid's golden dart transfix
> The tender soul of twenty-six
> The archer must have power divine
> To pierce the heart of sixty-nine."

June 17, in Vernon, Asa GIFFORD, Esq., of Sherburne, to Lucy ALBERT of Vernon.
June 12, at Guilford, Elias JOHNSON, graduate of Hamilton Theological Seminary, to Beulah BUCKINGHAM, of Guilford.
Sept. 17, in Hamilton, by Rev. Nath'l KENDIRCK, Richard WATERS to Hannah PIERCE.
Sept. 17, in Hamilton, James MUNROE to Almeda SKEELS.
Sept. 17, in Hamilton, D. TORRY to Sally NICHOLS.
Sept. 17, in Hamilton, Orrin PARKS to Polly PALMER.
Oct. 2, in Lebanon, by Rev. SHAW, Joel KENYON, of Brookfield, to Lavina MAXON, of Lebanon.
In issue of Oct. 15: At Bristol, PA, the Hon. Peter SMITH, of Peterboro, to Miss Sarah POGSON, of Charleston, SC.
Oct. 19, at Sherburne, by Rev. Amos KINGSLEY, Elijah SLOCUM, to Miss Eliza Ann SMITH, of Sherburne.
Oct. 15, in Hamilton, by Rev. KINGSLEY, Stephen HANMON, of Lebanon, to Melinda GOODALE, of Sherburne.
Nov. 13, in Lenox, by Rev. OLDS, Walter WHITE to Larny RATNOUR, both of Lenox.
Dec. 13, in Lenox, Israel OTCOTT to Loe ADAMS.

HAMILTON RECORDER - 1824

1824

Jan. 1, in Sullivan, by Rev. OLDS, Everitt VAN EPS to Electa HARRIS.

Jan. 1, in Lenox, by Rev. BOYD, Whitefield NORTHRUP to Ann FOWLER, of Lenox.

Jan. 4, in Lenox, by Rev. ADAMS, William E. FISKE to Miss Eliza OLCOTT.

Jan. 7, in Hamilton, Jason CORWIN to Daborah (sic) C. ORTON.

Jan. 15, at New Hartford, Dr. John A. PAINE, of Volney, to Amanda KELLOGG, daughter of Jacob KELLOGG.

Issue of Feb. 4th: In Williamsburg, IL, John EDGAR, of NJ, age 90 years, to Eliza STEVENS, age 14 years.

Feb. 22, in Hamilton, by Rev. Nathaniel STACEY, Mr. Lyman COLSON to Miss Lucy CRANE.

Feb. 21, in Sangerfield, Ashbel CADWELL, of Lenox, to Maria JEFFRIES, of Sangerfield.

Feb. 24, in Lenox, George JEFFRIES to Belinda CADWELL, by Rev. ADAMS.

Feb. 3, in Lenox, Alvan WALKER to Lucy GRAY.

Feb. 3, at Canastota, by Elder POWELL, Mr. Thomas PERKINS to Miss Lydia LEWIS.

Feb. 4, by Rev. HEATH, Mr. Wells STEDMAN to Miss Eliza WING.

Feb. 4, by Rev. Mr. BOID, Henry HOLLISTER to Harriet HALLOCK.

Feb. 17, by Rev. GOODWIN, Mr. Nathan CADY to Miss Emoline BEECHER.

Feb. 18, by Elder POWELL, Daniel D. WOLF to Widow MC MICHAEL.

Feb. 22, by Rev. ADAMS, Anson ALCOTT to Sabria NICHOLS.

Mar. 3, by Rev. KENDRICK, in Morrisville, George WILLIAMS to Miss Sarah BYER.

Apr. 18, in Madison, by Rev. Jesse MINOR, Joel NYE Jr. to Susan LIVERMORE.

Mar. 20, in Brookfield, by Rev. Jesse MINOR, Warren COWIN to Julia NYE.

May 5, in Log City, Clement LEACH to Laura HATCH, both of Log City.

At Danbe, Herkimer Co., Daniel ROOF, 3 ft. 8 in. tall, to Miss Mary PETTEN, 3 ft. 6 in. tall.

May 29, in Colchester, Mr. USHER to Miss FOOT.

May 29, in Lebanon, by Rev. Daniel HASCALL, Daniel SHAPLEY to Chloe BUDLONG.

June 2, in Westmoreland, Dr. Benjamin W. BABCOCK to Miss Hannah HAVENS.

HAMILTON RECORDER - 1824

May 27, in Log City, by Rev. KENDRICK, Rev. John SMITZER to Mary HATCH.

May 28, by Rev. HASCALL, John B. BALLARD, graduate of the Baptist Literary and Theological Seminary, to Miss Augusta GILMAN.

June 2, in Hamilton, Eber TUCKER to Martha, daughter of T. COX, Esq. He is a graduate of the Baptist Literary and Theological Seminary.

Issue of June 30: In Dayton, OH, Mr. Conrad REED to Miss Catherine WEAVER.

June 15, at Waterloo, NY, Mr. Lucas MORGAN, Att'y at Law, to Miss Charlotte BEAR.

June 5, in this village [Hamilton], by Dr. KENDRICK, Mr. Howland TURNER, graduate of the Baptist Literary & Theological Seminary, to Miss Amanda WHEELER.

June 8, in this village [Hamilton], by Dr. KENDIRCK, Mr. Gates DAVIS to Harriet JONES.

July 29, in this village [Hamilton], by Thomas WYLIE, Esq., Mr. Elijah OWEN to Mrs. Betsey DOTY.

Agu. 21, in this town [Hamilton], by Thos. WYLIE, Mr. Stewart BENEDICT to Miss Cena COLE.

Sept. 1, in this village [Hamilton], by Prof. HASCALL, Rev. Jacob KNAPP to Miss Electa PAYNE.

Sept. 2, in Lebanon, by Elder JERIL, Mr. Thomas STONE to Miss Abigail WEATHERLY.

Sept. 2, in Great Barrington, MA, by Rev. Mr. BURT, Mr. John G. STOWER, Esq., to Miss Amelia KELLOGG, of the former place.

Oct. 9, in Lebanon, Mr. Thomas DRAKE to Miss Chloe FORD.

Oct. 31, in Sangerfield, by Rev. Joel W. CLARK, Mr. James GOVE, of this village [Hamilton], to Miss Betsey TERRY, of Sangerfield.

Nov. 18, in this town [Hamilton], by Rev. Daniel HASCALL, Mr. Luther MABIN to Miss Mary PIERCE.

Nov. 25, in Lebanon, by Rev. Thos. JERIL, Mr. Leonard FELLOWS to Miss Arminda JOHNSON.

Dec. 21, in this village [Hamilton], by Rev. HASCALL, Mr. Newell HEMINGWAY to Miss Eliza DOW.

Dec. 10 (or 19), in Lebanon, by Rev. Thos. JERIL, Joel KIBBE to Miss Sophia BUYSBY.

Dec. 19, in Lebanon, Mr. Orrin STETSON to Miss Lucretia TENNY.

Dec. 20, in Lebanon, Mr. Nathaniel LYON to Miss Hannah JOHNSON.

Dec. 16, in Lebanon, Mr. Calvin BLISS to Miss Minerva LYON.

Dec. 6, in Lebanon, by Rev. KINGSLEY, Mr. Daniel ELLIS to Miss Sally COY.

HAMILTON RECORDER - 1825

1825

Feb. 21, in Albany, by Rev. FERRIS, Hon. James B. ELDREDGE, of this village [Hamilton], to Miss Sarah CARPENTER, of Albany.
Feb. 10, at Smithfield, by Elder BROWN, Mr. Silas AUSTIN to Miss Laura DEWY.
Feb. 16, at Smithfield, by Rev. PADDOCK, Mr. Nathan HARVEY, of Augusta, to Miss Aurel LYMAN, of Smithfield.
Feb. 23, in Augusta, by Rev. LYMAN, Mr. Clinton GAGE to Miss Rosannah COWDEN.
Mar. 3, in Augusta, by Rev. LANE, Mr. Ezekiel BARBER to Miss Anna LOVE.
Mar. 12, in this town [Hamilton], by Rev. STACY, Mr. Leonard HOADLY to Miss Elizabeth DUNHAM, both of Hamilton.
At the same time and place, by Rev. STACY, Mr. Asa DUNBAR, of New Berlin, to Miss Martha CAMPBELL, of Hamilton.
May 22, in Hamilton, by Rev. DOOLITTLE, Mr. Chauncey GRAY, to the amiable and accomplished Miss Melinda, daughter of Jonathan SKINNER, of Hamilton.

Vol. IV, No. 1

June 28, in Georgetown, by Rev. Mr. MORSE, Mr. Vine B. GILBERT, of Lebanon, to Miss Susan BROWN.
July 4, in Georgetown, Mr. Aylmer BALLARD to Miss Lydia UTTER, both of Georgetown.
Sept. 14, by Rev. Joel W. CLARK, in Hamilton, Zenas MORSE, Prin. of Hamilton Academy, to Miss Cemantha J. PARMELY, both of Hamilton.
Nov. 30, in Augusta, Mr. Tommy WYATT (an Indian) of Brothertown, to Mrs. Hannah, daughter of Mr. John GILBERT.
At Henrietta, NY, (no date), Capt. Samuel CURRIER, to Mrs. Mary ARCHER, his seventh marriage.

1826

Feb. 5, at Eaton, by Robert HENRY, Mr. Jacob TUCKERMAN, of Eaton, to Miss Delia BLACKMAN, of Hamilton.
Mar. 8, in Lebanon, by Rev. Matthias CAZEER, Mr. Joseph FORD to Miss Olive LINSEY, both of Lebanon.
May 3, in Madison, by Rev. Mr. LATHAM, Mr. Nathan PECK, of Hamilton, to Miss Phebe TOMPKINS, of Madison.

HAMILTON RECORDER - 1826

May 22, at Waterville, by Rev. Mr. HOPKINS, Philo GRIDLEY, Esq., of Hamilton, to Miss Susan WILLIAMS, of Waterville.

May 5, in Eaton, by Rev. Mr. CUMMINGS, Mr. Jonathan PRINCE to Miss Nancy MILLER, daughter of George MILLER, both of Eaton.

June 4, in Smyrna, by Joseph MUNSON, Esq., Mr. Elihu DICKS to Miss Miranda BILL, both of Smyrna.

Nov. 1, at Waterville, by Rev. E. BEARDSLEY, Mr. Julius CANDEE of Hamilton, to Lucia M. OSBORNE, of Waterville.

Nov. 1, in Hamilton, by Rev. Jacob KNAPP, Rev. Seth SMALLEY, of Amsterdam, to Miss Philena M. PAYNE, of Hamilton.

Oct. 24, near Cadiz, Harrison Co., OH, Napolean Bonaparte KENNEDY to Miss Mary GILMORE, daughter of Samuel GILMORE.

1827

Mar. 15, in Lebanon, by Thomas WYLIE, Esq., Mr. Zarah SIMMONS, age 82 years, to Mrs. Hannah STEBBINS, age 34 years.

Mar. 22, in Lebanon, by Rev. Dr. KENDRICK, Mr. Horace A. CAMPBELL to Miss Phila ANDRUS.

Vol. VI, No. 1

Aug. 6, in Hamilton, by Rev. Nathaniel KENDRICK, the Rev. William G. MILLER, of New York, to Miss Cynthia BACON, eldest daughter of Rufus BACON, Esq., of Hamilton.

Aug. 7, by Rev. Daniel HASCALL, Mr. William CHURCH, of Coventry, to Miss Betsy Ann EVERETT, of Hamilton.

Oct. 1, in Hamilton, by Lucus CRANE, Esq., Mr. Benjamin INGRAM, to Miss Betsey FARR, after a courtship of one-half day.

REPUBLICAN REGISTER
Published at Hamilton, Madison County, NY
Vol. 1, No. 1, Year 1828

Apr. 9, in Hamilton, by Rev. Daniel HASCALL, Mr. Daniel ALLEN to Miss Mary SMITH.

REPUBLICAN REGISTER - 1828

Apr. 10, at North Norwich, by Rev. ADAMS, Mr. Ebenezer S. TRACY, of this village [Hamilton], to Miss Eliza MEAD, of North Norwich.
Dec. 10, in this town [Hamilton], by Rev. Nathaniel STACY, Capt. Almor RICHARDSON to Miss Mary TURNER.
Dec. 17, in Newark, Tioga Co., NY, Mr. Frederick B. BEMENT to Miss Mary Ann, daughter of Francis ARMSTRONG.

1829

Jan. 1, by Rev. FIELD, Mr. H.B. FURNISS to Miss Dorothy DOW.
Jan. 1, by John FOOT, Esq., Mr. David BARBER to Miss C. ALDERMAN.
Jan. 1, by Rev. LATHAM, James POOLE to Miss B. H. BOON, all of Hamilton.
Jan. 1, in Sangerfield, by Rev. A. KINGSLEY, Mr. A. BEEBE, of Brookfield, to Miss Delight WILLIAMS, of Sangerfield.
Jan. 6, by Rev. Daniel HASCALL, Mr. Aaron C. WHEELER to Miss Miranda BEACH, all of this town [Hamilton].
Jan. 4, by Rev. Pindar FIELD, at Lebanon, Mr. Levi S. BACKUS, late of Hebron, CT, to Miss Anna R. ORMSBY, of Lebanon.
Jan. 4, in Lebanon, by same, Mr. Frederick FOX, of Canajoharie, to Miss Hannah ORMSBY, of Lebanon. [NOTE: The last two couples are deaf and dumb. The ladies were educated at the Deaf and Dumb Asylm at Canajoharie, and Mr. BACHUS is Prin. or teacher in the institution.]
Jan. 14, by Rev. P. FIELD, Dr. Henry LOCKWOOD to Miss Sophia S. PECK, all of Hamilton.
Jan. 15, in Butternuts, by Rev. WHEELER, Mr. Ferdinand WALKER to Miss Almira SMITH, of Butternuts.
Jan. 13, at Lebanon, by Rev. P. FIELD, Stephen OWEN, Esq., to Miss Mary SQUIRES, both of Lebanon.
Jan. 9, at Hamilton, by C. G. OTIS, Esq., Mr. --- BROWN, of Locke, Cayuga Co., NY, to Miss Sally PHINEY of Hamilton.
Jan. 22, in Eaton, by Rev. BEARDSLEY, Mr. --- WILSON, of Danville, to Miss Cordelia ENOS, of Eaton.
Feb. 5, in Kirkland, Mr. Thomas POTHICARY, of this village [Hamilton], to Miss Betsey PIERCE.
Jan. 30, at New York, by Rev. UPHOLD, James G. BROOKS, Esq., to Miss Mary Elizabeth, daughter of the late John AIKIN, Esq., of Duchess County, NY.

REPUBLICAN REGISTER - 1829

Feb. 17, at Troy, by Rev. HOWARD, Rufus BACON, Esq., to Miss Eliza BARTHOLOMEW, both of Hamilton.
Mar. 4, in Hamilton, by Rev. STACY, David OSGOOD to Miss Lucy PRESTON.
Mar. 8, Mr. Phineas CASE, of Candor, Tioga Co., to Miss Olive BUTTLER, of Hamilton.
Mar. 15, in Smyrna, by Rev. William GARDNER, Eli GREGORY to Miss Thankful REYNOLDS.
Mar. 4, in this town [Hamilton], by Rev. William GARDNER, Mr. GUSTIN to Widow TORRY.
Mar. 29, in Hamilton, Mr. Joseph CLARK to Sophronia IDE (Miss).
Aug. 5, in Augusta, Samuel ROSE to Mary E., daughter of Robert J. MORRIS.

HAMILTON COURIER
1834-1835

May 4, 1834, in Sherburne, by Rev. Mr. BARROWS, Arba K. MAYNARD, Esq., Attorney-at-Law, to Miss Minerva GATES, both of Sherburne.
June 3, at Western, Oneida Co., by Rev. Geo. S. BOARDMAN, of Watertown, John B. JERVIS, Esq., Chief Engineer on the Chenango Canal, to Miss Cynthia, daughter of George BRAYTON, Esq., of Western.
Sept. 27, in Toronto, U.C., by Rev. Dr. PHILLIPS, of the English Church, Franklin J. MUNGER, Esq., Attorney-at-Law, of this village [Hamilton], to Miss Hannah V., eldest daughter of Joseph TURTON, Esq., of the former place.
Oct. 20, in Newark Valley, NY, by Rev. Mr. COLBURN, Mr. Alfred H. FORD and Miss Elizabeth RICH, all of that place.

1835

Jan. 6, by Rev. A. M. WILSE, Mr. Nuell FULLER to Miss Louisa YEOMAN, both of East Hamilton.
Jan. 8, in Norwich, by Elder J. S. SWAN, Alfred SLOCUM, of this village [Hamilton], to Miss Amelia B. RANDALL, daughter of Deacon Charles RANDALL, of Norwich.
Jan. 29, in this village [Hamilton], by Elder Daniel HASCALL, Mr. Johnson SHAPLEY, merchant, to Miss Betsey WHEELER, all of this place.
Jan. 8, by Elder Daniel HASCALL, Mr. Eliakim SHERRILL, Merchant, of Salisbury, NY, to Miss Emily E., daugh-

ter of the Hon. James B. ELDREDGE, of this village [Hamilton]; marriage in this village.

THE HAMILTON EAGLE
1839-1840

In issue of Nov. 13, 1839: In Madison, on last Thursday, by Rev. Mr. PRATT, Mr. Aaron RANKINS, of Munnsville, to Miss Sarah G. SIMMONS, of Madison.

In issue of Nov. 20, 1839: In this village, on Tuesday last, by Rev. J. A. BRAYTON, Doct. Henry D. KENDALL, of Norwich, to Miss Marchia D.S. HAVENS, of this place [Hamilton].

Nov. 28, in this village [Hamilton], by Elder WARNER, Mr. Eli BUEL Jr., of this place, to Miss Phoebe LAMPHIRE, of Jefferson Co., NY.

Dec. 2, in this town [Hamilton], by Rev. Mr. WELTON, Mr. Amos T. GEER to Miss Sabrina Amelia PARKER, of Madison.

Dec. 29, by Rev. Alonzo WELTON, Mr. Henry PAWLETT to Miss Julia O. CLARK, all of this place [Hamilton].

1840

Feb. 5, in this town [Hamilton], by Rev. WELTON, Dr. James K. BOWEN, of Pitcher, Chenango Co., to Miss Cordelia, eldest daughter of Hubbard B. AVERY.

Feb. 17, in this village, by Rev. B. G. PADDOCK, Mr. Edmund R. COMBS, of Troy, to Miss Elizabeth GILBERT, of Watertown.

HAMILTON PALLADIUM
Vol. II, No. 1
1839

[Date not given], in Nantucket, Mr. Barnabas BOURNE, of Falmouth, to Miss Lydia B. LONG, by Benj. GARDNER, Esq.

Aug. 25, By Rev. J. A. BRAYTON, in Hamilton, Mr. Frederick T. GREENLY to Miss Elizabeth HIGGINS, both of Hamilton.

Aug. 25, in Lebanon, by the same, Capt. Lewis WICKWIRE, of Hamilton, to Miss Laura A. SHELDON, of Lebanon.

HAMILTON PALLADIUM - 1839

Aug. 20, in Depeauville, by Rev. Morgan GILLETTTE, Deyer E. PIERCE, M.D., to Miss Mary J. ACKET, both of Depeauville.

Sept. 4, in Earlville, by Rev. W. W. EVERTS, Mr. Elisha PHILLIPS, of Augusta, to Miss Lucy HUGHES, of Hamilton.

Aug. 25, at Madison, by Agur GILBERT, Esq., Mr. Truman J. HUGHES, of Hamilton, to Miss Nancy MC COMBER, of Eaton.

Sept. 24, in this village [Hamilton], by Rev. Alonzo WELTON, Mr. John J. FOOTE to Miss Mary CROCKER, both of Hamilton.

Oct. 10, at the Friends' Meeting House in Madison, Stephen ATWATER, of Lockport, to Mary L. WEAVER, daughter of Zebulon WEAVER, of Madison.

Oct. 24, in Hamilton, by Rev. Mr. WELTON, William FAIRCHILD to Miss Anna MAFFET.

Issue dated Nov. 22: In Hamilton, by Rev. J. A. BRAYTON, Henry D. KENDALL, M.D., of Norwich, to Miss Marcia D. S., daughter of Dr. P. B. HAVENS.

Dec. 2, in Hamilton, by Rev. Mr. WELTON, Mr. Amos T. GEER to Miss Sabrina Amelia PARKER.

1840

Jan. 15, in Pompey, by Rev. E. E. L. TAYLOR, Mr. James H. TAYLOR, of Delphi, to Miss Charlotte E., only daughter of Capt. Thomas DAVIS.

Feb. 5, in Lebanon, by Rev. Mr. WELTON, Dr. James K. BOWER, of Pitcher, to Miss Cordelia, eldest daughter of Hubbard B. AVERY.

Feb. 16, in Hamilton, at Mr. Horace PIERCE's home, by Rev. B. G. PADDOCK, Mr. Edward COMBS to Miss Betsey GILBERT.

Feb. 27, in Sherburne, by Rev. Elder BLODGETT, Mr. Alanson S. CRUMB, of Edmeston, only son of Silas CRUMB, to Miss Finnett PROBERT, second daughter of James PROBERT, of Sherburne.

Mar. 4, in Earlville, by Prof. A. C. KENDRICK, of the Hamilton Literary and Theological Institute, Mr. H. A. GARDNER, of DeRuyter, to Miss Minerva A. CALKINS.

Mar. 9, in Lebanon, by Rev. Mr. AYRES, Mr. Charles F. OWEN to Miss Susan Ann HEWS, all of Lebanon,

Apr. 1, in Hamilton, by Rev. WELTON, Mr. Charles SMITH to Miss Mary Ann SMITH.

HAMILTON PALLADIUM - 1839

Mar. 22, in Eaton, by Rev. B. G. PADDOCK, Mr. Chauncey S. SMITH, of Hamilton, to Miss Mary Ann ALBEE, of Eaton.

May 13, in Georgetown, by Rev. Mr. WOOLLEY, Mr. Palmer HOPKINS, of Eaton, to Miss Miranda FLETCHER, of Georgetown.

May 24, in Hamilton, by Rev. Benj. PUTNAM, of Lebanon, Mr. Henry COMPTON to Miss Caroline M. SMITH, all of Hamilton.

June 3, by Rev. L. FLETCHER, Mr. Joseph TOWNE, of Troy, Crawford Co., PA, to Miss Celestia A. CALKINS, of Hamilton.

June 10, in Hamilton, by Rev. B. G. PADDOCK, Hon. B. F. SKINNER, of Washington County, to Miss Eliza G. BLISH, of Hamilton.

June 9, in Silver Creek, Chautauqua Co., NY, by Rev. O. C. BEARDSLEY, Mr. Samuel P. RUSSELL, of Hamilton, to Miss Clarissa BIRDSLEY, of Silver Creek.

1841, Vol. II, No. 1

Aug. 9, by Prof. MAGINNIS, George POND, of Hamilton, to Ann HURD, of Lebanon.

Aug. 11, by Rev. BARTHOLOMEW, in Madison, Lyman P. ORTON, M.D., of Lebanon, to Julia M., youngest daughter of Gen. Erastus CLEAVELAND.

Aug. 25, in Sherburne, by Rev. BACHUS, Mr. E. R. BARKER, of Hamilton, to Almira H. GRAVES, of Sherburne.

Aug. 29, in Lebanon, Ormel HUTCHINS to Angeline BUEL, daughter of Mrs. Pamillia BUEL, all of Lebanon.

Sept. 15, in Madison, by Rev. PLATT, Oren WRIGHT, Esq., of Munnsville, to Calista SIMMONS, daughter of Cornelius SIMMONS, of Madison.

Sept. 22, in Madison, Dr. Amos K. WHITE, to Ann, daughter of Rev. Philip BROWN, of Madison.

Sept. 12, in Hamilton, by Rev. L. FLETCHER, Col. Nathaniel STANTON, of Hornby, Steuben Co., to Samantha TRACY, of Hamilton.

Sept. 22, in Hamilton, by the same, David F. PAYSON to Lucy A. FITCH, both of Eaton.

Sept. 6, in Homer, by Rev. L. BARROWS, of Norwich, Mr. H. N. PELLET, Editor of the *Chenango Telegraph*, to Malvina, daughter of Ira BOWEN, of Homer.

Sept. 9, in Verona, by Rev. A. B. GROSH, Mr. J. H. BROOKS, of Munnsville, to Miss E. Ann SHEPARD, daughter of Aaron SHEPARD of Verona.

Sept. 23, in St. Johnsville, by Rev. A. MYERS, Newton HAYS, of Earlville, to Anna LEONARD.

HAMILTON PALLADIUM - 1840

Sept. 29, in Hamilton, by Rev. L. FLETCHER, Mr. John R. BALDWIN, of Branford, CT, to Miss Harriet ROGERS, daughter of Medad ROGERS.

Oct. 20, in Madison, by Rev. Mr. PLATT, Mr. Ira SHIPMAN, of MI, to Miss Emergene BEACH, of Madison.

Oct. 13, in Coventry, Otsego Co., by Rev. Mr. WHITE, George F. SMITH, of Masonville, son of Ebenezer SMITH, to Miss Mary A., only daughter of Noah SMITH, of Coventry.

Oct. 7, in Lebanon, by Elder KENYON, Capt. J. H. WARRINER to Miss Jane E. LIVINGSTON, all of Lebanon.

Oct. 25, in Lebanon, by Rev. H. KENYON, Luke G. MAXSON to Cordelia Ann, youngest daughter of Jacob HARTSHORN, of Lebanon. He is Prin. of Coudersport Academy, PA.

Nov. 2, in Madison, by Rev. PLATT, Chester HOLCOMB, of Winfield, to Lucy TOMPKINS.

Nov. 1, in Hamilton, George KEMPTON, of Beaufort District, SC, to Sarah E. MOTT, of Hamilton, by Rev. MAGINNIS.

Nov. 10, in Clockville, by Rev. S. WRIGHT, B. Franklin CHAPMAN to Huldah WILCOX, daughter of Deacon A. WILCOX.

Nov. 28, in Clinton, by Rev. CLOWES, John B. LOOMIS, of Vernon, to Elizabeth Thompson, daughter of Amariah FENTON, Esq., of Clinton.

Dec. 2, in Georgetown, Elijah LONT to Margaret CONICK, both of Lebanon.

Dec. 16, in Brookfield, by D. HARDIN, Mr. Avery BROWN to Miss Almira CLARK, all of Brookfield.

[No date], in Albany, Mr. Henry L. WEBB, of the Hamilton Literary and Theological Institute, to Miss Ann Elizabeth HULL, of Hamilton. (See below.)

Dec. 24, in Hamilton Center, Capt. --- WOOLEY to Miss Mary PALMER, all of Hamilton.

Nov. 18, in Albany, Henry WEBB, of New Brunswick, NJ, to Anna Elizabeth HULL, of Hamilton, youngest daughter of the late Dr. C. W. HULL, of Eaton.

1842

Jan. 6, in Vernon, by Rev. ROBINSON, Hiram KENDALL to Elizabeth OSGOOD.

Jan. 12, in Poolville, by Rev. HOLMES, Allan N. WOOD to Calista M. EATON.,

Feb. 15, in Madison, Gilbert TOMPKINS to Julia MANCHESTER, both of Madison.

Feb. 23, in Hamilton, by Rev. YARRINGTON, Capt. James COE, of Stratford, CT, to Helen WEST.

HAMILTON PALLADIUM - 1842

Mar. 24, in Hamilton, by Rev. L. FLETCHER, Horace WELCH, of Sherburne, to Jerusha C. HUNT, of Hamilton.

Apr. 3, in Lebanon, by Avery Z. KINGSLEY, Capt. Nelson CARPENTER, of Sherburne, to Nancy WILLIAMS.

Apr. 14, in Madison, by Rev. LEACH, of Hamilton, Mr. George HUTCHINSON, of Newton, MA, to Loretta COE, of Madison.

May 5, in Bridgewater, by Rev. BROWN, David MANNERING, of Hamilton, to Maria DE WOLF.

Apr. 28, in Oswego, by Rev. R. W. CONDIT, Mr. Thomas S. MYRICK, of Cazenovia, Editor of the *Madison County Eagle*, and Miss Hannah B. SPRAGUE, of Oswego.

June 1, in Hamilton, by Rev. Robert DAY, John MITCHELL, of Norwich, to Caroline D. FOOTE, daughter of John FOOTE, Esq.

June 1, in East Hamilton, by Rev. HARTWELL, Elijah SMITH to Nancy E. HALL, both of East Hamilton.

June 14, at Dr. Noah FOOTE's in East Hamilton, by Rev. Andrew PECK, David MAINE Jr., of DeRuyter, to Mrs. Lodema PALMER of Branford, CT.

June 13, in Hamilton, Hiram NASH to Mary CADWELL.

June 16, in Sangerfield, by Rev. M. PLATT, of Madison, Col. Erastus T. HATCH, of Clayville, to Roxanna CAMP, of Sangerfield.

June 30, in this village [Hamilton], by Rev. Robert DAY, Mr. C. M. HAWLEY, of Penn Yan, to Miss Cornelia M. CROCKER, daughter of Amos CROCKER, Esq.

July 5, in Hamilton, by Rev. Robert DAY, Mr. Edward E. WELTON to Miss Emeline BONNEY, all of Hamilton.

Sept. 6, at Gilbertsville, Otsego Co., by Rev. Mr. WINKOOP, Mr. A. H. NILES, of Lebanon, to Miss Mary E., youngest daughter of Eli DONALDSON, Esq., of Gilbertsville.

Sept. 7, in this village [Hamilton], by Rev. B. M. LEACH, Mr. Moses S. MORSE to Miss Cornelia SCRANTON, all of this town.

Sept. 14, at Sherburne Village, Chenango Co., by Rev. BLODGETT, Mr. David RIGBY to Miss Betsey RAY, both of Georgetown, Madison County.

Sept. 6, in Munnsville, Mr. E. S. DAVIS, of Carroll, graduate of Hamilton Literary and Theological Institute, to Miss Angeline E. PARMELEE, of Munnsville.

July 26, at Morrisville, by Rev. Benj. PUTNAM, William S. PACKER, Esq., of New York, to Miss Harriet L. PUTNAM, youngest daughter of the officiating clergyman.

July 21, in East Hamilton, by Rev. Joseph HARTWELL, Mr. Oliver BENTLEY, of Brookfield, to Miss Mary E. BROWN, of E. Hamilton.

HAMILTON PALLADIUM - 1842

Sept. 5, in Peterboro, by Rev. Mr. SCOFIELD, Mr. John GLANVILLE, late of this village [Hamilton], to Miss Sarah A. WILBER, of the former place.

Oct. 5, in Hamilton, by Rev. B. N. LEACH, Mr. Willard JOSLIN to Miss Perces A. CALKINS, both of Hamilton.

Sept. 20, in Brooklyn, L.I., by Rev. R. R. RAYMOND, of Hartford, CT, George R. BLISS, of this village [Hamilton], to Mary A., daughter of Eliakim RAYMOND, Esq.

Nov. 17, in Eaton, by Rev. Samuel R. SHOTWELL, Mr. John BRIGHAM to Miss Lydia CASE, both of Hamilton.

Nov. 23, in Eaton, by Rev. Samuel R. SHOTWELL, Deacon Seth MINER to Miss Lucretia BLINN, both of Eaton.

Nov. 30, in this village [Hamilton], by Rev. L. FLETCHER, Mr. Clark DAWLEY to Miss Harriet WOODMAN, both of this village.

1843

Jan. 11, in Lebanon, at house of A. Z. KINGSLEY, Esq., by Rev. Mr. DAY, Mr. George JULIAND, of Greene, Chenango Co., to Miss Charlotte HYDE, formerly of Albany.

Jan. 15, in Norwich, by Rev. L. HOWARD, Mr. Paul R. BROWN to Miss Harriet S. ALEXANDER, all of Norwich.

Jan. 31, in Eaton, by Rev. Mr. DAY, Mr. Julius RISLEY to Miss Olive DIX, both of Madison.

Feb. 6, in this village [Hamilton], by Prof. Geo. W. EATON, Mr. Charles D. BLISH, of Watertown, Jefferson Co., NY, to Miss Amelia A., eldest daughter of Rev. Leonard FLETCHER, of this place.

Mar. 15, in Eaton, by Rev. S. R. SHOTWELL, Jason OWEN, Esq., of Lebanon, to Miss Abigail LEACH of Eaton: -- also--

Mar. 15, in Eaton, by Rev. Mr. PEARL, Mr. Benjamin COLTON and Miss Hannah CAMPBELL.

Apr. 1, in Brookfield, by Elder S. P. WAY, Capt. Lewis M. WILKINS, of New York, to Miss Sarah M. DELANCEY, of Brookfield.

Apr. 1, in Hamilton, by Rev. Prof. J. S. MAGINNIS, Mr. Henry MC CARDY to Mrs. Jane PRENTISS.

Mar. 26, in Henry Co., IL, by Rev. CHAPIN, Mr. William BENHAM to Miss Amanda ROGERS, formerly of this place [Hamilton].

May 4, in Vernon, by Rev. R. C. BRISBIN, Mr. A. JUDSON to Miss Emily S. NORTON, of Vernon.

HAMILTON PALLADIUM - 1843

Apr. 17, in Peterboro, by Rev. D. W. SMITH, Mr. P. N. GLIDDEN, of Peterboro, to Miss Margaret H. MANUEL, of Morrisville.

Apr. 20, in Smithfield, by the same, Mr. William H. DOWNER to Miss Lucinda LOOK, all of Smithfield.

June 7, in East Hamilton, by Rev. Wesley FOX, Mr. Julius WHITCOMB to Miss Aurelia R., daughter of Mr. Jared J. BEACH.

June 1, in Lebanon, by Rev. W. H. PEARNE, Mr. A. H. BRIGGS, of Earlville, and Miss Nancy STOWEL, of Lebanon.

June 3, in Earlville, by the same, A. S. NICHOLS, M.D., of Earlville, and Miss Bethina MC CANN, of Gilbertsville, Otsego Co.

June 4, in Earlville, by the same, Mr. Joseph SQUIRES to Miss Patty IDE, both of Lebanon.

June 17, in this village [Hamilton], by Rev. J. S. MAGINNIS, John HOGAN, Esq., of Hogansburg, to Miss Ann Margaret MASTERS, of Smith's Valley, youngest daughter of the late Hon. Judge MASTERS, of Renssalaer Co.

June 4, in this town [Hamilton], by Rev. H. TREMAIN, Mr. Llias (sic) FINCH, of Black Brook, Clinton Co., to Miss Frances M. CASE, of the former place.

Oct. 24, in Hamilton, by Rev. Prof. A. C. KENDRICK, Mr. Charles E. SHERRILL, of Lebanon, to Miss Achsa M. NILES, of Hamilton.

Oct. 23, in Trinity Church, Utica, by Rev. Dr. PROAL, Franklin L. FAY, Esq., to Miss Hannah, daughter of the late William BLACKWOOD, all of that city.

Oct. 24, in DeRuyter, by Rev. J. W. BURDICK, Mr. A. J. BURLINGAME, of Hamilton, to Miss Harriet F. WITHAM, of DeRuyter.

Sept. 26, in Sherburne, by Rev. Prof. P. B. SPEAR, Mr. Warren A. SKINNER, son of Deacon Isaac SKINNER, of East Hamilton, and Miss Amarintha MILLER, daughter of the last Esquire MILLER, of Sherburne.

DEMOCRATIC REFLECTOR,
Hamilton, NY
Vol. I, No. 2, issue of Nov. 1, 1842

Oct. 26, in Norwich, by Rev. L. HOWARD, Roswell A. RANDALL, formerly of Hamilton, to Miss Lurensa NEWTON, of Norwich.

Nov. 30, in Hamilton, by Rev. L. FLETCHER, Mr. Clark DAWLEY to Miss Harriet WOODMAN, both of Hamilton.

1843

Jan. 1, in Hamilton, by Rev. Mr. DAY, Mr. David A. SHAPLEY to Mrs. Hannah WILLARD, formerly of Portland, ME, but all of Hamilton, now.

Jan. 1, in Hamilton, by Rev. Mr. DAY, Mr. John T. MILLER to Miss Eunice L. STEBBINS.

Feb. 6, in Hamilton, by Prof. G. W. EATON, Mr. Charles D. BLISH, of Watertown, to Miss Amelia A., daughter of Rev. Leonard FLETCHER, of Hamilton.

Feb. 14, in Vernon, by Rev. Mr. BRISBANE, Mr. Miles NORTON, of Chilicothe, Ross Co., OH, to Miss Abbey SHERWOOD, of Vernon.

Apr. 1, in Hamilton, by Rev. J. S. MAGINNIS, Mr. Henry MC CARDY to Miss Margaret PRENTISS.

Apr. 12, in Norwich, by Rev. Mr. HOWARD, Mr. William F. WILLARD, of Hamilton, to Miss Clarissa MILLER, of Norwich.

May 4, in Vernon, by Rev. R. C. BRISBANE, Mr. A. JUDSON and Miss Emily S. NORTON, all of Vernon.

May 28, in Sherburne, by Rev. L. A. BARROWS, Mr. J. Antle WHITE, of Whitestown, to Miss Almira H., only daughter of Asa FOOTE, Esq., of Sherburne.

May 29, by Jedediah WOODWARD, Mr. L. W. CROSS to Miss Sarah Jane WATERHOUSE, both of Hamilton.

June 1, in Lebanon, by Rev. W. H. PEARNE, Mr. A. H. BRIGGS, of Earlville, and Miss Nancy STOWELL, of Lebanon.

June 2, in Earlville, Mr. A. S. NICHOLS, M.D., of Earlville, to Miss Bethia MC CARM, of Gilbertsville.

June 4, in Earlville, Mr. Joseph SQUIRES to Miss Patty IDE, both of Lebanon.

June 17, in Hamilton, by Rev. J. S. MAGINNIS, John HOGAN, Esq., of Hogansburg, to Ann Margaret MASTERS, of Smith's Valley, youngest daughter of the late Hon. Judge MASTERS, of Rens. Co.

July 6, in Fort Plain, by Rev. A. C. BARRY, Mr. Jonathan ORMSBY to Miss Margaret FOX, of Fort Plain.

Aug. 16, in Hamilton, by Rev. J. S. MAGINNIS, Mr. M. H. STANLEY, of Watertown, to Miss Cornelia E. OSGOOD, of Hamilton.

Aug. 21, in Hamilton, by Prof. J. S. MAGINNIS, Mr. J. C. BURROUGHS, of Shelby, NY, to Miss Alvira S. FIELDS, late of New Haven, CT.

Sept. 3, in Earlville, by Rev. Wright, Mr. Warren T. OVERHISER, of Big Flats, Chemung Co., to Miss Mary KING, of Augusta.

DEMOCRATIC REFLECTOR - 1843

Aug. 29, in Eaton, by Rev. H. TREMAIN, Mr. James M. BROWN to Miss Ann M. CHUBBUCK, all of Eaton.
Sept. 25, in Hamilton, by Prof. G. W. EATON, Mr. David PECKHAM, of Madison, to Miss Frances Jane GUTHRIE, of Smyrna.
Sept. 24, in Smyrna, by Rev. William S. COLLINS, Rev. H. L. HAMMOND, of Homer, MI, to Miss Jane MEAD, of Smyrna.
Oct. 12, in Hamilton, by Rev. B. N. LEACH, Mr. O. M. SHELDON to Miss Lydia Ann, eldest daughter of Theodore BURCHARD, all of Hamilton.
Oct. 11, in Hamilton, by Rev. Prof. G. W. EATON, Rev. Seymour W. ADAMS, of Vernon, to Miss Caroline E., daughter of Ichabod GRIGGS, Esq., of this place.
Oct. 19, in Hamilton, by Rev. S. EDSON, Mr. Amos F. CRANDALL, of Smithfield, to Miss Violet A. BURDICK, of Hamilton.
Oct. 24, in Hamilton, by Rev. Prof. A. C. KENDRICK, Mr. Charles E. SHERRILL, of Lebanon, to Miss Achsa M. NILES, of Hamilton.
Oct. 23, in Trinity Church, Utica, by Rev. Dr. PROAL, Franklin L. FAY, Esq. to Miss Hannah, daughter of the late William BLACKWOOD, all of Utica.
Oct. 24, in DeRuyter, by Rev. J. W. BURDICK, Mr. A. J. BURLINGAME, of Hamilton, to Miss Harriet P. WITHAM, of DeRuyter.
Oct. 26, in Sherburne, by Rev. Prof. P. B. SPEAR, Mr. Warren A. SKINNER, son of Deacon Isaac SKINNER, of East Hamilton, to Miss Amarantha MILLER, daughter of the late Esquire Miller of Sherburne.

DEMOCRATIC REFLECTOR
Published Wednesdays
Vol. II, No. 1, issue of Nov. 22, 1843

Nov. 19, in North Bainbridge, by Rev. Mr. HOYT, Mr. Levi SHEPARD Jr., of Hamilton, to Miss Caroline OLENDORF, of North Bainbridge.
Dec. 28, in Westmoreland, by Rev. Mr. KENYON, Mr. Benjamin F. PENDLETON of Vernon to Miss Delia A., eldest daughter of the late Hon. Pomroy JONES.
Dec. 31, in Brookfield, Mr. Solomon CROEL, of Hamilton, to Miss Nancy KENYON, of Brookfield.
Dec. 31, in Brookfield, Mr. Ransford CROEL, of Hamilton, to Miss Diadama COATES, of Brookfield.

1844

Jan. 9, in East Hamilton, by Rev. Z. COOK, Mr. Erastus THROOP to Miss Mary Ann NYE.

Jan. 4, by Rev. Mr. PLATT, Mr. Spencer PECKHAM to Miss Priscilla SIMMONS.

Jan. 2, in Eaton, by Rev. Mr. ADAMS, Mr. Harlow HOPKINS to Miss Sarah Jane TACKABERRY.

Jan. 16, in Hamilton, by Rev. Mr. SCOFIELD, Mr. William W. MORRIS, of Lebanon, to Miss Sarah L. STAFFORD.

Jan. 10, in DeRuyter, by Rev. James BAILEY, Dr. Noah B. FOOTE, of East Hamilton, to Mrs. Betsey AYRE, of DeRuyter.

Feb. 1, in Mt. Upton, by Rev. RANSOM, Justus Smith MASTERS, Esq., of Smith's Valley, to Frances Mary Upton MORRIS, daughter of Richard MORRIS, Esq. of Upton Park, Otsego Co., and granddaugther of the late Gen. MORRIS.

Jan. 31, at Leeville, by Rev. Mr. ADAMS, Mr. Moses STEWART to Miss Elizabeth OMANS.

Feb. 13, in Sherburne, by Rev. Mr. BROWN, Mr. John B. SUMNER to Miss Harriet Ann ROBINSON.

Feb. 6, in Sanford, Broome Co., by Rev. F. LILLY, Mr. Albert R. CRANDALL, of Sherburne, to Miss Sarah E. BEEBE, of Coventry.

At the same time, in the same place, and by the same, Mr. Charles W. SAWDEY, of Hamilton, to Miss Emily R. BENEDICT, of Coventry.

Feb. 14, in Eaton, by Rev. S. SHOTWELL, Rev. J. Wheeler OSBORN, Pastor of the Baptist Church of Scipio, Cayuga Co., to Miss Malintha Sophia SHORT.

Feb. 16, in Eaton, by Rev. C. H. HARVEY, William H. TOMPKINS, of Hamilton, to Miss Hannah SIMMONS, of Eaton.

Feb. 27, by Rev. Mr. ADAMS, Mr. John F. SHERWIN to Miss Mahrion GREEN, of Eaton.

Mar. 13, in Waterville, by Amos O. OSBORN, Esq. Mr. Albert N. SHELDON, of Waterville, to Miss Frances E., daughter of the late John B. LADD, of Hamilton.

Apr. 10, in Eaton, Mr. Syrenus WHITE to Miss Polly BULLUS, both of Eaton.

April 18, in Brookfield, Mr. Dewey DALRYMPLE to Mrs. Susan PALMITER.

June 11, in Homer, by Rev. C. DARBY, of Greene, Mr. E. H. WEAVER, of this village [Hamilton], to Miss Lucy A. SHORT, of Homer.

Sept. 5, in this village [Hamilton], by Rev. B. N. BEACH, Mr. J. Osgood PIERCE to Miss Cornelia M. COBB, daughter of Deacon William COBB.

DEMOCRATIC REFLECTOR - 1844

Sept. 22, in Smyrna, by Rev. D. A. BARROWS, Mr. D. B. LEAVENWORTH, of Albany, to Miss Almira G. STREW, of Smyrna.

Nov. 8, in Bouckville, Mr. William H. MIZE to Miss Sylvia E. HOWARD, all of Bouckville.

May 23, in Fabius, by Rev. J. HARTWELL, Mr. Chauncey STEVENS, of Hamilton, to Miss Eliza S., oldest daughter of John DOUBLEDAY, Esq.

May 28, in Eaton, Dr. B. W. MASON, of Canastota, to Miss Hannah CRAMPHIN, of Eaton.

May 23, in Earlville, by Rev. J. T. WRIGHT, Mr. George G. LOCKWOOD to Miss Elmima O. MERCHANT, both of Cazenovia.

May 30, in Hamilton, by Rev. C. H. HARVEY, Mr. Ira H. FLEMING to Miss Ceriza W. PALMER, both of Morrisville.

May 29, in Paris, by Rev. Isaac SWART, Mr. George F. HAVENS, formerly of Hamilton, to Miss Clarinda J., eldest daughter of Isaac WELTON, Esq., of Paris.

May 30, in Westmoreland, by the same, Mr. R. B. TURNER, of Hamilton, to Miss Catharine A., daughter of Mr. Joseph HAVENS, of Westmoreland.

July 1, in Pitcher, by Rev. I. ADAMS, Mr. Judson SANFORD, of Hamilton, to Miss Harriet L. CHATFIELD, of Pitcher.

Sept. 30, by Rev. L. BOWDISH, Mr. Mason MILLER, of Smithfield, to Miss Harriet SHEPARD, of Hamilton.

DEMOCRATIC REFLECTOR
Beginning Vol. III, No. 1
1844

Dec. 11, in Eaton, by Rev. Washington THATCHER, Mr. Abner W. NASH, of Earlville, to Miss Lucy Ann TORREY, of Poolville.

Dec. 29, in Hamilton, Dr. David MC WHORTER, of Pitcher, to Miss Sarah J. MURDOCK, of Madison, at Baptist Church.

Dec. 31, in Hamilton, by Rev. J. H. CHAMBERLAIN, Mr. Charles B. POST, of Hamilton Literary & Theological Institute, and Miss Mary Ann SIMONS.

DEMOCRATIC REFLECTOR - 1845

1845

Jan. 1, in Hamilton, by Rev. M. S. PLATT, Mr. George WICKWIRE, of Hamilton, to Miss Hannah W. HITCHCOCK, of Madison.

Jan. 2, by Rev. C. P. SHELDON, Rev. J. V. DE WITT, of Tioga, to Miss Louisa C. CHURCH, of Madison.

Jan. 9, in Poolville, by Rev. Mr. EDSON, Mr. William L. TAGGART, of Eaton, to Miss Lydia Florilla POOL, of Poolville.

Jan. 2, in Earlville, Dr. D. RANSOM to Miss Rosina TOWN, all of Earlville.

Jan. 4, in East Hamilton, by H. H. GREEN, Esq., Mr. Austin COLEMAN to Mrs. Lydia C. BRATLEY.

Jan. 8, by Rev. Mr. BOWDISH, Mr. Myron A. BISHOP, of Hamilton, to Miss Sarah L. SMITH, daughter of Samuel SMITH, Esq., of Smyrna.

Jan. 23, in Otselic, by Rev. H. A. REDFIELD, Marcin H. WEDGE, Esq., of Lebanon, to Miss Mary H. RAY, of Otselic.

Feb. 2, in Hamilton, by Rev. C. P. SHELDON, Mr. Seth T. BLAIR, of Madison, and Miss Sarah M. HARRIS, of Hamilton.

Feb. 27, in Hamilton, by Rev. Mr. BOWDISH, Mr. John TUCKER and Miss Lydia KNAPP, all of Hamilton.

Mar. 9, in Brookfield, by Nathan T. BROWN, Esqr., Mr. George W. TAYLOR to Miss Phebe M. SAUNDERS, all of Brookfield.

Mar. 5, in DeRuyter, by Rev. Mr. SMITH, Mr. J. Orlando DIBBLE, of East Hamilton, to Miss Rebecca T. AYERS, of DeRuyter.

Mar. 19, in Sherburne, by Rev. Mr. EDSON, Mr. Stafford GREEN, of Smithfield, to Miss Sabrina MILLER, of Sherburne.

Apr. 6, in East Hamilton, by Brother Benjamin F. GIBBS, of Madison, Mr. Nicanah BROWNELL, of Brookfield, to Miss Caroline Elizabeth, 2d daughter of Col. Sherebiah HUNT, of East Hamilton.

Mar. 19, in Bouckville, by Elder GIFFORD of Madison, Gov. William HEALY, of Otselic, to Eliza Ann SLOCUM, formerly of Earlville.

May 1, in Hamilton, by Rev. Mr. BOWDISH, Mr. Franklin WOODMAN to Miss Jane HAMMOND.

Apr. 26, at Poolville, by Rev. EDSON, Mr. Josiah W. CLARK to Miss Malvina TERWILLIGER, both of Earlville.

Apr. 24, in Rome, by Rev. H. C. VOGELL, Rev. Clesson P. SHELDON, Pastor of the Baptist Church in this vil-

DEMOCRATIC REFLECTOR - 1845

lage [Hamilton], and Miss Charlotte A. COLE, of Rome.

May 10, in Hamilton, by Rev. C. P. SHELDON, Rev. Roswell R. PRENTICE, of Berwick, PA, to Miss Harriet A. CALKINS, of Hamilton.

June 9, in Hamilton, by Rev. Dr. EATON, Hon. Lorenzo SHERWOOD to Caroline, 3d daughter of James B. ELDREDGE, Esq., all of Hamilton.

June 3, at East Hamilton, by Jedediah WOODWARD, Esq., Mr. Jonathan FORCE, of Alkin, IL, to Miss Louisa WAY, of New Hartford.

June 25, in Hamilton, by Rev. Mr. SHELDON, Br. Chester A. STEVENS, of Empire Tent, No. 77, to Miss Jane A. JOHNSON, only daughter of Mr. Timothy JOHNSON, of this place [Hamilton].

July 22, in Vernon, by Rev. Wayne GRIDLEY, of Clinton, Thomas Hart POND, of Rome, to Miss Eleanora G., youngest daughter of Mr. Amariah FENTON, of Vernon.

Aug. 17, in Madison, by Rev. M. S. PLATT, Lodowick Clark YORK, Principal of Brookfield Academy, to Miss Frances Degrass, oldest daughter of Dr. Samuel COLLISTER, of Madison.

Aug. 23, in Hamilton, by Rev. C. P. SHELDON, Mr. William BONNEY, late graduate of Hamilton Literary and Theological Institute, to Miss Irene B., daughter of Eli BUELL, Esq., of Hamilton.

Aug. 18, in Pittsfield, Mr. John Delos DENNISON, of Brookfield, to Miss Abigail R. LOVE, of Pittsfield.

Aug. 19, in Watertown, Mr. R. E. HUNGERFORD to Miss Helen M. OSGOOD.

Sept. 4, in Lebanon, by Rev. Mr. COPELAND Jr., Mr. M. B. WILLIAMS, Esq., of WI, to Miss Mary L. OWEN, of Lebanon.

Sept. 3, in Lenox, by Rev. Lyman WRIGHT, Rev. W. S. MIKELS, of New York City, to Miss Lydia A. ALLEN, of Lenox.

Sept. 3, in Madison, Mr. Solomon COVEY, of Fenner, to Miss Electa BONNEY, of Hamilton.

Sept. 3, in Eaton, by Rev. W. THATCHER, Mr. Alpheus MORSE, to Miss Marietta CRAMPHIN, daugther of the late Thomas CRAMPHIN, Esq., of MD.

Sept. 21, at Pratt's Hollow, by E. MANCHESTER, Esq., Stephen H. PLIMPTON, of Marshall, to Miss Mary ELMORE, of Madison.

Sept. 30, in Hamilton, by Rev. Mr. SHELDON, Mr. Almond HOLCOMB, of Westmoreland, to Mrs. E. H. MERRIFIELD, of this place [Hamilton].

DEMOCRATIC REFLECTOR - 1845

Oct. 1, in Sangerfield, by Rev. J. MURDOCK, Rev. Spencer S. AINSWORTH and Frances A., daughter of Mr. Daniel C. DOUGLAS, of Sangerfield.

Oct. 30, in Hamilton, by Rev. C. P. SHELDON, Mr. Horace M. MOSHER to Miss Susan CURTIS.

Nov. 1, in Hamilton, by Rev. Mr. THATCHER, Mr. Denison HATCH, of Eaton, to Miss Lucy Ann ALLEN, of Hamilton.

Nov. 2, Mr. William B. GARRATT, of Hamilton, to Miss Mary DAVIS, of Butternuts. (see below)

Oct. 20, at Whitewater, WI, by Rev. Mr. KINNEY, DeWitt C. GROVE, of Utica, to Miss Caroline L. PRATT, of Hamilton.

Nov. 3, in Hamilton, by Rev. M. M. TUKE, Brother William B. GARRATT, of Empire Tent No. 77, to Miss Mary Eliza DAVIS, of Butternuts. (see above)

Nov. 9, in Hamilton, Mr. James WICKWIRE to Mrs. Rachel ALDRICH.

Dec. 2, in Pharsalia, by Rev. WARREN, H. C. WILBER to Marcia COLE.

Nov. 9, in Lebanon, by Rev. E. D. REED, Mr. Charles ALLEN and Miss Laura J. HARTSHORN.

Nov. 20, in Eaton, by Rev. W. THATCHER, Mr. Henry H. BAGG to Miss Mary Ann STORRS.

Nov. 13, in Albion, by S. A. DAY, Esq., Mr. Henry BAKER to Miss Betsey Ann UPSTON, all of Albion.

Nov. 20, in Brookfield, by Rev. Mr. BRECKENRIDGE, Mr. Heman HILL to Miss Maria HINKLY, all of Brookfield.

Nov. 26, in Columbus, by Rev. Mr. CRANDALL, Mr. Silas LAMB, of Brookfield, to Miss Rhoda Ann TUTTLE, of Columbus.

Nov. 30, in Brookfield, by the same, Mr. Freeman P. CRANDALL, of Columbus, to Miss Adeline CUTLER, of Brookfield.

Dec. 28, in Hamilton, by Rev. Mr. EDSON, Mr. Mason CUSHMAN, of Chautauqua Co., NY, to Miss L. Melissa BEACH, daughter of E. H. BEACH, Esq., of Hamilton.

Dec. 25, in Fabius, by Rev. Mr. BLAKESLEE, Mr. Alfred HALL and Miss Electa, 6th daughter of Sol. Simon ROBBINS, Esq., all of Fabius.

1846

Jan. 13, in Hamilton, by Rev. Mr. BROOKS, Mr. William WYLIE to Miss Ann HUNTER, both of Westmoreland.

Jan. 14, in Lebanon, by Rev. G. W. EATON, Mr. Beriah W. WYLIE to Miss Julia ALLEN.

Jan. 29, in Oriskany Falls, by Rev. Pinder FIELDS, Mr. Corydon NASH, of Hamilton, to Miss Louisa STOCKING, of Oriskany Falls.

Jan. 29, at New Milford, Orange Co., NY, by Rev. Mr. TINLOW, Asa FOOTE, Jr., Esq., of Sherburne, to Mrs. Almeda A. GALE, of New Milford.

Jan. 29, in Eaton, by Rev. Mr. HARRINGTON, Mr. Elijah JOHNSON, of Sempronius, to Miss Sophia M. POWERS, of Eaton.

Feb. 26, in Brookfield, Mr. Benjamin GORTON and Miss Catherine YORK.

Mar. 4, in Eaton, by Rev. W. THACHER, Mr. I. Addison BARNES to Miss Julia Ann CRAIG.

Mar. 11, in Truxton, by Rev. Mr. HOAG, Mr. A. P. BENSON, of Fabius, to Miss Lydia PATRICK, of Truxton.

Mar. 15, in Hamilton, by Rev. Mr. SHELDON, Mr. W. B. STODDARD to Miss Emily C. SMITH, both of Hamilton.

Mar. 12, in Hamilton, by the same, Mr. Harleigh J. FOSTER to Miss Mary A. COREY, both of Hamilton.

Mar. 9, in Madison, by Rev. SHELDON, Mr. F. B. COATS, of Undadilla Forks, to Miss Caroline D., daughter of Amasa ROWELL, Esq., of Madison.

Mar. 19, in Hamilton, by Prof. MAGINNIS, Mr. Edward RICHMOND to Miss Elizabeth BRAINARD.

Mar. 18, in Morrisville, by Rev. Mr. PARKS, Edward MANCHESTER, Esq., to Miss Lucetta HAUGHTON, both of Eaton.

Mar. 6, in Lebanon, by Joseph A. NORTON, Esq., Mr. John LONT to Miss Elbecca BEACH, both of Lebanon.

Apr. 8, in Hamilton, by Rev. C. P. SHELDON, J. O. PIERCE, Esq. to Miss Chloe WILCOX, both of this place [Hamilton].

Apr. 29, in Hamilton, by Rev. A. L. BROOKS, John WAIT, Esq., of Norwich, to Miss Mary K. FOOTE, of Hamilton.

May 4, in Madison, by Rev. C. P. SHELDON, Mr. Henry H. BABCOCK, of Unadilla Forks, to Miss Catherine G., daughter of Amasa ROWELL, of the former place.

May 6, in Lebanon, by Rev. A. SCOFIELD, Mr. Ira C. OWEN to Miss Jenette P. BUEL, both of Lebanon.

May 13, in Hamilton, by Rev. Asahel L. BROOKS, Mr. Edwin C. BROOKS, of Norwich, to Miss Helen KEYES, of Hamilton.

May 27, in Pratts Hollow, by Rev. E. M. WOOLEY, Mr. Luther M. KENT, of Utica, to Miss Helen M. LEWIS, of the former place.

June 2, in Hamilton, by Rev. N. KENDRICK, D.D., Prof. in Madison University, the Rev. A. JUDSON, D.D., of

DEMOCRATIC REFLECTOR - 1846

Maulmain, Burma, to Miss Emily CHUBBUCK, daughter of Charles CHUBBUCK, of Hamilton.

May 28, in Hamilton, by Rev. Prof. MAGINNIS, Mr. Erastus F. WILLIAMS to Mary RUSSELL, both of Hamilton.

June 2, in Eaton, by Rev. Mr. TUKE, Mr. John STRINGER to Miss Rachel TUKE, both of Eaton.

June 10, in Oriskany, by Rev. B. W. WHITCHER, Mr. James MERRIMAN to Miss Elizabeth Mills GOSS, daughter of James GOSS, all of Oriskany.

June 13, in Quincy City, IL, by Rev. Mr. PARR, Mr. C. H. LILLYBRIDGE to Miss L. M. OSGOOD, both of Oneida County.

June 1, in Cortlandville, by Rev. J. P. SIMMONS, Mr. Francis H., 2d son of Mr. Dan HIBBARD, and Augusta L., 3d daughter of the late Lewis JOY, all of Cortlandville.

July 2, in Lebanon, by Rev. A. L. BROOKS, Mr. Vaulkert LAMPHERE, of Eaton, to Miss Francis M. DURFEE, of Lebanon.

June 29, in Madison, by Alfred MEDBURY, Esq., Mr. Wilson BROWN to Miss Thankful MILLARD, both of Georgetown.

July 5, in Madison, by Rev. M. S. PLATT, Manco Capac DICKINSON to Miss Charlotte HARVEY, all of Binghamton.

Aug. 10, in Hamilton, by Rev. Mr. BROOKS, Mr. Lafayette LEWIS to Miss Elnora, only daughter of Daniel B. SHAPLEY.

Aug. 5, in Augusta, by Rev. O. BARTHOLOMEW, Samuel L. ROSE, Counsellor at Law, to Miss Mary, daughter of Robert J. NORRIS, Esq.

Aug. 21, in Hamilton, by Rev. G. W. EATON, D.D., Mr. Freeman LILLYBRIDGE, of Annsville, late gradute of Madison University, to Miss Mary BRYANT, of Watertown.

Aug. 5, in Guilford, by Rev. T. H. PEARNE, Lyman N. ROOT, of Madison, to Miss Pheba Jane, daughter of Dr. J. GUERNSEY of Guilford.

Aug. 14, in DeRuyter, by A. Scott SLOANE, Esq., Mr. D. L. GLOVER, of Boston, to Miss L. Caroline, daughter of Arza GAGE, Esq., of DeRuyter.

Aug. 30, in Jordan, NY, by Rev. H. J. EDDY, Rev. Thomas G. WRIGHT, Pastor of the Baptist Church in that village, to Miss Julia A. S. GREEN.

Sept. 17, in Hamilton, by Rev. Dr. KENDRICK, Mr. Linus M. PECK, of Cazenovia, to Miss Cordelia C. KENDRICK, of Hamilton.

DEMOCRATIC REFLECTOR - 1846

Sept. 20, by Rev. Perry G. WHITE, of Earlville, Mr. Tabour TOBY of Butternuts, to Miss Betsey THOMPSON, of Hamilton, formerly of Exeter.

Oct. 6, in Smyrna, by Rev. Mr. SOULE, Mr. Edmund L. CALKINS, of Hamilton, to Miss Elizabeth, daughter of Mr. John TOBY, Esq., of Smyrna.

Oct. 7, in Hamilton, by Rev. A. L. BROOKS, Mr. Samuel STEERE, of New Berlin, to Miss Julia Ann SMITH, of Otsego Co.

Oct. 8, in Earlville, by Rev. Perry G. WHITE, Mr. J. D. FRANCIS and Miss Eliza, daughter of Charles G. OTIS, Esq.

Oct. 3, at the home of Mr. ANGELL in Sherburne, by Rev. Perry WHITE, Mr. John ELDRED and Miss Mary FRINK, both of Hamilton.

Oct. 15, in Eaton, by Rev. Marcena STONE, Mr. Guy CARTER, Jr., of Johnstown, WI, to Miss Catherine E. CHILDS, of Eaton.

Oct. 12, in Brookfield, at Henry C. BURDICK's, by Rev. Charles RANDALL, Mr. Perrin BURDICK, of Cassville, to Miss Susan DUTCHER, of Waterville.

Oct. 27, in DeRuyter, by Rev. E. D. TAYLOR, H. WHITTEMORE, a merchant, to Miss Mary Jane CALKINS, of Earlville.

Oct. 29, in Hamilton, by Rev. Mr. BROOKS, Mr. Jacob J. CHAPMAN to Miss Ann Vennette WILBER.

Oct. 27, in Eaton, by Rev. Isaac PARKS, Mr. James HARDER, of Lenox, to Miss Maria HOLBROOK, of Eaton.

1852

Dec. 16, in Herkimer, on Dec. 8th, by Rev. C. S. MEAD, Mr. Thomas L. JAMES, publisher of the *Madison County Journal*, to Miss Emily I. FREEBURN, of Herkimer.

1853

Jan. 17, in Smith's Valley, by Rev. George W. EATON, D.D., Rev. Henry E. RUGGLES, Pastor of the Presbyterian Church in Eaton village, to Miss Julia Ann, youngest daughter of Chanceller BIERCE, Esq., of the former place.

Jan. 14, in East Hamilton, by Rev. Job POTTER, Mr. Newell HYDE to Miss Eliza M. CHESEBRO, all of Brookfield.

Jan. 16, in Nelson, by Rev. G. BRIDGE, Mr. Morah M. JONES, of Eaton, to Miss Maria L. RICHARDSON, of Nelson.

DEMOCRATIC REFLECTOR - 1853

Jan. 26, at C. C. BRAND's, Earlville, by Rev. Perry G. WHITE, Mr. G. F. RISLEY, of Sangerfield, to Miss Evanna GREEN, of North Brookfield.

Feb. 17, at the Boarding Hall in Hamilton, by Rev. P. F. JONES, Mr. Albert M. PETTIS and Miss Sarah A. CRANDALL, both of Earlville.

Feb. 17, at C. C. BRAND's by Rev. P. G. WHITE, Mr. Daniel W. NILES to Miss Abby Eliza BOOTH, both of East Hamilton.

Mar. 9, at North Brookfield, by A. M. COREY, Esq., Mr. Christopher C. MASON to Miss Lydia JOHNSON, all of Brookfield.

Mar. 16, in this village [Hamilton], at St. Thomas' Church, by Rev. S. H. NORTON, Mr. John M. DE LANCEY to Miss Mary Ann, daughter of James K. LARKIN, all of Brookfield.

Mar. 13, at Truxton, Cortland Co., by Rev. E. D. REED, Mr. S. B. BURCHARD Jr., son of Hon. S. B. BURCHARD, of Eaton, to Miss Irene B. DUNHAM, of Truxton.

Mar. 20, in Lebanon, by Rev. Mr. SCHOFIELD, Mr. Hiram SEARS to Miss Mary A. GATES.

Apr. 5, at the Park House, by Rev. S. H. NORTON, Rector of St. Thomas' Church, Mr. Andrew M. CAREY, of Augusta, to Miss Elizabeth A. HOLLINGSWORTH, of Eaton.

Apr. 12, in this town [Hamilton], by Rev. A. PERKINS, Mr. Archibald BALLOU, of Deerfield, Oneida Co., to Miss Catherine HAGGERT, of this town.

Apr. 12, in East Hamilton, by Rev. Job POTTER, Mr. Jonathan MINER, of Brookfield, to Miss Roxey PENDOCK, of Hamilton.

Apr. 12, in Eaton, by Elder PUTNAM, Mr. Christopher E. SMITH of Williamsville, Erie Co., to Miss Marcella E. SMITH, of Eaton.

Apr. 7, in Sherburne, by Rev. Mr. E. TUTTLE, Mr. Frederick BRAINARD to Miss Amanda SIMMONS, of Eaton.

Oct. 11, (1852), Mr. Edwin WATROUS to Miss Betsey HAMMOND, both of Erieville.

May 8, in this village [Hamilton], by Rev. A. SEDGWICK, Mr. John WOODMAN to Mrs. Catherine RUSSELL, all of Hamilton.

May 4, in Clinton, by Rev. Mr. STOCKING, Mr. T. W. CALKING, of Hamilton, to Miss Mary Ann CARR, of Clinton.

May 4, in Nashville, (Brookfield), by Rev. E. BEEBE, Mr. Peleg SAUNDERS to Miss Esther ELLIS, daughter of Palmer ELLIS, Esq., of Nashville.

May 14, in this village [Hamilton], by Rev. A. SEDGWICK, Mr. Orlando GRIGGS to Miss Mary L. GARVER, both of Oriskany.

DEMOCRATIC REFLECTOR - 1853

May 18, at Rome, Oneida Co., Mr. Russell E. COMES, of Morrisville, Madison Co., to Miss Mary LYNCH, of Pratts Hollow.

June 1, in St. James Church, Brooklyn, by Rev. Alvah GUION, B. F. MATTESON, of Earlville, to Miss Matilda HOWARD, of Brooklyn.

June 1, in Norwich, by Rev. Walter JEROME, Mr. George H. WILLIAMS, of this place [Hamilton], to Miss Julia BARBER, of Norwich.

June 2, in Earlville, by Rev. Perry WHITE, Mr. Hiram E. GUSTIN to Miss Maria LYON, both of Sherburne.

May 12, at the residence of Nehemiah MERRITTT, by them-selves, Mr. Alfred C. HILLS and Miss Sarah A. MER-RITT, both of DeRuyter.

May 22, at Hubbard's Corners, by Uri N. RHODES, Esq., Brother Theron NYE to Sister Caroline M. COLSON, both of Hubbardsville Tent, I.O.R.

June 24, in Madison, by Rev. L. C. BATES, Mr. Hylon DOTY, M.D., of Utica, to Miss Louisa LIPPITT, of Madison.

July 19, in Onondaga, by Rev. COMFORT, Rev. Merrill W. RIPLEY, of Hamilton, to Miss Lucemia M. SPENCER, of Onondaga.

July 21, in Lebanon, by Rev. George W. EATON, D.D., Mr. Clinton C. BUELL, Prin. of Hamilton Academy, to Miss Mary A. NILES, daughter of John NILES, Esq., of Lebanon.

Aug. 4, by Rev. A. PERKINS, Mr. Ira WATKINS, of Smithfield, to Mrs. Lydia F. BURDICK, of Canastota.

Aug. 19, in this village [Hamilton], in Baptist Church, by Rev. A. PERKINS, D.D., John H. COLGATE, Esq., of New York, to Miss Frances L. GRIGGS, of Hamilton.

Aug. 16, in Clarksville, by Rev. Eli S. BAILEY, Capt. William BROWN to Miss Julia Ann BAILEY, of Clarkville (sic).

Aug. 22, in this village [Hamilton], by Rev. George W. EATON, D.D., Mr. M. RIDDLEBARGER, late of Madison University, and Miss Sarah A. FINCH, of Hamilton.

July 31, in East Hamilton, by Rev. Job POTTER, Mr. Nathan H. CHESEBRO to Miss Clarissa SAUNDERS, both of North Brookfield.

May 17, in Madison, at residence of Benjamin LOVEJOY, Esq., by Rev. Job POTTER, Mr. Ransom BACON and Miss Frances M. STURTEVANT, both of Madison.

Aug. 31, at Cazenovia, by Rev. A. H. GASTON, H. C. BINGHAM, of Brantford, C. W., to Miss Helen M. PARMELEE, of Cazenovia.

DEMOCRATIC REFLECTOR - 1853

Sept. 2, in East Hamilton, by Rev. Job POTTER, Mr. Martin R. COLSON and Miss Emer S. HUNT, both of East Hamilton.

Sept. 8, in Sherburne, by Rev. Mr. MUMFORD, Mr. W. H. FIRMAN, of Norwich, to Miss Betsy BARNES, of Sherburne.

Sept. 13, in Morrisville, by Rev. M. HARRINGTON, Henry C. THOMPSON to Miss H. Geraldine COOK, both of Morrisville.

Sept. 15, in Lebanon, by Rev. H. W. LEE, Mr. George FLETCHER, of Georgetown, and Louise BAKER, of Lebanon.

Oct. 2, in Hamilton, by Rev. Mr. SEDGWICK, Mr. J. W. CONSIDINE, of Earlville, to Miss Helen PLUMBLY, of Hamilton.

Oct. 6, at the house of D. RICHMOND, in Poolville, by Rev. P. G. WHITE, Mr. Luman GUSTIN, of Hamilton, to Miss Laura Jane JACKSON, of Brookfield.

Oct. 12, in Clockville, by Rev. W. L. PALMER, Mr. Eli S. CASEY (or COREY?) of Utica, to Miss Mary K. WALRATH, of Clockville.

Oct. 13, also in the same place, by Rev. W. L. PALMER, Mr. James B. CHAPIN to Miss Sarah S. REED, both of Nelson.

Oct. 21, in Poolville, by Rev. Perry WHITE, Mr. George BATES, of Brookfield, to Miss Sarah Ann WILBUR, of East Hamilton, formerly of Smyrna.

Oct. 31, in this village [Hamilton], by Rev. PERKINS, D.D., J. H. ABBOTT to Miss Celia P. ATKINS, all of this village.

Nov. 8, in Christ Church, Sackett's Harbor, by Rev. G. HUNTINGTON, Mr. John S. BLISH to Miss Margareta H. HENSHAW.

Nov. 17, at Johnson's Creek, by Rev. G. C. WALKER, Mr. Jonathan MORRIS of Lebanon, and Miss Frances D. CRANE, of Hartland.

Nov. 12, in West Edmeston, by Joshua MAXSON, Esq., Mr. William M. PALMETER and Miss Phoebe C. MAXSON, all of Connville.

Nov. 16, by Rev. A. SEDGWICK, Mr. James IRVING to Miss Elizabeth Ann MC MASTER, both of Hamilton.

Dec. 1, in this village [Hamilton], by Rev. Mr. BRIDGE, Mr. H. T. WILCOX to Miss Helen M. WILCOX, both of this place.

Dec. 1, in this village [Hamilton], by Rev. Mr. PERKINS, Mr. W. H. COULTS, of this place, to Miss Jennie HANLEY, of Waterville.

DEMOCRATIC REFLECTOR - 1853

Nov. 24, in this village [Hamilton], by Rev. E. S. GALLUP, Mr. William STOWELL, of Madison, and Miss Lucina FISHER, of this place.
Nov. 24, in this village [Hamilton], by Rev. G. BRIDGE, Mr. William BELL and Miss Charlotte PARSONS, both of Eaton.
Dec. 18, in this town [Hamilton], by Rev. H. SEDGWICK, Mr. N. P. SQUIRES, of Lebanon, to Miss N. M. PEEBLES, of Hamilton.
Dec. 15, in Tompkins, Delaware Co., NY, by Rev. L. HARTSOUGH, Mr. Charles H. SMITH, of Hamilton, to Miss Louise J. BAUMES, of Tompkins.
Dec. 25, in Church at Clarkville, by Rev. Mr. ROGERS, Mr. Bill SPOONER to Miss Antionett YORK.
Dec. 25, at Leonardsville, by N. T. BROWN, Esq., Mr. Lucien FULFORD to Miss Elizabeth WADDELL.

1854

Jan. 1, at Bensville, by N. T. BROWN, Esq., Mr. George THOMPSON, of Sangerfield, to Miss Mary CLARK, of the former place.
Jan. 3, in Morrisville, by Rev. Mr. TUCKER, Mr. Lewis WICKWIRE, Jr., son of Lewis WICKWIRE, of this place, to Miss Abigail C. SHAPLEY, daughter of Col. H. B. SHAPLEY, of Lebanon.
Jan. 4, at the same place, and by the same, Mr. Samuel DUNTON, of Sherburne, to Miss Rosa MC DONALD, of this place [Hamilton].
Jan. 5, at Sandy Creek, Oswego County, by Rev. Mr. BROWN, Mr. Alexander MC DONALD, of Hamilton, to Miss Helen FULLER, of Sandy Creek.
Jan. 17, in Plymouth, by Rev. Walter JEROME, Mr. Liester SACKETT to Miss Calphurnia GARRETT, all of Plymouth.
Feb. 1, in Poolville, by Rev. Perry WHITE, Mr. John C. TORREY to Miss Clara A. DUNBAR, all of Poolville.
Jan. 29, at the Park House, in Hamilton, by the same, Mr. John S. ROSS to Miss Josephine C. COLSON, of Poolville.
Jan. 30, in Eaton, by Rev. A. L. BRUCE, Mr. N. H. ROWLINSON to Miss Adaliza A. BROWN, of Eaton.
Feb. 7, by Rev. A. PERKINS, Mr. Peter V. KERN to Miss Cornelia EDDY, of this village [Hamilton].
Feb. 7, in Eaton, by Rev. C. BRIDGE, W. E. TOUSLEY, of West Eaton, to Miss Ellen M. TUKE, of Pratts Hollow.

DEMOCRATIC REFLECTOR - 1854

Feb. 9, in the Baptist Church at Hamilton, by Rev. W. G. EATON, Mr. C. S. SQUIRES to Miss Elizabeth J. BENTON, all of this village [Hamilton].

Feb. 9, in Columbus, by Rev. BEEBE, Mr. Melville ALCOTT to Miss Emily WILLCOX, all of Columbus.

Feb. 9, in East Hamilton, by Rev. Perry WHITE, Mr. Calvin M. BILLINGS, to Miss Mary M. BLAIR, both of Lebanon.

Feb. 16, in Deansville, by Rev. ELLIOT, Mr. A. D. MAYDOLE, of Hamilton, to Miss Clara M. FRYER, of Madison.

Feb. 13, in Eaton, by Rev. G. BRIDGE, Mr. James PUTNAM, of Hamilton, and Mrs. Lucy LILLIE, of Eaton.

Feb. 15, by Rev. A. SEDGWICK, Mr. Ephraim S. TUCKER to Miss Eunice HUBBARD, both of Earlville.

[No date], in Methodist Church at Earlville, by Rev. D. A. WHEDON, Mr. Samuel HUNT, of Ava, NY, to Mrs. Nancy E. S. BRIGGS, of Earlville.

Feb. 23, at the Eagle Hotel in this village [Hamilton], by Rev. George BRIDGE, Mr. Hugh GILLESPIE to Miss Lovina TEMPLE, both of Eaton.

Feb. 28, at the same place, by the same, Mr. Levi SHAW, of Eaton, to Miss Lucina WALDEN, of Otsego.

Feb. 27, in Sherburne, in Christ Church, Mr. H. S. WILCOX, of Utica, to Miss Lavina ELSBRE, of Sherburne.

Feb. 24, in Erieville, by Rev. J. S. KIBBE, Mr. Thomas M. RICHARDSON to Miss Maria E. PINKERTON, of Eaton.

Feb. 8, at the Eagle Hotel, in Hamilton, by Rev. A. W. BRUCE, Mr. G. W. ROBIE to Miss Emily BROWN, both of Eaton.

Mar. 6, in Poolville, by Rev. Perry WHITE, Mr. Robert T. GIBSON, of Plymouth, to Miss Ellen L. SMITH, of Smyrna.

Mar. 18, in this village [Hamilton], by Rev. George BRIDGE, Mr. S. T. CHURCH to Mrs. Mary WHITCOMB, both of this village.

Mar. 23, at the home of Cyrus THOMPSON, in Madison, by Rev. D. T. ELLIOTT, Mr. John VICKERY, of Sauquoit, to Miss Emily THOMPSON, of Madison.

Mar. 29, in Pratts Hollow, by Rev. George BRIDGE, Mr. Henry BARNS, of Bouckville, to Miss Sarah A. TOOKE, of Pratts Hollow.

Apr. 5, in Poolville, by Rev. H. W. LEE, Mr. H. F. SKINNER, of Indianapolis, IN, and Miss Orra S. TORREY, of Poolville.

Apr. 12, in Waterville, Mr. William COE, of Madison, and Miss Abigail FISHER, of Hamilton.

Apr. 14, by Rev. A. PERKINS, D.D., Rev. Rodolphus BARD, of Brimfield, OH, to Mrs. Harriet L. SANFORD, of Hamilton.

DEMOCRATIC REFLECTOR - 1854

May 3, in Eaton, by William F. BONNEY, Esq., Mr. Benjamin CRAWFORD to Mrs. Philena TENNANT, both of Eaton.

May 18, in West Eaton, by Rev. G. BRIDGE, Mr. Philo WALDEN to Mrs. Mary Jane WELLINGTON, both of West Eaton.

May 30, at Georgetown, by Rev. SCOFIELD, J. M. GRAY, Esq., of Hamilton, and Harriet A., only daughter of Samuel W. BARNETT, Esq., of Georgetown.

May 23, in this village [Hamilton], by Rev. George BRIDGE, Mr. Henry S. PALMER, of Lebanon, to Miss Susan M. DANFORTH, of West Eaton.

Issue of June 8th: In Brookfield, by Elder J. CLARK, Mr. Abel CONGER to Mrs. Harriet MINER, of Brookfield.

June 27, in Waterville, by Rev. D. T. ELLIOTT, O. F. CALKINS, Esq., of Earlville, and Miss Anna Maria WILLIAMS, of Fremont, OH.

June 13, in Trinity Church, Geneva, by Rev. BISSELL, Mr. Charles Wells HAYES, Rector, St. Thomas' Church, Hamilton, and Miss Frances E. GLADDING, of Geneva.

July 10, at the Eagle Hotel in Hamilton, by Rev. G. BRIDGE, Mr. Lewis MOSES, of Florence, Oneida Co., to Miss Delia MORGAN, of Smithfield, Madison Co.

July 4, at Oriskany Falls, by Rev. Orlo BARTHOLOMEW, Mr. Charles GILBERT to Miss Jenette BRIGGS, of Lebanon.

July 13, in Hamilton, by Rev. George BRIDGE, Mr. Orson BUNO, of Nunda, to Miss Sarah F. BENTLEY of Hamilton.

July 8, in Hamilton, by Prof. George W. EATON, D.D., Mr. Robert P. UPHAM, of LeRoy, Genesee Co., to Miss Rhodie FISHER, of Hamilton.

July 18, at Stanwyx Hotel, Rome, NY, by Rev. George W. EATON, D.D., W. W. CHUBBUCK, Esq., of this village [Hamilton], and Miss Julia Allin TROWBRIDGE, oldest daughter of George TROWBRIDGE, Esq., of Camden, NY.

July 24, in this village [Hamilton], by Prof. G. W. EATON, D.D., Mr. J. D. DENISON, foreman in this office, and Miss Miranda J. ATKINS, both of this village.

July 15, in Albany, by Rev. C. P. POST, Augustus SIMONS, Esq., Steward of Madison University, and Mrs. Emily Maria CROCKER, of this place [Hamilton].

July 31, in Sherburne, by Rev. T. APPLEGATE, Mr. James M. SCARRITT, of Buffalo, to Miss Almeda C. TACKABERRY, of Eaton.

Aug. 16, at York Mills, by Rev. HOLMES, Mr. Samuel R. WILLIAMS, of Morris, IL, to Miss Elizabeth COTTRELL, of Madison.

Aug. 4, in North Adams, MA, by Rev. Miles SANFORD, Mr. W. H. KING, of this village [Hamilton], to Miss Amanda J. CHAPEL, of North Adams.

Sept. 24, in DeRuyter, by Charles H. MAXSON, Esq., Mr. Joseph BAILEY to Miss Mary B. TRIPP, all of DeRuyter.

Sept. 24, in Buffalo, by C. P. SHELDON, Mr. Ansel CHAMBERLAIN to Mrs. Amanda P. STANDISH. Also by same:

Sept. 23, in Hamburg, Erie Co., Mr. Isaac C. TRYON, of Buffalo, to Miss Julia A. CHILCOTT, of Hamburg.

Sept. 30, in Hamilton, Mr. Daniel BUTCHERS, of Madison, to Miss Phebe KELLEY, of Augusta.

Oct. 29, in Earlville, by Rev. Perry WHITE, Mr. M. W. HUBBARD to Miss Betsey C. CROSS, both of Hamilton.

Nov. 8, by Rev. Perry G. WHITE, Mr. Orsemus SAWDY to Miss Deborah S. FULLER, both of Hamilton.

Nov. 9, by the same, Mr. John DOWELL to Miss Mary A. SAWDY, both of Hamilton.

Nov. 16, in Lebanon, by Rev. Perry G. WHITE, Mr. Andrew J. BARNEY to Miss O. Sophia SHERMAN, both of that place.

Nov. 28, at Bergen, Genesee Co., NY, by Rev. A. O. WIGHTMAN, Mr. Ambrose COAN, of this village [Hamilton], to Miss Lovisa W. BURNHAM, of Bergen.

Dec. 20, in Hamilton, by Rev. George BRIDGE, Mr. John L. BOWEN, of Eaton, to Miss Mary E. CRANDALL, of Stockbridge.

Dec. 21, in Sherburne, by Rev. Mr. APPLEGATE, Mr. Martin K. SHAW, of Hamilton, to Miss L. Jane MERRITT, of Leeville.

At the same time, and by the same, Mr. Ezra D. MOTT, of Hamilton, to Miss Louisa MERRITT, of Leeville.

Dec. 24, in DeRuyter, by Charles H. MAXSON, Esq., Mr. Benjamin F. REYNOLDS, of Otselic, to Miss Lucetta SHERMAN, of DeRuyter.

Dec. 31, at the home of C. C. BRAND, Earlville, by Rev. Perry WHITE, Mr. Lester STEVENS and Miss Cordelia MARICLE, both of Lebanon.

Dec. 21, in Syracuse, by Rev. C. E. HEWES, of Cazenovia, Charles T. BROWN, of Eaton, to Alzina HARP, of Oneida.

1855

Jan. 2, at Earlville, by the same, (Rev. Perry WHITE), Mr. Thomas O. STODDARD, of Chenango Forks, and Mrs. Elizabeth A. THOMAS, of Earlville.

On the same day, at the home of C. C. BRAND, Earlville, by the same, Mr. Lyman FOWLER and Miss Harriet W. WHITE, both of Sherburne.

DEMOCRATIC REFLECTOR - 1855

Jan. 9, in Oxford, by Rev. H. CALLAHAN, Mr. Dwight BYINGTON, of Norwich, to Miss Emily Jane EGGLESTON, eldest daughter of Levi EGGLESTON, Esq., of that village.

Jan. 1, in Nelson, by Rev. William CLARK, Mr. Joseph C. MASON, of Wayne, Erie Co., PA, and Miss Fanny H. BOOTH, of Nelson.

Jan. 16, in Hamilton, by Rev. George BRIDGE, Mr. Albert EASTMAN, of Augusta, and Miss Harriet M. COOK, of Augusta.

Jan. 17, in Hamilton, by Rev. A. W. BRUCE, of Poolville, Mr. Harvey CRANE and Miss Roxana CORY, both of this place [Hamilton].

Jan. 17, in Camden, by Rev. O. M. LEGATE, Mr. Cyrus M. MORSE, of Annsville, to Miss Hannah SEYMOUR, of Camden; both deaf mutes.

Jan. 17, in Perryville, by Rev. Charles E. BROWN, Mr. Orson C. FAY, of Fenner, to Miss Mary E. SEARS, of Perryville.

Jan. 30, in Hamilton, by Prof. GALLUP, Mr. Murray HALL, of Preston, and Clarissa T. HAIGHT, of this village [Hamilton].

Jan. 21, in Chittenango, by Rev. James ABEL, Mr. S. James COBB, Editor of the *Chittenango Herald*, to Miss Josephine, daughter of the late Fletcher BARRON, of Danville.

Feb. 15, in DeRuyter, by Charles H. MAXSON, Esq., Mr. Rufus A. BUGBEE, of Tully, to Miss Martha A. JONES, of Apulia.

Feb. 19, in Georgetown, by Rev. W. C. HUBBARD, Mr. Charles CLARK, of WI, and Miss Polly WESTCOTT, of NY.

Feb. 19, in Morrisville, by Rev. Mr. JEWEL, Mr. John BABCOCK, of Hamilton, to Miss Adeline GOODING, of Morrisville.

Feb. 19, in Cortlandville, by Rev. Henry BOWEN, Mr. D. W. KELSEY, formerly of this village [Hamilton], to Miss A. M. WOOD, of Manlius.

Feb. 21, in Sangerfield, by Rev. C. P. SHELDON, Mr. George TYLER, of Hamilton, to Miss Mary A., daughter of Stephen WOOD, of Sangerfield.

Mar. 15, in Madison, by Rev. George BRIDGE, Mr. George B. WOODMAN and Miss Mary SIMMONS, both of Madison.

Mar. 8, at the home of H. A. CAMPBELL, Esq., in Earlville, by Rev. P. G. WHITE, Mr. Otis FOLLETT and Mrs. Mertia HAY, both of Lebanon.

On the same day, and by the same, at the home of Elias FELT, Esq., in Earlville, Mr. Horace THOMPSON, of Fenner, to Mrs. Matilda LOVELAND, of Hamilton.

DEMOCRATIC REFLECTOR - 1855

Mar. 13, in Earlville, by Rev. S. C. AINSWORTH, Mr. DeWitt INGALLS and Mrs. Amarintha SKINNER, both of Earlville.

Mar. 8, in Hamilton, by Rev. C. P. SHELDON, Mr. Solomon WARING, of Annapolis, MD, to Mrs. Harriet M. THURSTON, of Hamilton.

Mar. 18, in North Brookfield, by Rev. Mr. CASSLER, Mr. James BURDICK, of South Brookfield, to Miss Marcelia B. KEITH, of North Brookfield.

Mar. 13, in the town of Madison, by Rev. Mr. PLATT, Mr. Edward B. MORSE, of Hamilton, to Miss Mary A. ARMSTRONG, of Waverly.

Mar. 18, in Madison, by Rev. Dwight WILLIAMS, Mr. Edwin M. COLSON, of East Hamilton, to Miss Caroline SEYMOUR, of Sangerfield.

Apr. 1, at Hubbard's Corners, by U. N. RHODES, Esq., Mr. Benjamin BONNEY, of Georgetown, to Mrs. Nancy BONNEY, of Hamilton.

Apr. 26, in Lebanon, by Rev. George W. BRIDGE, Mr. Joseph CURTIS, Jr., of Hamilton, to Miss Helen OWEN, of Lebanon.

Apr. 25, at Belmont, Allegany Co., NY, by Rev. W. H. RANDALL, James NORTON, Esq. to Miss Elizabeth H. BURNHAM, of Angelica. He is one of the proprietors of the *Morrisville Observer*.

Apr. 26, in Peterboro, by W. B. DOWNER, Mr. Spencer S. BURDICK, to Miss Mary Jane ROWLINGS.

May 14, in Hamilton, by Rev. Mr. WADSWORTH, G. S. ELDREDGE, Esq. to Miss Maria MOSELY, all of Hamilton.

Apr. 3, in Clarkville, by Rev. William H. CARD, Mr. George WHITE to Miss Lucy M. HILLS, all of Clarkville.

Apr. 17, by Rev. CLARK, Mr. Charles CRANDALL and Miss Frances DENNISON, of the above place.

May 21, in Earlville, by Rev. S. C. AINSWORTH, Mr. Lewis E. WHEELER, of Belvidere, IL, and Miss Sarah A. SHEFFIELD, only daughter of Joseph W. SHEFFIELD, of Earlville.

June 25, in Madison, by Rev. D. WILLIAMS, Mr. Henry M. BLOSSOM, of St. Louis, MO, and Miss Sue H. BRIGHAM, of Madison

July 1, in Hamilton, by Rev. George BRIDGE, Mr. Alonzo DUTCHER to Miss Caroline E. SAMPSON, both of Hamilton.

July 9, in Brookfield, by Rev. Mr. PHILLIPS, Mr. Ambrose PHILLIPS, of Plainfield, to Miss Lucy M. BROWN, of Brookville.

July 8, in Peterboro, by Hon. A. C. STONE, Mr. Charles JOHNSON and Miss Jane TITUS, both of Hamilton.

July 28, in Hamilton, by Rev. C. P. SHELDON, Mr. Healy BROWN to Miss Harriet A. SMITH, both of Eaton.

July 31, at Hamilton, by Rev. S. M. CAMPBELL, Rev. J. T. WHITTEMORE, of Ira, Cayuga Co., to Miss Mary A., daughter of Mr. F. W. STILLMAN, of Hamilton.

July 10, at Palmer, MA, Austin BAILEY, of Agawam, to Miss Sophronia WILLIS, of Wilbraham; deaf mutes.

July 19, in Madison, by Rev. Walter JEROME, Rev. Dwight WILLIAMS to Miss Keziah LANE, both of Madison.

Aug. 7, in Newburyport, MA, Wilson WHITON, Esq., Instructor in the American Asylum for the Education of Deaf Mutes at Hartford, to Miss Sybil Smith RICHARDS; both deaf mutes.

[No date], in Dresden, OH, by Rev. A. T. MC MURPHY, Mr. Oscar T. EDWARDS, formerly of Lebanon, to Miss Jemima OSBORN, of Dresden.

Sept. 4, in Hamilton, by Rev. L. HARTSOUGH, Henry BAILEY, Jr., of Otselic, to Miss Angeline E. SPRAGUE, of Plainfield, Otsego Co., NY.

By the same, at the same time and place, William W. SHAW, of Smyrna, to Miss Mary E. SPRAGUE, of Plainfield, Otsego Co., NY.

Sept. 15, in Eaton, by W. F. BONNEY, Esq., Mr. Willis H. CARPENTER and Miss Celesta A. FOX, both of Pompey.

Sept. 10, in Middlebury, VT, by Rev. A. P. WRIGHT, Mr. James C. AUSTIN, of Swanton Falls, VT, and Miss Lucetta WRIGHT, of Middlebury; both deaf mutes.

Sept. 24, in Hamilton, by Rev. C. P. SHELDON, Mr. Matthias LONT, of Delhi, IA, and Mrs. Irene B. JOHNSON, of Hamilton.

Sept. 24, in Mottville, Onondaga Co., by Rev. J. M. AUSTIN, Dr. Amasa LORD, Jr., of this place, to Mrs. Ada Miranda NYE, of Mottville.

Sept. 20, in Hamilton, by Rev. M. S. PLATT, Mr. Cornelius L. DURFEE and Miss Amanda P. SIMMONS.

Sept. 19, in Lyons, by Rev. G. R. RUDD, Mr. O. K. KLINCK, formerly of this village [Hamilton], to Sophia J., daughter of David R. ROZELL, Esq., of Lyons.

Sept. 19, in Clarkville, by Rev. J. CLARK, George W. HOLMAN, of Clarkville, to Miss Barbara M., daughter of Hosea B. CLARK, of Clarkville.

Sept. 9, in Brookfield, by Rev. L. CASSLER, Mr. George SMITH, of Monroe Co., to Miss Sarah STOCOUM, of Brookfield.

Oct. 9, in Bridgewater, by Rev. Mr. THATCHER, Mr. Otis S. CAMPBELL, of Hamilton, and Miss Elizabeth P., daughter of Deacon John THOMPKINS, of Bridgewater.

DEMOCRATIC REFLECTOR - 1855

Aug. 24, in Fabius, by Rev. L. S. LIVERMORE, Mr. Charles Milas GROW, of Rawleigh, NC, to Miss Lucinda E. HILL, of Fabius; deaf mutes.

Oct. 24, by Rev. A. W. BRUCE, in Hamilton, Alexander L. DUNHAM to Esther L., daughter of Willard NASH, Esq., both of Hamilton.

Sept. 15, in Sacramento City, CA, Mr. George I. LYTLE, formerly of Kingston, Ulster Co., and later of South Hartford, Washington Co., NY, and Miss Mary SMITH, Albany.

Oct. 31, in Poolville, by Rev. Perry WHITE, Mr. James J. NICHOLS, of East Hamilton, to Miss Lora C. HOBBS, of Poolville.

INCOMPLETE FILES OF VARIOUS NEWSPAPERS

ALBANY GAZETTE

Issue of Jan. 18, 1829: At Washington, Hon. John H. EATON to Mrs. Margaret TIMBERLAKE, widow of the late J. TIMBERLAKE, U.S. Navy.

DEMOCRATIC UNION
Hamilton

Issue of Sept. 4, 1862: In this village [Hamilton], on the 2d inst., by Rev. M. S. PLATT, Enos CLARK, Esq., of St. Louis, MO, and Miss Mary Annette FOOTE, eldest daughter of Hon. John J. FOOTE, of Hamilton.

1872
Oneida, NY

Mar. 26, in Canastota, by Rev. L. C. ROGERS, Abram KILTS and Addie WELLS, both of Canastota.

Mar. 20, in Madison, by Rev. KEELER, Addison J. CUSHMAN and Frankie ROOT, both of Madison.

Mar. 14, in Cazenovia, by Rev. C. P. SMITH, Franklin DURFEE and Kittie DEAN, all of Cazenovia.

Mar. 1, in Cazenovia, by Rev. John WARD, George F. MARTIN and Nettie E. MARIKLE, both of Cazenovia.

Mar. 14, in Poolville, Harry BIXBY, of Poolville, and Miss Mary SIMMONS, of Hubbardsville.

Feb. 26, in Poolville, by Rev. J. H. MC GOHEN, Mr. Henry LUCAS and Miss Fanny TABOR, both of Cazenovia.

DEMOCRATIC UNION - 1872

Mar. 25, in Lincklaen, by Rev. A. W. COON, Millard DAVIS and Frankie DAVIS, all of Lincklaen.
Mar. 26, in DeRuyter, by Rev. William PIKE, George E. SAVAGE, of Delphi, and Emma GREENMAN, of DeRuyter.

MADISON COUNTY JOURNAL
1851-1852

Aug. 26, 1851, at Bouckville, by Rev. D. T. ELLIOTT, Theron THOMPSON, son of Roswell THOMPSON, of Morrisville, to Miss Cornelia A., second daughter of J. J. EDGARTON, Esq., of Bouckville.
Aug. 21, 1851, at the White House, Bouckville, by Rev. D. T. ELLIOTT, Delos TWIST, of Fenner, to Miss Delia Ann WILBER, of the same place.
July 1, 1852, in East Hamilton, by the Rev. Job POTTER, Mr. Hubbard HART and Miss Elizabeth L. COLLINS.
July 4, 1852, in Sherburne, by Rev. P. G. WHITE, James D. CROWELL, of East Hamilton, and Miss Harriet HOWARD, of Sherburne.

DEMOCRATIC REPUBLICAN
Hamilton
Scattered Issues
1856

Aug. 24, Gilman D. WILLEY, of Croagville, WI, and Hattie A. TORREY, formerly of Hamilton, NY.
Oct. 20, at Lambertville (NJ?), Rev. John C. WARD and Jane S. HADNETT, of Lewis County, NY.
Oct. 3, George N. FOOTE, of Beaver Dam, WI, and Celett T. HARVEY, formerly of Morrisville, NY.
Oct. 21, George P. AVERY and Cornelia R. PRATT, both of Sherburne, NY, at the home of O. B. GILBERT, Lebanon, NY.

1857

April 21, at Peterboro, Eliphalet ALESWORTH, Esq. and Margaret C. KLINCK, both of Peterboro.
Apr. 21, at Sherburne, David S. MILLER, of Sherburne, and Harriet L. HALL, daughter of Col. S. S. HALL, of Earlville.

1858

Sept. 15, George R. MORRISON and Miranda C. GARDNER, both of Cernon, at the home of Nelson GARDNER.
Sept. 22, at Lenox, A. K. KINGSLEY and Mary E. LEWIS.
Oct. 5, at New Berlin, Alvin D. SERGEANT, of Butternuts, and Cordelia E. CORBIN, of New Berlin.
Sept. 22, in East Hamilton, William W. SHELDON and Anna Maria ALDRICH, both of Sherburne.
Sept. 22, in Brookfield, Lewis PERKINS, of Sherburne, and Mrs. Rispy P. BACON, of Brookfield.

1859

July 27, in Lenox, Rev. George R. BUTLER, of Lenox, and Mrs. Lucy BALDWIN, of Lenox.

1862

Feb. 11, in Otselic, Avery FISH, of Otselic, and Lois J. TAYLOR, of Hamilton.
Feb. 11, in Morrisville, Dr. Seymour CURTIS and Rosetta HARVEY.
Mar. 12, in Madison, at the home of the bride's father, Deacon Phillip TOMPKINS, Herman W. TOMPKINS, of Paris Hill, and Cynthia F. TOMPKINS, of Madison.
ITEM: Miss Alida Cornelia AVREY, is mentioned as a recent graduate of New England Female Medical College.
Aug. 14, Myron PERRY, of Prairieville, MN, and Nancy B., oldest daughter of James CAREY, of Smithfield.

1863

Feb. 1, in New London, OH, Thomas FARGHER, M.D., Surgeon, USA, and Sophia JACKSON, recently of Hamilton.
Feb. 3, in Earlville, Levi DELINE, of Alderly, WI, and Cynthia L. EDDY, of Lebanon.
Feb. 3, in Morrisville, Thomas GREEN and Amelia SANDERSON.
Feb. 3, in Smithfield, Judson SMITH and Josephine E. WAKELEE.
[No date], in Hamilton (?), M. V. B. CURTIS, of Madison, and Frances A. MORSE, of Nelson.
Feb. 8, in Georgetown, Dwight E. WHITMORE and Mary SAUNDERS.
Feb. ?, in Lebanon, Albertus J. GUTHRIE and DeEste E. CARD.

DEMOCRATIC REPUBLICAN - 1863

Feb. 12, in Bouckville, Preston C. HOWARD and Almira CARTER.

Feb. 25, at Hamilton, Charles GALE, of Binghamton, and Emma S. LAY, of Hamilton.

Mar. 15, George M. ABBERT, of Hamilton, and Eveline HEAD, of Madison.

Mar. 16, George B. ABBERT and Jane M. RUSSELL, both of Hamilton.

Mar. 19, John BAKER, Sr. and Mary A. MOTT, both of Hamilton.

Apr. 5, at the residence of William M. PLUM, near Poolville, by T. P. HALSTED, Mr. Reuben BACON and Miss Abbie HAMILTON, both of Hamilton.

Mar. 28, at Underhill Cottage on Alderbrook, by Rev. S. N. WESTCOTT, Mr. Silas L. DANFORTH and Miss N. Jennie STEWART, both of Eaton.

May 25, in Eaton, by Rev. M. S. PLATT, Mr. Cyrus P. BUCKLEY, of Marshall, and Miss Lorinda S. HATCH, of Eaton.

May 31, at Cazenovia, by Rev. E. G. ANDREWS, Mr. Lewis L. RICHMOND and Miss Mary E. LASELLE, both of Lebanon.

[No date], at the Baptist Parsonage in Edmeston, by Rev. S. N. WESTCOTT, Mr. George C. KERN and Miss Delia A. TOWNSLEY, both of Pratts Hollow.

June 2, in West Eaton, by Rev. O. TAINTOR, Mr. Charles B. HAUGHTON, of Morrisville, to Miss Amelia B., daughter of Deacon Joseph TAINTOR, of West Eaton.

June 10, at the Congregational Parsonage in Hamilton, by Rev. M. S. PLATT, Mr. Ansel HOWARD and Miss Sarah E. RICHARDS, both of Madison.

June 9, in Eaton, by Rev. M. V. WILSON, Mr. N. H. SHORT of Greene, to Miss Martha A. COLE, of Eaton.

June 1, at the Eaton Baptist Church, by Rev. H. WHEAT, Mr. J. J. BENNETT, of Sherburne, and Miss Eilen J. WHITE, of Eaton.

June 25, at Speigletown, NY, by Rev. A. T. TWING, Mr. C. M. MOTT, of this village [Hamilton], and Miss Belle EDDY, of the former place.

June 24, at the residence of the bride's father, by Rev. H. A. SMITH, O. B. WILCOX, M.D., of Earlville, and Sarah L. BURGESS, eldest daughter of Alfred BURGESS, of Richfield.

July 8, at North Brookfield, by Rev. CHURCH, Mr. O. M. GORTON and Miss Helen M. BURDICK.

July 18, at the residence of the bride's father, by Rev. B. W. SHARTS, Mr. William J. BREWER, of MI, and Miss Mary J. HADCOCK, of Madison.

DEMOCRATIC REPUBLICAN - 1863

Aug. 2, in Madison, by Rev. S. S. WEBBER, Mr. George W. SKINNER and Miss Eliza C. WOODMAN, both of Madison.

Aug. 12, in Hamilton, by W. R. BROOKS, Mr. E. R. MIDDLEBROOK and Miss Emily S. PAYNE.

Aug. 12, in Earlville, by H. A. CAMPBELL, Esq., Mr. William FELT and Miss Phebe A. PHELPS, both of Lebanon.

Aug. 19, at Cazenovia, by Rev. G. S. BOARDMAN, Mr. Ezra T. WILLIAMS and Miss Eliza T. WHIPPLE, daughter of Col. WHIPPLE.

Aug. 20, at St. Thomas' Church in Hamilton, Mr. Richard M. BAKER, of Oneida, and Miss Frank M. RICE, of Hamilton.

Aug. 30, at the M. E. Parsonage in Hamilton, by Rev. T. Jefferson BISSELL, Mr. Isaac S. FORD and Miss Mary A. GUTHRIE, both of Madison.

Sept. 2, at Oriskany Falls, by Rev. C. BARSTOW, Mr. Charles P. DAY, of Lebanon, and Miss Myra A. CLARK, of Otselic.

Sept. 23, at the residence of the bride's father at Eaton, by Rev. T. J. BISSELL, Mr. Jerry WEEDEN, of Madison, and Miss Anna M. LILLIE.

Oct. 6, at the home of the bride's father in Smyrna, by Rev. M. S. PLATT, Mr. John N. HOLMES, of West Eaton, and Miss Althea M. MEAD, of Smyrna.

Sept. 30, in Brookfield, by Rev. E. TODD, Mr. Jackson L. HOWARD and Miss Mary E. RAMSDELL, daughter of Silas RAMSDELL.

Oct. 6, in West Eaton, by Rev. George SMITH, Mr. Isaac C. HOPKINS and Miss Lucinda F. BEDELL, both of West Eaton.

Oct. 13, at the residence of the bride's father, by Rev. Bela PALMER, R. Olmstead NILES and Mary E. KINGSLEY, eldest daughter of A. Z. KINGSLEY, all of Lebanon.

Oct. 14, in Hamilton, by Rev. A. LOUDERBACK, Mr. William C. GARDNER and Miss Libbie C. WHEELER, all of Hamilton.

Oct. 24, in Hamilton, by J. Sterling SMITH, Esq., Mr. Charles A. MAIN, of Brookfield, and Miss Ellen J. ALDRICH, of Sherburne.

Nov. 11, at the residence of George WOODMAN, Esq., Madison, by Rev. T. J. BISSELL, Mr. Samuel C. EMERY, of Westmoreland, Sergeant, Co. A, 117th NY Vol., and Miss Merebah WOODMAN, of Madison.

Nov. 16, at Brookfield, by Rev. J. M. TODD, Mr. Clark BURDICK and Mrs. Lucinda CLARK, all of Brookfield.

Nov. 4, in Hamilton, by Rev. W. R. BROOKS, Mr. Joseph CURTIS, of Fitchville, OH, and Mrs. Laura J. ALLEN, of Hamilton.

DEMOCRATIC REPUBLICAN - 1863

Nov. 12, at the residence of Sherman SAWDEY in Poolville, by Rev. T. P. HALSTEAD, Mr. James R. HASH and Miss Emogene C. SAWDEY, both of Hamilton.

Nov. 25, at the residence of the bride's father, by Rev. M. S. PLATT, Mr. Gerrit S. SIMMONS and Miss Mercell D. RISLEY, both of Madison.

Dec. 3, in Hamilton by Rev. W. R. BROOKS, Mr. Albert BRAMER, of Fabius, and Miss Emma ANDERSON, of Hamilton.

Dec. 9, at the residence of the bride's mother, by Rev. S. D. BURCHARD, Mr. Francis T. PIERCE, of Hamilton, and Miss Louisa BURCHARD, of Hamilton.

Dec. 23, at the residence of the bride's father, by Rev. George FOSTER, Mr. Franklin A. SIMMONS, of Hamilton, to Miss Adda L. MERRITT, only daughter of E. MERRITT, Esq., of Oswego.

Dec. 28, at the residence of Mrs. CAMPBELL in Hamilton, by Rev. J. DONNELLY, Jr., Mr. Giles A. PENNY, of Unadilla Forks, and Miss Phebe L. CLARK, of Brookfield.

Dec. 28, in Madison, by Rev. Mr. FARGO, Mr. Fred L. BASHER, of Augusta, to Miss Julia M. HAMLIN, of Madison.

Dec. 23, at the Parsonage in East Hamilton, by Rev. T. P. HALSTEAD, Mr. George S. JENKS to Miss Martha J. HOWARD, both of Sherburne.

1864

Jan. 11, at the residence of Amos CAMPBELL, Hamilton, by Rev. T. Jefferson BISSELL, Mr. Andrew J. HENDERSON, late of the 176th Reg. NY Vols., and Miss Elizabeth M. SMITH, both of Madison.

Dec. 31, 1863, in Yonkers, by Rev. E. M. HULBERT, Mr. Charles M. HATCH, of Eaton, and Miss Louia M. DE FOREST, of Hartford, CT.

Dec. 30, 1863, in Columbus, by Rev. S. S. CADY, Mr. Calvin S. CARRIER and Miss Maggie BOYD, all of Columbus.

Jan. 18, 1864, at St. Thomas's Church, Hamilton, by Rev. A. LOUDERBACK, Mr. A. A. PIERCE and Miss Lucinda MOTT, daughter of Smith MOTT, all of Hamilton.

Jan. 19, by Rev. H. C. BEEBE, Mr. Adelbert CHEESBRO and Miss Abigail ROWE, both of Brookfield.

Jan. 31, in Hamilton, at the home of the bride's sister, by Rev. M. S. PLATT, Mr. David H. MOORE, of Cincinnatus, and Miss Mary Ann BATEMAN, of Sherburne.

DEMOCRATIC REPUBLICAN - 1864

Feb. 7, in Hamilton, by Rev. M. S. PLATT, Mr. Justus DICKINSON, of Preston, and Miss Addie F. CARR, of Norwich.

Feb. 9, at the residence of Mrs. ABBOTT, in Hamilton, by Rev. T. P. HALSTEAD, Mr. Newel HYDE, of Brookfield, and Mrs. Addie NORTON, of Hamilton.

Feb. 10, at the residence of J. HOLMES, Esq., Poolville, by Rev. T. P. HALSTEAD, Mr. Marcus T. PHILLIPS, of Villanovia, NY to Miss Hattie E. HOLMES, of Hamilton.

Feb. 14, by O. B. LORD, Esq., at his residence, Mr. John W. RUSS, of Poolville, to Miss Annette L. BABCOCK, of Vernon, NY.

Feb. 15, at the residence of the bride's father, by Rev. T. J. BISSELL, Mr. Frank L. CARPENTER, of Michigan City, IN, and Miss Lettie M. BRONSON, of Hamilton.

Feb. 15, at the residence of Amos CAMPBELL, by Rev. T. P. HALSTEAD, Mr. Deloss H. BILLINGS, of Lebanon, and Miss Lorain M. CAMPBELL, of Hamilton.

Feb. 12, at the residence of M. Tyler BROWN, Esq., in Brookfield, by Rev. J. DONNELLY, Jr., Mr. Charles B. GRIFFIN, of Utica, and Miss Ann E. CARPENTER, adopted daughter of N. T. BROWN.

Feb. 15, at the home of the bride's father in Sherburne, by Rev. N. C. MALLORY, Lieut. Edwin R. SLATER, of North Norwich, Co. D, 38th Reg., NY Vol., and Miss Addie E. WATERS.

Feb. 16, in Hamilton, by Rev. M. S. PLATT, Mr. John T. MYERS and Mrs. Mary STONE, both of Madison.

Feb. 18, in Hamilton, by the same, Mr. Martin B. ALBERT and Miss Almira R. TAYLOR, both of Madison.

Feb. 18, in Madison, by the same, Mr. Humphrey HAMMOND, and Miss Sarah E. BRIGGS, both of Madison.

Issue of March 3d: At the M.E. Parsonage, in Hamilton, by Rev. T. J. BISSELL, Mr. Edward F. RYAN and Miss Sarah E. LOWE, both of Madison.

Feb. 23, in Lebanon, by Rev. D. W. SHARTS, Mr. Nelson J. SEATON, of Allegany, and Miss Maria SHARTS, of Lebanon.

Feb. 14, at the Baptist Parsonage, in Norwich, by Rev. A. N. BENEDICT, Mr. Josiah E. FULLER to Miss Mary A. SAUNDERS, both of Hamilton.

Mar. 8, at Lebanon, at the residence of the bride's father, by Rev. B. PALMER, Mr. Herman SNELL, of Stockbridge, to Miss DeEtte O. PARTRIDGE, of Lebanon.

DEMOCRATIC REFLECTOR - 1843

DEMOCRATIC REFLECTOR
Scattered Issues 1843-1854
1843

Jan. 1, at the Presbyterian Church in Hamilton, by Rev. DAY, Mr. David SHAPLEY and Mrs. Hannah WILLARD, formerly of Portland, ME, all of Hamilton.
Jan. 1, in this village [Hamilton], by Rev. DAY, Mr. John T. MILLER and Miss Eunice L. STEBBINS, all of Hamilton.

1848

Feb. 7, 1848, in this village [Hamilton], by T. H. GREENLY, Esq., Mr. Truman HILDRETH, of Fayetteville, to Miss Mary HUBBELL, of Brookfield.
Mar. 14, in Madison, by Elder HARTSHORN, Dr. John HEFFRON, of Erieville, to Miss Ann CURTISS, of Madison.
Mar. 16, by Rev. Perry WHITE, Mr. L. H. MILLER, of Sherburne, to Miss H. Maria DANIELS, of Hamilton.
Aug. 28, in Hamilton, by Rev. Francis D. HIGGINS, Mr. Randall WILCOX to Mrs. C. TERRY, all of Hamilton.
Dec. 28, at Emmuel (Episcopal) Church, Norwich, by Rev. Samuel GOODALE, Mr. Charles W. OLENDORF to Miss Justine PELLET.
Dec. 28, in Truxton, Cortland Co., NY, by Rev. Caleb CLARK, Mr. James SCHEMERHORNE, of Cortland Village to Miss Sarah M. PARKER, of the former place.
Dec. 28, in Earlville, at the house of H. B. HOYT, by Rev. Perry G. WHITE, Mr. Chester WENTWORTH to Miss Sarah M. OWEN, both of Lebanon.

1850

May 14, 1850, in the Episcopal Church at Sherburne, by Rev. Dr. WILSON, Henry N. MARCHISI, of Utica, and Miss Emily, daughter of Elijah B. MERRILL.
Aug. 27, in Hamilton, by Rev. J. POTTER, Mr. Hiram R. ACKLEY to Miss Julia A. COMSTOCK.

1852

July 10, 1852, in this village [Hamilton], by Rev. Dr. EATON, Mr. A. T. ROSE to Miss Mary CAMPBELL.

DEMOCRATIC REFLECTOR - 1852

July 1, by Rev. A. PERKINS, Mr. John BROWN to Miss Cassadan M. HATCH, both of the town of Lebanon.

Aug. 19, at Herkimer, by Rev. C. S. MEAD, Mr. Jacob S. HAYS, Forman in the Madison Co. *Journal* office, and Miss Sarah J., only daughter of Cyrus SHAW, Esq., of the former place.

Aug. 17, in Morrisville, by Rev. Mr. RICHARDS, Otis P. GRANGER, Esq. and Mrs. Elizabeth L. CROSS, all of that place.

1855

Jan. 17, 1855, in Camden, by Rev. O. M. LEGATE, Mr. Cyrus M. MORSE, of Annsville, to Miss Hannah SEYMOUR, of Camden; both deaf-mutes.

Jan. 17, in Perryville, by Rev. Charles E. BROWN, Mr. Orson C. FAY, of Fenner, to Miss Mary E. SEARS, of Perryville.

DEMOCRATIC REPUBLICAN
1864 Complete

Mar. 12, in West Martinsburg, by Rev. R. BARBER, Mr. Charles D. V. CARTER, printer, and Miss Theresa HOPSEGER, both of Lowville.

Mar. 31, in the Methodist Parsonage, in this village [Hamilton], by Rev. T. J. BISSELL, Mr. Hiram A. DUNHAM, of Hamilton, and Miss M. Louise PECKHAM, of Madison.

Apr. 7, in Hamilton, by Rev. M. S. PLATT, Mr. Charles W. PALMER and Miss Sarah P. STILLMAN.

Apr. 13, in Smyrna, by Rev. M. S. PLATT, Mr. Dennison A. KELSEY, of Quincy, IL, and Miss Cornelia A. MEAD, of Smyrna.

Apr. 13, in Smyrna, by Rev. M. S. PLATT, Mr. Nathan MARTINIS, of New Hampton, NJ, and Miss M. Gertrude KELSEY, of Smyrna.

Apr. 2, by O. B. LORD, Esq., Nathan PALMER, of Sherburne, and Kate PUGH, of Augusta.

May 1, by O. B. LORD, Esq., Albertus JENKS and Maria PALMER, both of Sherburne.

Mar. 19, by Elder A. SCOFIELD, Elder L. P. DAY and Miss Betty F. DAY.

June 12, in Lebanon, by M. N. CAMPBELL, Esq., Mr. Lemuel WATTLES and Mrs. Elizabeth WRATTEN.

DEMOCRATIC REPUBLICAN - 1864

June 22, at Hamilton, by Elder A. SCOFIELD, of Lebanon, Mr. Richard SIMON, of Canada, NY, and Miss Ellen M. VAN DEUSEN, of Hamilton.

June 22, in Madison, by Rev. M. S. PLATT, Mr. Melville SNOW, of North Brookfield, and Miss Flora A. RISLEY, of Hamilton.

July 4, at Bridgewater, by A. BROWN, Esq., Mr. Gilbert B. WIRES, of Lebanon, and Miss Louisa CARPENTER, of Eaton.

Sept. 1, at Hamilton, by Rev. M. LAUDERBACK, Mr. Edward B. MOTT, and Miss Lena FAIRCHILD, both of Hamilton.

Sept. 14, in Poolville,, by Rev. T. P. HALSTEAD, Mr. George A. WILLEY, of Crown Point, IN, to Miss Lauraine F. NASH, of Hamilton.

Sept. 27, in Eaton, by Rev. M. S. PLATT, Mr. Loyal TABER and Miss Mary E. SMITH, both of Eaton.

Oct. 11, in Earlville, by Rev. T. P. HALSTEAD, Mr. C. L. COTTON to Miss Louisa L. FELT.

Oct. 9, in Hamilton, by Rev. R. R. PRENTICE, Mr. F. W. CALKINS, of Rockford, IL, and Miss M. Irene PIERCE, of Hamilton.

Oct. 18, in Hamilton, by Rev. W. R. BROOKS, Mr. William ROBERTS, of Hamilton, and Miss Angeline JACKSON, of Milford, WI.

Sept. 27, in Lebanon, by Rev. I. PARKER, Mr. Julius I. BAKER, son of S. BAKER, Esq., to Miss Dexa E. BILLINGS, daughter of Bradley BILLINGS, Esq.

Oct. 16, in Lebanon, in the Baptist Church, by Rev. I. PARKER, Mr. Samuel B. BENEDICT to Miss Julia CADY.

Oct. 1, in Hamilton, by Rev. T. P. HALSTEAD, Mr. Andrew R. LEWIS, of Bay City, MI, to Miss Carrie E. CUSHMAN, of Hamilton.

Sept. 28, at Norwich, by Rev. S. SCOVILLE, Mr. E. Lawrence LEWIS, of Lebanon, to Miss Glicera L. SHERMAN, of Otselic.

1865

Jan. 2, in Hamilton, by Rev. T. P. HALSTED, Mr. Charles D. PLUMBLEY, of Buffalo, to Miss Sarah C. LAY, of Hamilton.

Jan. 5, in Smyrna, by Rev. T. P. HALSTED, Mr. John W. INGALLS, of Groton, to Miss Mary A. WILCOX, of Smyrna.

Jan. 12, in Hamilton, by Rev. P. E. FIELD, Mr. James L. BISHOP to Miss Hannah L. PUTNEY, both of Fenner.

DEMOCRATIC REPUBLICAN - 1865

Jan. 31, by Rev. James PARKE, Mr. Hartley POOLE to Miss Sarah WILLIAMSON, daughter of Thomas WILLIAMSON, of South Hill, Lebanon.

Feb. 8, in Hamilton, by J. Sterling SMITH, Esq., Mr. John ROCKWELL, late of PA, to Miss Lucy PAYSON, of Smyrna.

Feb. 9, in Hamilton, by Rev. W. R. BROOKS, Miles MC COMBER, of Eaton, to Cynthia D. CLARK, of Hubbardsville.

Feb. 8, at Eaton, by Rev. W. E. STANTON, E. W. CARTER, of Greene, to Libbie H. SHORT, of Eaton.

May 28, in Hamilton, by Rev. W. R. BROOKS, M. A. ABBEY, of Preston, C.W., to Mrs. A. M. RUSSELL, of Hamilton.

May 3, in Lincklaen, by Rev. Charles BASTOW, Mr. D. Brainard WHITNEY, of Taylor, Cortland Co., NY, to Miss Frank E. POOLE, of the fomer place.

June 1, by Rev. Samuel MILLER, Mr. George BURDIN to Miss Seleria E. SALISBURY, both of Nelson; marriage in Eaton.

June 17, in Earlville, by Rev. L. V. ISMOND, Mr. J. P. OWENS, of Earlville, to Miss Sophronia M. LEE.

June 29, in Sherburne, by Rev. Mr. WADSWORTH, Mr. John LOVEJOY, of Hamilton, to Miss Mary SWIFT, of Sherburne.

July 1, in Earlville, by Rev. L. V. ISMOND, Mr. Delavan B. WAY, to Miss Mary E. PECKHAM, both of Georgetown.

July 12, in Hamilton, by Rev. T. M. DAWSON, Mr. William V. BRAND to Miss Emily A. HUNT, both of Smyrna.

July 17, in Hamilton, by Rev. W. R. BROOKS, Mr. Wilson A. REYNOLDS, of Lebanon, to Miss Emily E. BENNETT, of Hamilton.

Feb. 1, in Bouckville, by Rev. E. C. BROWN, Mr. Austin M. TIBBITTS, of Ithaca, to Miss Matilda L. GORHAM, of Sherburne.

Aug. 3, in Earlville, by Rev. L. V. ISMOND, Mr. Clinton S. GALPIN, of Falls Church, VA, to Miss Martha A. YOUNG.

Aug. 3, in Poolville, by E. B. LORD, Esq., Mr. Smith HILL, of Sherburne, to Miss Mary WILCOX, of Columbus.

Aug. 13, in Georgetown, by Solander PELLET, Esq., Mr. Jacob ODELL and Miss Mary Ann KINNEY, all of Georgetown.

Aug. 18, in Hamilton, by Rev. T. M. DAWSON, Mr. E. Selden MATHER to Miss Mary KINGSBURY, both of Cazenovia.

Aug. 26, in Hamilton, at the home of Henry POWERS, by Rev. C. E. HEWES, Mr. W. R. HANDY, of Sherburne, to Mrs. Polly PERKINS, of Columbus.

DEMOCRATIC REPUBLICAN - 1865

Sept. 4, in Earlville, at the home of Leonard PIERCE, by Rev. ISMOND, John W. HOUGHTON to Samantha L. ADAMS, all of Earlville.

Sept. 6, in Hamilton, by Rev. W. R. BROOKS, Prof. N. L. ANDREWS, of Madison University, to Miss Cynthia S. BURCHARD.

Sept. 12, in Hamilton, by Rev. W. R. BROOKS, Rev. E. Arthur WOODS, of Little Falls, to Miss Mary BLAIR, only daughter of the late Alexander KENNEDY, Esq., of Edinburgh, Scotland.

Sept. 29, in Whitewater, WI, by Rev. Dr. POPE, Mr. Israel T. BONNEY, of Eaton, and Miss Susan C. HALL, daughter of the Hon. Solomon HALL, of Smyrna.

Oct. 11, in Georgetown, by Rev. J. R. HASCALL, Mr. Palmer NEWTON, of Sherburne, and Miss Sarah H. AVERY, of Georgetown.

Oct. 7, in Pharsalia, by Rev. Lewis LAWTON, Mr. Samuel G. PECKHAM, of Madison, to Miss Helen MC GRAW, of Eaton.

Oct. 31, in Hamilton, by Rev. W. R. BROOKS, Mr. Harry W. JONES, of Ilion, to Miss Isadore COAN, of Hamilton.

Dec. 12, in Hamilton, by Rev. W. A. SMITH, Mr. William STERNBERG and Miss Viola DIABEL, both of Georgetown.

Dec. 16, in Hamilton, by Rev. W. A. SMITH, Nathan J. ALLEN and Emma V. FERREL, both of Georgetown.

Dec. 26, in Hamilton, by Rev. W. A. SMITH, Mr. Delancey W. JENKS, of Plymouth, and Helen STEINBERG, of Smyrna.

Dec. 14, in Lebanon, by Rev. L. V. ISMOND, Benjamin R. JENKS, of Cazenovia, to Miss Polly MARVIN, of Nelson.

Dec. 25, in Earlville, by the same, Elisha W. STEBBINS, of Smyrna, and Cordelia RINGLEKA, of Otselic.

Dec. 27, by George BALCOM, an evangelist, in East Hamilton, Major Willard KEECH and Miss Francelia E. ACKLEY.

Dec. 7, in Hamilton, by Rev. William GRANNIS, Mr. E. L. MOSELEY, of Fairport, to Miss Addie A. BEACH, of Hamilton.

Dec. 31, in Earlville, by Rev. L. V. ISMOND, Mr. Abram BLIVEN, of Brookfield, to Miss Nancy M. HOLMES, of South Hamilton.

Dec. 19, in Chicago, by Rev. CUMMINGS, Mr. N. J. FAIRCHILD, of St. Louis, MO, to Miss Carrie H. HARRIS, of Hamilton.

Dec. 26, at Oriskany Falls, by Rev. A. M. LAKE, Mr. Bradford HESS, of Hamilton, to Miss Kate JOHNSON, of Oriskany Falls.

DEMOCRATIC REPUBLICAN - 1866

1866

Jan. 3, in this village [Hamilton], by Rev. W. H. BROOKS, Lieut. Hiram D. GATES of St. Paul, MN, to Lydia G. ROGERS.

Jan. 9, in Madison, by Rev. W. A. SMITH, Mr. H. S. LILLIE, of Pine Woods, to Miss Lucy B. TOMPKINS, daughter of Sidney TOMPKINS.

Jan. 23, in Hamilton, at the residence of Henry POWERS, by Rev. W. A. SMITH, Mr. L. E. BEEBE and Miss Mary J. JOHNSON, both of Brookfield.

Jan. 30, at the residence of the bride's father, by Rev. W. R. BROOKS, Mr. Oscar J. MOSELY to Miss Amrylis T. ROGERS, all of Hamilton.

Feb. 5, in Georgetown, by Solander PETTIT, Esq., Mr. STEVENS to Mrs. Aliza M. ALLEN, both of Solon.

Feb. 14, at Hamilton, by Rev. W. A. SMITH, Frederick YOUNGLOVE, of Lebanon, to Lucy GREY, of Smyrna.

Feb. 22, at Hamilton, by Rev. W. A. SMITH, Albert C. BALLOU, of WI, to Celia M. PUTNEY, of North Norwich.

[No date], in Earlville, Mr. Jacob G. REESE to Miss Orcelia MILLER, of Earlville.

[No date], in Lebanon, by Rev. E. PERKINS, Capt. Charles J. JOHNSON, late of the 148th Reg't., to Miss Abbie D. GREY, of Lebanon.

Mar. 28, in Hamilton, by Rev. Dr. ARNOLD, Edward VAN FRADENBURGH to Miss Sarah J. EDDY, all of Hamilton.

Apr. 9, in Earlville, by Rev. William H. COBB, Rev. L. V. ISMOND to Miss Annie E. NASH.

Apr. 10, in Hamilton, by Rev. W. R. BROOKS, Rev. John A. EDGREEN, of Stockholm, Sweden, to Miss Anna CHAPMAN, of Hamilton.

***Dec. 25, 1865, in Smyrna, by Rev. J. H. NASON, Mr. Henry H. GROVES, of Eaton, to Miss Sarah A. HYDE, of Smyrna.

May 2, in Madison, by Rev. T. COOPER, Mr. Benjamin F. CASE, of Hamilton, and Miss Annie B. WOODMAN.

Apr. 26, in Hamilton, by Rev. W. R. BROOKS, Mr. George MENZA, of Canastota, to Mrs. Esther BEACH, of Hamilton.

May 3, in Newark, NJ, Mr. David G. OATMAN, of Angola, Erie Co., NY, to Miss Aletta J. ARNESON, of Newark, NJ.

May 28, in Hamilton, by Rev. W. R. BROOKS, Mr. Thomas STRADLING, of Madison, to Miss Ellen THOMPSON, of Halifax, England.

June 12, in Hamilton, by Rev. C. E. HEWES, John A. MC DANIELS, of Vinton, IA, to Florence A. HEWES, eldest daughter of the officiating clergyman.

DEMOCRATIC REPUBLICAN - 1866

June 13, in Hamilton, by Rev. T. COOPER, Mr. William SHIRLEY to Miss Mittie L. LA MUNION, both of Stockbridge.

June 16, in Hamilton, by Rev. COOPER, Nathan M. COON, of Solsville, to Mary D. BLUNT, of Oriskany Falls.

May 22, in Vineland, NJ, by Rev. M. S. PLATT, Mr. William HOXIE, of Lincoln, DE, to Miss Maria DEMMON, of Vineland.

June 7, at Sing Sing, NY, by Rev. Dr. GEER, Rev. W. H. DeLancey GRANNIS, Rector of St. Thomas' Church, Hamilton, to Harriet GREEN, of Sing Sing, daughter of Dr. Horace GREEN.

June 12, in Earlville, by Rev. D. A. WHEDON, of Newport, RI, Albert N. TURNER, of Utica, to Delia A. PARSONS, of Earlville.

June 10, at Westmoreland, by Rev. E. M. DUNHAM, Edwin H. RISLEY, of Hamilton, to Miss Hattie A. METCALF, of Westmoreland.

July 18, in Cazenovia, by Rev. J. D. CHILDS, Mr. J. P. RHODES, of Hamilton, to Miss Sarah A. WAKELEY, of Cazenovia.

Aug. 2, in Hamilton, by Rev. Lyman WRIGHT, Rev. A. Edward REYNOLDS, Pastor of the Baptist Church in East Jaffrey, NH, to Miss Franc M. BANCROFT, of Hamilton.

Aug. 7, in Sherburne, by Rev. J. PEDDIE, of Watertown, Mr. A. E. LEWIS, of Hamilton to Miss M. S. POTTER, of Sherburne.

Aug. 20, in Georgetown, by Rev. Mr. BROOKS, George W. HARRIS, M.D. and Miss Viola GREEN, of Lebanon.

Sept. 18, in Hamilton, by Rev. W. H. D. GRANNIS, Mr. Charles E. THORNE, of St. Louis, MO, and Miss Ella M. MASON, daughter of Hon. Charles MASON, of Hamilton.

Sept. 19, in Georgetown, by Rev. J. R. HASKINS, Mr. Milton D. ALLEN to Miss Mary MOSELEY, daughter of Z. J. MOSELEY, all of Georgetown.

Sept. 13, in Zumbrota, MN, a the residence of C. Page BONNEY, by Rev. A. B. DE GROAT, Mr. William R. DORMAN, of Zumbrota, to Miss Christiana FULKERSON, of Hamilton.

Sept. 27, in Morrisville, by Rev. S. S. UTTER, Mr. A. A. RICHARDSON to Miss Nettie ISBELL, of West Eaton.

Oct. 4, in Madison, by Rev. S. S. WEBBER, Mr. J. W. BUNCE, of Hartford, CT, to Miss Louisa CLARK, formerly of Madison.

Oct. 9, in Hamilton, by Rev. P. T. HUGHSTON, Mr. Orville HALL to Miss Helen GILBERT, both of Hamilton.

DEMOCRATIC REPUBLICAN - 1866

Oct. 17, in Hamilton, by Rev. P. T. HUGHSTON, Mr. Allen VANDERPOOL, of Yates, to Miss Cynthia M. BOOTH, of Hamilton.

Oct. 22, in Hamilton, by Rev. W. A. SMITH, Mr. John J. COLEY, of Syracuse, to Miss Eva E., daughter of William FAIRCHILD, of Hamilton.

Oct. 30, in Hamilton, by Rev. W. A. SMITH, Robert WRIGHT, of Vienna, Fairfax Co., VA, to Miss Mary MANCHESTER, of Hamilton.

Oct. 22, by Rev. L. V. ISMOND, in Earlville, Mr. A. Alymer LA SELLE, of North Plain, MI, to Mrs. Roxana PECKHAM, of Earlville.

Nov. 1, at the residence of H. P. RANGER, by Rev. Theron COOPER, Mr. C. Erastus WHITMORE to Miss L. Maryette RANGER, all of Hamilton.

Oct. 14, in Hamilton, by T. Jefferson BISSELL, Mr. Ira R. HILL, of Hubbardsville, and Mrs. Maria H. HITCHCOCK, of Waterville.

Nov. 7, at the residence of the bride's father, Deacon William RICHARDSON, by Rev. O. TAINTOR, of West Eaton, Mr. Herbert WILLIAMSON to Mrs. Loretta CHASE, both of Nelson.

Oct. 22, in Smyrna, by Rev. Mr. COCHRANE, Mr. Charles BORDWELL, of Cazenovia, to Miss Nettie E. GEER, of Smyrna.

Nov. 10, in Hamilton, by Rev. Theron COOPER, Mr. Corriden E. NASH, of Smyrna, to Miss Sarah HEWES, of Madison.

Nov. 13, in Hamilton, by Rev. COOPER, Mr. Orlando A. WEDGE to Miss Sarah A. SHARP, both of Georgetown. He was in the Civil War and drew a pension.

Nov. 6, in Syracuse, at the residence of Mrs. HERRICK, by Rev. Samuel J. MAY, Frederick W. TERHUNE and Miss Edith M. SEYMOUR, all of Syracuse.

Nov. 10, in Hamilton, by Rev. COOPER, Mr. Coryden E. CASH, of Smyrna, to Miss Sarah E. HUGHES, of Madison.

Nov. 21, in Madison, by Rev. D. WILLIAMS, of Clinton, Mr. Joseph H. SANFORD to Miss Meroa C. BRIGGS, both of Madison.

Nov. 20, in Utica, by Rev. D. G. COREY, Mr. James BALL, of Hamilton, and Miss Eliza ROWLAND, of Madison.

Dec. 1, at the Methodist Parsonage, by Rev. T. COOPER, Mr. Irving W. DEITZ, of Sherburne, to Miss Mary A. COLLINS, of West Eaton.

Dec. 4, at the residence of John MORGAN, of Lebanon, by Rev. H. W. JONES, Mr. Samuel D. COSMER, of Fredericktown, OH, to Miss Libbie E. HARTSHORN, of Lebanon.

DEMOCRATIC REPUBLICAN - 1866

Dec. 18, in Earlville, by Rev. Thomas P. TYLER, D.D., Rector of St. Thomas' Church, Hamilton, Mr. J. LeRoy NASH, of Hamilton, and Miss Louisa HECOX, daughter of Mr. Jacob HECOX, of Sherburne.

Dec. 11, in Hamilton, by Rev. D. W. SKINNER, Mr. Sereno WILLEY to Miss Hattie STANTON, both of Poolville.

Dec. 25, in Madison, by Rev. W. R. BROOKS, Mr. Edwin B. SHERRILL, of Hamilton, and Miss Florence A. RICHMOND.

Dec. 25, in San Francisco, CA, by Rev. Dr. SCUDDER, Harvey S. HUNTINGTON, Esq., to Miss Eusebia N. CAMPBELL, daughter of H. A. CAMPBELL, Esq., of Earlville.

1867

Jan. 1, in Hamilton, by Rev. L. V. ISMOND, Mr. Hiram S. WARNER, of Pitcher, to Miss Emma A. THOMPSON, of Otselic.

Jan. 9, in Hamilton, at the residence of D. W. INGALLS, by Rev. W. BROOKS, Mr. Judson L. FOLLETT, of Sioux City, IA, to Miss Viola WICKWIRE, of Hamilton.

Jan. 3, at Lebanon, by Rev. H. W. JONES, Mr. J. Eugene WEDGE, of Hamilton, to Miss Evaleen M. GROSVENOR, of Lebanon.

Jan. 15, in Earlville, by the same, Mr. Caleb S. PAGE to Miss Katie POTTER, both of Earlville.

Feb. 2, in Madison, by Rev. Theron COOPER, Mr. Thomas STAPLETON to Miss Mary M. SKINNER, both of Madison.

Jan. 31, in East Hamilton, by Rev. W. R. BROOKS, Mr. Wolcott HUBBARD, of Hamilton, to Miss Mary WILBUR.

Feb. 6, in Earlville, by Rev. ISMOND, Mr. Norman W. TORREY to Miss Helen BROOKS, both of Earlville, at the residence of N. W. BROOKS.

Feb. 7, at Knoxboro, by Rev. W. KNOX, Mr. E. D. MANCHESTER to Miss Fannie WHITNEY, of Knoxboro.

[No date], in Otselic, by Rev. R. O. BEEBE, Mr. William C. UTTER, of Georgetown, to Miss Lettie I. CARD, of Otselic.

Feb. 26, in Hamilton, by Rev. BROOKS, Mr. William FULKERSON to Miss Rebecca RANSOM, of Hamilton.

Feb. 25, in Georgetown, by Rev. W. M. MOREY, Mr. Elnathan ELLIS, of Georgetown, to Mrs. Diana EVANS, of Norwich.

Mar. 2, in Poolville, at the residence of Mr. BROWN, by Rev. ISMOND, Mr. George M. BURDICK to Miss Clara L. SNOW, both of Norwich.

DEMOCRATIC REPUBLICAN - 1867

Mar. 6, in Earlville, by Rev. L. V. ISMOND, Mr. George E. ANDREWS, of Eaton, to Miss Sarah M. EGGLESTON, of Attica.

Feb. 24, in Sherburne, by Rev. E. CURTIS, Mr. George H. BRADLEY, of Eaton, to Miss Lydia C. BRAINARD, of Poolville.

Mar. 14, in Georgetown, by Rev. James H. SAGE, Mr. Spencer B. SHAPLEY, of Lebanon, to Miss Dora C. STEWART.

Mar. 6, in Georgetown, at the residence of H. HILL, by Rev. Mr. BROOKS, Mr. Reuben MORTON, of Herkimer Co., to Miss Mary WHEELER, of Otselic.

Mar. 6, in Georgetown, by Rev. BROOKS, Mr. George H. HUNT, of DeRuyter, to Miss Dorleska TUTTLE, of Georgetown.

Mar. 26, in West Eaton, by Rev. O. TAINTOR, Mr. Spencer HARRIS to Miss Olive C. BEEBE, both of Erieville.

Apr. 7, in Hamilton, Mr. Eli POND to Mrs. ORMSBY.

Mar. 30, in West Eaton, by Rev. G. W. MITCHELL, Mr. Virmilye GRIFFIN to Miss Lucy A. GAGE, both of Pierceville.

Apr. 17, in Webster, Monroe Co., NY, by Rev. J. C. HITCHCOCK, Mr. Charles W. WARNER, of Lebanon, to Miss Cordelia A. SUTTON, of Webster.

May 7, in Hamilton, by Rev. Mr. GRANNIS, Mr. N. Wilson PARKER to Miss Genevieve H. WHEELER, daughter of the late Erastus WHEELER, both of Hamilton.

From *NY Tribune*: Apr. 24, by Rev. Dr. Thomas S. HASTINGS, J. Crocker FOOTE, of Hamilton, to Helen GARVIN, daughter of the Hon. Samuel B. GARVIN, of this city.

May 9, in Hamilton, by Rev. R. R. PRENTICE, Mr. Edgar M. BARNES, of Versailles, KY, to Miss Jennie A. PRENTICE, of Hamilton.

May 16, in Erieville, at the residence of J. G. NORTON, by A. MEDBURY, Esq., Mr. Davis NORTON, of Nelson, and Mrs. Mary STILES, of Georgetown.

June 5, at the residence of John KERN, of Hamilton, by Rev. A. G. FARGO, William H. JOHNSON and Mary Jane MARSHALL, both of Georgetown.

Mar. 12, in Otselic, by Rev. BROOKS, Mr. George BROWN to Miss Mary E. BACON, all of Otselic.

Mar. 16, at Deansville, by Methodist Minister, Mr. Leander BUTTERFIELD to Miss Harriet BABCOCK, both of Madison.

[No date], in Earlville, at the home of James WENTWORTH, by Rev. ISMOND, Mr. Adelbert C. BURLINGAME to Miss Hattie LAPHAM, both of Clinton.

Mar. 19, in Madison, by Rev. E. S. DAVIS, Mr. Elisha J. BLINN, of Eaton, to Miss Nettie A., daughter of George C. CLARK, of Hubbardsville.

DEMOCRATIC REPUBLICAN - 1867

Mar. 21, at Bouckville, by Rev. A. P. FARGO, Waulstean P. WARD, of Madison, to Lottie A. COOK, of Bouckville.

Feb. 28, in South Otselic, by J. H. STANBRO, Esq., Mr. A. B. GARDNER to Miss Adelia A. CARPENTER, both of DeRuyter.

Apr. 4, in Hamilton, by Rev. W. A. SMITH, W. H. KINNEY to Emma M. SUMNER, both of Munnsville.

June 4, in Georgetown, at the Baptist Church, by Rev. Mr. CRAIN, Mr. George CARVER, of Boston, MA, to Miss Maryella WHITMORE, of Georgetown.

June 8, in Hamilton, by Rev. Mr. SMITH, Mr. A. L. SLAWSON, of Detroit, MI, and Miss Hattie WALDRON, of Hamilton.

June 26, in Morrisville, by Rev. H. DUDLEY, Mr. Wilbur HOLMES, of Cincinnatus, Cortland Co., NY, to Miss Annette DUTTON, daughter of N. F. DUTTON, Esq.

June 19, in Hamilton, by Rev. E. B. HULBERT, of Manchester, VT, Mr. O. W. COLE, of Carmel, to Miss Nellie A. WALKER.

June 26, in Earlville, by Rev. SHELDON, of Troy, NY, Mr. William J. RUSSELL, of New York, to Miss Francella M. FELT, of Hamilton.

June 11, in Hamilton, by Rev. E. S. GALLUP, Mr. Philip WEEDEN, of Madison, to Mrs. Abigail J. COE, of Hamilton.

June 26, in Lebanon, by Rev. H. A. MARSHALL, Mr. Addison B. BAKER, of East Sumner, IL, to Miss Julie E. HEAD, of Lebanon.

June 26, in Rochester, by Rev. E. P. BRIGHAM, of Penn Yan, Mr. A. A. HOPKINS, of Hamilton, to Miss Adell R. ALLEN, daughter of Lewis ALLYN [sic], of Rochester.

July 9, in the Baptist Church in North Brookfield, by Rev. S. N. WESTCOTT, Mr. H. D. SCOTT to Miss L. M. MASON, both of North Brookfield.

Aug. 8, in Hamilton, by Rev. W. R. BROOKS, Mr. E. J. WARRINER to Miss Fannie THOMPSON, of Hamilton.

Aug. 8, in Madison, by Rev. W. S. DAVIS, Mr. W. H. HAIGHT, of Cleveland, OH, to Marian E. LIVERMORE.

Aug. 27, by Rev. W. A. SMITH, Mr. Henry H. HILL and Miss Emma P. LAY, both of Hamilton.

Sept. 4, by Rev. Theron COOPER, Mr. David SWIFT, of Emporium, PA, to Miss Celia G. HUNT, of Hamilton.

Sept. 11, by the same, Mr. Adoniram J. TUCKER to Alvira B. THOMPSON, both of Hamilton.

Aug. 22, in West Eaton, by Rev. O. TAYNTOR, Mr. Everett BLISS, of Georgetown, to Miss Rosall RAYLOR, of West Eaton.

DEMOCRATIC REPUBLICAN - 1867

Sept. 20, in North Otselic, by G. S. MASON, Esq., Mr. Ira HOLMES, of DeRuyter, to Mrs. Jane E. PEVIE, of Georgetown.

Sept. 25, in Eaton, by Rev. E. D. REED, Mr. Henry M. LOOMIS, to Miss Mary A. WILLIAMSON, both of Lebanon.

Oct. 1, by Rev. Theron COOPER, Mr. Edward W. PRICE and Miss Cornelia BAKER, both of Lebanon.

Oct. 1, by Rev. D. K. BERTLETT, of Plymouth, Major George G. WANZER, of Rochester, and Miss Frances T. Lewis, daughter of Dr. W. B. BROWN, of Palmyra (sic).

Oct. 3, in Eaton, by Rev. Samuel MILLER, Mr. H. E. EATON, of Fayetteville, to Miss C. Olivia, daughter of A. N. WOOD, Esq., of Eaton.

Oct. 3, in Eaton, by Rev. Samuel MILLER, Mr. Sylvester GILMAN, of Oriskany Falls, to Julia A. DANFORTH, of Eaton.

***From the issue of Oct. 31, a column, perhaps containing marriage or death notices, had been cut out.

Nov. 5, in Sherburne, by Rev. M. BENNETT, Mr. Edward FAULKNER, of Brookfield, and Miss Sarah E. CARPENTER, of Sherburne.

Nov. 5, in Canastota, by Rev. A. M. LAKE, Mr. William MACK, of Georgetown, to Miss Frankie SOULE, of Lebanon.

Nov. 19, in Madison Village, by Rev. D. W. SKINNER, Mr. Henry PEBBLES, of Oriskany Falls, to Miss Fedora M. CURTIS, of Madison.

Nov. 21, in Monroe Center, OH, by Rev. W. H. HOVEY, Mr. Arnold CRANSTON to Miss Phebe SKINNER, both of Hamilton.

Nov. 14, in Nelson, by Rev. C. S. GRAIN, Mr. Thomas RIGGAL, of Georgetown, to Miss Adella PATTERSON.

Nov. 28, in Rochester, by Rev. Dr. CAMPBELL, J. S. PIERCE, Esq., of Hamilton, to Miss Nellie E., only daughter of William HANNA, of Rochester.

Dec. 3, in Manchester, OH, by Rev. W. NORTHRUP, Mr. J. D. EDDY, of Delaware, OH, to Miss Hattie LONT, of Hamilton.

Dec. 24, at the residence of the bride's father in Madison, by Dr. TAYLOR, of St. Thomas' Church, Mr. Newton E. WICKWIRE, of Hamilton, and Miss Phebe A. PECKHAM, of Madison.

Dec. 24, at the residence of the bride's father, L. B. FOSTER, of Hamilton, by Rev. W. A. SMITH, Mr. Frank BENEDICT and Miss Adella FOSTER, of Hamilton.

Dec. 18, in Scheneateles (Skaneatles), by Rev. Mr. BOWEN, Mr. Henry A. STEWART and Miss Sarah A. NYE, both of Hamilton.

DEMOCRATIC REPUBLICAN - 1867

Dec. 26, in Hamilton, by Rev. W. A. SMITH, Hamilton RHODES, of Oneida, to Nellie OGDEN, of Munnsville.

Dec. 31, in Hamilton, by Rev. W. A. SMITH, Mr. Nicholas HARP to Miss Lucy SKELLENGER, all of Hamilton.

Dec. 31, in Lebanon, by Rev. W. E. BROOKS, William H. JONES, of Boonville, Oneida Co., NY, to Ida A. CAMPBELL.

Dec. 26, in St. Joseph, MO, Dr. Dewitt HUMPHREY, of Delhi, NY, to Miss Flora A. LASELL, of Lebanon.

1868

Jan. 7, in Earlville, by H. A. CAMPBELL, William WOODREDGE to Miss Jane Jenette ELWELL, both of Plymouth, Chenango Co.

Jan. 1, in Lebanon, by Rev. James H. SAGE, Mr. Charles BOWEN, of Willet, to Miss Amelia CHAPIN.

Jan. 1, in Georgetown, by Rev. Mr. CRAIN, Mr. Ira TRUMAN, of Otselic, to Miss Julia BROWN, of Lebanon.

Jan. 22, in town of Hamilton, by Rev. P. T. HUGHSTON, Mr. Elmer J. PARTRIDGE, of Hamilton, to Miss Mary PIERCE, of Madison.

Jan. 28, in town of Eaton, by Rev. S. N. WESTCOTT, Mr. Smith D. MARSH, of North Brookfield, to Miss Tacy A. MOORE, of Morrisville.

Mar. 11, in Sangerfield, by Rev. L. W. NICHOLS, James W. TURNER, of Pawling, NY, to Mary Ellen NICHOLS, daughter of the officiating clergyman.

Mar. 10, in Georgetown, by Rev. Mr. BROOKS, Mr. Allen FERGUSON to Mrs. Jenett CHAPHE, of Georgetown.

In issue of April 9, 1869: By the Hon. J. W. LIPPITT, Mr. Alonzo CURTIS and Miss Louisa SPENCER, the widow of Noah SPENCER, who died in the army. (She thus forfeits receipt of her husband's pension.)

Mar. 31, at Solsville, Mr. Aaron BLISS and Miss Alseba PHILLIPS, by Rev. Mr. MARSHALL,; Mr. BLISS was a good Union Soldier.

Apr. 6, in Lebanon, by Rev. H. S. REDFIELD, Mr. Orson BUNO to MIss Ellen R. MELROY, of Lebanon.

May 20, in Lebanon, by Rev. J. W. BARR, Mr. Corydon B. NASH, of Hamilton, to Mrs. Mary E. WARNER, of Phoenix, Otsego Co.

June 11, by Rev. R. YALE, in Madison, L. Walker CURTIS to Miss Annie M. VAN DUSEN, of Fishkill, Dutchess Co., NY.

DEMOCRATIC REPUBLICAN - 1868

June 16, at St. Thomas' Church, Hamilton, by Rev. Dr. TAYLOR, William H. HARWOOD, of Utica, and Inez S. BILLINGS, of Bennington, VT.

June 24, in North Brookfield, by Rev. S. N. WESTCOTT, Mr. David JENKS, of Sherburne, to Miss Fannie CUTLER, of Columbus.

June 24, by Rev. S. N. WESTCOTT, Mr. Emory MORGAN to Miss Alice, eldest daughter of William TALCOTT, all of North Brookfield.

July 9, in Newark, OH, by Rev. J. W. WHITE, Mr. Edward B. GASKILL, of this village [Hamilton], to Miss Elizabeth R., daughter of Rev. P. H. O'BANNON, of Newark.

July 14, at the residence of E. AYLESWORTH in Peterboro, by Rev. William BRIDGE, Dr. E. W. LOVELAND, of Wampsville, to Miss Emma J. RICE, daughter of Carlton RICE, Esq., of Hamilton.

Sept. 29, at the residence of the bride's father in this village [Hamilton], by Rev. W. R. BROOKS, Mr. I. Irving BURN, of Washington, DC, to Miss Mary C. RUSSELL, of Hamilton.

Sept. 30, at the Baptist Church in this village [Hamilton], by Rev. Dr. ARNOLD, Mr. H. R. TRAVER, of Waterford, to Miss Mary E. RHODES, of Hamilton.

Oct. 8, in Hamilton, by Rev. W. H. BROOKS, John Y. BONNEY to Miss Mattie A. HILL, all of Hamilton.

[No date], in Newburyport, MA, by Rev. P. Randolph CAMPBELL, Mr. Waldo B. SMITH to Miss Eliza LOWE, both of Newburyport.

Oct. 9, in Hamilton, by Rev. A. L. YORK, Mr. G. W. BARBER, of Hamilton, to Miss Emma SMITH, of Madison, NY.

Oct. 21, in Hamilton, by Rev. C. BARSTOW, Mr. Burdett J. SIMONS to Miss Deette CADY, both of New Berlin.

Oct. 21, in Hamilton, by Rev. Dr. TYLER, at Mr. DEWEY's, Mr. George WILLIAMS, of Buffalo, to Miss Charlotte PEARL, of Hamilton.

***From the issue of Oct. 29th, a piece of a column had been cut.

Nov. 5, in Earlville, by Rev. A. C. SMITH, Charles S. NECOMBER, of Eaton, to Minnie HART, of Sherburne.

Nov. 4, in Brookfield, by Rev. D. MOORE, Mr. Frederick J. OBERG to Miss Anna Louise, daughter of the late George P. WILLARD, of Hamilton.

Nov. 24, in Plymouth, NY, at the residence of the bride's father, by S. S. ANTHONY, Esq., Byron J. ORMSBY, M.D. to Mary L. ANTHONY, all of Plymouth.

Issue of Dec. 24, 1868: In Morrisville, at the residence of S. S. DUNTON, Esq., by Rev. H. F. DUDLEY, Mr.

DEMOCRATIC REPUBLICAN - 1868

Charles E. FRY to Miss Maggie MC DONALD, all of Morrisville. [No date given.]

Dec. 22, at Solsville, by Rev. MARSHALL, Mr. Alexander COULTIS, of Hamilton, to Miss Jane, youngest daughter of Oliver BUTTERFIELD, Esq.

Dec. 25, at Greene, Chenango Co., by Rev. HAMMOND, Luther D. CROWELL, of Lebanon, to Miss Cynthia M. TUTTLE, of Greene.

1869

Jan. 26, at Hamilton, by Rev. A. L. YORK, Mr. O. C. WICKWIRE, of Sioux City, IA, to Miss Frances K. CUSHMAN, of Hamilton.

Jan. 27, in Hamilton, by Rev. Dr. HARVEY, Mr. Brooks CHAPIN to Mrs. Sarah M. MOSELEY, all of Hamilton.

Jan. 13, in Hamilton, at the residence of the bride's grandfather, Ethan BEACH, Esq., by Rev. MARSHALL, Mr. Carlton D. GREEN(E) to Miss Flora M. WELLS, both of Hamilton.

Jan. 14, in Sherburne, by Rev. S. MILLER, Mr. J. D. PRESTON to Miss Theresa PALMER, both of Hamilton.

Feb. 9, at the residence of the bride's father in Madison, by Rev. BURNS, Mr. J. LOWDEN, of Brooklyn, NY, to Miss Hellen WHEELER, youngest dauther of H. C. WHEELER, Esq.

Feb. 3, at the Parsonage of St. Thomas' Church, Hamilton, by Rev. Dr. TYLER, Frederick DUNBAR to Mary EDBERT, both of this town.

Feb. 4, in Cooperstown, by Rev. MC HARG, Jay M. FELT, of Grand Rapids, MI, to Miss Hattie HALL, of Cooperstown.

Mar. 8, by Rev. Dr. TYLER, Rector of St. Thomas' Church, George W. RICE, of Lebanon, to DeEtte MAXON, of Smith's Valley.

Apr. 20, in Morrisville, by Mr. F. G. RICE, of Hamilton, --- and Miss Lois MOORE, of Morrisville.

Apr. 11, in Earlville, by the same, Mr. A. C. RICHARDSON to Miss Lou BUTTON, both of Poolville.

May 14, at the residence of A. SIMONS in this village [Hamilton], by Prof. E. S. GALLUP, Joseph TAYNTOR, of West Eaton, to Miss Minerva POST, of Jersey City, NJ.

June 1, at the residence of the bride's father in Cazenovia, by Rev. A. L. YORK, Mr. J. E. WELTON, of the firm of Welton & Bonney, of Hamilton, to Miss Mary A. JONES.

DEMOCRATIC REPUBLICAN - 1869

June 1, in this village [Hamilton] at the residence of the bride's father, by Hon. Charles MASON, Mr. I. D. CHAPIN, of Oneida, to Miss Hattie MASON, of Hamilton.

June 11, in Waterville, by Rev. W. CLARK, Mr. Francis M. SANDERS, of Norwich, to Miss Ellen A. HUBBARD, of Poolville.

May 1 (sic), in South New Berlin, George BICE, of Sherburne, to Mrs. Lydia WRENCH, of New Berlin.

May 25, in Sherburne, by Rev. J. L. BURROWS, Mr. Frederick S. GAYLORD to Miss Harriet E. UPHAM.

June 16, at the residence of George WILBUR in Marysville, OH, by Rev. BRADLEY, Mr. Samuel MARSH, of OH, to Miss Abbie PIERCE, of Madison.

July 10, in Fenner, by Rev. E. M. BARBER, Mr. Benjamin BATEMAN and Mrs. Mary J. ELDRED, both of Hamilton.

July 19, in Hamilton, at the Park House, by G. HYDE, Esq., Mr. John WHALEN and Miss Mary JOHNSON.

July 5, in St. Thomas' Church, by Rev. Dr. TYLER, Rev. Jebez SNASHALL, A.B., of Evansville, WI, and Miss Julia H. SHAPLEY, of this village.

June 22, at East Springfield, by Rev. S. P. GRAY, of Weedsport, NY, H. P. MILLER, M.D., of Eaton, to Miss Celia GRAY, of East Springfield, Otsego Co., NY.

Aug. 4, in this village [Hamilton], by Rev. W. S. TITUS, James B. JOHNSON to Miss Catherine FOLTS, both of Frankfort, NY.

Aug. 8, in Earlville, by Rev. D. D. BROWN, Lamott COLE, of North Brookfield, to DeEtte PALMER, of East Hamilton.

Aug. 12, at Lake Superior, by Dr. D. A. RANDALL, Mr. John W. SPEAR and Miss Sarah RAMPTON, all of Marquette. Mr. SPEAR is a son of Dr. SPEAR, and a former resident of Hamilton.

Sept. 15, in Hamilton, at the residence of the bride's father, by Rev. C. BARSTOW, Mr. Charles F. HULL, of New York, to Miss Martha BOYD, daughter of William BOYD, Esq. of Hamilton.

Sept. 23, at the parsonage of the M.E. Church in this village [Hamiton], by Rev. W. S. TITUS, Isaac H. RINGGE, of Norwich, to Miss Kittie NIEDOCK, of Oxford.

[No date], in issue of Sept. 30, 1869: At the residence of the bride's father in town of Madison, by Rev. W. S. TITUS, Rev. Nelson SUTTON, A.B., of the class of '69, Madison University, now of Reading, East Genesee Conference, M.E. Church, to Miss Frances A. SIMONS, youngest daughter of Zarah SIMONS, Esq.

DEMOCRATIC REPUBLICAN - 1869

Sept. 23, at the Park House, by Rev. Charles BARSTOW, Mr. Clark A. MACK and Miriam C. SEELEY, both of Marathon, NY.

Sept. 22, in Hamilton, at the residence of the bride's father, Daniel READ, Esq., by Rev. W. R. BROOKS, Mr. Luther O. KENDALL, of Alton, IL, to Miss Louisa M. READ, of Hamilton.

Oct. 12, in Otselic, by Rev. E. D. REED, Mr. Walter BRIGGS to Miss E. Vanella BOWEN.

Oct. 12, in Truxton, by the same, Mr. Henry M. BILLINGS to Miss Pamela GEWYE.

Oct. 2, by Rev. J. D. PEASLEY, in Waterville, Mr. W. M. HART, of Hubbardsville, to Miss Almeda HOUSE, of Brookfield.

Oct. 27, in St. Thomas' Church in this village [Hamilton], by Rev. Dr. TYLER, Mr. George F. FOOTE and Miss Genny BAKER.

Nov. 12, in Utica, by T. D. COOK, Mr. H. S. THOMPSON to Miss Helen A. DUNHAM, both of Hamilton.

Nov. 6, in Madison, at the residence of the bride's father, by Rev. W. S. TITUS, Mr. David BANNARD, of Waterville, to Miss Anna E. FISHER, of Madison.

Nov. 24, in the M.E. Parsonage at Hamilton, by Rev. W. S. TITUS, Mr. Stephen COON to Miss Fannie A. PALMITER, both of Brookfield.

Dec. 8, at the residence of Elijah THOMPSON, near this village [Hamilton], by Rev. W. S. TITUS, Mr. Allen E. ENOS to Miss Mary E. THOMPSON, both of Hamilton.

Dec. 15, in Hamilton, at the residence of Mrs. E. NICHOLS, by Rev. C. BARSTOW, Mr. William COBB, of Schoolcraft, MI, to Miss Louisa M. NICHOLS, of Hamilton.

Dec. 25, in Solsville, at the residence of the bride's father, by Rev. Hiram GEE, Mr. Adelbert BRIDGE to Miss Elizabeth KERSHAW, daughter of Marsden KERSHAW.

Dec. 28, in Hamilton, at the residence of the bride's father, by Rev. W. R. BROOKS, Mr. Samuel BROWNELL, of Madison, to Miss Nettie A. HARRIMAN, of Hamilton.

Dec. 29, in Eaton, by Rev. M. L. BENNETT, at the residence of the bride's father, Mr. J. A. ALLEN to Miss Adella STORES, both of Eaton.

Dec. 30, in South Hamilton, at the residence of the bride's mother, by Rev. J. O. GIFFORD, Mr. George SHERMAN to Miss Elvina KIMBALL, all of Hamilton.

1870

Jan. 1, at the bride's residence in this city, by Rev. W. R. CHAMBERLIN, Mr. S. Brownie HEWES and Miss Mary C. PALMER, both of Vinton. [Vinton, Iowa, *Eagle*]

Jan. 12, in Gloversville, by Rev. J. L. CLARK, Mr. Charles GODFREY, formerly of this village [Hamilton], to Miss Emma LAMB, of Gloversville.

[No date], at Sangerfield Center, by Rev. J. D. PEASLEY, Mr. Alburtus SAWDEY, of Poolville, to Miss A. M. SEELEY, of Sangerfield.

Mar. 26, in Utica, at the American Hotel, by Rev. H. A. SMITH, of Hamilton, Mr. Riley J. VEDDER and Miss Harriet E. DAGGETT, both of Oneida.

Mar. 21, by Rev. S. S. UTTER, in Morrisville at the Exchange Hotel, Mr. George PULVER, of Oswego, to Miss Lucena C. WELCH, of Hamilton.

Apr. 7, in Hamilton, by Rev. W. S. TITUS, Truman J. ELLINGWOOD, of Richwood, OH, to Miss Mary J. WILCOX, of Hamilton.

May 8, at the residence of the bride's father, at Solsville, Mr. Charles LEWIS, of Knoxville, to Miss Janet RUNDELL, youngest daughter of Abel RUNDELL.

June 1, at the residence of Zelotus ACKLEY, Esq., in Hamilton, by Rev. W. R. BROOKS, Mr. Lauriston B. GREEN to the bereaved widow of Eustice L. PARKS. "May her second husband prove to be as worthy and upright as her first. Peace and prosperity be theirs."

June 16, in Hamilton, by Rev. C. BARSTOWN, Mr. Heman HOTCHKIN, of Pekin, NY, to Mrs. Emeline J. WARNER, of Hamilton.

June 16, in Eaton, at the residence of the bride's father, by Rev. W. S. TITUS, Mr. Henry J. MAYNARD to Miss Susan R. JOHNSON, both of Eaton.

June 22, at the residence of the bride's father in Hamilton, by Rev. W. R. BROOKS, Rev. C. C. SMITH, of Cooperstown, NY, to Miss Alcesta LEWIS.

Aug. 10, at the Country Seat of the bride's father in Hamilton, NY, by Rev. Charles BARSTOW, Theodore F. W. TAYLOR to Helen T., daughter of Adon SMITH, Esq., all of New York City.

Aug. 9, at Dr. P. B. SPEAR's, Homer H. KEITH, Esq., and Miss Mary SPEAR, all of Hamilton.

Aug. 17, at the residence of the bride's mother, by Rev. W. R. BROOKS, Mr. Eugene P. SISSON, Prin. of the Union School, to Miss Mary A. WICKWIRE, of Hamilton.

DEMOCRATIC REPUBLICAN - 1870

[No date], at the Roman Catholic Church in this village [Hamilton], by Rev. A. P. LUDDEN, Mr. John BROWN to Miss Anna MC QUADE, both of Hamilton.

[No date], at the residence of the bride's father, by Rev. William H. PENDLETON, of New York, assisted by Rev. E. T. HISCOX, D.D., of Brooklyn, Rev. J. V. OSTERHOUT, of Webster, MA, to Miss Annie E. BEMAN, only daughter of R. BEMAN, Esq., of Brooklyn.

Oct. 15, in Hamilton, by Rev. W. S. TITUS, Mr. Ira PIERCE, of Canadea, Alleghany Co., NY, to Miss Rachel Maria PIERCE, of Eaton, Madison Co.

[No date], at the residence of William M. HARTSHORN, Delaware, IA, by Rev. A. PRESCOTT, Mr. K. W. KINGSLEY, of Delaware, and Miss Delight BEEBE, of Hamilton.

Oct. 23, at the residence of Frank STREVER, in Newark, NJ, by Rev. Dr. FISK, Mr. Homer B. WEDGE, of Plymouth, CT (Co?), to Martha M. WARNER, of Hamilton.

Nov. 7, at the residence of Mr. A. P. KERN, of Madison, NY, by Rev. W. S. TITUS, William BYRD to Miss Elizabeth COOK, of Madison.

Nov. 10, at the residence of the bride's father, Charles GREEN, of Hubbardsville, by Rev. James O. GIFFORD, Mr. I. Duane BRAINARD to Miss Geneva GREEN, both of Hamilton.

Nov. 16, in Hamilton, by Rev. W. S. TITUS, Mr. Menzo BRAINARD of Madison to Mrs. Jennie BURNAP.

Nov. 10, in Hamilton, at the residence of the bride's father, by Rev. W. R. BROOKS, Mr. Eaton CHRISTMAN, of Virgil, NY, to Miss Helen F. HOLDREDGE, of Hamilton.

Nov. 15, at the Roman Catholic Church, by Rev. A. P. LUDDEN, Mr. James HOPKINS to Miss Bridget LYON, both of Hamilton.

Nov. 10, at the residence of the Hon. William Pitt DEWEY, Lancaster, WI, by Rev. W. S. EATON, Mr. William W. EASTMAN, of Bloomington, IL, to Miss Frances A. DEWEY, of Lancaster, WI.

Dec. 13, in Brookfield, by Rev. R. R. PRENTICE, Mr. Adelbert E. CROWELL and Miss Deette WILLIAMS, both of Brookfield.

1871

Jan. 13, in Jackson City, MI, by Rev. O. B. TAYLOR, of Salipa, MI, Mr. O. B. TAYLOR, Jr., of Dansville, MI,

DEMOCRATIC REPUBLICAN - 1871

to Miss Sarah A. KEYES, of Norwich, Chenango Co., NY.
Jan. 10, in this village [Hamilton], by Samuel SCOVILLE, Peter TOUSSAINT and Jane Elizabeth COSTELLO, both of Norwich. (From *Chenango Telegraph*, Norwich, NY)
Jan. 19, in Lebanon, at the residence of the bride's parents, by Rev. E. G. REED, Mr. Eugene A. PERRY, of Georgetown, and Miss Achsah NILES, of Lebanon.
Feb. 4, in Earlville, at the residence of the bride's father, by Rev. R. A. WARNER, Nelson ADAMS to Smanatha ALLEN.
Feb. 7, at the parsonage in Deansboro, by Rev. A. C. SMITH, Mr. A. E. STONE to Miss Mary A. BABCOCK, both of Lebanon.
Feb. 9, at the same place, Mr. D. BRIGGS to Miss Nettie E. WILBUR, of Lebanon.
Feb. 14, in Smithfield, by Rev. Mr. TOWNSEND, Mr. William CHAFEE and Miss Ella ARMOUR, both of Smithfield.
Feb. 8, In Eaton, by Rev. Mr. DAVIS, Mr. F. R. ALLEN and Miss Ada MOSELEY, both of Eaton.
Mar. 9, at the residence of F. H. INGALLS in Hamilton, by Rev. W. R. BROOKS, Joshua D. BLISS, of Groton, Tompkins Co., NY, to Miss Mary E. STEVENSON, of Hamilton.
Apr. 19, in Eaton, by Rev. Judson DAVIS, Mr. F. L. BRIGGS to Miss Kate A. BOOTH, all of Eaton.
May 10, in Hamilton, by Rev. Dr. EATON, Mr. Asa J. WILCOX to Miss Phebe LAMPHERE, of Hamilton.
May 11, in Hamilton, by Rev. I. D. PEASLEE, John WOODMAN to R. Myra BYER, all of Hamilton.
May 31, In Waterville, by Rev. Mr. ADAMS, Mr. Thomas WILLIAMS, of Hamilton, to Miss Liza EGBERT, of Sangerfield.
June 14, by Rev. P. B. SPEAR, Mr. Frank SPEAR, of Marquette, MI, to Miss Sarah S. KENYON, of Pittsburgh, PA. Frank's many friends, since he left his home in Hamilton, and the University, rejoice to hear of his prosperity and this happy event of his marriage.
June 21, in Fenner, by Rev. Mr. TAYNTOR, Mr. William BAILEY, of California, to Miss Theresa COVEY, daughter of S. H. COVEY, of Fenner.
June 22, at West Eaton, at the residence of the bride's father, by Rev. Judson DAVIS, Mr. Leroy WOOD, of Killington, CT, to Miss Bell E. TAYNTOR, of West Eaton.
June 28, in East Hamilton, by Rev. Dr. BROOKS, Capt. Charles W. UNDERHILL, of Hamilton, to Miss Mary E., daughter of Dr. F. W. ROOT, of East Hamilton.

DEMOCRATIC REPUBLICAN - 1871

July 3, in Sherburne, by Rev. Mr. HALLSTEAD, Mr. John HILL, of Madison, to Miss Amanda J. ODELL, of Hamilton.

June 29, in this village, at the residence of the father, Mr. L. B. FOSTER, by Rev. Charles BARSTOW, Mr. William KELLOWAY to Miss Hattie M. FOSTER.

July 1, in Brookfield, at the residence of the bride's father, DeWitt C. COON, by Rev. J. M. TODD, Mr. Harvey A. BABCOCK to Miss Eulie COON, both of Brookfield.

Aug. 3, at the residence of the bride's parents, in Hamilton, by Rev. W. R. BROOKS, Prof. James M. TAYLOR, of Madison University, and Miss Mary PADDOCK.

May 20 (sic), in Earlville, by Rev. Mr. STOW, of Cleveland, OH, Mr. G. H. PERKINS, of Madison to Miss Fannie P. COVEY, of Hamilton.

Sept. 5, at the residence of the bride's father, Gurdon HYDE, in Hamilton, by Rev. Mr. PAYNE, Rector of St. Thomas' Church, Rev. William M. LAWRENCE, of Amsterdam, NY, to Miss Belle E. HYDE, of Hamilton.

Sept. 8, in Hamilton, by Rev. I. D. PEASLEE, Mr. Irvin J. PRESTON, of Oneida, to Miss Nettie E. CROMMIE, of Unadilla Forks.

Sept. 19, in Sangerfield, at the residence of the bride's father, by Rev. A. M. PRENTICE, Mr. R. Y. HIBBARD to Miss Adella F. SPENCER, of Sangerfield.

Oct. 2, at the residence of the bride's mother in Earlville, by Prof. H. HARVEY, D.D., Mr. Irvin I. HARRIS, of Sherburne, and Miss Millie R. BERKIN, of Earlville.

Oct. 4, in Eaton, by Rev. Judson DAVIS, Mr. James CARVER to Miss Sarah C. WENTWORTH, both of Bridgewater, MA.

[No date], in Eaton, by Rev. Judson DAVIS, Mr. Heamon PERDY, of Oswego, to Miss Ella A. WILCOX, of Eaton.

Aug. 31, in Illion, by Rev. Judson DAVIS, Mr. Corey JOHNSON to Miss Nettie AUSTON, both of Ilion.

Sept. 10, in West Eaton, by Rev. Judson DAVIS, Mr. F. J. WHITE, of Georgetown, to Mrs. F. M. RUSSELL, of Eaton.

Sept. 20, in Eaton, by Rev. Judson DAVIS, Mr. Adelbert MOSELEY to Miss Kate LYNDON, both of Eaton.

Sept. 27, in Hamilton, by Rev. I. D. PEASLEE, Mr. Thomas NEWMAN to Miss Jerusha HEAD, both of Madison.

Oct. 11, at the residence of H. D. BONNEY in this village [Hamilton], by Rev. I. D. PEASLEE, Jr., J. E. SHEPARDSON and Miss Jennie E. NICHOLS, both of Hamilton.

DEMOCRATIC REPUBLICAN - 1871

Oct. 31, in Eaton, at the residence of the bride's father, by Rev. W. R. BROOKS, Mr. William H. ALBERT, of Hamilton, to Miss Emma J. LAMPHERE, of Eaton.

Oct. 25, at the residence of the bride's parents near Suffern, NY, by Rev. George A. MAGIE, Mr. George R. CONY, of ME, and Miss Margaretta, daughter of C. W. CHRISTIE.

Oct. 26, in West Eaton, by Rev. Judson DAVIS, Mr. Lywellyn H. LEWIS to Miss Sarah G. GREEN, both of West Eaton.

Nov. 8, by Prof. H. HARVEY at South Hamilton, Mr. Ralph E. THOMPSON, of South Otselic, to Miss Ella C. REYNOLDS, of South Hamilton.

Nov. 15, in Earlville, by Rev. Dr. HARVEY, Mr. John BARSTOW, of Lebanon, to Miss Deette WATERS, of Earlville.

Nov. 14, at the residence of the bride's father at Jersey City Heights, by Rev. L. L. NOBLE, Rector of the Holy Trinity Church, Capt. Judson L. POWERS, formerly of Hamilton, to Eva A., only daughter of Ex-Mayor B. F. SAWYER, of Jersey City.

Nov. 14, in West Eaton, by Rev. Judson DAVIS, Mr. Adelbert ANDREWS to Miss Mary F. WILCOX, both of Eaton.

Nov. 20, in Eaton, by Rev. Judson DAVIS, Mr. Abram S. ELMER, of Erieville, to Miss Anet R. ORVIS, of Poland, Herkimer Co.

Nov. 22, in West Eaton, by Rev. Judson DAVIS, Mr. Wilson SLOCUM, of Eaton, to Miss Olive FISK, of West Eaton.

Nov. 16, at the residence of A. M. BAKER, Bloomington, IL, by Rev. Dr. MORRISON, Washington STICKNEY, formerly of Canastota, to Mrs. Harriet BAKER, formerly of Hamilton.

Dec. 20, in West Eaton, by Rev. Judson DAVIS, William W. LYON to Miss Nettie E. RICHARDSON, both of Nelson.

Dec. 26, in Eaton, by Rev. Judson DAVIS, Mr. Godfrey WOODHEAD to Miss Mary M. TURPIN, both of Eaton.

Dec. 31, at the residence of the bride's father, by Rev. I. D. PEASLEE, Mr. David NELSON to Miss Mary LAMB, both of Hamilton.

Dec. 31, in Hamilton, by Rev. Dr. HARVEY, Mr. Charles L. DRAKE, of Oxford, to Miss Josephine RISLEY, of East Hamilton.

1872

Jan. 1, in Hamilton, by the same, at the residence of the bride's father, Mr. Orren P. PIERCE, of Genoa, IL, to Miss Mary E. PYNE, of Hamilton.

DEMOCRATIC REPUBLICAN - 1872

Jan. 18, in Eaton village, at the residence of the bride's father, by Rev. Judson DAVIS, Mr. J. J. BENJAMIN to Miss Etta A. JOSLIN, all of Eaton.

Jan. 15, in Madison, by Rev. I. D. PEASLEE, R. R. NORTON, of Norwich, to Miss Addie FRYOVER, of Madison.

Jan. 17, in Madison, at the residence of the bride's father, by Rev. I. D. PEASLEE, Mr. M. STEVENS to Mary A. CARTER, both of Madison.

Jan. 28, in Eaton, by Rev. Judson DAVIS, Mr. Addison SEYMOUR, of New Woodstock, to Miss Ellen E. PENCE, of Eaton.

Feb. 15, in Eaton, by Rev. Judson DAVIS, Mr. Jefferson LEONARD, of DeRuyter, to Miss Jannie BROWN.

Feb. 26, at the residence of the bride's foster mother, Mrs. S. HAYES, of Columbus, by Rev. J. H. MC GAHEN, of Hamilton, Mr. Henry V. LUCAS to Miss Fannie L. TABER, all of Columbus.

Feb. 26, at the residence of Prof. Alfred TAYLOR, by Rev. W. R. BROOKS, Mr. George Dorrance SCOTT to Miss Kittie OSGOOD, oldest daughter of David OSGOOD, both of Hamilton.

Mar. 14, at the residence of Adon SMITH, by Rev. C. BARSTOW, B. C. BRISTOL, of Lebanon, to Mrs. Mary P. HARMON, of Hamilton.

Mar. 14, at Lebanon, by Rev. D. E. REED, assisted by Rev. W. R. BROOKS, Mr. Calvin G. BEACH, of Blue Rapids, KS, and Miss Charlotte M. REED, daughter of the officiating clergyman.

Mar. 15, at the residence of the bride's mother in New Berlin, by Rev. R. W. VAN SCOTT, Mr. Frank WHEATON, of Killawog, Broome Co., NY, and Miss Emma LORD, of New Berlin.

Apr. 16, in Hamilton, by Rev. P. FIELD, Mr. Leveritt PERKINS to Miss Mary DAVIS, both of Madison.

Apr. 9, in Brookfield, by Rev. R. R. PRENTICE, Mr. John T. CRANDALL and Mrs. Ruth ADAMS, both of Brookfield.

May 14, at the residence of the bride's mother in Hamilton, by Rev. I. D. PEASLEE, Mr. S. Judson WARNER to Miss Ella L. FELT, both of Hamilton.

June 6, in Liberty, MO, at the residence of the bride's father, W. P. LEWRIGHT, by Rev. J. HITCHMAN, Prof. J. R. EATON, of William Jewel College, 2d son of George W. EATON, D.D., of this place [Hamilton], and Miss Mattie E. LEWRIGHT.

June 13, in West Eaton, by Rev. Judson DAVIS, Mr. Marshall NILES, of Union City, PA, to Mrs. Elizabeth R. CAMPBELL, of West Eaton.

DEMOCRATIC REPUBLICAN - 1872

June 10, in Hamilton, by Rev. I. D. PEASLEE, Mr. Charles A. PETERSON, of Stockbridge, and Miss Ella BRIGGS, of Lebanon.

June 27, in Lebanon, by Rev. Judson DAVIS, Mr. C. C. PATRAGE, of Eaton, to Miss Hattie MORY, of Lebanon.

July 7, in Eaton, by Rev. Judson DAVIS, Mr. L. G. BROOKS, of Peterboro, and Miss Mary E. WILCOXSON.

Aug. 15, at the residence of the bride's mother in Hamilton, by Rev. W. R. BROOKS, William A. LEWIS, City Attorney of Jersey City, NJ, and Miss Virginia POST, of Hamilton.

Sept. 18, in this village [Hamilton], by Rev. I. D. PEASLEE, Mr. J. S. KIMBERLEY to Miss Hattie M. POTTER, of Hamilton.

Sept. 18, at St. Thomas' Church in Hamilton, by Rev. H. R. PYNE, Mr. Frank S. WICKWIRE, of Hamilton, and Miss Mary E. SANFORD, of Bouckville.

Sept. 22, at the residence of the bridegroom's mother, by Rev. J. H. MC GAHEN, Mr. William E. HOLT, of South Hamilton, to Miss Adell R. PIERCE of Columbus.

Sept. 21, at the Eagle Hotel, by Rev. I. D. PEASLEE, Mr. Albert J. BLUNT, of Madison, to Miss Martha A. HARVEY, of Detroit.

Sept. 26, at the residence of the bride's father, in Newark, OH, by Rev. H. M. HENRY, Mr. F. G. RICE, of Hamilton, to Miss Nellie O'BANNON, daughter of Rev. P. N. O'BANNON.

Sept. 24, in Earlville, by Rev. Dr. HARVEY, Mr. Welk M. LEE, of Bridgeport, CT, (Query: Is this name meant to be Welcome?), and Miss Franc A. SMITH, of Earlville.

Sept. 21, in West Eaton, by Rev. Judson DAVIS, Mr. Frank G. BABCOCK and Miss Maggie E. JONES, both of West Eaton.

Sept. 29, in Hannibal, Oswego Co., NY, by Rev. Judson DAVIS, Mr. R. M. JOHNSON, of Bangor, ME, and Miss Tryphena STARK, of Hannibal.

Oct. 12, at the residence of the bridegroom's father in South Hamilton, by Rev. James H. MC GAHEN, Mr. John F. FLETCHER and Miss Ida M. USHER, all of South Hamilton.

Oct. 13, in Lebanon, by Rev. J. W. BARR, Mr. George S. LASELLE, of Lebanon, and Miss Florence D. WEDGE, of this place.

Oct. 10, in Hamilton, by Rev. Dr. HARVEY, Mr. Myron TOMPKINS and Miss Harriet Eva VAN HOUSEN, all of Hamilton.

DEMOCRATIC REPUBLICAN - 1872

Oct. 9, in the Baptist Church at Sloansville, Schoharie Co., NY, by Rev. Judson DAVIS, Mr. J. W. HUNTER, 1010 Lafayette Ave., Brooklyn, and Miss Emma B. TEEPLE, of Sloansville.

Oct. 9, in the First Baptist Church of Troy, by Rev. George C. BALDWIN, assisted by Rev. C. P. SHELDON, Mr. William Lee CHURCH, of New York, to Miss Birdie BECKWITH, daughter of Edgar BECKWITH, of Troy.

Oct. 16, at the residence of the bride's father, by Rev. Dr. HARVEY, Mr. Charles H. PERKINS, of Cazenovia, and Miss Alice C. KINGSLEY, of Hamilton.

Oct. 10, at the residence of the bride's father, in Morrisville, by Rev. Samuel MILLER, of Sherburne, Mr. Henry G. NEWELL, of Groton, Tompkins Co., NY, and Miss Cornelia J. DUNTON, of Morrisville.

[No date], in Hamilton, at the residence of the bride's father, by Rev. Dr. BROOKS, Mr. Charles S. OMSBY, of Eaton, and Miss Fannie S. BARDIN, of Hamilton.

Oct. 29, in Lebanon, by Rev. E. D. REED, Mr. Henry M. WILLIAMSON and Miss Addie M. WARNER, of the same place.

Oct. 24, in Hamilton, at the residence of the bride's father, by Rev. Mr. PYNE, Rector of St. Thomas' Church, Mr. William C. THURSTON, of Norwich, and Miss Emma A. BAKER, of Hamilton.

Oct. 30, in West Eaton, by Rev. Judson DAVIS, Mr. R. A. SIMPSON, of Fairport, and Miss Cora E. FLEMING, of West Eaton.

Nov. 3, at the residence of Thomas R. GORTON, North Brookfield, by Rev. L. CASLER, Mr. Edward HUGHES and Miss Louisa DURANT, both of Hubbardsville.

Nov. 12, at the residence of the bride's father in Nelson, by Rev. Mr. WHITNEY, Mr. George G. GROSVENOR, of Lebanon, and Miss Sarah MACKIN, of Nelson.

Nov. 6, in Durhamville, at the residence of the bride's father, by Rev. Frank H. NEWTON, Mr. A. F. LAWRENCE to Miss Sophia HESS, both of Durhamville.

In issue of Nov. 21, 1872: By Rev. Judson DAVIS, Mr. John NEAL and Miss Delia PATRIDGE, both of Georgetown.

Dec. 4, in Hamilton, at the residence of C. R. PALMITER, by Rev. Mr. NORTHRUP, of Clarkville, Mr. William STANBRO, of Brookfield, and Miss Ett[a?] C. PALMITER, of Hamilton.

Dec. 4, in Eaton, by Rev. Judson DAVIS, Mr. Albert WILCOCKSON and Mrs. Nellie A. WAMPLE, both of Eaton.

Dec. 12, in Eaton, by Rev. Judson DAVIS, Mr. David N. SMITH and Miss Lydia RAILEY, both of Eaton.

DEMOCRATIC REPUBLICAN - 1872

Dec. 18, in Hamilton, by Rev. H. HARVEY, Mr. E. F. ATWOOD, of Oberlin, OH, and Miss H. M. ROGERS, of Hamilton.

Dec. 24, at the Baptist Church in Hamilton, by Rev. W. R. BROOKS, Mr. William D. HENRY, of New York, and Miss Annie L. SWIFT, daughter of A. S. SWIFT, of Hamilton.

Dec. 24, in Eaton, by Rev. Judson DAVIS, Mr. H. J. FOSTER, of Hamilton, and Miss Mary A. WINCHESTER, of Eaton.

1873

Jan. 1, in this village [Hamilton], by Rev. W. R. BROOKS, Mr. J. Moss SMITH, of Danbury, CT, and Miss Adelaide G. BROOKS, of this village.

Jan. 1, at the residence of the bride's mother in Hamilton, by Rev. Mr. PYNE, Mr. Charles A. BARBER and Miss Mary SWIFT, of Hamilton.

Jan. 1, in Hamilton, by Rev. I. D. PEASLEE, Mr. William MC LEAN and Miss Ella COLLINS, both of Augusta, NY.

Jan. 1, in Hamilton, by Rev. I. D. PEASLEE, Wallace ELPHIC, of Hamilton, and Miss Frankie JOHNSON, of Peterboro.

Jan. 5, in Pierceville, at the residence of Mr. John BENNETT, by Rev. Judson DAVIS, Mr. Niles REYNOLDS and Miss Maggie RICHMOND, both of Otselic.

Jan. 8, in West Eaton, by Rev. O. TAYNTOR, at the residence of D. M. DOWELL, Mr. Lucian H. OSGOOD to Miss M. Matilda WICKWIRE, both of Rose, Wayne Co., NY.

Jan. 21, in Eaton, by Rev. Judson DAVIS, Mr. Silas S. CLARK and Miss Lavina A. HOPKINS, youngest daughter of L. HOPKINS, both of Eaton.

Jan. 22, in Morrisville, by the same, Mr. E. D. SHIPMAN and Miss Gussie A. WALES, both of Morrisville.

Feb. 20, at West Eaton, by Rev. O. TAYNTOR, A. Z. KINGSLEY, of Hamilton, to Mrs. Mary E. SMITH, of Madison, Branch Co., MI.

Feb. 26, in this city, at the residence of A. M. CHURCH, by Rev. C. P. SHELDON, H. M. BOSWORTH, of New York City, to Miss Lizzie D. ANDREWS, of Troy. (From Troy paper.)

Feb. 19, in Eaton, by Rev. Judson DAVIS, Mr. Elijah BLINN and Mrs. Cornelia MORSE, both of Eaton.

Feb. 15, in this village [Hamilton], at the M. E. Parsonage, by Rev. I. D. PEASLEE, Mr. Asa P. WHITE, of Bouckville, to Miss Fannie E. TIBBETTS, of Hamilton.

DEMOCRATIC REPUBLICAN - 1873

Feb. 15, in Flint, MI, by Rev. D. B. EDDY, Mr. Charles B. WAIT, of Norwich, and Miss Nellie ORR, of the same place.

May 5, in Hamilton, by Rev. W. R. BROOKS, Mr. James P. BROWNELL, of Madison, and Miss Mary M. THROOP, of Hamilton.

May 12, at the residence of the bride's father in Hartford, CT, by Rev. Mr. SIMPSON, Mr. A. L. GEER, of South Manchester, CT, formerly of Lebanon, NY, and Miss Allie J. HUNT.

June 3, in Eaton, by Rev. Judson DAVIS, Mr. Fred SHORT and Miss Myra FINNEY, all of Eaton.

June 10, in West Eaton, by Rev. Judson DAVIS, Mr. C. H. HOWE and Miss Jennie E. RICHARDSON, both of West Eaton.

June 15, at the Baptist Church in South Hamilton, by Rev. J. H. MC GAHEN, Mr. William PROCTOR and Miss Grace HOLMES, both of Earlville.

June 11, at the residence of the bride's father in Burlington Flats, by Rev. L. CASLER, Mr. Dorr C. CHAPMAN and Miss Sarah A. THOMPSON, all of Burlington Flats.

July 12, in Morrisville, at the residence of the bride's father, by Rev. Judson DAVIS, Mr. B. F. SANFORD, of Eaton, and Miss Libbie E. BROWN, of Morrisville.

July 20, at the Baptist Parsonage, in South Hamilton, by Rev. J. H. MC GAHEN, Mr. George W. RAY, of East Hamilton, and Miss Ella A. PIERCE, of South Hamilton.

Aug. 10, at the Baptist Parsonage in South Hamilton, by Rev. J. H. MC GAHEN, Mr. Sanford D. PALMER, of North Brookfield, and Addie R. ELPHICK, of East Hamilton.

Aug. 6, in Hamilton, by Rev. L.B. BARKER, of Fairfax, VT, Mr. B. Walters BARKER, Class of 1873 of Madison University, and Miss Kittie A. OSBORN, daughter of Prof. L. M. OSBORN of the University.

Aug. 21, in Hamilton, by Rev. J. H. MC GAHEN, Mr. Albert BATES, of Hubbardsville, and Miss Carrie S. ELDRED, of Hamilton.

Sept. 7, at North Brookfield, by Rev. L. CASLER, Mr. Theodore HALSEY and Miss Carrie FOGUS, both of Waterville.

Sept. 7, at North Brookfield, by Rev. L. CASLER, Mr. James YOUNG and Miss Nora A. DEANE, both of Earlville.

Sept. 8, at the residence of the bride's father in Bridgewater, by Rev. D. W. SKINNER, of Hamilton, Mr. James S. HASCALL, Jr., of Boone, IA, and Miss Delia WALDO, of Bridgewater, NY.

DEMOCRATIC REPUBLICAN - 1873

Oct. 2, at the residence of the bride's mother in Hamilton, by Rev. I. D. PEASLEE, Mr. Henry H. HARRIS, of Knoxboro, and Miss Nellie G. BRIGGS, of Hamilton.

Sept. 28, at Madison, by Rev. I. D. PEASLEE, of Hamilton, Mr. Jerome David BAKER, of Lebanon, and Miss Mary A. DAILEY, of Madison.

Sept. 28, at Eaton, by Rev. Judson DAVIS, Mr. Johnathan ODELL and Miss Mary SHATTUCK, both of Erieville.

Oct. 8, at the residence of the bride's father in Fleming, NY, by Rev. W. A. MAYNARD, the Rev. J. H. MC GAHEN, of South Hamilton, and Miss Florence D. GRIGGS, of Fleming.

[No date], at the residence of the bride's mother in Mexico, Oswego Co., NY, by Rev. Judson DAVIS, Mr. John JONES and Miss J. R. TIFFANY, both of Mexico.

Oct. 16, at Earlville, by Rev. Dr. HARVEY, Mr. Norman W. TORREY to Miss Mary, daughter of Orville SMITH, of Earlville.

[No date], in Poolville, by Rev. Dwight WILLIAMS, at the residence of the bride's father, Mr. H. N. PIERCE, of Hamilton Center, and Miss Clara A. SMITH, of Poolville; in issue of Dec. 4th.

Issue of Dec. 4, 1873: On Nov. 28, at the residence of D. W. INGALLS, by Prof. L. M. OSBORN, Oliver IDE, of IA, and Miss Catherine WARRINER, of Hamilton.

1874

Jan. 1, in Hamilton Center, at the residence of the bride's father, by Rev. D. W. SKINNER, Mr. Lewis D. NEWTON, of Brooklyn, to Miss Cynthia L. PIERCE.

Dec. 10, 1873, at the M. E. Parsonage in Sherburne, by Rev. H. FOX, Mr. Smith M. HANSON, of Poolville, to Miss Mandane LARKIN, of Hubbardsville. (NOTE: This announcement really gave the date of marriage as Dec. 10, 1872.)

Jan. 14, in Earlville at the residence of the bride's father, by J. H. FULLER, Justice of the Peace, G. O. DAGGETT, of Jones Co., and Helen L. RICHMOND. (From *Manchester Press*, IA)

Jan. 21, at St. Thomas' Church in Hamilton, by Rev. E. P. SMITH, Rector, Mr. John BARBER, of Rome, NY, and Miss Genevieve CAMPBELL, of Hamilton.

Feb. 11, in Eaton, by Rev. Judson DAVIS, Deacon A. BOOTH, of Eaton, and Mrs. Sarah B. SLATER, of Smyrna.

Feb. 21, in Hamilton, by Rev. A. R. BEACH, Mr. B. H. CRANDALL, of Battle Creek, MI, and Miss Ann Eliza

DEMOCRATIC REPUBLICAN - 1874

BEACH, of Hamilton, daughter of the officiating clergyman.

Jan. 1, at the home of the bride in Brookfield, by Rev. R. H. NORTHRUP, Mr. Alvin CHESBRO and Miss Hattie A. HUNTLEY.

Feb. 25, at Richfield Springs, by Rev. E. M. PECK, Andrew J. BEEBE, of Norwich, to Miss Lizzie E. MINER, daughter of Paul R. MINER, of the former place. (From *Norwich Telegraph*)

Feb. 25, at the residence of the bride's parents near Earlville, by Rev. J. O. GIFFORD, Mr. Charaloise W. BRAINARD, of Poolville, to Miss Lettie J. CUSHMAN.

Apr. 7, at the residence of the bride's father, George M. RHODES, Grand Rapdis, MI, by Rev. J. Morgan SMITH, Mr. W. H. MC CREDY and Miss Della C. RHODES, both of Grand Rapids.

June 18, at the Baptist Church in Hamilton, by Rev. Dr. BROOKS, Mr. Marcus E. MASON, Missionary to Assam, Asia, and Miss Fidelia S. HOWES, of Hamilton.

At the same time and place, by the same clergyman, Mr. K. G. PHILLIPS, Missionary to Assam, Asia, and Miss Ella V. HOWES, of Hamilton.

June 27, by Rev. Judson DAVIS, A. J. CADY to Elizabeth POTTER, of Madison.

June 25, in Vernon, by Rev. E. H. PAYSON, Mr. Eben CURRY, Esq., of Little Falls, to Miss Julia A. PIERCE, of Vernon.

July 22, in Hamilton, by Rev. Dr. BROOKS, Mr. C. Egbert VAUGHAN, of IL, and Miss Emma J. RICE, of Hamilton.

Aug. 11, in Hamilton, at the residence of the officiating clergyman, Rev. J. O. GIFFORD, Mr. A. L. DUNHAM, of South Hamilton, and Miss Lottie M. NASH, of Poolville.

Aug. 8, in Eaton, by Rev. Judson DAVIS, Mr. E. P. STORRS and Miss Joie (sic) HENRY, all of Eaton.

Aug. 25, at the M. E. Parsonage in this village [Hamilton], by Rev. Gordon MOORE, Mr. Franklin B. REYNOLDS and Miss Hannah D. FARNUM.

Sept. 1, in Eaton, by Rev. Judson DAVIS, Mr. H. G. DODD and Miss Ida M. SEELEY, both of Georgetown, NY.

Aug. 13, at the residence of the bride's father at Upper New York Mills, by Rev. N. WOODWARD, Mr. Amasa LORD, of New York, to Mrs. Mary E. READ, of Utica.

Oct. 3, in Eaton, by Rev. Judson DAVIS, Mr. Wesley DAWLNIE, of Waterville, and Miss Fannie MINTIE, of Eaton.

Oct. 27, at Little Falls, NY, by Rev. A. LE ROY, assisted by Rev. R. R. PRENTICE, Rev. A. M. PRENTICE, of

DEMOCRATIC REPUBLICAN - 1874

Brockport, NY, and Miss Jennie WHITTEMORE, of Little Falls.
Oct. 19, in Hartford, CT, by Rev. A. H. MEAD, Charles D. ALDERMAN, of East Hamilton, and Miss Annie L. TRESCOTT, of that city.
Nov. 22, in Erieville, by Rev. Judson DAVIS, Mr. Burdette ARNST and Miss Etta B. JONES, both of Morrisville.
Nov. 18, in West Eaton, by Rev. Judson DAVIS, Mr. T. R. JONES and Miss Mary A. JONES, both of West Eaton.
Nov. 18, at the Eagle Hotel in Hamilton, by Rev. R. T. CROSS, Devillo PALMER and Lilla BATES, both of Brookfield.
Dec. 17, at the residence of the bride's father, by Rev. J. H. MC GAHEN, Mr. Emory B. MC GAHEN (brother of the officiating clergyman), to Miss Emma E. LOOMIS, both of South Hamilton.
Dec. 22, at the residence of the bride's father in Hamilton, by Rev. R. T. CROSS, Mr. Albert W. EVANS, of Oneida, to Miss Ella A. RICE, of Hamilton.
Nov. 19, at the residence of the bride's father, Col. S. WAIT, of Homer, MO, Mr. Fred GREENLEY, formerly of this village [Hamilton], now of Homer, to Miss Augusta S. WAIT.
Dec. 30, in Hamilton, by Rev. E. P. SMITH, rector of St. Thomas' Church, Mr. George PRATT and Miss Emeline FRINK, all of Hamilton.
Dec. 30, at Hamilton, by Rev. Father LUDDEN, Mr. Peter HAND and Miss Eliza HURLEY, all of Hamilton.
Dec. 30, at the residence of the bride's father in Brookfield, by Rev. J. H. MC GAHEN, Mr. Simon BROWN and Miss Mary A. BEECHER, both of Brookfield.

1875

Jan. 6, in Hamilton, by Rev. J. O. GIFFORD, Mr. M. D. SCOVAL and Miss M. A. THOMPSON, all of Hamilton.
Jan. 12, in Lebanon, at the residence of the bride's father, by Rev. N. S. JONES, Mr. Frank VOSBURG, of Stockport, to Miss Mattie E. DYE, of Lebanon.
Jan. 20, at the Congregational Parsonage in Hamilton, by Rev. R. T. CROSS, Mr. George W. NEWMAN, of Chenango, to Miss Eugenia S. HOLT, of Columbus.
Jan. 28, at the residence of the bride's father in Erieville, by Rev. Judson DAVIS, Mr. M. D. HOPKINS to Miss Susan J. BLAIR, of Erieville.
Feb. 4, at the home of the bride's mother in this village [Hamilton], by Rev. Gordon MOORE, Mr. William A.

DEMOCRATIC REPUBLICAN - 1875

BOYD, of Lebanon, and Miss Nellie SWIFT, of Hamilton.

Feb. 11, at the residence of the bride's father, by Rev. Mr. BAKER, Mr. J. L. GOULD, of Royal Oaks, MI, to Miss Sophia J. BLAIR, of Onondaga Valley, NY.

Mar. 2, at the home of the bride's parents in Madison, by Rev. Gordon MOORE, Mr. Dealton E. BURLINGAME and Miss Clara A. LAMB, both of Madison.

Mar. 2, in Hamilton, by Rev. G. J. TRAVIS, Mr. Alanson C. MOREY and Clara H. HUGHES, both of Lebanon.

Mar. 9, in Hamilton, by Rev. R. T. CROSS, DeWitt OSBORN and Julia J. BATES, both of Hamilton.

Mar. 4, in Eaton, by Rev. Mr. CLEVELAND [probably the brother of President Grover Cleveland], Mr. Seymour LA MUNION and Miss Eliza ALLEN, both of Stockbridge, NY.

Mar. 17, in Hamilton, by Rev. R. T. CROSS, Chauncey D. SMITH and Hattie SQUIRES, both of Hamilton.

Mar. 31, in Pierceville, NY, at the residence of the bride's father, by Rev. Judson DAVIS, Mr. Harti H. NORTHRUP and Miss Jennie M. PARKER, both of the town of Eaton.

May 4, in East Hamilton, by Rev. Dwight WILLIAMS, Mr. Arthur J. PARTRIDGE, of Hubbardsville, to Miss Ella NILES, of East Hamilton.

May 20, in Norwich, by Rev. D. H. LOVERIDGE, Mr. Augustus H. GOODWIN to Miss M. Nellie BEEBE, daughter of A. J. BEEBE, Esq., of Norwich, NY.

May 27, in Vienna, at the bride's home, by Rev. J. O. GIFFORD, Mr. Joseph M. PHERIS to Miss Ellen E. STARKWEATHER.

[No date], at the parsonage in McConnellsville by the same, Mr. Wright F. WASHBURN, of Constantia, NY, to Miss Sarah J. SNIDER, of Vienna, NY.

June 23, at the residence of the bride's parents in Vienna, NY, by Rev. J. O. GIFFORD, Mr. J. ROANTREE and Miss Carrie FOX, both of Vienna.

June 27, at the residence of the bride's father, in Madison, by Rev. R. T. CROSS, N. H. TOWER, of Waterville, to Phoebe T. HITCHCOCK.

July 7, in Hamilton, by Rev. S. J. MATTESON, D.D., Mr. Albert M. BAKER, of Hamilton, to Miss Ada E. LONT, of North Versails.

June 17, at Buchanan, MI, by Rev. Mr. RUSSELL, at the residence of the bride's sister, Mrs. Dr. R. PIERCE, Mr. M. I. B. RICHMOND, of Earlville, to Miss E. A. HOAG.

DEMOCRATIC REPUBLICAN - 1875

Aug. 11, in Chicago, IL, by Rev. J. P. BATES, Jacob LeRoy WHITE, Esq., of Franklin, IN, and Augusta F. PAYNE, of Hamilton.
June 23, at the residence of the bride's father in Hamilton, by Rev. P. B. SPEAR, D.D., Rev. G. E. WEEKS, pastor-elect of the Baptist Church, Belmont, NY, to Miss Julia C. KEITH.
Aug. 4, in Hamilton by Rev. Dr. DODGE, Rev. B. F. LEIPSNER, late pastor of the Baptist Church at Rhinebeck, NY, and Miss Viola FELT of Hamilton.

"Rev. B. F. LEIPSNER, TO E. D. VAN SLYCK, Dr.
To balance on bill for printing one number of
"The Cuirassier"
900 copies, in June 1872 . . . . $5.00
To binding two magazines 1.80

                                        $6.80
We wish we could receipt the bill."

Aug. 23, in the M. E. Parsonage in this village [Hamilton], by Rev. Gordon MOORE, Mr. Peter D. HUGHES and Miss Sarah C. JONES, both of Nelson, Madison Co.
Aug. 25, at the residence of the bride's foster father, N. P. SQUIRES, Esq., in Hamilton, by Rev. Mr. HARDEY, of Madison, NY, Mr. Adelbert BEEBE and Miss Eva SQUIRES, both of Hamilton.
June 22, at the old home of the bride in Eaton, NY, by Rev. Dr. BROOKS, Mr. Backus I. LEACH, of Hamilton, and Mrs. Etta A. PHILPOT, of Eaton.
Aug. 25, at the residence of the bride's father in Madison, by Rev. G. W. BARNES, assisted by Rev. Prof. J. J. LEWIS, Rev. R. T. JONES, pastor of the Baptist Church at Ballston Spa, NY, and Miss Mary P. LUCAS, of Madison.
Aug. 25, 1874 (sic), by Rev. Charles SIMPSON, Frank J. ROOT, of Hamilton, of Class '73, Cornell University, and Clara E. SIMPSON, of Ithaca.
Sept. 8, at the residence of the bride's father in Madison, by Rev. W. R. TOMPKINS, Mr. Adon N. SMITH, of Hamilton, and Miss Ella J. TOMPKINS of Madison.
Sept. 11, in Eaton, by Rev. Judson DAVIS, Frank KINGSBURY, of Bouckville, and Miss Ida BRADSHAW, of Fulton.
Sept. 20, in Hamilton, at the residence of the bride's parents, by Rev. R. T. CROSS, Mr. Allen N. LEACH, of Lebanon, and Miss Hattie M. SQUIRE, of Hamilton.
Oct. 6, at the residence of the bride's parents near Poolville, by Rev. Gordon MOORE, G. S. COMSTOCK,

DEMOCRATIC REPUBLICAN - 1875

M.D., of Hamilton, and Miss Adelle BANNING, of Poolville.

Oct. 10, at the Park Hotel in Hamilton, by Rev. Gordon MOORE, Mr. Thomas SHEPARD, of Waterville, and Miss Harriet READ, of Sangerfield.

Oct. 17, at the M. E. Parsonage in this village [Hamilton], by Rev. Gordon MOORE, Mr. William RICH, of Augusta, NY, and Miss Mary HOLMAN (HOLZMAN), of Hamilton.

Oct. 20, at the M. E. Parsonage in this village [Hamilton], by Rev. Gordon MOORE, Mr. Mirton YOUNG and Miss Nellie SHEPARDSON, both of Hamilton.

Oct. 27, in Hamilton, by Rev. C. Venton PATTERSON, James E. CADY, of Lebanon, and Mrs. Abbie H. JENNESS, of Brookfield, VT.

Nov. 2, at the house of the bride's mother in Eaton, by Rev. Mr. SHAW, Mr. James D. COLLISTER, of Madison, and Miss Emma JEFFS, of Eaton.

Nov. 5, at the home of the bride in Lebanon, by Rev. J. D. WOODRUFF, Mr. Frank J. BENEDICT and Miss Mary L. BENEDICT, both of Lebanon.

Nov. 2, in Brookfield, by Rev. J. M. TODD, Mr. Henry M. COLLINS and Miss M. Velona CARRINGTON.

Nov. 7, at the M. E. Parsonage in East Hamilton, by Rev. S. M. FISK, Mr. A. Coleson SHEPARDSON, of Poolville, to Miss Mary CUTLER, of Columbus.

Nov. 10, at the American Hotel in Utica, by Rev. Judson DAVIS, Mr. T. C. HINDS and Miss Libbie E. DAVIS, both of Otsego Co., NY.

Nov. 23, at the residence of the bride's father, by Rev. D. W. SKINNER, Mr. Charles E. MONTGOMERY and Miss Julia A. BIXBY, both of Smith's Valley, NY.

Nov. 30, in Hamilton, at the residence of the bride's mother, by Rev. Gordon MOORE, Mr. Adelbert WEEDEN, of Madison, and Miss Mary M. JOHNSON, of Hamilton.

Dec. 7, at the M. E. Parsonage in Hamilton, by Rev. Gordon MOORE, Mr. Sanford W. CRANDALL and Miss Sarah J. MELVIN, both of Marshall, NY.

Dec. 6, at the M. E. Parsonage in Hamilton, by Rev. Gordon MOORE, Mr. Albert A. CLARK, of Chateaugy, NY, and Miss Mary E. FOLAND, of Durhamville, NY.

Dec. 2, in Hamilton, at the residence of the bride's mother, by Rev. R. T. CROSS, Mr. James Whittier HURN, of New York, member of the Class '73, Madison University, and Miss Hattie Evelyn WICKWIRE, of Hamilton.

DEMOCRATIC REPUBLICAN - 1875

Dec. 30, at the residence of the bride's parents, in Lebanon, by Rev. J. D. WOODRUFF, Mr. John HARMON, of Hamilton, and Miss Olive M. GROSVENOR, of Lebanon.

Dec. 26, at residence of the bride's parents at Smith's Valley, by Rev. R. T. CROSS, Edward D. WEBSTER, of Norwich, and Jennie L. WICKWIRE, of Smith's Valley.

Dec. 30, at bride's residence at 178 Court St., by Rev. Albert F. LYLE, Mr. Frank L. EVERTS, of Eaton, to Miss Rosa C. KEIM, of Utica, NY.

[No date], in Eaton, at the residence of the bride's mother, by Rev. C. Venton PATTERSON, assisted by Rev. George A. SMITH, Mr. Calvin T. KINNEY, of New Woodstock, and Ida L. SCOTT, of Eaton.

Dec. 22, in Pierceville, NY, at the residence of the bride's father, by Rev. Judson DAVIS, Mr. Jerome E. LEE, CT, and Miss Jennie E. WALKER.

Dec. 25, in Eaton, by Rev. Judson DAVIS, Mr. C. W. SOULE and Miss Emma STONE, both of Lebanon.

Dec. 25, in Brookfield, at the residence of Samuel CLARK, Esq., by Pastor SAULSBURY, of the Methodist Church, Mr. Otis YORK and Miss Mary Jane CLARK.

1876

Jan. 12, at the residence of Mr. H. K. BIDWELL, by Rev. Gordon MOORE, Mr. Albert FAGAN, of Eaton, and Miss Libble D. BIDWELL, of Madison.

Feb. 16, in Waterville, by Rev. G. J. TRAVIS, Mr. Addison MORSE, of Hamilton, and Miss Anna REYNOLDS, of Waterville.

Feb. 23, in Hamilton, by Rev. A. P. LUDDEN, Mr. THOMAS to Miss Nellie STRAUBE, all of Hamilton.

Feb. 27, at the M. E. Parsonage in East Hamilton, by Rev. S. M. FISK, Mr. Hoxie T. CRUMB, of Brookfield, and Miss Irena S. DUTCHER, of Hamilton.

Feb. 27, at the Baptist Parsonage in Hamilton, Sunday morning, by Rev. J. M. STIFLER, D.D., Mr. Alfred W. SLOCUM and Miss Katie A. THOMPSON.

Feb. 20, in the Baptist Church in Erieville, by Rev. J. DAVIS, Mr. James M. MALTBY and Miss Agnes M. WILKINSON, both of Fayetteville.

Mar. 9, at the residence of Mr. Warren BUELL near Hamilton, by Rev. R. T. CROSS, Sidney TOMPKINS, of Madison, and Mrs. Lucinda RICHARDS, of Hamilton.

June 18, at the residence of the bride's mother in Madison, by Rev. George L. HARDY, Mr. William C. SIM-

DEMOCRATIC REPUBLICAN - 1876

MONS, of Buffalo, and Jennie L. BROWNELL, of Madison.

May 17, at the residence of the bride's parents in Hamilton, by Rev. R. T. CROSS, Mr. William C. MORSE, of Watertown, NY, to Miss Nettie G. BAKER, of Hamilton.

June 1, at the residence of the bride's father at Solsville, by (blank), Mr. Henry GOSLEY, of Pratt's Hollow, to Miss Delia KELLY.

June 14, at the residence of the bride's sister in Camillus, NY, by Rev. G. F. GENUNG, Mr. Arthur CADY, of Hamilton Theological Seminary, and Mrs. Belle R. LOCKHEART, of Hamilton.

June 26, at the Baptist Church in West Eaton, by Rev. Judson DAVIS, Mr. Adelbert RUGG to Miss Mary MINER, of Georgetown, NY.

June 29, in this village [Hamilton], at the residence of the bride's father, Mr. G. R. WALDRON, Esq., Editor of the *Democratic Volunteer*, by Rev. R. T. CROSS, Mr. Henry A. MILLER, of Southwick, MA, and Miss Ida Belle WALDRON, of Hamilton.

June 28, in the Baptist Church at Cazenovia, by Rev. S. H. GREENE, Prof. James W. FORD, of Cook Academy, Havana, NY, to Miss Katie E. JONES, of Cazenovia.

July 26, in Hamilton, by Rev. Dr. HARVEY, Mr. Arthur C. RICE to Miss Ella L. WILLIAMS, all of Hamilton.

July 12, from the *Kankakee, IL, Gazette*: In this city, by Rev. J. H. BARNDARD, Mr. S. B. BURCHARD to Mrs. Carrie HOUSTON, both of this city. Mr. BURCHARD is an old resident of Kankakee, and highly esteemed. They left for Hamilton, NY, the home of the former, whence they will proceed to New York City and the Centenniel.

Aug. 2, in Hamilton, by Rev. D. DODGE, D.D., William L. KOLB, of New York, to Harriet, youngest daughter of the late Horatio ROGERS, Esq., of Providence, RI.

Aug. 14, in Cooperstown, Andrew W. CLARK, A.M., of Gilbertsville, late of Hamilton Theological Seminary, to Miss Alna (sic) B. TRIPP, of Cooperstown.

Aug. 19, at the bride's parents, by Rev. O. J. ROSE, of Smithport, Andrew V. CRUMB, of Brookfield, to Hattie E. HIBBARD. of Corryville, PA. (From *Brookfield Courier*). He was lately a graduate of the Hamilton Theological Seminary, and was ordained to the Gospel ministry at Brookfield last week. Twelve churches were included in the council where Rev. E. D. REED, of North Brookfield was moderator and J. H. MC GAHEN, of Richfield, clerk.

DEMOCRATIC REPUBLICAN - 1876

Sept. 5, in Hamilton, at the residence of F. B. NEWTON, Esq., by Rev. Dr. PORTER, Mr. George BEAL, of Hamilton, and Miss Eliza A. WHAN, of Neustadt, Ontario.

[No date], in Madison, at the residence of the bride's parents, by Rev. Dr. HARVEY, Hon. Robert HOSEA, of Cincinnati, OH, to Miss Lucy KLINCK.

Oct. 11, at the residence of C. W. UNDERHILL, in Hamilton, by Rev. John James LEWIS, Oliver B. PRESCOTT, of New Hartford, NY, to Elizabeth C. SMITH, of Hamilton.

Oct. 23, in South Hamilton, by Rev. E. D. CLOUGH, Mr. Daniel T. CRUMB, and Miss Annie E. GREEN, both of Brookfield.

Oct. 11, in Watertown, at the residence of the bride, by Rev. J. H. PUTNAM, Mr. J. H. HOLDRIDE, of Ilion, and formerly of Hamilton, to Mrs. M. CHARGO (sic), of Watertown.

Nov. 1, at the residence of the bride's father, by Rev. D. W. SKINNER, Mr. J. Archie CAMPBELL to Miss Jennie M. ROSS, both of Lebanon.

Oct. 17, in North Parma, NY, by Rev. J. S. OLCOTT, of Rochester, Rev. R. R. PRENTICE, of Parma, and formerly of this place, and Lucy NEWELL.

Nov. 14, in Lebanon, at the residence of J. A. HEAD, Esq., by Rev. Dr. BROOKS, Hull S. GARDINER, M.D., of Hamilton, and Miss Calista R. HEAD, of San Francisco, CA.

Nov. 19, in Hamilton, by Rev. E. W. JONES, Mr. Otis T. SIMMONS and Miss Carrie FELT, both of Hamilton.

Nov. 19, in Hamilton, by Rev. E. W. JONES, Mr. Charles LOOMIS, of Lebanon, and Miss Ellen RAMSDELL, of Brookfield.

Nov. 22, in Hamilton, by Rev. E. W. JONES, Mr. H. I. HILLS and Elsie S. WOODMAN, both of Hamilton.

Dec. 6, at the residence of the bride's parents in Hamilton, by pastor of the Baptist Church, Rev. J. M. STIFLER, assisted by Rev. John James LEWIS, the Rev. Charles P. FOX, pastor of the Baptist Church at Moriah, NY, and Miss Nellie P. SPENCER, of Hamilton.

Dec. 21, at the residence of the bride's parents in Madison, by Rev. J. M. STIFLER, Mr. Robert WALLACE, of M. U., to Miss Lizzie A. ROWLANDS.

[No date], in West Eaton, at the residence of the bride's father, S. PAYNE, Esq., by Rev. Judson DAVIS, Mr. Chancey F. CARTER, of Oriskany Falls, to Miss Mary L. PAYNE, of West Eaton.

[No date], in Eaton, at the residence of the bride's father, Jerome WHEELER, Esq., by Rev. Judson DAVIS,

DEMOCRATIC REPUBLICAN - 1876

Frank G. WHEELOCK, M.D. of Preble, Cortland Co., NY, to Miss Emma G. WHEELER, of Eaton.

1877

Jan. 1, in Utica, at Mrs. Jessie WOODARD's, by Rev. N. R. EVERTS, Ores RANNEY, Esq., of Oneida, to Mrs. Elmora M. COAN, of Oneida Lake.

Jan. 25, at the Baptist Parsonage in Hamilton, by Rev. J. M. STIFLER, Mr. James KENYON and Miss Marion DECKER, both of Eaton.

Jan. 25, in Eaton, Mr. GREEN, of Smyrna, to Miss Lillie HOOPER.

Feb. 8, at the residence of the bride's parents in the town of Madison, by Rev. E. W. JONES, William E. LAMB and Miss Ella BURLINGAME, both of Madison.

By Rev. W. H. HOPKINS, of St. John's Episcopal Church, Hon. Charles H. CURTIS and Miss Sophie BAKER, all of Chicago. (*Chicago Tribune*, of Feb. 3d.)

[No date], at the residence of the bride's mother in Brooklyn, by Rev. Dr. R. DURYEA, William H. SCHRODER to Mary E. HENRY, formerly of this place [Hamilton].

[No date], in West Eaton, at the residence of the bride's parents, by Rev. Judson DAVIS, George CLARK, of Madison, and Miss DeEtta S. HUDSON, of West Eaton.

Mar. 9, at the residence of the bride's parents in Eaton, by Rev. J. M. STIFLER, Frederick ALLEN and Miss Rosaleia ERSKINE, both of Eaton.

Mar. 9, in Eaton, at the home of George TYLER, by Rev. Judson DAVIS, Erastus H. WOOD, of Shed's Corners, and Mrs. M. H. SWIFT, of Cazenovia.

Feb. 28, in Lebanon, at the residence of the bride's parents, by Rev. C. Vinton PATTERSON, Frank C. P. BILLINGS to Miss Jennie TALLET, both of Lebanon.

Mar. 15, at the residence of the bride's sister in Grant, NY, by Rev. M. D. V. WALES, Ervin E. WALKER, of Middleville, and Miss Jennie A. DE LONG, of Grant.

Mar. 21, at the Congregational Church in Morrisville, by the pastor, Rev. W. A. SMITH, Mr. J. Dixon AVERY to Mrs. Mary Y. TIDD.

Apr. 15, at the residence of the bride's parents, Madison Center, NY, by Rev. HARDY, Mr. Robert HAWLEY, of Adams, NY, and Miss Frank PERKINS, of Madison.

May 1, in Columbia Springs, NY, by Rev. D. M. RANKIN, Mr. James BRIGHT, of Hamilton, and Mrs. Josephine L. HAYWARD, of Columbia Springs.

DEMOCRATIC REPUBLICAN - 1877

May 14, in Hamilton, at the M.E. Parsonage, by Rev. E. W. JONES, Warren J. TALCOTT, of Hamilton, and Miss Nellie M. BROWN of Madison.

May 14, in Hamilton, at the residence of L. R. CLARK, by Rev. JONES, William LUCAS and Mary E. DALEY, both of Hamilton.

May 27, in Brookfield, by Elder BARRY, Mr. A. B. RICE, of Hamilton, and Miss Ella LOOMIS, of North Brookfield.

May 29, at the bride's home in Lebanon, by Rev. WILSON of Eaton, Mr. J. T. CRAMPHIN and Miss Florence A. BALLARD, both of Lebanon.

May 23, in Hamilton, by Rev. J. A. RICE, of Unadilla Forks, Mr. Martin L. RUGG, of Grafton, VT, and Miss Lille A. MOSELEY, Hamilton.

May 20, in Hamilton, by Rev. J. M. STIFLER, Eugen MAHAN and Clara S. TAFT, both of Hamilton.

June 11, in Hamilton, by Rev. E. W. JONES, William C. COE, of Madison, and Miss Cora L. BUELL, of Hamilton.

June 20, in Eaton, by Rev. Judson DAVIS, A. D. MORTON and Miss M. Francelia DAVIS.

June 25, in Hamilton, by Rev. E. W. JONES, Daniel D. SHARMAN, of Hamilton, and Miss Lizzie G. THOMPSON, of Argyle, NY.

June 20, at the home of the bride's mother in Bridgeport, CT, by Rev. E. W. MAXEY, James H. HEWITT, of Hamilton, and Miss Ella C. TOMLINSON, of Bridgeport, CT.

June 19, in Hamilton, by Rev. James M. STIFLER, assisted by Rev. J. J. LEWIS, C. H. WATSON, of Oswego, and Miss Ada BARDEEN, of Hamilton.

June 12, at the residence of O. PECKHAM, by Rev. A. E. WILSON, Mr. Orson PECKHAM and Abigail BIGELOW, of Scriba, NY.

July 25, in Hamilton, by Rev. A. P. LUDDEN, Mr. Daniel J. MARVIN, of Utica, to Miss Mary E. STRAUBE, of Hamilton.

Aug. 8, in Hamilton, by Rev. Dr. DODGE, Bradford P. MARKHAM, of Springfield, MA, and Lily F. WHITMORE.

Aug. 15, in Medina, NY, at the bride's home, by Rev. FREEMAN, of Lockport, and Rev. H. O. ROLLINS, of Whitestown, Prof. W. R. ROLLINS, Prin. of the Union School in Hamilton, and Miss Helen UNDERHILL, of Medina.

Aug. 16, at the home of the bride's parents in Hamilton, by Rev. Dr. STIFLER, Rev. S. A. NORTHRUP, Class of '76 M.U., Pastor of the Baptist Church at Fenton, MI, and Miss Lettie A. JOSLIN, Hamilton.

DEMOCRATIC REPUBLICAN - 1877

Aug. 23, at the Baptist Church in Hamilton, by Rev. J. M. STIFLER, Mr. Arthur FROTHINGHAM, of Scranton, PA, and Miss Laura FITZ RANDOLPH, of Hamilton.

Sept. 19, in Poolville, by Rev. Dr. STIFLER, Frank J. KELLOWAY, of Hamilton, and Miss Mary A. WELLS, of Poolville.

Aug. 22, in Madison, by Rev. STIFLER, C. A. NICHOLS, of Ridgefield, CT, and Miss Jennie S. ROOT, of Madison.

Sept. 18, at the residence of the bride's parents in Elmira, by Rev. S. T. CLARK, Mr. Charles B. BROWNELL, of Chicago, and Miss Fannie FULLER, of Elmira.

Sept. 26, at Saratoga Springs, by Rev. D. COREY, Henry C. WELTON and Miss Annie L. GEORGIA, both of Utica.

Oct. 29, at the M. E. Parsonage in Hamilton, by Rev. E. W. JONES, Adelbert E. HERRICK, of West Eaton, and Miss Josephine A. STREETER, of Pratt's Hollow.

Nov. 7, at the residence of the bride's father in Eaton, by Rev. Judson DAVIS, Delos STEBBINS, of Oneida, and Miss Ida M. LEACH, of Eaton.

Dec. 18, in Eaton, Mr. Allen VANDERPOOL, of Lyndenville, NY, and Miss Nettie E. NICHOLS, of Eaton.

Dec. 25, in Lebanon, by Rev. Judson DAVIS, Daniel S. PORTER and Miss Emma A. CADWELL, both of Lebanon.

On New Year's Eve, in Bouckville, by S. E. SCRANTON, William F. LOGAN, of Hamilton, and Miss Chloe RALPH, of Eaton.

1878

Jan. 3, in Hamilton, by Rev. E. W. JONES, Mr. E. Whitford THOMPSON, of Madison, and Miss G. Gertrude LAMB, of Hubbardsville.

Jan. 10, at the residence of the bride's parents in Madison, by Rev. A. G. FARGO, Mr. J. Arthur YOUNGLOVE and Miss Sophia FULLER, both of Madison.

Jan. 22, at Hamilton, by Rev. E. W. JONES, Mr. Hiram H. TUCKER, of Norwich, and Jane E. CRUMB, of Hamilton.

Jan. 10, by Rev. J. M. STIFLER, D. N. FOSTER, of Fort Wayne, IN, to Miss Sarah PYNE, of Hamilton.

On the evening of Feb. 2, at the residence of C. P. BONNEY, Lake City, MN, by Rev. ANDERSON, Mr. Frank W. FULLERSON and Miss Viola J. DICKASON.

Feb. 18, at the M. E. Parsonage in Hamilton, by Rev. E. W. JONES, Walter CHRISPELL and Miss Ettie S. FAGAN, both of Madison.

Feb. 21, in Hamilton, by Rev. Charles H. WATSON, of Oswego, the Rev. A. Wayland BOURN, Pastor of the Sherman

DEMOCRATIC REPUBLICAN - 1878

Avenue Baptist Church of Newark, NJ, to Miss Emma BARDEEN, daughter of Dr. A. V. BARDEEN of Hamilton.
Feb. 18, by Rev. E. W. JONES, Mr. Robert W. ROBERTS, of Irontown, WV, and Miss Mary Libbie KENYON, of Poolville.
Mar. 6, in Hamilton, at the M. E. Parsonage, by Rev. E. W. JONES, Mr. James JONES, of Sauquoit, NY, and Miss Jennie VAN DUSEN, of Hamilton.
Mar. 12, at the bride's residence in Hamilton, by Rev. STIFLER, D.D., Alfred L. BROWN, of Lebanon, and Sarah J. FULKERSON, of Hamilton.
Mar. 20, at the M. E. Parsonage, Hamilton, by Rev. E. W. JONES, Edgar W. CRANDALL and Miss Lucy REYNOLDS, both of Lebanon.
June 6, at the residence of the bride's mother in Canajoharie, NY, by Rev. Richard R. WILLIAMS, Fannie, eldest daughter of the late Hon. David SPRAKER, to Walter P. BONNEY, of Herkimer, NY. (From the *Utica Republic*.)
June 6, in Cortland, by Rev. Mr. IGER, O. B. LORD, of Hamilton, and Mrs. S. A. EGGLESON, of Cortland.
June 18, in Cazenovia, at the home of the bride's mother, Mrs. J. A. JOHNSON, by Rev. W. W. STAPLES, Charles O. MORGAN, of Earlville, to Miss Lizzie M. CHAPHE.
June 11, at the Baptist parsonage in Hamilton, by Rev. J. M. STIFLER, Mr. David P. TABER to Miss Lillie TOOGOOD, both of Lenox.
June 5, at Brooklyn, NY, by Rev. Wayland HOYT, Paul H. BATE to Geneva, daughter of Samuel P. RUSSELL, all of Brooklyn.
June 26, in Brooklyn, Francis A. HYATT, of Fenner, NY, to Mrs. Elizabeth BENEDICT, of Brooklyn.
July 2, by Rev. James COOTE, at the residence of Amos TICHENOR, Joseph FRANKLIN, of Hamilton, and Mrs. Mary EDWARDS, of Eaton.
July 4, in Eaton, by Rev. Judson DAVIS, Fred H. WELCH and Jane R. COLLINS, both of Lebanon.
July 11, at the First Baptist Church in Hamilton, by Rev. W. R. BROOKS, Rev. H. C. WOODS, of Minneapolis, MN, to Miss Mary H. EATON, daughter of Rev. George W. EATON, President of Madison University.
July 18, in Sangerfield, by Rev. J. G. TRAVIS, Mr. Lewis RUSSELL to Miss Helen A. MILLS, both of Hamilton.
Sept. 19, at the bride's residence, by Rev. J. M. STIFLER, Bradley BILLINGS and Mrs. E. C. SIMONS.
Oct. 4, in Hamilton, by Rev. W. D. ELWELL, Henry KELLEY and Mary E., youngest daughter of Alexander SMITH, both of Otsego.

DEMOCRATIC REPUBLICAN - 1878

Oct. 9, by Rev. James COOTE, Ernest C. BUTLER and Miss Lois E. FOSTER, all of Hamilton.
Oct. 31, at Morrisville, by Rev. W. H. MAYNARD, J. E. SLAUGH, M.D. of Hamilton, and Miss Nellie D. COMAN, of Morrisville.
Nov. 3, in Hamilton, by Rev. Dr. HARVEY, Jacob R. MILLER, of Augusta, KS, and Mrs. Rebecca REESE, of South Hamilton.
Nov. 6, in Lebanon, at the residence of the bride's mother, by Rev. Seward M. DODGE, Mr. Charles H. CLOSE to Miss Lyda A. STEWART, all of Lebanon.
Dec. 2, by Rev. James COOTE, Mr. Francis A. SWEATMAN, of Camden, Oneida Co., and Miss Mary A. KEATING, of Camville, Ontario Co., Canada.
Dec. 11, in Lebanon, by Rev. G. B. SIMONS, Edward M. COOK and Mrs. Jennie R. COLE, both of Lebanon.
Dec. 25, by Rev. G. A. RAWSON, Mr. C. W. SMITH, of Cincinnatus, NY, and Mary C., daughter of H. P. HARTSHORN, of Hamilton.

1879

Jan. 1, at Morrisville, by Rev. George B. SIMMONS, George H. PARTRIDGE to Clara J. QUAIL, both of Lebanon.
Jan. 1, by Rev. J. E. NASMITH, Mr. Darwin N. OLCOTT, of Pompey, to Miss Mary A. LAW, of Stockbridge.
Jan. 29, at North Brookfield, by Rev. A. H. MARSHALL, Charles F. SHERMAN to Fannie L. HOLMES, both of Hubbardsville.
Feb. 12, in Hubbardsville, by Rev. O. M. TODD, Romaine RISLEY and Miss Ada CRANDALL, both of Hubbardsville.
Feb. 27, in Hartwick, NY, by Rev. CASLER, George H. COBBIN, of Fair Haven, CT, and Miss Ruth G. SLAYTON, of Cossockton [Coshocton?], OH.
Mar. 31, in West Eaton, by Rev. J. W. WILSON, Mr. Lee AUDSLEY to Rose, youngest daughter of Samuel SELFE.
Mar. 16, at Avon, NY, by Rev. F. A. WOODARD, George M. WAITE, of Hamilton, and Minnie M. DAHM, of West Branch, NY.
Apr. 2, at the Park House, by Rev. J. M. STIFLER, Andrew J. SHAUL, of Morrisville, and Miss May E. BAKER, of Siloam, NY.
Apr. 8, at Lebanon, by Rev. S. M. DODGE, Miss Annie C. WAGNER, of Lebanon, to George T. HOXIE, of Providence, RI.
May 7, in Utica, by Rev. James COOTE, Mr. Zarah SIMONS, of Madison, and Mrs. Rhoda CLARKE, of Hamilton.

DEMOCRATIC REPUBLICAN - 1879

May 8, at the residence of Dr. J. M. STIFLER, officiating clergyman, Mr. J. Byron ROLLINS and Miss Hattie J. JAQUAY, both of Poolville.

May 24, at the residence of Mrs. C. E. STORRS at Eaton, by Rev. Thomas WILSON, Charles W. RICH and Alida M. THROOP, both of Eaton.

May 29, in Eaton, by Rev. J. J. W. WILSON, William HANNA, of West Eaton, and Mrs. HARDACRE, of Utica.

June 10, in Hartford, NY, by H. L. ANDREWS, Seneca B. BURCHARD, of Grant Park, IL, to Miss Hannah MILLER, of New Hartford.

June 10, at the home of the bride's father, by Rev. George B. SIMONS, George H. MORTON to Adell RICHARDSON, all of Eaton.

June 15, in West Eaton, by Rev. Judson DAVIS, James CADY and Mrs. Nancy R. TAYLOR, of West Eaton.

June 20, in Hamilton, by Dr. OSBORN, Mr. Myron W. HAYNES, of Madison, and Miss Florence FELT, of Hamilton.

June 24, in Clinton, by Rev. T. B. HUDSON, F. N. TOMPKINS, of Hamilton, to Minnie A. MYRICK, of the former place.

July 3, in Lebanon, by Rev. S. M. DODGE, William G. COLVIN to Miss Nancy E. SPOONER, both of Eaton.

[No date], by Rev. O. D. TAYLOR, W. H. WILLIAMS, of Hamilton, and Susan E. BOLAND, of Oswego. (Issue of July 17th.)

Aug. 18, in West Eaton, by Rev. Judson DAVIS, Arthur G. BRADSHAW, of Wales, St. Clair Co., MI, and Miss Rosetta H. STABBINS, of Whitesville, Alleghany Co., NY.

Aug. 13, in Eaton, by Rev. Judson DAVIS, Albert COSTELLO, of Eaton, and Miss Ida S. STEVENS, of Earlville.

Aug. 30, in Hamilton, by Rev. J. M. STIFLER, Frank W. WINTER (? paper torn) of Preston, Ontario, and Miss Ida B. RISLEY, of Hamilton. Best wishes of her friends go with the bride to her foreign home.

Sept. 11, in Lebanon, by Rev. S. M. DODGE, Addison W. HEAD, of Prescott, AZ, and Alida S. BENEDICT, of Lebanon.

Sept. 28, in Friendship, Alleghany Co., NY, by Rev. F. M. ALVORD, George CASTIDAY, of Binghamton, NY, to Miss Sarah D. FISHER.

Oct. 8, in Stockbridge, by Rev. James COOTE, of Hamilton, William B. ELDRIDGE, of Oriskany Falls, and Mrs. Alice E. SNELL, nee Eaton, of Stockbridge.

Oct. 8, in Sherburne, by Rev. R. R. RIDDLE, of Boston, assisted by Rev. G. R. BURNSIDE, Rev. John GREEN, of Waterford, NY, to Annie D. REESE, of Sherburne.

DEMOCRATIC REPUBLICAN - 1879

Oct. 14, in Hamilton, by Rev. G. A. RAWSON, William S. BURDICK, of Springfield, MA, and Augusta S. SMITH, of Eaton.

Oct. 22, at the residence of Mrs. Juline PIERCE, of Hamilton, by Rev. Dr. BROOKS, Mr. Marvin STEWART, of Lebanon, and Honora HANSEN, of Hamilton.

Nov. 27, by Rev. James COOTE, Herbert E. FULLER and Gertie PUTNAM, both of Madison.

Nov. 27, in Lebanon, by Rev. S. M. DODGE, Otto P. MOOR, of Middlebury, VT, to Katie SEVERANCE, of Lebanon.

Dec. 10, in Lebanon, by Rev. DODGE, Isaac B. MARSH, of South Hamilton, and Mary COLVIN of Lebanon.

Dec. 8, in Hamilton, by Rev. Mr. PURRINGTON, Fred DUNHAM and Nellie BANNING, both of Hamilton.

Dec. 20, in Hamilton, by Rev. James COOTE, Frank E. CUMMINS and Myrta SINTON, both of Columbus, NY.

Dec. 30, at Bouckville, by Rev. Mr. HUBBARD, of Madison, Frank BENJAMIN to Rose COLE, both of Solsville.

Dec. 21, in Aurora, TX, Mr. L. W. TAYLOR, formerly of Eaton, and Miss Alice CHERITRE, of Coxsackie, NY.

1880

Jan. 1, at the M. E. Parsonage, Hamilton, by Rev. James COOTE, Orson P. MANCHESTER and Ernestine M. BETHKE, both of Hamilton.

Feb. 10, at the residence of the bride's father, H. C. HOWE, of West Eaton, by Rev. J. W. WILSON, Elmer E. HALSTEAD, of Waterloo, IA, to Etta C. HOWE of West Eaton.

Feb. 11, in Hamilton, by Rev. S. T. FORD, J. W. BROWNING, of Earlville, and M. Jenette HAYWARD, of Hamilton.

Feb. 12, in East Hamilton, at the home of the bride's parents, Mr. and Mrs. William GREEN, by Rev. W. S. PURRINGTON, Jay D. CURTIS, of Poolville, and Miss Addie GREEN, of East Hamilton.

Mar. 18, in Hamilton, by Rev. Dr. HARVEY, Albert N. REYNOLDS, of Springfield, MA, and Mrs. Elvira C. MINER.

Apr. 13, at the residence of George H. BAKER, Madison Center, by Rev. James COOTE, Henry D. RISLEY and Elizabeth M., only daughter of Edmund WOODMAN, of Madison.

April 7, at the residence of the bride's father in West Eaton, by Rev. J. W. WILSON, John BROWN of Pitcher, Chenango Co., NY, and Ada BEEBE, only daughter of Asa C. BEEBE.

DEMOCRATIC REPUBLICAN - 1880

[No date], at Vernon, Oneida Co., by Rev. H. HARVEY, Rev. James A. CUBBERLY to Miss Viola G. BROWN, daughter of A. J. BROWN, of Vernon. (Issue of April 23d.)

May 4, in West Newark, NY, by Rev. H. L. HUBBARD, B. F. CASE, of Hamilton, and Miss M. E. PIERCE, of West Newark.

May 18, in Watertown, at the residence of the bride's parents, by Rev. G. J. PORTER, Lamott L. PIERCE and Fannie CROSS, all of Watertown.

June 2, at the residence of the bride's parents in Lebanon, by Rev. S. M. DODGE, W. H. PATTERSON and Miss Ernestine R. RICHMOND.

June 21, in Hamilton, by Rev. James H. BENEDICT, Frank L. SMITH and Miss Emma G. HALL, both of Boston, MA.

June 6, at the residence of the bride in Erieville, by Rev. E. E. REED, Joshua A. WELLS, of West Eaton, and Mrs. Clark WELLS, of the former place.

July 5, at Solsville, by F. H. MANCHESTER, Jesse TOUSLEY and Dora GREEN, both of Augusta, Oneida Co., NY.

July 14, at the residence of the bride's parents in this village [Hamilton], by Rev. W. H. MAYNARD, Rev. S. E. WILCOX, pastor of the Baptist Church at Homer, NY, and late of the Hamilton Theological Seminary, and Miss Sarah BAKER, of Hamilton.

ANNIVERSARY: The 10th anniversary of the marriage of Mr. and Mrs. H. H. KEITH, of Hamilton, was Aug. 9th.

Aug. 19, at the residence of the bride's father, by Rev. BURCHARD, of New York, Prof. Eugene P. SISSON, of Colgate Academy, to Miss Jennie A. BUELL, daughter of Warren F. BUELL.

Sept. 7, in Hamilton, at the M. E. Parsonage, by Rev. H. M. CHURCH, George GLAZIER and Ida MANN, all of Hamilton.

Aug. 28, at Reedsbury, WI, by Clergyman J. H. WHITNEY, Frank C. ELLIOTT, of Ironton, WI, to Miss Lizzie STOWE, formerly of Hamilton.

Sept. 30, in Hamilton, at the home of the bride's parents, by Rev. S. WILCOX, pastor of the Baptist Church, Homer, NY, Eugene NILES, of Franklin, and Lillian BAKER, youngest daughter of John BAKER, Jr.

Nov. 9, in Madison, by Rev. A. J. WALWORTH, John H. PIERCE, of Lincklaen, Chenango Co., NY, and Miss Alice R. TUTTLE, of Madison.

Nov. 24, in Hamtilon, by Rev. A. M. BEEBE, William SMITH, of Lebanon, to Estelle LEACH, of Hamilton.

DEMOCRATIC REPUBLICAN - 1881

1881

NOTE: This year's file lacks issues from 24th Feb., 1881, to 16th June, except for issue of April 14.
Last issue of 1880 was Dec. 30th
1881 starts with issue of Jan. 13th

Jan. 12, at the Presbyterian Church at Milford, NY, by Rev. Seward W. DODGE, assisted by Rev. D. C. OLMSTEAD, Almon D. BLAKELY, M.D. and Jennie ROBINSON, both of Milford.

Feb. 23, in Hamilton, by Rev. A. M. BEEBE, Marcus P. SCHENCK, of Fulton, and Miss Hannah HARTSHORN, of Hamilton.

Apr. 17, by Prof. M. L. ANDREWS, Mr. Sidney TOMPKINS, of Madison, to Mrs. Eunice B. NICHOLS, of Hamilton.

June 14, in Hamilton, by Rev. Robert G. SEYMOUR, Mr. E. T. FLETCHER, of Boston, and Laura T. WILBUR, of Hamilton.

July 5, at the Methodist Parsonage in Hamilton, by Rev. H. M. CHURCH, Peter PULVER, of Volney, Otsego Co., and Mrs. H. Adella CLARKE, of Hamilton.

Aug. 3, in Juniata, NE, by Rev. O. A. BUZZELL, William D. SEWELL and Miss Cora E. WOOD, of Juniata.

Aug. 16, at the residence of the bride's parents in Madison, by Rev. H. C. CRONIN, Samuel R. MOTT, Jr., of New York, and Miss Nettie C. PECKHAM.

Aug. 25, at the residence of the bride's mother, in Lebanon, by Prof. A. M. BEEBE, Charles S. WOODMAN, of Madison, and Miss Alice LEACH.

Sept. 28, at the Baptist Church in Hamilton, by Rev. H. A. HAZSEN, assisted by Pres. DODGE, Mr. Wells B. SIZER and Miss Mae HOWES, daughter of Prof. O. HOWES, of Hamilton.

Oct. 2, at South Hamilton, by Rev. E. HOLROYD, Mr. J. M. KING, of Columbus, and Mrs. C. M. JOHNSON, of Hamilton.

Sept. 20, in San Francisco, CA, Mr. D. R. ORMSBY and Miss Tillie M. BOYLER, both of San Francisco.

Sept. 28, at the residence of Dwight LELAND in Madison, by Rev. I. D. PEASLEE, Ira M. GARRISON, of Albany, and Carrie A. BRAITHWAITE, of Ann Arbor, MI.

Oct. 5, at the residence of the bride's father in Madison, by Rev. I. D. PEASLEY, J. N. WOODMAN and Francena A. STOWELL, both of Madison.

Oct. 6, at the residence of the bride's parents in Hamilton, by Rev. S. BURNHAM, Charles F. HAHN and Miss Hattie A. HOWE, both of Hamilton.

DEMOCRATIC REPUBLICAN - 1881

[No date], in Lebanon at the residence of the bride's father, George W. SMITH, by Rev. E. D. REED, Charles E. BILLS and Mary R. SMITH.

Nov. 1, at the home of the bride in Albion, WI, by Rev. Mr. WILLIAMS, Mr. Dolf L. BABCOCK, of Hamilton, and Miss Harrie J. LANGWORTHY, of Albion.

Nov. 8, at the residence of T. B. CHASE, by Rev. L. M. OSBORN, Charles L. OSBORN, of Hamilton, and Miss Martha E. SHEFFIELD, of Rose, Wayne Co., NY.

Nov. 16, in Milford, NY, by Rev. S. M. DODGE, E. D. SQUIRES and Mrs. Ada L. ADAMS, daughter of Samuel BENEDICT, of Lebanon.

Dec. 21, in Hamilton, Edgar WESTCOTT, of Sherburne, and Miss Georgie HALL, granddaughter of Deacon Joseph BANNING, of Hamilton.

Dec. 8, in Palmyra, NY, by Rev. J. G. WEBSTER, George S. POSSEE, of Palmyra, and Carrie A. HUGHES, of Hamilton.

Dec. 27, in Utica, at the residence of the bride's mother, by Rev. A. BRAMLEY, James H. MC CARTHY, of Oriskany Falls, and Mary Ella RICHARDS, of Utica.

1882

Jan. 15, at the Messenger House in Smyrna, by Rev. C. T. JOHNSON, James K. KENNEDY to Miss Carrie R. BROGAN, both of Hamilton.

Feb. 22, at the residence of Zarah SIMMONS, in Madison, by Rev. W. H. CHURCH, George K. HALL, of Earlville, and Miss Janette SIMMONS, of Madison.

Feb. 23, at the M. E. Parsonage in Hamilton, by Rev. I. D. PEASLEY, Robert LLOYD, of Madison, and Miss Mary E. BENNETT, of North Brookfield.

Mar. 8, in Hamilton, by Rev. H. C. CRONIN, LeRoy FAIRCHILD and Miss Della SMITH, all of Hamilton.

Mar. 15, at the residence of the bride's parents in Hamilton, by Rev. W. F. PURRINGTON, George W. ABBEY, of Madison, and Miss Inez COREY, of Hamilton.

Mar. 8, in Madison, at the residence of Henry LEWIS, by Rev. I. D. PEASLEY, Mr. Dell WOODHULL to Anna BUTTERFIELD, all of Madison.

Mar. 16, in Madison, at the residence of Mrs. CARTER, by Rev. I. D. PEASLEY, John DYE to Mrs. Harrie CAMP, all of Madison.

Apr. 8, at the M. E. Parsonage in Waterville, by Rev. James COOTE, William J. JOHNSON and Ella L. HYDE, of Eaton.

DEMOCRATIC REPUBLICAN - 1882

June 20, in Waterville, by Squire CHURCH, Frank L. CULVER, of Bay City, MI, and Miss Dena J. BEEBE, of Hamilton.

June 29, at the residence of Mr. B. W. SAWDY, Main St., by Rev. J. Allen MAXWELL, Mr. L. LANE, of Youngstown, OH, and Mrs. C. A. WICKWIRE, of Madison.

July 4, at the Methodist Parsonage in Hamilton, by Rev. A. M. CHURCH, Charles R. TANNER, of New Milford, PA, and Miss Anna WOOD, of Portland, Canada.

Aug. 9, in Poolville, by Rev. R. K. SMITH, William P. SAUNDERS and Mrs. Lida SHERMAN, both of Poolville.

Aug. 17, at the residence of the bride's sister, Mrs. Thomas RUSHMER, by Rev. Milton F. NEGUS, Marvin W. WILCOX and Miss Mary H. CROSSMAN, both of Hamilton.

Sept. 4, at Eaton, by Rev. Judson DAVIS, S. H. PAYSON, of Norwich, and Mrs. Lutie PAYSON, of Eaton.

Sept. 13, at the bride's home, by Rev. R. J. SMITH, John B. BUELL, of States Corners, WI, formerly of Hamilton, and Mrs. Matilda A. BUELL, of Hamilton.

Sept. 20, at Lebanon, by Rev. Henry C. CRONIN, Ladurna BALLARD to Fallie C. HITCHCOCK, both of Lebanon.

[No date], in St. Thomas's Church, Hamilton, by Rev. Dr. MURRAY, William M. WEST and Alice GRAY, all of Hamilton.

Sept. 27, in Madison, by Rev. I. D. PEASLEY, A. TUBBS, M.D. and Geneva M. BROWN, both of Oriskany Falls.

Sept. 28, at the Park Hotel, Waterville, by Rev. I. D. PEASLEY, George LATTIMER, of Madison, and Mary NIEDICK, of Oxford, NY.

Oct. 6, in Binghamton, William H. MANCHESTER, of Hamilton, and Miss Emma A. BARRETT, of Binghamton.

Oct. 9, at the residence of the bride's father at Maple Grove, Earlville, Oct. 9, by Rev. A. M. BEEBE, Walter J. ALLEN, of Toledo, OH, and Minnie S. MORGAN, of Lebanon.

Oct. 25, at Hamilton, by Rev. H. C. CRONIN, Frank OGILVIE, of Smithport, PA, and Lillian M. BUSH, of Hamilton.

Nov. 1, at St. Mary's Church, Hamilton, by Rev. Father HANNETT, Martin MC DONALD, of Hamilton, and Miss Nora MORAN, of Sherburne.

Oct. 31, in Lebanon, by Rev. C. P. P. FOX, George E. HITCHCOCK and Libbie L. BOYD, both of Lebanon.

Oct. 28, in this village [Hamilton], by Rev. H. M. CHURCH, Hiram HITCHCOCK, of Pompey, and Miss Ann SMITHERS, of Otselic.

Nov. 5, in West Eaton, by Rev. C. M. JONES, George SMITH to Cora WESTCOTT.

DEMOCRATIC REPUBLICAN - 1882

Nov. 8, at the residence of Walker CURTIS in Madison, by Rev. I. D. PEASLEY, John WOOD, of Hamilton, and Mrs. Mary A. WATTS, of Madison.
Nov. 22, at the residence of Solomon BAKER, in Eaton, by Rev. J. B. MURRAY, Vinson R. HOWARD, of Saratoga, and Mrs. Lida O. CAMPBELL, of Hamilton.
Dec. 20, in Hamilton, by Rev. J. B. MURRAY, Charles WICKWIRE and Louise PARKER, all of Hamilton.
Dec. 19, in this village [Hamilton], by Rev. H. S. STACKPOLE, Mr. NICHOLSON, of Rome, and Mrs. Nettie WILLIAMS, of Hamilton.
Dec. 20, at the residence of Dr. OSBORN near Hamilton, J. C. BRICKER, of Schenectady, and Miss Minnie OSBORN, of Hamilton.

1883

Jan. 4, at the residence of the bride's father at Pittstown, by Rev. H. H. DAVIS, William A. RHODES, of Hubbardsville, to Anna F. BOSWORTH, of Pittstown.
Jan. 10, at West Eaton, by Rev. C. M. JONES, Charles W. ELLIS, of Smithville, and Nettie, eldest daughter of H. A. WADSWORTH.
Jan. 17, at his residence in Diana, NY, by Rev. H. C. DIKE, Mr. Otis A. DIKE and Miss Ada A. SHELDON, of Hamilton.
Jan. 31, at St. Mary's Church in this village [Hamilton], by Rev. Father HANNET, W.F. CLEVELAND and Ella HOGAN, both of Hamilton.
Feb. 15, in Hamilton, by Rev. H. C. CRONIN, Emory A. TIBBETTS and Julia A. SHELTON, both of Hamilton.
Feb. 28, near Poolville, by Rev. W. T. GALLOWAY, Uri RHODES, of Hubbardsville, and Mattie BRONSON.
Mar. 7, in Lebanon, by Rev. W. R. BROOKS, Thomas H. CADY and Addie C. KIMBALL, both of Lebanon.
Apr. 12, at the residence of the bride's father in Poolville, J. F. BLAKEMAN, of Hamilton, and Hattie A. CURTIS, of Poolville, by Rev. Dwight WILLIAMS, of Cazenovia.
Apr. 3, at Brown's Valley, MN, by Rev. G. D. BALLANTINE, Orlo ROGERS, formerly of Hamilton, and Mrs. Julia G. POTTS, of Brown's Valley.
May 9, at the residence of the bride's mother at New York Mills, by Rev. Mr. COBB, of the M. E. Church, Chauncey E. TALMAN, of Solsville, and Anna CLARK, of New York Mills.

DEMOCRATIC REPUBLICAN - 1883

May 29, in Hamilton, by Rev. Dr. MURRAY, of the Episcopal Church, Newton R. WICKWIRE and Mattie S. WRIGHT, all of Hamilton.

GOLDEN WEDDING: On Wed., June 20, Mr. and Mrs. GIPSON celebrated their 50th wedding anniversary at their home on Payne Street, Hamilton.

July 1, in Hamilton, by Rev. Henry C. CRONIN, Albert B. PLUMB, of Hubbardsville, to Lura THAYER, of Hamilton.

June 28, in the West Eaton Church, Charles HOWE, of Elmira, and Miss Anna, daughter of S. W. LAWRENCE, of West Eaton.

July 5, in Madison, by Rev. Albert MARSHALL, W. H. MATHESON of Panora, Guthrie Co., IA, and Hattie EATON, of Hamilton.

July 14, at the M. E. Parsonage in Hamilton, by Rev. G. G. DALNES, Samuel TUCKER and Cora KELLEY, both of Solsville.

July 17, in Hartford, CT, by Rev. William F. NICHOLS, David DAMON, of Morrisville, to Christine ROBERTS, of Hartford.

Aug. 15, in Manlius, by Rev. G. M. HARDY, Charles E. DONNER, of Cazenovia, and Nellie ALLEN, of Fayetteville.

Sept. 15, in Eaton, by Rev. Judson DAVIS, G. H. BUCKLEY, of Madison, to Miss Hattie T. SIMPSON, of Hamilton.

Oct. 13, by Rev. D. G. DAINS, George R. SLACK, of Greene, to Sarah E. WATERSON, of Hamilton.

Oct. 10, in Earlville, by Rev. J. G. BENSON, Gaylord A. BUTTLES and Mary LOOMIS, both of Hubbardsville.

Oct. 17, at the residence of the bride's brother near Poolville, by Rev. J. G. BENSON, Hamilton J. WHITFORD, of Leonardsville, and Carrie SAWDY, of Waterville.

Nov. 15, in Ilion, by Rev. Judson DAVIS, E. G. STODDARD and C. FARRINGTON, both of Ilion.

Nov. 21, by Rev. Mr. WALWORTH, James KELLEY to Hattie TUCKER, both of Solsville.

Nov. 21, in Solsville, by Rev. A. H. MARSHALL, William SALISBURY, of St. Louis, to Mary CURTIS, of Solsville.

Nov. 22, in South Hamilton, by Rev. Judson DAVIS, C. H. BRONSON, of Poolville, and Miss Nora D. NICKHAM, of South Hamilton.

Oct. 14, in Earlville, by Rev. J. George BENSON, John R. PARSONS of Earlville, and Viola E. COOK of Poolville.

DEMOCRATIC REPUBLICAN - 1883

Nov. 29, at the Baptist Parsonage in Eaton, by Rev. Judson DAVIS, Edwin FLEMING and Miss Altie GREENE, both of Lebanon.
Nov. 29, at Lambertsville, NJ, by Rev. W. P. S. STICKLAND, assisted by the Rev. William JOHNSON, Burt P. SPERRY, of Hamilton, and Martha C. JOHNSON, of Lambertsville, NJ.
Dec. 19, in Lebanon, by Rev. W. R. BROOKS, Gillette I. WILCOX, of Erieville, and Mamie E. GREENE, of Lebanon.
Dec. 18, in Madison, by Rev. A. W. MARSHALL, Clarence RISLEY and May COREY, both of Hamilton.
Dec. 18, at the residence of the bride's parents in Pratt's Hollow, by Rev. W. F. TOOKE, Ex-Assemblyman E. C. PHILPOT and Libbie CRITCHEL, both of Pratt's Hollow.
Dec. 27, in Madison, by Rev. Mr. WALRATH, Prof. Arthur M. PRESTON, Principal of the Madison Union School, and Miss Nettie L. BABCOCK, of Madison.
Dec. 27, at the residence of Mr. T. LEONARD in this village [Hamilton], by Rev. G. T. DAINS, Albert F. FLINT, of Colesville, Broome Co., NY, and Miss Lizzie BRADY, of Randallsville.

1884

Jan. 30, in Hamilton, by Rev. S. BURNHAM, Edward KINGSBURY and Miss Sarah FOSTER, all of Hamilton.
Jan. 26, in Earlville, by Rev. J. G. BENSON, Elmer A. HUFF and Miss Jennie M. TOOKER, both of Hamilton.
Jan. 31, at Pittsfield, MA, by Rev. Mr. TERRETT, assisted by Rev. ANDREWS, William L. PADDOCK, M.D., of Groton, MA, and Miss Lizzie L. CRAINE, of Dalton, MA.
Feb. 13, at the residence of the bride's parents, by Rev. G. G. DAINS, Emmett A. TOOKE, of Pratt's Hollow, and Miss Emma M. KELLOWAY.
Mar. 9, at the M. E. Parsonage in Hamilton, by Rev. G. G. DAINS, Jay D. SERGANT and Miss Nettie BLAIR, both of Madison.
Mar. 12, at the residence of the bride's parents in Madison, by Rev. G. G. DAINS, Charles S. WOODMAN and Miss Eveleen LAMB, both of Madison.
Mar. 18, at the residence of the bride's parents in East Hamilton, by Rev. J. G. BENSON, Bert J. NEWTON, of Earlville, to Gertie M. SHEPARDSON, of East Hamilton.

DEMOCRATIC REPUBLICAN - 1884

Mar. 16, in Eaton, by Rev. Judson DAVIS, Charles B. LEACH, of Eaton, and Miss Mina V. ROACHE, of Pratts Hollow.

Mar. 26, in Hamilton, by Rev. S. BURNHAM, Frank P. WATERS, of Groton, NY, and Mary A. STARK, of Hamilton.

Mar. 30, in Cazenovia, by Rev. James R. THOMAS, Walter W. FELT, of Hamilton, and Miss Blanche L. HART, of Morrisville.

Apr. 6, in Hamilton, by Rev. G. G. DAINS, DeWitt ARNOLD, of Hamilton, and Florence CORNICK, of Chenango Bridge, NY.

Apr. 8, in Hamilton M. E. Parsonage, by Rev. G. G. DAINS, Jesse L. SMITH, of Hamilton, and Miss Rebecca TOMLINSON, of Pine Woods.

Apr. 16, in Toledo, OH, by Rev. W. W. WILLIAMS, Mary E. SPENCER and Homer SPENCER-COMSTOCK, of Cazenovia.

Apr. 19, in Hamilton, by Rev. H. C. CRONIN, Frank M. CASH, of Earlville, to Ella M. TALCOTT, of Hamilton.

Apr. 21, in the Congregational parsonage at Hamilton, by Rev. Henry CRONIN, Will Foster MERRILL, of Oneida, to Gertrude E. NASH, of Oneida.

May 26, in Hamilton village, by Rev. G. G. DAINS, Dennis A. POPE and Anna P. RUNDELL, both of Solsville.

June 2, at the M. E. Parsonage in Hamilton, by Rev. G. G. DAINS, Joseph A. BANKER, of Battle Creek, MI, and Nettie R. BISHOP, of Bouckville.

June 2, at the M. E. Parsonage in Earlville, by Rev. J. G. BENSON, Arthur WOOD and Sarah F. BELL, both of Lebanon.

June 8, in South Hamilton, by Rev. Judson DAVIS, George D. THOMAS, of Otego, and Carrie A. COMSTOCK, of South Hamilton.

June 11, in Hamilton, by Rev. G. G. DAINS, Granger E. FULLER, of Central Square, and Fannie W. HAYDEN, of Coughdenony, NY.

July 3, in Eaton, by Rev. Judson DAVIS, Henry A. BROWN, of New Woodstock, and Mrs. Hattie BROWN, of DeRuyter.

July 1, in Hamilton, by Rev. Mr. W. R. BROOKS, DeWitt STONE and Miss Frankie CARPENTER, both of Randallsville.

July 23, in Hamilton, by Rev. G. G. DAINS, Stanton DAVIS, of Verona, and Miss Etta D. CROWELL, of Poolville.

Aug. 8, in Hamilton, by Rev. Henry CRONIN, Willis E. MONTANA, of Pine Woods, to Viola M. DUELL, of Lebanon.

Aug. 6, at Oriskany Falls, by Rev. A. A. PIERCE, Samuel WOOD to Jennie Rose MANCHESTER, of Solsville.

DEMOCRATIC REPUBLICAN - 1884

Aug. 12, in Hamilton, by Rev. W. H. MAYNARD, F. W. COLE-GROVE, Prin. of Marion Institute, and Miss Mabel DART, of Hamilton.

Sept. 3, in Hamilton, by Rev. S. H. STACKPOLE, Prof. A. G. HARKNESS and Miss Katherine Margaret BEEBEE, both of this village [Hamilton].

Sept. 4, at the Congregational parsonage in Madison, by Rev. George E. SOPER, Edgar WELDER and Miss Hattie BURGDOFF, both of Albion, Oswego Co., NY.

[No date], at the Congregational parsonage in Madison, by Rev. SOPER, Amasa J. HOLMES and Sophronia BLOWERS, both of Lincklaen, Chenango Co., NY. (In issue of Sept. 11th.)

Oct. 8, at Chicago, by Rev. W. M. LAWRENCE, Howard H. TOMPKINS, of Throp, WI, and Miss Eliza M. COLEMAN, of Hamilton.

Oct. 12, at the home of Mrs. Ellen HOLT, by Rev. Judson DAVIS, Charles E. HOLT, of South Hamilton, and May ANDERSON, of North New Berlin.

Oct. 26, in West Eaton, by Rev. Mr. ERWIN, Allison GATES and Miss Carrie C. SEELEY, both of Lebanon.

Oct. 13, in Madison, at the residence of Joshua ROOT, by Rev. A. J. WALRATH, F. S. FOWLER, of Oriskany Falls, and Lulu ROOT, of Madison.

Nov. 6, at the residence of Margaret POND in this village [Hamilton], by Rev. S. H. STACKPOLE, Edward W. HUNT and Miss Annie SMITH, both of Madison.

Dec. 3, in South Hamilton, at the bride's uncle's, J. MILLER, by Rev. Judson DAVIS, Mr. J. Jay KIMBALL to Miss Elle J. BUGBEE, both of South Hamilton.

Dec. 31, in this village [Hamilton], by Rev. W. R. BROOKS, Elmer Eugene BEEKMAN, and Minnie Eloise BEEKMAN, both of Sherburne.

1885

Jan. 28, at St. Thomas's Church in Hamilton, by Rev. J. E. WILKINSON, Walter J. BANNING and Mrs. Lida H. GATES, both of Hamilton.

Feb. 12, in Eaton, by Rev. Judson DAVIS, Howard MURPHY and Caroline JOHNSON, all of Eaton.

Feb. 11, in Hamilton, by Rev. J. Fletcher BROWN, Dwight HULETT and Flora PARLER, of Hamilton.

Feb. 18, in this village [Hamilton], by Rev. J. W. HAMMOND, F. C. BEST, of Hamilton, and Miss Winnie EVANS, of Whitestown, NY.

DEMOCRATIC REPUBLICAN - 1885

Mar. 19, at the residence of the bride in Hamilton, by Rev. C. Winton PATTERSON, of Rochester, John G. PATTERSON to Miss Ella S. TRACY, both of Hamilton.

Apr. 27, at the M. E. Parsonage in Hamilton, by Rev. J. F. BROWN, M. S. PENNOCK, of West Eaton, to Eliza BROWN, of East Hamilton.

May 20, at the bride's home in Hamilton, by Rev. J. F. BROWN, Allen N. ENOS to Rose D. THOMPSON, both of Hamilton.

June 8, at Earlville, by Rev. L. W. JACKSON, Samuel RAY and Miss Louise M. WHEELER, all of Hamilton.

June 17, at Oswego, by Rev. A. H. PRISER, Charles VAN HOUSEN, of Hamilton, and Miss Louisa YORKER, of Oswego, NY.

Aug. 7, in Utica, Jesse APPLEGATE and Mary BRASS, both of Hamilton.

Oct. 28, at the residence of the bride's parents in Lebanon, by Rev. Dr. BROOKS, Milton WOODMAN, of Madison, and Lelia RICE, daughter of DeWitt RICE, of Lebanon.

Oct. 26, at St. Mary's Church, Hamilton, by Rev. Father HANNETT, John WHITE and Alice MURPHY, both of Hamilton.

[No date], in Eaton, by Rev. Thomas WILSON, John MILLS, of Hamilton, and Mary CLOSE, of Randallsville.

Dec. 23, at the bride's home in Madison, by Rev. R. FLINT, Fred S. COLLISTER, of Cleveland, OH, to Nellie M. ALLEN, of Madison.

Dec. 24, in Penn Yan, by Rev. Mr. LORD, Edward S. CURTIS, of Chicago, and Miss Gertrude JOHNSON, of Lambertsville, NJ.

Dec. 29, in Munnsville, by Rev. M. L. DALTON, Arthur C. TALCOTT and Maggie FENTON, both of Hamilton.

Dec. 31, in Hamilton, by Rev. H. STACKPOLE, Will CASE and Miss Adria KERN, both of Hamilton.

1886

Jan. 7, in Lebanon, by Rev. H. G. ALLABAN, Walter R. INGALLS, of Hamilton, to Angie BENEDICT, of Lebanon.

Jan. 7, in Madison, by Rev. R. FLINT, Benjamin F. HEAD, of Poolville, to Miss Malvina W. SMITH, of Madison.

Jan. 19, in Hamilton, Alvah B. RORABACK, of Castleton, NY, to Kate METTLER, of Hamilton.

Feb. 23, at Sherburne, by Rev. A. K. BATCHELLOR, Willard W. BOWERS to Isaphine J. WATERS, both of Sherburne.

Jan. 30, at Hamilton, by Rev. J. F. BROWN, William BASSETT and Ada WILBUR, both of Madison.

DEMOCRATIC REPUBLICAN - 1886

Feb. 22, in Clinton, by Rev. L. GOLDEN, Benjamin L. THOMPSON, of McDonough, to Mrs. Mary E. CASITY, of Clinton.

Mar. 3, at the home of the bride, by Rev. J. F. BROWN, W. D. WOODMAN and Miss Ada LAMB, of Madison.

Feb. 9, at Canastota, by Rev. E. A. TUTTLE, Will ARNOLD and Winnie FANCHER, all of Canastota.

Feb. 17, at Smithville, by Rev. O. G. H. PHILLIPS, William WARNER, of Lenox, and Miss Katie F. CLUTE, of Smithville.

Feb. 17, at Canastota, by Rev. J. C. DUNCANSON, William H. BRITTON and Bertha M. NASH.

Jan. 21, in Syracuse, by Rev. G. SPAULDING, E. P. BEVILLARD and Miss Sarah DODGE, both of Oneida.

Mar. 2, in Brookfield, by Rev. R. J. THOMPSON, Ernest REYNOLDS and Miss Lucy LAMB, both of Brookfield.

Mar. 3, in DeRuyter, by Rev. J. CLARK, Mr. Bert YAP, of Portsville, NY, and Miss Lizzie CRANDALL, of DeRuyter.

Feb. 22, in Hamilton, Mr. Ashel M. BURLISON and Miss Anna J. DURKEE, all of Augusta.

Mar. 3, in Utica, by Rev. R. L. BACHMAN, Henry C. DENNISON, of Knoxboro, and Miss Italia T. CRIM, of Mohawk.

Feb. 16, at Lansing, by Rev. I. J. NOURSE, George W. LAMB, of Hamilton, and Tilda CLARE, of Lansing, NY.

Mar. 10, at Klockville, by Rev. G. F. BUCKLEY, Charles A. DOUGLASS, of Mile Strip, and Carrie D. WHITE, of Vernon.

Mar. 18, at Vernon, by Rev. W. C. TAYLOR, Bert J. DODGE and Cora L. BEECHER, both of Verona.

Mar. 17, at Durhamville, by Rev. A. COCHRAN, Solomon A. CAMPBELL, at Painted Post, and Sarah J. WITTER, of Durhamville.

[No date], at Lebanon, by Rev. H. G. ALLABEN, John HYLAND and Nellie TEW.

Feb. 17, near Columbus City, IA, John A. GRIFFIS, formerly of Fenner, and Miss Ellen EVANS.

Mar. 16, in Brookfield, by Rev. R. J. THOMPSON, John N. HOGLE to Alice A. HOLCOMB, both of Brookfield.

Mar. 14, at West Edmeston, by Rev. Clayton A. BURDICK, Dorr P. SPENCER to Miss Estella M. POPLETON, both of Brookfield.

Mar. 17, at Brookfield, by Rev. J. H. TODD, George W. BURDICK, of Verona, and L. Lenora CLARKE.

Mar. 23, at Peterboro, NY, by Rev. O. G. H. PHILLIPS, Harvey A. AUSTIN, of Fenner, and Miss Eva WILKINSON, of Smithville.

DEMOCRATIC REPUBLICAN - 1886

Mar. 3, at Bennett's Corner, by Rev. Ellis ANDREWS, Abram L. RICKARD, of Pendleton, Niagara Co., NY, to Jennie M. BROTLE.

Mar. 18, in Utica, by Joseph LAMB, William H. BENSTED, of Madison, and Mary J. MAXSTED, of Lent Co., England.

Mar. 10, at Madison, by Rev. A. S. WALRATH, Andrew S. BENNETT, of Waterville, and Hattie E. TYNELL, of Madison.

Mar. 3, at Augusta, by Rev. M. COOK, Albert FELLOWS, of Solsville, and Henrietta HAYWARD, of Augusta.

Mar. 25, in the town of Vernon, by Rev. Wayne BREWSTER, George E. CORNEY, of Vernon, and Alice MAHANEY, of Vienna.

Mar. 31, in Hamilton, by Rev. N. L. ANDREWS, Hiram WRIGHT and Lucinda GARDNER.

Mar. 30, in Eaton, by Rev. W. P. OMANS, Luther SANDERSON and Mrs. Sophia HUDSON, both of Eaton.

Mar. 31, by Rev. O. G. H. PHILLIPS, Frederick HYLAND, of State Bridge, NY, and Minnie M. MORGAN, of Pratts Hollow.

Mar. 27, at Knoxboro, NY, by Rev. E. H. DICKENSON, Fred E. WING and Anna H. MORGAN, both of Augusta.

Mar. 24, at the residence of A. M. STEVENS, Madison Center, by Rev. R. FLINT, William H. BENJAMIN, of Solsville, and Valetta BRIGGS, of Madison.

Mar. 30, at the home of the bride, by Rev. M. WELLS, Frank J. KRETZ, of New York City, and Katie J. GILBERT, of State Bridge, NY.

Mar. 30, at the home of the bride, by Rev. M. WELLS, Mr. Harlan B. BEECRAFT, of Utica, NY, and Mary E. GILBERT, of State Bridge.

Apr. 4, at Brookfield, by Rev. J. G. BROOKS, Harley PALMITER to Edna B. BUCKLEY, all of Brookfield.

Apr. 6, at Augusta, by Rev. H. M. DODD, Alpha F. ORR, of Camden, and Eva E. GREEN.

Apr. 17, in Morrisville, by Rev. M. MERRILL, Fred NICHOLSON and Nellie RUNDELL, both of Hamilton.

Apr. 10, in Oxford, by Rev. B. F. BRADFORD, Asa P. HYDE and Mary F. JACOBS, all of Oxford.

Apr. 8, in Norwich, by Rev. A. G. UPTON, Herbert D. BARR and Alice May SCOTT, both of Norwich.

Mar. 30, in Ithaca, Orange BOOTH, of Candor, to Mrs. Sarah BLIVEN, of Ithaca; formerly waitress in the American Hotel in Norwich.

Apr. 7, in Oneida, by Rev. W. G. ROGERS, Charles L. MONROE and Mary ARNOLD, all of this village [Hamilton].

Apr. 6, in Canastota, by Rev. F. P. WINNIE, Theodore T. VISSEL and Jeanie C. SHELDON, both of Canastota.

DEMOCRATIC REPUBLICAN - 1886

Apr. 22, in Hamilton, by Rev. MAYNARD, Frank GODFREY and Kate MURPHY, all of Crescent, NY.

Apr. 18, in Smyrna, by Rev. C. A. BENJAMIN, Olivia F. SIMMONS to E. J. SPRAGUE, of Central Square.

Apr. 22, in Earlville, by Rev. L. W. JACKSON, Willis PAYNE to Lizzie M. BAYLIS, all of Madison County.

Apr. 14, at Elmira, by Rev. W. T. HENRY, Enos W. RUTAN, of Elmira, and Nellie ELWELL, formerly of Oneida.

Apr. 27, in Oneida, by Rev. Samuel JESSUP, James ANDERSON of Pittston, PA, and Carrie A. WESTCOTT, of Oneida.

Apr. 21, at Canastota, by Rev. J. C. DUNCANSON, Benjamin J. BURR and Lizzie E. CLUTE.

May 11, at the Powell House in Sherburne, by Rev. T. A. STEVENSON, Fred ROWLEY, of Earlville, and Hattie E. MASON, of Sherburne.

June 1, in Oneida, by Rev. E. H. DICKENSON, Arthur HAY and Helen D. E. DODGE, of Oneida.

June 2, in Oneida, by Rev. W. G. ROGERS, J. Laister JOYCE and Anna S. STEBBINS, both of Oneida.

June 2, at Canastota, by Rev. E. P. WINNIE, George E. JOHNSON and Carrie E. VAN AMAN, all of Canastota.

June 16, in this village, by Rev. N. A. COLEMAN, of Half Moon, NY, John O'NEIL, of Chappell, Cheyenne Co., NE, and Allie WARNER, of Hamilton.

June 10, at Madison, Ernest DAVIS and Miss Nellie MC CARTHY, both of Madison.

June 18, at Waterville, by Rev. H. NELSON, James MOTT, of Sangersfield, and Grace BEARDSLEY, of Waterville.

June 20, at Clinton, by Rev. R. FLINT, Herbert A. WAGNER, of Peterboro, and Flora P. AVERY, of Clinton.

June 20, at Cazenovia, by Rev. L. A. EDDY, J. COONZER and Hattie GORTON, both of Fenner.

June 20, at East Hamilton, by Rev. William WILLIAMS, Will STAPLETON and Miss Etta CLARK.

June 29, at Oneida, at St. John's Church, by Rev. J. Everist CATHALL, C. Edward EAGER, of Syracuse, and Marion, daughter of Mr. and Mrs. Seymour HARVEY, of Oneida.

June 28, at St. John's Church, by the rector above, Leander A. ROGERS, of Troy, NY, to Hattie, daughter of Asa KNOWLTON, of Durhamville.

June 22, at the residence of the bride's parents, by Rev. C. O. THATCHER, Clarence G. ADAMS and Miss Ada CARL, both of Chittenango, NY.

July 1, at Oneida, by Rev. A. COCHRAN, Mr. John S. LEONARD of Worcester, NY, and Miss Lizzie May LOOMIS, only daughter of Mr. and Mrs. John J. LOOMIS.

DEMOCRATIC REPUBLICAN - 1886

June 30, at Leeds, NY, by Rev. E. N. SEBRING, Mr. Stephen H. FARNAM, of Oneida, to Mrs. Sarah L. NEWKIRK, of Leeds.

June 30, in Oriskany Falls, by Rev. S. A. WORDEN, Mr. Horace SHEAD, of Oswego, and Frances A., daughter of K. J. WILLARD, of Oriskany Falls.

June 29, in DeRuyter, by Rev. A. C. SMITH, the Rev. John F. AMES and Miss Sophie A. WALL, both of DeRuyter, also

Fred O. HENDEE, of Sloan, IA, and Miss Zella E. WALL, of DeRuyter.

June 27, in DeRuyter, by Elder T. FISHER, Frank BRODERICK and Miss Mary CASE, both of Pompey, NY.

July 7, in Scranton, PA, by Rev. David SPENCER, Albert E. BAXTER, of Greene, NY, to Miss L. May PARKER, of Sherburne.

July 8, in Utica, by Rev. Dr. A. B. GOODRICH, Mr. Hubert J. PEEBLES, of Fulton, formerly of Oriskany Falls, and Miss Annie E. LONGLEY, of Utica.

July 3, at DeRuyter, by Rev. L. J. WHEELOCK, Ira D. MERRITT, of Georgetown, and Miss Sophronia A. WILLIAMS, of DeRuyter.

June 29, in the village of Manlius, by Rev. L. A. EDDY, Mr. Ehle FOX, of Cazenovia, and Miss Lucy A. PADDOCK, of Manlius.

June 29, at New Woodstock, by Rev. C. A. SMITH, Marshall W. TAYLOR and Miss Leta CONE, both of DeRuyter.

July 14, in Oneida, at the residence of the bride's parents, by Rev. Samuel JESSUP, Mr. Charle SEGAR and Miss Lulu A. SAGENDORF, both of Oneida.

July 22, in Brookfield, by Rev. E. J. THOMPSON, Charles A. TEFFT and Miss Mattie A. STILLMAN.

July 10, in Cazenovia, by G. H. BENJAMIN, Esq., Mr. Elias POWELL, of New Woodstock, and Miss Alice OAKE, of Erieville.

July 18, in Tully, NY, by Rev. JONES, Mr. Edward S. SHULTS, of Cazenovia, and Miss Flora B. NEGUS, of Fabius.

July 21, in Oneida, by Rev. S. JESSUP, at the residence of T. F. HAND, Sr., Mr. W. W. MC DONALD, of Pierre, SD, and Mrs. Lyman G. SHEPARD, of Buffalo.

July 28, at the residence of the bride's parents in Madison, by Rev. W. TISDALE, father of the bride, Josiah R. BENNETT, of Camden, NY, and Jennie M. TISDALE, of Madison.

July 28, in Utica, by Rev. M. D. MC DOUGALL, Mr. Charley O. WEDGE, of Hamilton, and Miss Mary E., daughter of the officiating clergyman, of Utica.

DEMOCRATIC REPUBLICAN - 1886

Aug. 10, in Hamilton, at the residence of Clarence RISLEY, by Rev. H. C. CRONIN, Mr. Martin R. COLSON, of Hubbardsville, and Miss Ida COREY, of Hamilton village.

Aug. 12, at the home of the bride, by Rev. H. C. CRONIN, Dr. P. B. HAVENS to Miss Lyra FOOTE, all of Hamilton.

Aug. 11, in Nelson, at the home of the bride's aunt, Mrs. S. L. JONES, Mr. Henry THOMAS, of Madison, and Miss Anna DAVIS, of Nelson.

July 29, at Allentown, PA, Mr. John BALLENTINE and Miss Sarah G. HOXWORTH.

Aug. 18, at the home of the bride, by Rev. Dr. BROOKS, Mr. Herbert S. MINER, of Hamilton, and Miss Mary A. ARMSTRONG, of Randallsville.

Aug. 31, at Hamilton, by Rev. Dr. H. HARVEY, assisted by President E. DODGE, D.D., L.L.D., Prof. DeWitt D. FORWARD, of Burlington College, IA, to Miss Grace A. HARVEY, of Hamilton.

Sept. 1, at the residence of the bride's parents in Lebanon, Frank F. HATCH and Miss Anna HATCH, all of Lebanon. [NOTE: the notice at the beginning of this read "HATCH-HEAD," so perhaps this should read Miss Anna HEAD.]

Sept. 6, in Morrisville, by Rev. J. D. MERRELL, Delos H. WILLIAMS, of Fort Plain, to Miss Elsie A. HATCH, of Oneida.

Sept. 8, in Oriskany Falls, Charles E. HATHAWAY and Miss Cynthia M. MOWERS, both of Oriskany Falls.

Sept. 5, in Chittenango, by Rev. C. O. THATCHER, Mr. Charles W. KNOWLTON, of Durhamville, and Miss Eliza E. KINNEY, of Chittenango.

Sept. 12, in Brookfield, by Rev. J. M. TODD, at his residence, Mr. Herman D. CHESEBRO, of South Hamilton, to Miss Minnie F. PALMER, of Brookfield.

Sept. 16, in North Brookfield, by Rev. M. L. BENNETT, Mr. Henry BARTRAM and Miss Mary G. TOWNSEND, both of Theresa.

Sept. 16, at the Congregational parsonage in Madison, by Rev. H. WAITE, John A. DITCH, of Syracuse, and Julia PENDOCK, of Brookfield.

Sept. 3, in the town of Hamilton, by Rev. Father HANNETT, Mr. Harvey BRIGGS and Miss Johanna MURPHY.

Oct. 6, in Randallsville, by Rev. W. R. BROOKS, D.D., Mr. J. D. ARMSTRONG and Miss May STONE, both of Randallsville.

Oct. 13, at the residence of the bride's parents in North Brookfield, Oct. 13, by Rev. M. L. BENNETT, Mr.

DEMOCRATIC REPUBLICAN - 1886

William E. STILLMAN, of Morrisville, and Miss Libbie CHESBRO, of North Brookfield.

Oct. 3, at Fife Lake, MI, Mr. Lorance YOUNG and Miss Nettie J. ANDERSON, of Hamilton.

Oct. 14, at Valley City, Dakota, Frank F. SANFORD, of Odell, Dakota, and Miss Helen T. KINGSLEY, of Cooperstown, Dakota. Mrs. SANFORD is a daughter of William KINGSLEY, and granddaughter of A. Z. KINGSLEY.

Oct. 13, in Sherburne, at the residence of the officiating clergyman, Rev. S. S. CADY, Orris HOWARD to Mrs. Emily FARRER, both of New Berlin.

Oct. 13, at the residence of the bride's mother in Johnstown, by Rev. J. H. BROWN, George W. WALDRON, of New York City, formerly of Sherburne, and Miss Florence A. BURNS.

Oct. 19, in Jamesville, NY, by Rev. James DOWNE, Mr. Will T. WEBBER and Miss Flora V. WHEELER, both of Munnsville.

[No date], in Georgetown, at the home of the bride, Arthur A. HARTSHORN, of Lebanon, to Miss Lydia B. UTTER, of Georgetown, by Rev. J. H. SAGE, pastor of the Baptist Church in Georgetown.

Oct. 26, in Norwich, by Rev. A. VAN CLEFT, Benjamin LEWIS, of Hubbardsville, and Mrs. Helen HERRINGTON, of Hamilton.

Oct. 25, in Sherburne, by Rev. S. W. MEVIS, Benjamin G. SISSON to Mrs. Mary O. A. WOODS, both of Sherburne.

Oct. 26, at the bride's home, by Rev. C. O. THATCHER, Alfred E. ROOT and Beatrice K. WALRATH, both of Chittenango.

Oct. 30, in Eaton, by Rev. Judson DAVIS, Eugene FAIRBANKS, of Lisle, NY, and Miss Alice WOOD, of Poolville.

Nov. 2, in Eaton, by Rev. Judson DAVIS, William BRANNAN and Miss Hattie DENNEY, both of Easton.

Nov. 10, in Randallsville, by Rev. W. R. BROOKS, U. G. CARPENTER and Miss Hattie HOPKINS, all of Randallsville.

Nov. 3, in Fenner, by Rev. L. W. JACKSON, Robert WILLIAMSON, of Earlville, and Miss Nannie D. LOOMIS, of Fenner. He is a member of the firm of Williamson & Rhodes, of Earlville. She is a daughter of Alfred LOOMIS, of Fenner, Madison Co., and a sister of George LOOMIS. They were married in the Baptist Church at Fenner, and will live in Earlville.

Nov. 10, at the pastoral residence of St. Francis de Sales' Church in Utica, John F. TEESDALE, of Hamilton, married Miss Anna C. BELL, daughter of John

DEMOCRATIC REPUBLICAN - 1886

BELL, of Utica. They have come to reside on Eaton St. in Hamilton, and he has lately opened a boot and shoe store on Lebanon St.

Nov. 6, in Brookfield, at the residence of Clark BURDICK, by Rev. J. M. TODD, Andrew S. TRACY, of Hamilton, and Miss Nora A. PALMITER, of Brookfield.

Nov.10, at the home of the bride in Waterville, by Rev. Thomas JENKINS, Louis FUESS, of Madison, and Miss Lizzie JENKINS, daughter of the officiating clergyman.

In Brookfield, Nov. 11, by Rev. B. D. SNYDER, William STANBRO, Jr., and Miss Maude E. POPPLETON.

Nov. 10, at the residence of Hon. Wait CLARKE, in Brookfield, by Rev. R. J. THOMPSON, John TELFER, of New Lisbon, and Mary C. MOTT, of Hartwick.

Nov. 25, in Brookfield, by Rev. B. DeForest SNYDER, Albert C. MILLER and Miss Luva E. LAMB.

Nov. 24, in Woodstock, at the residence of the bride's father, by Rev. O. G. H. PHILLIPS, Mr. Winfield S. WILSON, of Erieville, and Miss Libbie M. SMITH.

Nov. 21, in Sherburne, by Rev. D. W. TELLER, Orrin D. PARTRIDGE of Lebanon, and Mrs. Harriet A. HAYWARD, of Sherburne.

Nov. 25, in Waterville, by Rev. J. M. HUTCHINSON, William M. WALTER, of Oriskany Falls, and Miss Allie CHESEBRO, of Waterville.

Dec. 1, in Madison, at the residence of the bride's sister, by Rev. W. L. TISDALE, Mr. Lewis M. PHINNEY, of Deansville, and Miss Anna E. DAHN, of West Branch.

Dec. 3, in Oneida, by Joseph BEAL, Esq., Daniel PEILTZ and Fanny LONIS. (Miss)

Dec. 7, in Eaton, by Rev. C. E. HAMILTON, Mr. John JONES and Mrs. LAMB.

Dec. 4, in Eaton, by Rev. C. E. HAMILTON, Willard DURFEE and Miss Alice PETTET.

Dec. 8, in Utica, at the residence of the bride's mother, by Rev. Dr. A. B. GOODRICH, Mr. William Elmer MONTGOMERY, of Hamilton, and Miss Mary Newell ENQUEST.

Dec. 13, in Earlville, by Rev. L. W. JACKSON, C. M. HEBBARD, of Rochester, and Miss Sarah A. SAWYER, of Eaton.

Dec. 23, in Hamilton, by Rev. E. DODGE, D.D., L.L.D., Norman BROWER and Mrs. Fidelia A. STAPLES.

Dec. 28, at the residence of the bride's parents, Mr. and Mrs. M. C. WAITE, Rev. George P. PERRY, pastor of the First Baptist Church, Westerly, RI, to Miss Emma L. WAITE. The ceremony was performed by the groom's father, Rev. Owen F. PERRY, of Remsen, assisted by

DEMOCRATIC REPUBLICAN - 1886

Rev. W. L. SWAN, of Delhi. Josiah PERRY is a brother of the groom. Rev. George PERRY is a graduate of the Theological Seminary, class of '86, and is one of the best orators the University has ever produced. He occupied the position of Prof. of Elocution in the Academy and College for several years. The Church at Westerly is his first parish since graduation.

[No date], at the residence of the bride's parents, Mr. and Mrs. W. J. MAC MURRAY, James WINTERS, of Scott, PA, to Miss Martha MAC MURRAY, by Rev. W. R. BROOKS, of Madison University.

Dec. 30, at the Baptist Church in Madison, by Rev. Dr. LLOYD, of Madison University, Mr. Mereness ALLEN, of Titusville, PA, and Miss Clara PERKINS, of the same place, formerly of Madison. The reception was held at the home of the bride's aunt, Mrs. David POTTER.

Dec. 26, in Mannsville, Mr. G. L. CLARK, of Eaton, and Miss Belle STONE, of Munnsville.

****

Miscellaneous Newspapers Added to Archives during late 1953 and 1954, after copying was started.

MADISON COUNTY GAZETTE, printed by John B. JOHNSON & Son, Morris' Flats:
Issues of April 16, May 7, June 16 and June 25, 1818
No statistics

Name changed to *GAZETTE & MADISON COUNTY ADVERTISER*; same printer.
Issues of July 30 and Aug. 29, 1818; this latter issue contains the following notice:
DIED: in Nelson, Aug. 10, 1818, Mrs. Sarah LORD, wife of Deacon John LORD, age 75 years.

Name changed to *MADISON COUNTY ADVERTISER*; same printer.
Issue of July 5, 1820. No statistics.

OBSERVER & RECORDER; printed at Morrisville, Madison County, NY, by Bennett BICKNELL:
Issue of June 18, 1828 contains the following: Married at Ellicottville, Cattaraugus Co., NY, on the 25th ult., by the venerable Elder VINING, Mr. D. JONES, of Fabius, Onondaga Co., NY, to the amiable and

OBSERVER & RECORDER - 1828

    accomplished Widow, Mary SQUIRES, of the former place.
Died, at Wampsville, on the 10th inst., after a short illness, Miss Cynthia, second daughter of Levi BLOSSOM, age about 13 years.
Drowned, at Lenox, on the 7th inst., John NELLIS, son of Mr. John I. D. NELLIS, at about 8 years of age.
Issue of October 15, 1828 contains: Died, in Madison, on the 2d inst., Rachel PARKER, age 20 years.
Married, in this village, last evening, by Elder BLAKESLEY, Mr. Julius W. HATCH, of Sherburne, to Miss Harriet BICKNELL, daughter of Bennet BICKNELL, of this village [Morrisville].

THE MADISON FARMER; Printed in Hamilton at the New Printing Office in Hamilton Village. No statistics.

OBSERVER & RECORDER; Morrisville; Nov. 5, 1828. No data.

THE CIVILIAN, Hamilton: Oct. 5, 1830, Vol. I, No. 11; printed by L. DEWEY. Also Oct. 26, 1830. No data.

HAMILTON SENTINEL; printed by J. P. VAN SICE; Vol. II, No. 20. No data.

MADISON OBSERVER; printed by James NORTON, Morrisville, Vol. 17, No. 863; Aug. 21, 1838, contains:
Died, on the morning of the 17th, Carmi W. CARRUTH was killed in Mcdonough, Chenango Co., by lightening. He was a son of Levi CARRUTH, Esq., about 18 years of age, a student at Oxford Academy. (From *Oxford Republican*)
At Stockbridge, on the 13th, Mr. Daniel HADCOCKS, aged 89 years. He was a Soldier of the Revolution, and fought valiantly under the brave Col. GANSEVOORT at Fort Stanwix, under Gen. HERKIMER at Oriskany and in numerous other places along the valley of the Mohawk.

THE UNION HERALD, published by Luther MYRICK, Cazenovia, Madison Co., NY; Vol. III, No. 24, Dec. 29, 1838. No data.

THE FRIEND OF MAN, published by NY State Anti-Slavery Society at 177 Genesee St., Utica, NY; Vol. V, No. 24. Issue of April 13, 1841 contains:

THE FRIEND OF MAN - 1841

Married, in White[s]boro, on the 7th inst., by Rev. D. L. OGDEN, James W. NELLIS to Miss Caroline, daughter of John SPRIGGS, Esq., all of White[s]boro.
Also, by the same, on the same evening, Philip H. BOICE, Jr., to Miss Isabella, daughter of Hugh MITCHELL, Esq., all of Whitesboro.

MADISON COUNTY ABOLITIONIST, by Luther MYRIC, Publisher, Cazenovia, NY. Vol. I, No. 7; Nov. 2, 1841. No data.
Same; No. 9; issue of Nov. 16, 1841 contains:
DIED, in this village [Cazenovia], on the 13th inst., infant son of Philo E. and Eliza BLAIR.
(Also an article, "Historical," Lecture II, upon "Men and Events connected with the early history of Oneida County, NY."

THE LIBERTY PRESS, Utica, NY; James C. JACKSON, Editor, contains:
MARRIED, in Syracuse on the 29th ult., by Dr. J. W. ADAMS, Theodore F. ANDREWS, Esq., of Whitesboro, to Miss Jane Agnes, daughter of the Dr. T. R. HOPKINS, of Skaneatelas.
At Watervale, on the 19th ult., by the Rev. M. BARNUM, Judson LEWIS to Julia HAWES.
Issue of Apr. 15, 1847: Chenango County: "An Anti-slavery Convention will be held at Smyrna, on Wednesday, the 21st of April next, commencing at 10 o'clock A.M. The business of the meeting will be to discuss the subject of American slavery in its moral and political relations to the citizens of the County; and likewise, to nominate a County Judge and Surrogate, and a District Attorney. A full attendance is solicited from the Liberty men and women of the different towns. E. C. PRITCHETT of Cazenovia, and S. R. WARD, of Cortland, are especially invited to attend and adress the Convention.
                       W. W. CHAPMAN
                       Sherburne, March 26, 1847.
                       Ch'n of County Committee
Cortland American please copy.

UTICA LIBERTY PRESS, issue of June 1, 1848, contains:
MARRIED, in this city [Utica] on the 30th ult., by Rev. W. H. SPENCER, Mr. Cornelius MC LOUGHLIN, of Albany, and Miss Mary Ann, daughter of Noah WHITE, Esq., of this city.
In Westmoreland, on Wednesday, May 24th, by Rev. F. A. SPENCER, Mr. J. S. BLISS, of Whitestown, to Miss

UTICA LIBERTY PRESS - 1848

Marietta, youngest daughter of Jacob PHELPS, of Westmoreland.
Also on Thursday, May 25th, by the same, Mr. Arthur P. DOUGLASS, of Whitestown, to Miss Esther L. HEWITT, of Westmoreland.
DIED, in this city, on the 24th ult., of scarlet fever, Clarissa Fidelia, daughter of John MILLER, in the 3d year of her age.
In New Berlin Village, March 13, Mrs. Harriet C. COLBURN, wife of Mr. Johnson COLBURN, age 31 years.
Issue of June 22, 1848 contains:
MARRIED, in Trenton Village, on Monday, June 19th, Mr. T. P. OTTAWAY, Printer, of this city, and Miss Caroline CARTER, of the former place.
DIED, at his residence in the town of Green, Chenango Co., on the 10th of June, Mr. Stephen SHERWOOD, aged 29 years, son of Mr. Isaac SHERWOOD, of said town, after a painfull illness of two weeks. A large circle of friends and relatives mourn.
In Milford, Otsego Co., on June 6th, Mrs. Cammilliad WELLMAN, wife of William WELLMAN, in the 55th year of her age.
Issue of November 2, 1848 contains:
The Chenango Free Democrat is the title of the new paper just started at Norwich, Chenango Co., by J. D. LAWYER, of the *American Christian*, of Leesville, Schoharie Co., NY.

CHRISTIAN CONTRIBUTOR, Utica, NY, issue of March 21, 1849, contains:
MARRIED, at Henrietta, Feb. 22, by the Elder S. W. STREETER, Mr. Peter MARTIN and Miss Louisa J. ELLIS.
In Chicago, IL, by Elder W. H. RICE, Mr. Joseph S. CAVERT and Miss Mary E. AMBROSE.
DIED, Mrs. Mary BROWN, wife of Jonathan BROWN, formerly of Sutton, VT, at LaGrange, OH, Jan. 25, 1849, aged 61 years. She left husband and four daughters.
In Solon, Feb. 24, 1849, Mrs. Stephen POTTER, age 71 years.
In Methuen, MA, Mr. Richard CURRIER, age 99 years, 11 months, 6 days.
[No date given], in North Reading, MA, Mr. Eliab PARKER, age 80 years.
[No date given], died in Chelsea, MA, Mrs. Elizabeth BRAY, aged 83 years.
[No date given], in Royalston, MA, Mrs. Mary PIPER, aged 79 years.
[No date given], in Middlefield, MA, Mrs. Fanny SMITH, wife of Deacon O. S. SMITH, aged 53 years.

CHRISTIAN CONTRIBUTOR - 1849

[No date or age given], in Boston, MA, Joshua CRANE, Esq.
[No date given], in Providence, RI, S. B. MUMFORD, Esq., age 59 years.

DEMOCRATIC REFLECTOR, issue of May 10, 1849; no data.

DEMOCRATIC REFLECTOR, issue of March 6, 1856, (Thursday) contains:
MARRIED, At the Baptist parsonage in Norwich, Feb. 28, 1856, by Rev. L. WRIGHT, Mr. Charles S. WATERS to Miss Janette M. LYON, both of North Norwich.
By Rev. W. R. COBB, on Thursday evening, in Madison, Mr. Cephus LONT, of Lebanon, to Miss Harriet PECKHAM, of Madison.
DIED, in Madison, Mar. 3d, Stillman M. WHITE, son of Alexander WHITE, Esq., aged 21 years.

DEMOCRATIC UNION, Hamilton, NY, issue of Aug. 25, 1859 contains:
DIED, at Smith's Valley, on the 23d, after a long and painful illness, Mr. W. D. MC GUIRE, aged 43 years.
In Georgetown, on the 10th, Harriet, youngest daughter of Ephraim and Sibill TRACY, aged 17 years.
In the town of Eaton, on the 14th, Miss Mary CRITCHLEY, aged 38 years.
In Lebanon, on the 4th, John, son of Philander and Maria HYDE, age 2 years, 10 months.

THE ONEIDA SACHEM, issue of May 2, 1861, (Thursday), contains:
MARRIED, at the residence of her mother in Verona, on the 17th, by Rev. Henry HICKOCK, Charles VANESS, of MI, to Miss Harriet BARBER, of the former place.
In Bridgeport, on the 25th, by Levi COLLINS, Esq., Mr. Ellen (sic) RECTOR to Miss Elizabeth DENNIS, of Bridgeport.
DIED, In this place, Apr. 28, 1861, Susannah, wife of John SHERWIN, age 71 years, 10 months.
In Munnsville, Wednesday, Mrs. Betsy HOLMES, wife of Daniel HOLMES, in her 43d year.
In Cazenovia, Apr. 18, Mrs. Lamon H. STILES, age 41 years.
In Grand Rapids, MI, on Tuesday, Apr. 16, of consumption, Mrs. Cecelia REMINGTON, wife of George REMINGTON, and daughter of William MERCHANT, formerly of Fenner.
DIED, in Cazenovia, Apr. 22, Mrs. Mehitable DODGE, widow of Stephen DODGE, age 81 years.

THE ONEIDA SACHEM - 1861

At Bridgeport, Apr. 17, D. Theresa, only daughter of Dr. David DUNHAM, aged 11 years, 10 months.
At Frankfort, on the 25th, of diphtheria, Nellie, only daughter of Delevan and Sarah A. HUBBARD, aged 2 years.

DEMOCRATIC UNION, Hamilton: Thursday, Feb. 19, 1863, contains:
MARRIED, in Bouckville, at the residence of the bride's father, on the 12th, by Rev. E. C. BROWN, Mr. Preston C. HOWARD and Miss Almina CARTER, both of Bouckville.
In Hamilton, at the Park House, by Rev. W. R. BROOKS, Mr. M. V. B. CURTIS, of Madison, and Miss Frances A. MORSE, of Nelson.
In Morrisville, on the 10th, by Rev. A. L. YORK, Mr. J. Franklin BUYES, of Lenox, and Miss Charity E. FORT, of Peterboro.
In DeRuyter, on the 5th, by Rev. W. H. CURTIS, Mr. W. F. DRAKE, of Georgetown, to Miss Mary HUNT, of DeRuyter.
In Hamilton, on the 20th, by Rev. Mr. BEEBE, Mr. Joel CUTLER, of Brookfield, and Miss Wealthy A. SPAULDING of Columbus.
In Utica, on the 16th, by Rev. D. G. HOAG, Capt. D. L. BECKWITH, formerly of Hamilton, and Miss Allie H. HARRINGTON, both of Utica.
In Earlville, at the Felt House, on the 3d, by Rev. T. T. HALSTEAD, Mr. Levi DELINE, of Alderly, WI, and Miss Cynthia L. EDDY, of Lebanon, NY.
In New London, OH, on the 1st, Thomas FARGHER, M. D., Surgeon in the USA General Hospital, of Philadelphia, and Miss Sophia JACKSON, recently of Hamilton.
DIED, in Peterboro, on the 15th, of diphtheria, Frankie Clarence, aged 10 years, 11 months; and also
On the 25th, Jay A., aged 5 years, 5 months, 16 days, sons of Joseph G. MARSH.
At Underhill Cottage, on Alder Brook, on the 28th, Miss O. Anna STUART, aged 27 years.

THE MADISON OBSERVER, issue of Dec. 2, 1863 contains:
DIED, at Nelson Flats, on the 14th, Mrs. Lydia HYATT, wife of Aaron S. HYATT, aged 60 years.
In Madison, on the 16th, Mr. George SIMONS, aged 92 years.
In Lebanon, on the 12th, Mrs. Louisa, wife of Samuel B. BENEDICT, age 36 years.

WALDRON'S DEMOCRATIC VOLUNTEER - 1869

WALDRON'S DEMOCRATIC VOLUNTEER, Wednesday, published at Hamilton, NY; issue of Aug. 25, 1869, contains:

MARRIED, in East Springfield, June 22, by Rev. S. P. GRAY, Dr. H. P. MILLER, of Eaton, and Miss Celia GRAY, of East Springfield, Otsego County, NY.

In Boston, MA, on the 27th, by Rt. Rev. John J. WILLIAMS, Major G. F. EMERY and Miss Lizzie F., widow of the late Capt. O. H. TILLINGHAST, of Morrisville.

DIED, in Oneida, Aug. 16, 1869, at the residence of her son, I. N. MESSENGER, Esq., Mrs. Phebe Gage MESSENGER, aged 69 years, widow of the late Gen. John N. MESSENGER.

At Knoxboro, on the 17th, of typhoid fever, Martin BRIGHAM, in his 65th year.

In Cazenovia, on the 5th, Mrs. Harriet PORTER, aged 66 years.

Near Eaton Center, Aug. 13th, Mr. Solomon HART, aged 74 years.

At Pratt's Hollow, suddenly, July 27th, Emily, widow of the late Lyman HADDEN, aged 49 years.

DEMOCRATIC VOLUNTEER, Hamilton, March 25, 1874 issue contains:

A long obituary of Adon SMITH, who died in New York City on Monday last, Mar. 18th. He was buried in Greenwood Cemetery in New York beside eldest son and former wife; age 70 years.

DEMOCRATIC REPUBLICAN, Hamilton, Thursday, March 26, 1874:

DIED, in Madison County, NY, near this village, Mar. 23, 1874, George H. STONE, aged 39 years.

In Lebanon, Mar. 21, Pardon CLARK, aged 54 years.

GEOGRAPHICAL LOCATOR GUIDE

Inasmuch as many readers will not be familiar with all the placenames appearing in this work, nor will they have immediate access to necessary finding aids, the following locator list has abeen developed for their convenience.

We must assume that the majority of names of villages, towns, etc., used in this work are located in Madison Co. or the adjacent counties of Chenango, Oneida or Onondaga, unless otherwise stated.

The following references were consulted for names of geographical locations included herein: J. H. French, *Gazetteer of the State of New York...* (Syracuse, NY, 1860); Bishop Davenport, *A New Gazetteer or Geographical Dictionary of North America and the West Indies...* (Baltimore, MD, 1835); and *Lippincott's Pronouncing Gazetteer of the World...* (Philadelphia, 1895). These early gazetteers were used as many of the villages named no longer appear on a road map or have a post office.

As a matter of convenience, the following abbreviations are used:

```
Co. - county              l. - locality
t.  - town or township    v. - village
c.  - city                p.o. - post office
s.  - settlement
```

The reader should keep in mind that in New York State, the word "town" denotes a township.

Adams, Jefferson Co., NY
Agawam, v., Plymouth Co., NY; also v., Hampden Co., MA
Albion, v., Oswego Co., NY
Alderbrook, l., Madison Co., NY
Allegany, t. & v., Cattaraugus Co., NY
Amsterdam, t. & v., Montgomery Co., NY
Angelica, t. & v., Allegany Co., NY
Annsville, v., Oneida Co.
Argyle, t. & v., Washington Co., NY
Attica, t. & v., Wyoming Co., NY
Auburn, v., Cayuga Co., NY
Augusta, t., Oneida Co., NY
Augusta Center, Oneida Co., NY
Ava, t., Oneida Co., NY
Avon, t. & v., Livingston Co., NY
Bacon Hill, a very high hill south of New Woodstock, Madison Co., NY
Baldwinsville, v., Onondaga Co., NY
Ballston Spa, v., Saratoga Co., NY
Baltimore, city, MD
Baton Rouge, city, LA
Belmont, t., Franklin Co., NY
Bennett's Corner, early p.o., Madison Co., NY
Bensville (Not Found)
Bergen, t., Genesee Co., NY
Big Flats, t. & v., Chemung Co., NY
Binghamton, t. & c., Broome Co. NY
Black Brook, t. & v., Clinton Co., NY
Boonville, v., Oneida Co., NY
Boston, l. between Canaseraga and Canastota, Madison Co., NY
Bouckville, v., Madison Co., NY
Bridgeport, v., Madison Co., NY
Bridgewater, t. & v., Oneida Co., NY
Brisbane, p.o., Chenango Co., NY
Brockport, v., Monroe Co., NY
Brookfield, t. & v., Madison Co., NY
Brooklyn, L.I., NY
Brothertown, p.o., Calumet Co., WI
Brown's Valley, v., MN; also former p.o., CA
Buffalo, c., erie Co., NY
Burlington Flats, v., Otsego Co., NY
Burmah, state, India
Butternuts, T. & p.o., Otsego Co., NY
C. W. - Canada West
Camden, v., Oneida Co., NY
Camillus, v., Onondaga Co., NY
Canada, l., Cayuga Co., NY
Canajoharie, t. & v., Montgomery Co., NY
Canastota, v., Madison Co., NY
Candor, v., Tioga Co., NY
Caneada, t. & v., Allegany Co., NY
Cape May, c. & co., NJ
Carmel, t., Putnam Co., NY
Carroll, t., Chautauqua Co., NY
Carthage, Jefferson Co., NY
Cassville, v., Oneida Co., NY

222

Castleton, v., Rensselaer Co., NY; v., Ontario Co., NY; t. i Richmond Co. NY
Cazenovia, t. & v., Madison Co., NY
Cedar Lake, p.o., Herkimer Co., NY
Central Square, v., Oswego Co., NY
Cernon (Not Located)
Chateaugy, t. & v., Franklin Co., NY
Chenango, c. & t., Chenango Co., NY
Chenango Bridge, p.o., Broome Co., NY
Chenango Forks, v., Chenango Co., NY; also, Broome Co., NY
Chicago, c., IL
Chittenango, v., Madison Co., NY
Chittenango Falls, fall, Chittenango Creek, 4 mi. n. of Cazenovia, NY; formerly a p.o.
Clarksville, several v., Albany, Allegany, Cayuga, Maidson, Otsego and Rockland Cos., NY
Clifton Springs, v., Ontario Co., NY
Clinton, v., Oneida Co., NY
Clyde, v., Wayne Co., NY
Colchester, t., Delaware Co., NY
Columbia Springs, v., Herkimer Co., NY
Columbus, t. & v., Chenango Co., NY
Connville, should be Coonsville, l., Ontario Co., NY
Constantia, t. & v., Oswego Co., NY
Cooperstown, v., Otsego Co., NY

Cortland, v., Cortland Co., NY
Cortlandville, v., Cortland Co., NY
Coughdenony, [Caughdenoy], v., Oswego Co., NY
Coventry, t. & v., Chenango Co., NY
Coventry, Otsego Co.
Coxsackie, t. & v., Greene Co., NY
Crescent, v., Saratoga Co., NY
Danbe, Herkimer Co., NY
Deadwood, c., SD
Deansville, v., Oneida Co., NY
Deerfield, t., formerly a p.o., Oneida Co., NY
Delhi, t. & v., Delaware Co., NY
Delphi, v., Onondaga Co., NY
Depeauville, v., Jefferson Co., NY
Deposit, v., Broome Co.; v., Delaware Co., NY
DeRuyter, t. & v., Madison Co., NY
Detroit, c., MI
Diana, t. & former p.o., Lewis Co., NY
Durhamville, v., Madison Co., NY
Earlville, v. on line between Madison & Chenango Cos., NY
East Hamilton, former p.o., Madison Co., NY
East Springfield, v., Otsego Co., NY
Eaton, t. & v., Madison Co., NY
Eaton Center, s., Madison Co., NY
Eaton Township, Madison Co., NY
Edmeston, t., Otsego Co., NY

Elmira, v., Chemung Co., NY
Erieville, v., Madison Co., NY
Exeter, t., Otsego Co., NY
Fabius, t. & v., Onondaga Co., NY
Fairport, Monroe Co., NY
Falmouth, v., MA
Fayetteville, v., Onondaga Co., NY
Fenner, t. & former p.o., Madison Co., NY
Fish Creek, v., Oneida Co., NY
Fleming, t. & v., Cayuga Co., NY
Florence, t. & v., Oneida Co., NY
Fort Plain, v., Montgomery Co., NY
Fort Stanwix, pre-Revolutionary War fort near Rome, Oneida Co., NY
Frankfort, t. & v., Herkimer Co., NY
Franklin, t. & v., Delaware Co., NY
Friendship, t. & v., Allegany Co., NY
Fulton, v., Oswego Co., NY; t., Schoharie Co., NY
Fultonville, v., Montgomery Co., NY
Gaines, t. & v., Orleans Co., NY
Galesburg colony, IL (settled by group from Madison Co., NY)
Garwood Station, R.R. Station, Stueben Co., NY
Geneva, c., Ontario Co., NY
Georgetown, t. & v., Madison Co., NY
Gilbertsville, v., Otsego Co., NY

Gloversville, v., Fulton Co., NY
Governeur, v., St. Lawrence Co., NY
Grant, v., Herkimer Co., NY
Green[e], t. & v., Chenango Co., NY
Greenwood, t. and v., Steuben Co., NY
Groton, t. & v., Tompkins Co., NY
Guilford, t., Chenango Co., NY
Half Moon, t. & former p.o., Saratoga Co., NY
Hamburg, t. & v., Erie Co., NY
Hamilton, v., Madison Co., NY
Hamilton Center, v., Madison Co., NY
Harpersfield, t. & v., Delaware Co., NY
Hartford, t. & v., Washington Co., NY
Hartland, t. & former p.o., Niagara Co., NY
Hartwick, t. & v., Otsego Co., NY
Havana, v., Schuyler Co., NY
Henrietta, t. & former p.o., Monroe Co., NY
Herkimer, t. & v., Herkimer Co., NY
Higginsville, v., Oneida Co., NY
Hogansburg, v., Franklin Co., NY
Homer, t. & v., Cortland Co., NY
Hornby, t. and p.o., Steuben Co., NY
Hubbard's Corners, s., Madison Co., NY
Hubbardsville, v., Madison Co., NY
Ilion, v., Herkimer Co., NY

Ira, t. & v., Cayuga Co., NY
Jamestown, v., Chautauqua Co., NY
Jamesville, v., Onondaga Co., NY
Jay, t. & v., Essex Co., NY
Jersey City, NJ
Jersey City Heights, NJ
Johnson's Creek, v., Niagara Co., NY
Johnstown, t. & v., Fulton Co., NY
Jordan, v., Onondaga Co., NY
Juniata, several villages, U.S., most, PA
Keeler's Corners, Madison Co., NY
Kingston, t. & v., Ulster Co., NY
Kirkland, t. & former p.o., Oneida Co., NY
Klockville, v., Madison Co., NY
Knoxboro, NY
Knoxville, v., Madison Co., NY
Lamsons, v., Onondaga Co., NY
Lansing, t., Tompkins Co., NY
Lebanon, t. & v., Madison Co., NY
Leeds, v., Greene Co., NY
Leeville [Leesville], v., Schoharie Co., NY
Lenox, t. & former p.o., Madison Co., NY
Leonardsville, v., Madison Co., NY
LeRoy, v., Genesee Co., NY
Lima, v., Livingston Co., NY
Lincklaen, t. & v., Chenango Co., NY
Lisbon, l., St. Lawrence Co., NY
Lisle, t. & v., Broome Co., NY
Little Falls, t. & v., Herkimer Co., NY
Lockport, t. & v., Niagara Co., NY
Log City, derisive local name for Eaton, Madison Co., NY
Lowville, t. & v., Lewis Co., NY
Lyndenville, v., Orleans Co., NY
Lyons, t. & v., Wayne Co., NY
Madison, t. & v., Madison Co., NY
Madison Center, s., Madison Co., NY
Madison University, Hamilton, Madison Co., NY; now Colgate University
Manlius, t. & v., Onondaga Co., NY
Mannsville, v., Jefferson Co., NY
Marathon, t. & v., Cortland Co., NY
Marquette, several counties & villages, WI & MI
Marshall, t. and former p.o., Oneida Co., NY
Masonville, v., Delaware Co., NY
Maulmain, Burma
McConnellsville, v., Oneida Co., NY
McDonough, t. & v., Chenango Co., NY
Medina, v., Orleans Co., NY
Meredith, t. & v., Delaware Co., NY
Meridian, v., Cayuga Co., NY
Middleport, v., Niagara Co., NY; l., Madison Co., NY

Middleville, v., Herkimer Co., NY
Mile Strip, strip of land one mile wide across the south part of the town of Stockbridge, purchased from the Indians
Milford, t. & former p.o., Otsego Co., NY
Mohawk, t., Montgomery Co., NY; river through east central NY
Moriah, t. & v., Essex Co., NY
Morris, t. & p.o., Otsego Co., NY
Morrisville, v., Madison Co., NY
Mottville, v., Onondaga Co., NY
Mt. Upton, v., Chenango Co., NY
Munnsville. v., Madison Co., NY
Nantucket, Co. & v., MA
Napoli, t., Cattaraugus Co., NY
Nashville (Brookfield), v., Madison Co., NY; also a v., Chautauqua Co., NY
Nelson, t. and p.o., Madison Co., NY
Nelson Flats, v., Madison Co., NY
New Berlin, v., Chenango Co., NY
New Hartford, t. & v., Oneida Co., NY
New Lisbon, t. & p.o., Otsego Co., NY
New Orleans, c., LA
New Woodstock, v. south of Cazenovia, Madison Co., NY
New York, c. & co., NY
New York Mills, v., Oneida Co., NY
Newark, c., OH

Newark Valley, v., Tioga Co., NY
Newark, v., Wayne Co., NY
Ninevah, p.o., Broome Co., NY
North Bainbridge, l., south part of town of Bainbridge, Chenango Co., NY
North Brookfield, l., Madison Co., NY
North Norwich, t. & p.o., Chenango Co., NY
North Otselic, l., Chenango Co., NY
North Parma, v., Monroe Co., NY
North Versails [Versailles], s., Cattaraugus Co., NY
Norway, t. & v., Herkimer Co., NY
Norwich, t. & v., Chenango Co., NY
Nunda, t. & v., Livingston Co., NY
Oneida, v., Madison Co., NY
Oneida Castle, v., Oneida Co., NY
Oneida Community, communal community about 3 mi. south of Oneida, NY
Oneida Depot, railroad stopping place, Oneida Co., NY
Oneida Lake, large lake which forms north border of Madison Co., NY; also a former p.o., Madison Co., NY
Oneonta, t. & v., Otsego Co., NY
Onondaga, t. & p.o., Onondaga Co., NY
Onondaga Valley, v., Onondaga Co., NY
Oriskany, v., Oneida Co., NY

Oriskany Falls, v., Oneida Co., NY
Orleans, t. & v., Jefferson Co., NY
Oswego, t., Oswego Co., NY
Otego, t. & v., Otsego Co., NY
Otsego, t., Otsego Co., NY
Ovid, t. & v., Seneca Co., NY
Oxford, t. & v., Chenango Co., NY
Painted Post, v., Steuben Co., NY
Paris Hill [Paris], p.o., Oneida Co., NY
Pawling, t. & v., Dutchess Co., NY
Pecksport, l., town of Eaton, Madison Co., NY
Pekin, v., Niagara Co., NY
Pendleton, t. & v., Niagara Co., NY
Penn Yan, v., Yates Co., NY
Perry, v., Wyoming Co., NY
Perrysburg, t. & v., Cattaraugus Co., NY
Perryville, v., Madison Co., NY
Peterboro, v., Madison Co., NY
Pharsalia, t. & v., Chenango Co., NY
Philadelphia, t. & v., Jefferson Co., NY; c., PA
Phoenix, v., Otsego Co., NY
Pierceville, l., town of Eaton, Madison Co., NY
Pine Woods, p.o. & l., Madison Co., NY
Pitcher, t. & v., Chenango Co., NY
Pittsfield, t. & p.o., Otsego Co., NY
Pittstown, t. & p.o., Rensselaer Co., NY
Plainfield, t., Otsego Co., NY
Plymouth, t. & v., Chenango Co., NY
Poland, t. & v., Herkimer Co., NY
Pompey, t. & p.o., Onondaga Co., NY
Poolville, v., Madison Co., NY
Portsville [Portville], t. & v., Cattaraugus Co., NY
Pratt's Hollow, v., Madison Co., NY
Preble, t., Cortland Co., NY
Preston, t. & p.o., Chenango Co., NY
Preston Hill, hill, t. of Preston, Chenango Co., NY
Pulaski, v., Oswego Co., NY
Quality Hill, v., Madison Co., NY
Randallsville, former p.o., t. of Lebanon, Madison Co., NY
Reading, t. & p.o., Schuyler Co., NY
Remsen, t. & v., Oneida Co., NY
Rhinebeck, t. & v., Dutchess Co., NY
Richfield, t. & v., Otsego Co., NY
Richfield Springs, v., Otsego Co., NY
Rio, v., WI, IL, KY & MS
Rochester, c., Monroe Co., NY
Rome, c., Oneida Co., NY
Sackett's Harbor, v., Jefferson Co., NY
Salem X Roads, l., Washington Co., NY; l., Chautauqua Co., NY
Salisbury, t. & p.o., Herkimer Co., NY

Sandy Creek, t. & p.o., Oswego Co., NY
Sanford, t. & p.o., Broome Co., NY
Sangerfield, t. & p.o., Oneida Co., NY
Sangerfield Center, v., Oneida Co., NY
Saratoga, t., Saratoga Co., NY
Saratoga Springs, v., Saratoga Co., Ny
Sauquoit, p.o., Oneida Co., NY
Schenectady, c., Schenectady Co., NY
Scipio, t. & v., Cayuga Co., NY
Scriba, t. & p.o., Oswego Co., NY
Sempronius, t. & p.o., Cayuga Co., NY
Shed's Corners, former p.o., Madison Co., NY
Shelby, t. & p.o., Orleans Co., NY
Sherburne, t. & v., Chenango Co., NY
Siloam, p.o., Madison Co., NY
Sing Sing, p.o., Westchester Co., NY
Skaneateles, t. & v., Onondaga Co., NY
Sloansville, v., Schoharie Co., NY
Smith's Valley, l., Madison Co., NY
Smithfield, t. & v., Madison Co., NY
Smithport, PA
Smithville, v., Jefferson Co., NY; t., Chenango Co., NY; v., Genesee Co., NY
Smyrna, t. & v., Chenango Co., NY
Sodus Point, v., Wayne Co., NY

Solon, t. & v., Cortland Co., NY
Solsville, v., Madison Co., NY
South Augusta, l., Oneida Co., NY
South Brookfield, former p.o., Madison Co., NY
South Hamilton, former p.o., Madison Co., NY
South Hill, former p.o., Steuben Co., NY
South New Berlin, former p.o., Chenango Co., NY
South Otstlic, v., Chenango Co., NY
Speigletown, v., Rensselaer Co., NY
Springfield, t. & former p.o., Otsego Co., NY
Spuyten Duyvill, v., Westchester Co., NY
St. Johnsville, t. & v., Montgomery Co., NY
State Bridge, v., Oneida Co., NY; l., Cortland Co., NY
Stockbridge, t. & v., Madison Co., NY
Stockport, t. & v., Columbia Co., NY
Stockwell, prob Stockwell Settlement, Oneida Co., NY
Suffern, v., Rockland Co., NY
Sullivan, t. & former p.o., Madison Co., NY, originally called Canaseraga
Syracuse, c., Onondaga Co., NY
Theresa, t. & v., Jefferson Co., NY
Tompkins, t., Delaware Co., NY
Trenton Village, v., Oneida Co., NY
Troy, c., Rensselaer Co., NY

Truxton, t. & v., Cortland Co., NY
Tully, t. & v., Onondaga Co., NY
U. C., Upper Canada
Unadilla, t. & v., Otsego Co., NY
Unadilla Forks, v., Otsego Co., NY
Upper New York Mills, l., Oneida Co. NY
Upton Park, l., Otsego Co., NY
Utica, c., Oneida Co., NY
Vernon, t. & v., Oneida Co., NY
Vernon Center, v., Oneida Co., NY
Vernon Mills, l., Oneida Co., NY
Verona, v., Oneida Co., NY
Vienna, t. & v., Oneida Co., NY
Villanova, t. & former p.o., Chautauqua Co., NY
Vineland, v., NJ
Virgil, t. & v., Cortland Co., NY
Volney, t. & v., Oswego Co., NY
Volney, Otsego Co., error - see above
Wampsville, v., Madison Co., NY
Washington, t. & former p.o., Dutchess Co., NY
Waterford, t. & v., saratoga Co., NY
Waterloo, t. & v., Seneca Co., NY
Watertown, t. & v., Jefferson Co., NY
Watervale [Waterville], v., Oneida Co., NY
Watkins, v., Schuyler Co., NY
Waverly, villages, Cattaraugus, Tioga & Westchester Cos., NY

Weedsport, v., Cayuga Co., NY
West Branch, v., Oneida Co., NY
West Eaton, v., Madison Co., NY
West Edmeston, v., Otsego Co., NY
West Martinsburg, v., Lewis Co., NY
West Meredith, former p.o., Delaware Co., NY
West Newark, former p.o., Wayne Co., NY
West Troy, v., Albany Co., NY
West Winfield, v., Herkimer Co., NY
Westborough, v., MA
Western, t., Oneida Co., NY
Westfield, t. & v., Chautauwua Co., NY; t., Richmond Co., NY
Westmoreland, t. & former p.o., Oneida Co., NY
Whitesboro, v., Oneida Co., NY
Whitestown, t. & former p.o., Oneida Co., NY
Wilbraham, t., MA
Willet, t. & former p.o., Cortland Co., NY
Williamsville, v., Erie Co., NY
Winfield, t. & p.o., Herkimer Co., NY
Woodman's Pond, pond, Madison Co., NY
Woodstock, See New Woodstock
Worcester, t. & v., Otsego Co., NY
Wyoming, v., Wyoming Co., NY
Yates, t. & p.o., Orleans Co., NY
York Mills, probably New York Mills, Oneida Co., NY

INDEX

ABBERT, Elizabeth 40
  Eveline (HEAD) 150
  George 59
  George B. 150
  George M. 150
  Jane 59
  Jane M. (RUSSELL) 150
ABBEY, A. M. 157
  George W. 199
  Inez (COREY) 199
  M. A. 157
ABBOTT, --- (Mrs.) 153
  Celia P. (ATKINS) 139
  Clarissa 35
  J. H. 139
  Lola P. 29
  Mary C. 29
  Samuel S. 29
ABEL, James 144
ABERT, Celinda 5, 14
  Charles Perrin 14
  George 5, 14
ACKET, Mary J. 121
ACKLEY, --- (Rev.) 112, 113
  Artelissa M. 54
  B. C. 84
  D. 11
  Ellen R. 35
  Francelia E. 158
  Harriet 112
  Hiram R. 35, 154
  Julia 35
  Julia A. (COMSTOCK) 154
  Philo 57
  Zelotus 54, 171
ADAMS, --- (Rev. Mr.) 129, 173
  --- (Rev.) 114, 118
  Ada (CARL) 209
  Ada L. (BENEDICT) 199
  Caroline 11
  Caroline E. (GRIGGS) 128
  Clarence G. 209
  Flavilla 11
  I. 130
  J. W. 216
  Joseph Cyril 43

ADAMS, Larinza 96
  Loe 113
  Moses 11
  Nelson 173
  Ruth 176
  Samantha L. 158
  Seymour W. 128
  Smanatha (ALLEN) 173
  William 56
AIKIN, John 118
  Mary Elizabeth 118
AINSWORTH, Frances A. (DOUGLAS) 133
  S. C. 145
  Spencer S. 133
ALBE, John 12
  Josephine 59
  Rachel 21
  Ruie A. 54
ALBEE, Mary Ann 122
ALBERT, Almira R. (TAYLOR) 153
  Emma J. (LAMPHERE) 175
  George 31
  George Morris 85
  Lucy 113
  Martin B. 153
  William H. 175
ALCOTT, Anson 114
  Emily (WILLCOX) 141
  Melville 141
  Sabria (NICHOLS) 114
ALDERMAN, Annie L. (TRESCOTT) 183
  C. 118
  Charles 108
  Charles D. 183
ALDRICH, Anna Maria 149
  Ellen J. 151
  Rachel 133
ALESWORTH, Eliphalet 148
  Margaret C. (KLINCK) 148
ALEXANDER, Harriet S. 125
ALLABAN, H. G. 206
ALLABEN, H. G. 99, 207
ALLEN, --- (Col.) 4
  --- (Mrs.) 97
  Ada (MOSELEY) 173

231

ALLEN, Adell R. 164
 Adella (STORES) 170
 Aliza M. 159
 Aurelia 26
 Charles 133
 Clara (PERKINS) 214
 Daniel 117
 Delia D. 55
 Eliza 184
 Emma V. (FERREL) 158
 F. R. 173
 Francis 15
 Frederick 190
 Frederick Washington 99
 George 72
 Ira 22
 Ira B. 72
 J. A. 170
 J. C. 76
 Janette (WHEELER) 25
 John 97
 John W. 20
 Julia 133
 Julia J. 76
 Laura J. 151
 Leonard 93
 Lewis F. 25, 86
 Lucy Ann 133
 Lydia A. 132
 Marcus C. (PECK) 80
 Mary (MOSELEY) 160
 Mary (SMITH) 117
 Mary E. 97
 Mereness 214
 Milton D. 160
 Minnie S. (MORGAN) 200
 Nathan J. 158
 Nellie 202
 Nellie M. 206
 Philip 23
 Rosaleia (ERSKINE) 190
 Roxana V. 70
 Sally 15
 Smanatha 173
 Stephen 23
 Walter J. 200
ALLSTON, Jacob 78
 Lucy 78
ALLYN, Lewis 164
ALVERSON, Benjamin 32

ALVORD, F. M. 195
AMBROSE, Mary E. 217
AMES, David 89
 John F. 210
 Sophie A. (WALL) 210
ANDERSON, --- (Rev) 192
 Carrie A. (WESTCOTT) 209
 Clark D. 56
 Emma 152
 James 209
 May 205
 Nettie J. 212
ANDREWS, --- 38
 --- (Rev.) 203
 Adelbert 175
 Barnard 38
 Cynthia B. 92
 Cynthia S. (BURCHARD) 158
 E. G. 150
 Ellis 208
 F. L. 92
 George E. 163
 Gertrude A. 86
 H. L. 195
 Herbert 28
 James H. 86
 Jane Agnes (HOPKINS) 216
 Joel 37
 Lizzie D. 179
 M. L. 198
 Mary F. (WILCOX) 175
 N. L. 158, 208
 Nathaniel 93
 Sarah M. (EGGLESTON) 163
 Theo. 28
 Theodore F. 216
ANDRUS, Asahel 7, 9
 John T. 71
 Lydia 54
 Phila 117
ANGELL, --- (Mr.) 136
ANTHONY, Mary L. 167
 S. S. 167
APPLEFORD, William 74
APPLEGATE, --- (Rev. Mr.) 143
 Jesse 206
 Mary (BRASS) 206
 Pliny 107
 T. 142

APPLETON, Jeddie 51
  Thomas 51
ARCHER, Mary 116
ARITY, James B. 54
ARMISTEAD, Addie 79
ARMOUR, Ella 173
ARMSTRONG, Almira 71
  Charles T. 16
  Charlotta 52
  Clarissa E. 35
  Francis 118
  J. D. 211
  Mary A. 145, 211
  Mary Ann 118
  May (STONE) 211
ARNESON, Aletta J. 159
ARNOLD, --- (Col.) 4
  --- (Rev. Dr.) 159, 167
  Charles H. 22
  DeWitt 204
  Florence (CORNICK) 204
  Mary 44, 208
  V. M. 44
  Will 207
  Winnie (FANCHER) 207
ARNST, Burdette 183
  Etta B. (JONES) 183
ATKINS, Amos 23
  Celia P. 139
  Miranda J. 142
ATKYNS, Elijah 40
ATWATER, Mary L. (WEAVER) 121
  Stephen 121
ATWOOD, Clarissa 11
  E. F. 78, 179
  Frank Eugene 78
  H. M. (ROGERS) 179
  Hannah (ROGERS) 78
  John 11
  John Marshall 11
AUDSLEY, Lee 194
  Rose (SELFE) 194
AUSS, Soren 112
AUSTIN, Eva (WILKINSON) 207
  Harvey A. 207
  J. M. 146
  James C. 146
  Jay F. 111

AUSTIN, Laura (DEWY) 116
  Lucetta (WRIGHT) 146
  M. A. 110
  Silas 116
AUSTON, Nettie 174
AVERY, Abbie (DUNHAM) 38
  Charles 38
  Charles Barclay 60
  Constant 10
  Cordelia 120, 121
  Cornelia R. (PRATT) 148
  Fannie D. 65
  Fannie O. 48, 60
  Flora P. 209
  George P. 148
  Georgie K. 48
  Hubbard B. 120, 121
  J. D. 51
  J. Dixon 48, 60, 65, 190
  Mary Y. 190
  Russell 57
  Sarah H. 158
  Williams 35
AVREY, Alida Cornelia 149
AYER, Jerry 14
AYERS, Rebecca T. 131
AYLESWORTH, E. 167
AYRE, Betsey 129
AYRES, --- (Rev. Mr.) 121
BABBOT, John 18
BABCOCK, Abigail W. 91
  Adeline (GOODING) 144
  Alfred 12
  Annette L. 153
  Benjamin 101
  Benjamin W. 114
  Benjamin Wait 11
  Catherine G. (ROWELL) 134
  Charles 30
  Deborah S. 93
  Dolf L. 199
  Eulie (COON) 174
  Frank G. 177
  Gideon P. 102
  H. R. (Mrs.) 99
  Hannah 11, 100, 101
  Hannah (HAVENS) 114
  Harrie J. (LANGWORTHY) 199
  Harriet 163

BABCOCK, Harvey A. 174
  Henry H. 134
  John 28, 144
  Laura 12
  Lydia 102
  Maggie E. (JONES) 177
  Mary A. 173
  Nettie L. 203
  Sarah A. 30
  Sidney S. 38
  W. B. 11
BACHMAN, R. L. 207
BACHUS, --- (Mr.) 118
  --- (Rev.) 122
BACKUS, Anna R. (ORMSBY) 118
  Jabez 21
  Levi S. 12, 118
BACON, Abbie (HAMILTON) 150
  Anna R. 64
  Anson 66
  Charles 22
  Charlie R. 30
  Clark 69
  Curtis (Mrs.) 87
  Cynthia 117
  Eliza (BARTHOLOMEW) 119
  Frances M. (STURTEVANT) 138
  Frances W. 61
  Franklin 37
  George 85
  Greenly 104
  Jerome 26
  Laura 52
  Lillie 91
  Luther 74
  Mary E. 163
  Melissa 37
  Minnie 69
  Ransom 138
  Ranson 61
  Reuben 150
  Rispy P. 149
  Rufus 117, 119
  Solomon 22
BAGG, Henry H. 133
  Mary Ann (STORRS) 133

BAILEY, Angeline E. (SPRAGUE) 146
  Anna 55
  Austin 146
  Eli S. 138
  Eunice V. 63
  Henry 146
  James 129
  Joseph 143
  Julia Ann 138
  Mary B. (TRIPP) 143
  Sophronia (WILLIS) 146
  Theresa (COVEY) 173
  William 173
BAKER, --- (Mrs.) 33
  --- (Rev. Mr.) 184
  A. M. 175
  Ada E. (LONT) 184
  Addison B. 164
  Albert M. 184
  Arthur M. 38
  Benjamin 57
  Bessie Louisa 74
  Betsey Ann (UPSTON) 133
  Cornelia 165
  D. E. 74
  Dexa E. (BILLINGS) 156
  Ellen C. 50
  Emma A. 178
  Florence Estella 93
  Frank M. (RICE) 151
  Genny 170
  George 40
  George H. 196
  Harriet 175
  Harry 83
  Henry 133
  Henry A. 29
  J. I. 74, 108
  Jerome David 181
  John 83, 87, 150
  John, Jr. 197
  Julie E. (HEAD) 164
  Julius I. 156
  Lewis 50
  Lillian 197
  Louise 139
  Mary 87
  Mary A. (DAILEY) 181
  Mary A. (MOTT) 150

BAKER, May E. 194
  Nelson 46
  Nettie G. 188
  Richard M. 151
  Rose 40
  S. 156
  Samuel 33
  Sarah 197
  Solomon 201
  Sophie 190
  Warren 31
  Willie 40
BALCOM, George 158
BALDWIN, C. 98
  Cynthia M. 98
  George C. 178
  Harriet (ROGERS) 123
  James 100
  John R. 123
  Louisa A. 100
  Lucy 149
BALL, Daniel 71
  Eliza 81
  Eliza (ROWLAND) 161
  J. H. 81
  James 161
  Martha 55
BALLANTINE, G. D. 201
BALLARD, Augusta (GILMAN) 115
  Aymler 116
  Fallie C. (HITCHCOCK) 200
  Florence A. 191
  John B. 115
  Ladurna 200
  Lydia (UTTER) 116
BALLENTINE, John 211
  Sarah G. (HOXWORTH) 211
BALLOU, Albert C. 159
  Archibald 137
  Catherine (HAGGERT) 137
  Celia M. (PUTNEY) 159
  Edith 47
BANCROFT, Franc M. 160
BANKER, Joseph A. 204
  Nettie R. (BISHOP) 204
BANNARD, Anna E. (FISHER) 170
  David 170
BANNING, Adelle 186

BANNING, Joseph 199
  Lida H. 205
  Nellie 196
  Walter J. 205
BANTON, Amanda 44
  J. F. 106
  John 53
  Jonas 44, 52
BARBER, Alice 49
  Alsbro 12
  Alsbrow 73
  Amasa 98
  Anna (LOVE) 116
  Arthur G. 74
  Betsey 60
  C. (ALDERMAN) 118
  C. B. 57
  Calvin B. 71
  Caroline 46
  Charles A. 74, 179
  Charlotte 98
  Charlotte L. 57
  Cornelia 97
  Cornelia M. 49
  David 118
  David B. 46, 73
  E. M. 169
  Eli 73
  Elizabeth 12
  Emma (SMITH) 167
  Ezekiel 116
  G. W. 167
  Genevieve (CAMPBELL) 181
  Harriet 218
  Isabelle 46
  J. C. 107
  Joel 60
  John 181
  Joshua 46
  Julia 138
  Lorenzo A. 49
  Mary (SWIFT) 179
  Mary E. 74
  R. 155
  Thomas J. 23
  William 12
BARCHET, S. P. 108
BARD, Hannah (LAINING) 112
  Harriet L. (SANFORD) 141
  Palatiah 112

BARD, Rodolphua 141
BARDEEN, A. V. 38, 193
  Ada 191
  Cyrus 38
  Emma 193
  Sally 65
BARDIN, Fannie S. 178
BARDINE, E. R. 33
  Jennie S. 33
  May F. 33
BARKER, Almira H. (GRAVES) 122
  B. Walters 180
  Daniel 13
  E. R. 122
  Electa (WEST) 113
  Hannah H. 69
  Kittie A. (OSBORN) 180
  L. B. 180
  William 113
BARNARD, Ann W. 64
BARNDARD, J. H. 188
BARNES, Amanda (PALMER) 113
  Betsy 139
  Chauncey 113
  Edgar M. 163
  G. W. 185
  Hattie 81
  I. Addison 134
  Jennie A. (PRENTICE) 163
  Julia Ann (CRAIG) 134
BARNETT, Eleanor 6
  Ezra 16
  Harriet A. 142
  M. Emeline 16
  S. W. 59
  Samuel 6
  Samuel W. 142
BARNEY, Andrew J. 143
  O. Sophia (SHERMAN) 143
BARNS, Henry 141
  Sarah A. (TOOKE) 141
BARNUM, M. 216
BARR, Alice May (SCOTT) 208
  Herbert D. 208
  J. W. 166, 177
  Nathaniel 84
  Samuel 97

BARRETT, Emma A. 200
  Jacob 14
BARRON, Fletcher 144
  Josephine 144
BARROWS, --- (Rev. Mr.) 119
  D. A. 130
  L. 122
  L. A. 127
BARRY, A. C. 127
BARSTOW, C. 151, 167, 169, 170, 176
  Charles 170, 171, 174
  Deette (WATERS) 175
  John 175
BARSTOWN, C. 171
BARTHOLOMEW, --- (Rev.) 122
  Eliza 119
  O. 135
  Orlo 142
BARTLE, William 112
BARTON, Nancy 112
BARTRAM, Henry 211
  Mary G. (TOWNSEND) 211
BASHER, Fred L. 152
  Julia M. (HAMLIN) 152
BASS, Seth 84
BASSETT, Ada (WILBUR) 206
  William 206
BASTIAN, Ziba F. 63
BASTOW, Charles 157
BATCHELLOR, A. K. 206
BATE, Paul H. 193
BATEMAN, Benjamin 45, 169
  Mary 45
  Mary Ann 152
  Mary J. 169
BATES, Albert 180
  Archibald 103
  Carrie S. (ELDRED) 180
  Elizabeth 4
  George 139
  J. P. 185
  Jonathan 4
  Julia J. 184
  L. C. 138
  Lilla 183
  Sarah Ann (WILBUR) 139
BAUMES, Louise J. 140

BAXTER, Albert E. 210
  L. May (PARKER) 210
BAYLIS, Lizzie M. 209
BEACH, --- (Mr.) 1
  A. R. 181
  Aaron F. 29
  Addie A. 158
  Adelia 29
  Alice L. 29
  Allen R. 74
  Ann Eliza 182
  Aurelia R. 126
  B. N. 129
  Calvin G. 176
  Charlotte M. (REED) 176
  D. (TYLER) 112
  E. H. 133
  Elbecca 134
  Emergene 123
  Esther 159
  Ethan 168
  Jared J. 126
  Justus 112
  L. Melissa 133
  Merton 29
  Millard (Mrs.) 96
  Miranda 118
  Nellie L. 29
  Sophia 36
BEAL, Charles 73
  Eliza A. (WHAN) 189
  George 73, 189
  John 91
  Joseph 213
  Lizzie 73
BEAR, Charlotte 115
BEARDSLEY, --- (Rev.) 118
  E. 117
  Grace 209
  O. C. 122
BEBEE, Helen M. 95
BECKWITH, Allie H.
  (HARRINGTON) 219
  Barak 11
  Birdie 178
  D. L. 219
  Edgar 178
BEDELL, --- (Mr.) 97
  Lucinda F. 151
BEEBE, --- (Rev. Mr.) 219

BEEBE, --- (Rev.) 141
  A. 118
  A. J. 184
  A. M. 197, 198, 200
  Ada 196
  Adelbert 185
  Albert 42
  Ama M. 54
  Andrew J. 182
  Anna Louisa 42
  Annie 95
  Asa C. 196
  Delight 172
  Delight (WILLIAMS) 118
  Deloss 95
  Dena J. 200
  E. 137
  Eleazer 99
  Elizabeth 79
  Eva (SQUIRES) 185
  F. D. 99
  H. C. 152
  Juliaette 42
  Justin 63
  L. E. 159
  LeRoy 99
  Lizzie E. (MINER) 182
  Lois S. 99
  M. Nellie 184
  Mary J. (JOHNSON) 159
  Olive C. 163
  R. O. 162
  Sarah E. 129
  Sophrona 92
  Zadoc 39
BEEBEE, Katherine Margaret
  205
BEECHER, Cora L. 207
  Emoline 114
  Hilda 78
  Mary A. 183
BEECRAFT, Harlan B. 208
  Mary E. (GILBERT) 208
BEEKMAN, Elmer Eugene 205
  Minnie Eloise 205
BELDEN, A. Russel 22
  Sally 28
BELL, Anna C. 212
  Charlotte (PARSONS) 140
  John 212

BELL, Sarah F. 204
  William 140
BELLOW, Abigail 53
BELLOWS, Alfred 94
  Alfred D. 53
  Laura L. 94
BEMAN, Annie E. 172
  R. 172
BEMENT, Frederick B. 118
  Mary Ann (ARMSTRONG) 118
BENEDICT, A. N. 153
  Ada L. 199
  Adella (FOSTER) 165
  Alida S. 195
  Amelia 19
  Angie 206
  Cena (COLE) 115
  Della F. 53
  Desire 19
  Elizabeth 193
  Emily R. 129
  Frank 165
  Frank J. 186
  Frank S. 53
  J. Foster 53
  James H. 197
  James K. 30
  John 1
  Julia (CADY) 156
  L. A. 19
  Louisa 28, 219
  Mary L. 186
  Mary L. (BENEDICT) 186
  S. B. 19
  Samuel 199
  Samuel B. 28, 156, 219
  Stephen 112
  Stewart 115
  Zar 19
BENHAM, Amanda (ROGERS) 125
  William 125
BENJAMIN, C. A. 209
  Etta A. (JOSLIN) 176
  Frank 196
  G. H. 210
  J. J. 176
  Rose (COLE) 196
  Valetta (BRIGGS) 208
  William H. 208

BENNETT, --- (Mrs.) 100
  Abijah 67
  Andrew S. 208
  Daniel 94
  Eilen J. (WHITE) 150
  Emily E. 157
  Hattie E. (TYNELL) 208
  Henry 100
  J. J. 150
  Jennie M. (TISDALE) 210
  John 179
  Josiah R. 210
  M. 165
  M. L. 170, 211
  Mary E. 199
  Ray 100
BENNING, John M. 89
BENSON, A. P. 134
  J. G. 202, 203, 204
  J. George 202
  Lydia (PATRICK) 134
BENSTED, Mary J. (MAXSTED) 208
  William H. 208
BENTLEY, David P. 52
  Mary E. (BROWN) 124
  Oliver 124
  Sarah F. 142
BENTON, Amelia R. 59
  Anna 72
  Clara E. 72
  David 72
  Elizabeth J. 141
  Jason M. 59
  Rollen C. 59
BERKIN, Millie R. 174
BERRY, Ellen P. Barnett (PAINE) 70
  Lockert 3
  S. W. 70
BERTLETT, D. K. 165
BEST, F. C. 205
  Frank 111
  Winnie (EVANS) 205
BETHKE, Ernestine M. 196
BETSINGER, Thomas H. 24
BEVILLARD, E. P. 207
  Sarah (DODGE) 207
BEVINS, Charlotte 68
BICE, George 169

BICE, Lydia 169
BICKNELL, Bennet 215
  Bennett 214
  Harriet 215
  Melissa S. 97
BIDWELL, H. K. 187
  John 36
  Libbie D. 187
BIERCE, Chanceller 136
  Chancellor L. 81
  Charles O. 69
  Julia Ann 136
BIGELOW, Abigail 191
BILL, Miranda 117
BILLINGS, Bradley 156, 193
  Calvin M. 141
  Deloss H. 153
  Dexa E. 156
  E. C. 193
  Esther 89
  Frank C. P. 190
  Henry M. 170
  Inez S. 167
  Jennie (TALLET) 190
  Lorain M. (CAMPBELL) 153
  Mary M. (BLAIR) 141
  Pamela (GEWYE) 170
  Polly 18
  Truman 18, 89
BILLS, C. S. 109
  Charles E. 199
  Mary R. (SMITH) 199
BINGHAM, H. C. 138
  Helen M. (PARMELEE) 138
BIRCHARD, Lucinda 19
BIRD, James 92
BIRDGE, Benjamin S. 74
BIRDSLEY, Clarissa 122
BIRGE, --- (Mrs.) 29
  J. W. 29
BISBEE, Cyrenus 107
  Reuben 34
  Ruth 41
BISBY, Cyrus 109
BISHOP, Abigail 41
  Alanson 9
  Anna Norris (SMITH) 52
  Asa 10
  George G. 52
  Hannah L. (PUTNEY) 156

BISHOP, Hepzibah 9
  James 41
  James L. 156
  Mary 10
  Myron A. 131
  Nettie R. 204
  Sarah L. 131
  W. F. 52
BISSELL, --- (Rev.) 142
  Mary A. (GUTHRIE) 151
  T. J. 153, 155
  T. Jefferson 151, 152, 161
BIXBY, --- (Mrs.) 81
  Goodwin 8, 9
  Harry 147
  Julia A. 186
  Mary (SIMMONS) 147
BLACK, Samuel C. 98
BLACKMAN, Deborah 82
  Delia 116
BLACKWOOD, Hannah 126, 128
  William 126, 128
BLAIR, Catharine 15
  David 76
  DeAlton 15
  Dwight 51
  Eliza 216
  Erskin 15
  Gertrude 15
  Harvey 27
  Henry N. 27
  Mary 158
  Mary M. 141
  Nettie 203
  Philo E. 216
  Sarah M. (HARRIS) 131
  Seth 19, 52
  Seth T. 131
  Sophia J. 184
  Susan J. 183
BLAKELY, Almon D. 198
  Jennie (ROBINSON) 198
BLAKEMAN, Ara 56
  Cornelia J. (COLLISTER) 45
  Hattie A. (CURTIS) 201
  J. F. 201
  Lyman 45
BLAKESLEY, --- (Elder) 215

BLAKSLEE, --- (Rev. Mr.) 133
BLANCHARD, Azarial 2
  Calvin 2
  Elizabeth 2
  Walton 49
BLANCON, Eliza Dielle 79
BLANDING, Ella 61
BLINN, Cornelia 179
  Elijah 179
  Elisha J. 163
  Lucretia 125
  Nettie A. (CLARK) 163
BLISH, Amelia A. (FLETCHER) 125, 127
  Charles D. 125, 127
  Eliza G. 122
  John D. 40
  John S. 139
  Margareta H. (HENSHAW) 139
  Prudence O. 40
BLISS, Aaron 166
  Alseba (PHILLIPS) 166
  Calvin 115
  Everett 164
  George R. 125
  J. S. 216
  Joshua D. 173
  Marietta (PHELPS) 217
  Mary A. (RAYMOND) 125
  Mary E. (STEVENSON) 173
  Minerva (LYON) 115
  Rosall (RAYLOR) 164
BLIVEN, Abram 158
  Nancy M. (HOLMES) 158
  Sarah 208
BLODGETT, --- (Rev. Elder) 121
  --- (Rev.) 124
  Alathea (CROCKER) 101
  Carrie 101
  H. W. 101
  Warren 101
BLOOM, George W. 54
BLOSSOM, Cynthia 215
  Henry M. 145
  Levi 215
  Sue H. (BRIGHAM) 145
  T. C. (Mrs.) 16
BLOWERS, Sophronia 205
BLUNT, Albert J. 177
  Martha A. (HARVEY) 177
  Mary D. 160
BOARDMAN, B. G. 106
  G. S. 151
  George S. 119
BOICE, Isabella (MITCHELL) 216
  Philip H. 216
BOID, --- (Rev. Mr.) 114
BOLAND, Susan E. 195
BOND, Henry W. 93
  Israel 68
  Sophia 68
  William 95
BONNER, Harriet 82
BONNEY, Abigail (BISHOP) 41
  Albert F. 81
  Angie L. (CADY) 31
  Aurelia 38
  Beaulah A. 61
  Benjamin 43, 145
  C. P. 61, 87, 192
  C. P. (Mrs.) 62
  C. Page 160
  Charles L. 41
  Edward 7, 41
  Electa 132
  Emeline 124
  F. E. 109
  F. S. 38
  Fannie (SPRAKER) 193
  Gelusia 12
  H. D. 174
  Hannah 5
  Hannah (FINCH) 41
  Hannah B. 71
  Harriet F. 14
  Harwood 41
  Heman 19
  Irene B. 132
  Israel 31
  Israel T. 158
  J. M. 31
  James 41
  Jethro 39
  Jethro M. 75
  Jethro May 41

BONNEY, Job 41
  John Y. 75, 167
  Lavina C. 74
  LeRoy H. 75
  Leroy 37
  Levell 31
  Levi 41
  Levi B. 79, 90
  Levi Bisbee 41
  Lillian Eva 38
  Lucina R. 79
  Lucinda 41
  Lucretia 41
  M. 79
  Mattie A. 75
  Mattie A. (HILL) 167
  Nancy 145
  Neman 41
  Perez 41
  Perez H. 5
  Ruhama 41
  Ruth (BISBEE) 41
  Sarah 42
  Sophia (JUDD) 79
  Susan C. (HALL) 158
  Susan G. 90
  Syril 20
  W. F. 146
  Walter P. 193
  William 132
  William F. 6, 14, 63, 142
  William Finch 41
  William Henry 6
  William P. 71
BOON, B. H. 118
  S. 9
  Sanford Orsino 9
BOONE, Will 108
BOOTH, A. 181
  Abby Eliza 137
  C. A. 18
  Cynthia M. 161
  Fanny H. 144
  Kate A. 173
  Laura 46
  Orange 208
  Sarah 208
  Sarah B. (SLATER) 181
BORDEN, Jane E. 103
BORDWELL, Charles 161

BORDWELL, Nettie E. (GEER) 161
BOSWORTH, Anna F. 201
  H. M. 179
  Lizzie D. (ANDREWS) 179
BOTSFORD, Martha A. 82
BOURN, A. Wayland 192
  Emma (BARDEEN) 193
BOURNE, Barnabas 120
  Lydia B. (LONG) 120
BOWDISH, --- (Rev. Mr.) 131
  L. 130
  Nancy 65
BOWEN, --- (Rev. Mr.) 165
  Amelia (CHAPIN) 166
  Charles 166
  Cordelia (AVERY) 120
  E. Vanella 170
  Ella E. 85
  Harriet M. 15
  Henry 144
  Ira 122
  James K. 120
  John L. 143
  Malvina 122
  Mary E. (CRANDALL) 143
BOWER, Cordelia (AVERY) 121
  James K. 121
BOWERS, Emma G. 58
  Isaphine J. (WATERS) 206
  Willard W. 206
BOYCE, --- (Mr.) 13
  --- (Mrs.) 13
  Clarissa K. 13
  David A. 91
  Ella T. 91
  Ruth 13
BOYD, --- (Rev.) 114
  Ada L. 73
  Adell 73
  Libbie L. 200
  Maggie 152
  Martha 169
  Nellie (SWIFT) 184
  Roger D. 73
  William 169
  William A. 77, 184
BOYDEN, Samuel F. 24

BOYLER, Tillie M. 198
BRADFORD, B. F. 208
BRADLEY, --- (Rev.) 169
  George H. 163
  Lydia C. (BRAINARD) 163
BRADSHAW, Arthur G. 195
  Ida 185
  Rosetta H. (STABBINS) 195
BRADY, Lizzie 203
  Thomas (Mrs.) 79
BRAINARD, Amanda (SIMMONS) 137
  Charaloise W. 182
  Clarissa 99
  Elizabeth 134
  Everett 77
  Ezra 39
  Frederick 137
  Geneva (GREEN) 172
  I. Duane 172
  Jennie 172
  Lettie J. (CUSHMAN) 182
  Lydia C. 163
  Menzo 172
  Olive 18, 39
  Samuel A. 33
  Stephen 18
BRAITHWAITE, Carrie A. 198
BRAMER, Albert 152
  Emma (ANDERSON) 152
BRAMLEY, A. 199
BRANAGAN, John 65
  Margaret 65
  Thomas 65
BRAND, C. C. 137, 143
  Emily A. (HUNT) 157
  William V. 157
BRANNAN, Hattie (DENNEY) 212
  William 212
BRASS, Mary 206
BRASSE, Charles W. 85
BRATLEY, Benjamin 94
  Lydia C. 131
BRAY, Elizabeth 217
BRAYTON, Cynthia 119
  George 119
  J. A. 120, 121
BRECKENRIDGE, --- (Rev. Mr.) 133

BREED, Joshua 22
BRENAN, Mary 98
BRENNAN, Mary 90
BRESEE, William 26
BRETT, Charles E. 79
BREWER, Mary J. (HADCOCK) 150
  William J. 150
BREWSTER, Wayne 208
BRICKER, J. C. 201
  Minnie (OSBORN) 201
BRIDGE, --- (Rev. Mr.) 139
  Adelbert 170
  Benjamin 70
  C. 140
  Elizabeth 70
  Elizabeth (KERSHAW) 170
  G. 136, 140, 141, 142
  George 141, 142, 143, 144
  George W. 145
  William 167
BRIGGS, A. H. 126, 127
  Addison 52
  Andrew 18
  Ann 21
  D. 173
  E. Vanella (BOWEN) 170
  Ella 177
  F. L. 173
  Harvey 211
  J. M. 21, 30
  James E. 57
  Jane A. 21
  Jenette 142
  Jennie 47
  Johanna (MURPHY) 211
  Kate A. (BOOTH) 173
  Leonard 47
  Meroa C. 161
  Morris 30, 59
  Nancy (STOWEL) 126
  Nancy (STOWELL) 127
  Nancy E. S. 141
  Nellie G. 181
  Nettie E. (WILBUR) 173
  Phebe (SIMONS) 73
  Sarah E. 153
  Valetta 208
  Walter 30, 105, 170
BRIGHAM, --- (Mrs.) 66

BRIGHAM, Clarinda 89
  E. P. 40, 164
  John 125
  Lydia (CASE) 125
  Martin 220
  Mary A. (HOPKINS) 40
  Samuel 16
  Sue H. 145
BRIGHT, George 16
  James 66, 190
  Josephine L. 190
  Melissa 66
BRISBANE, --- (Rev. Mr.) 127
  R. C. 127
BRISBIN, R. C. 125
BRISTOL, B. C. 176
  Mary P. 176
BRITTON, Bertha M. (NASH) 207
  William H. 207
BROCKET, L. A. 32
  Lydia P. 32
BROCKETT, Allie L. 50
  Alvah 31
  David Z. 28
  Elizabeth 28
  Leonard A. 31
  Lydia 31
BRODERICK, Frank 210
  Mary (CASE) 210
BROGAN, Bridget 34
  Carrie R. 199
  James 34
BRONSON, --- (Elder) 25
  C. H. 202
  John 44
  Lettie M. 153
  Lucretia 44
  Marian 82
  Mattie 201
  Nora D. (NICKHAM) 202
  Westel 34
BROOKE, Nelson 88
BROOKS, --- (Capt.) 31
  --- (Rev. Dr.) 178, 182, 185, 189, 196, 206, 211
  --- (Rev. Mr.) 133, 160, 163, 166
  A. L. 134, 135, 136

BROOKS, Adelaide G. 179
  Asahel L. 134
  Charles H. 35
  E. Ann (SHEPARD) 122
  Edwin C. 134
  Helen 162
  Helen (KEYES) 134
  J. G. 208
  J. H. 122
  James G. 118
  James W. 60
  L. G. 177
  Mary E. (WILCOXSON) 177
  Mary Elizabeth (AIKIN) 118
  N. W. 162
  Nelson 29
  W. 162
  W. E. 166
  W. H. 158, 167
  W. R. 35, 151, 152, 156, 157, 158, 159, 162, 164, 167, 170, 171, 172, 173, 174, 175, 176, 177, 179, 180, 193, 201, 203, 204, 205, 211, 212, 214, 219
BROTLE, Jennie M. 208
BROWER, Fidelia A. (STAPLES) 213
  Norman 213
  Norman (Mrs.) 85
BROWN, --- (Elder) 116
  --- (Mr.) 118, 162
  --- (Rev. Mr.) 129, 140
  --- (Rev.) 124
  A. 156
  A. J. 197
  A. Judson 29
  A. L. 46
  Ada (BEEBE) 196
  Adaliza A. 140
  Alfred 26
  Alfred L. 193
  Alice M. (HOSTLER) 98
  Almira (CLARK) 123
  Alzina (HARP) 143
  Ann 122
  Ann M. (CHUBBUCK) 128
  Anna (MC QUADE) 172
  Avery 123

BROWN, Bertie 93
  Cassadan M. (HATCH) 155
  Charles 34
  Charles E. 144, 155
  Charles H. 98
  Charles T. 143
  D. D. 169
  Duane 55
  E. C. 157, 219
  Edward 74
  Eliza 206
  Elmira 37
  Emily 141
  Frances T. Lewis 165
  Frankie 75
  Fred E. 85
  Geneva M. 200
  George 163
  H. Philander 27
  Harriet A. (SMITH) 146
  Harriet S. (ALEXANDER) 125
  Hattie 204
  Healy 146
  Henry A. 204
  J. F. 206, 207
  J. Fletcher 205
  J. H. 93, 212
  James 7, 9, 34
  James M. 128
  James R. 46
  Jannie 176
  Jennie 63
  John 106, 108, 109, 155, 172, 196
  John H. 85
  Jonas 17
  Jonathan 217
  Joseph 19
  Julia 166
  Julia Ann (BAILEY) 138
  Libbie E. 180
  Lucas 66
  Lucy M. 145
  Lydia 10
  Maria 95
  Martha E. 46
  Mary 98, 217
  Mary A. (BEECHER) 183
  Mary E. 124

BROWN, Mary E. (BACON) 163
  Mary Jane 49
  Minnie A. 34
  N. T. 140, 153
  Nathan T. 131
  Nellie M. 191
  Nicanor 75
  P. P. 27, 29
  Paul R. 125
  Phebe 75
  Philip 122
  Ruth 55
  Sally (PHINEY) 118
  Samuel 49
  Samuel (Mrs.) 76
  Sarah J. (FULKERSON) 193
  Simon 183
  Sophia 66
  Susan 116
  Thankful (MILLARD) 135
  Timothy G. 85
  Tyler 153
  Viola G. 197
  W. B. 165
  W. E. 88
  William 138
  Wilson 135
BROWNELL, Alvin 48
  Amelia 48
  Caroline Elizabeth (HUNT) 131
  Charles B. 192
  Fannie (FULLER) 192
  Genevieve 52
  J. B. 68
  James P. 180
  Jennie L. 188
  Mary M. (THROOP) 68, 180
  Nathan 37
  Nettie A. (HARRIMAN) 170
  Nicanah 131
  Samuel 92, 170
  Sarah M. 49
  Willie H. 38
BROWNING, J. W. 196
  M. Jenette (HAYWARD) 196
BROWNSON, Herman 24
BRUCE, A. L. 140
  A. W. 141, 144, 147
  B. F. 85

BRUCE, Nancy A. 85
BRYANT, Mary 135
BUCKINGHAM, Beulah 113
BUCKLEY, Cyrus P. 150
  Edna B. 208
  G. F. 207
  G. H. 202
  Hattie T. (SIMPSON) 202
  Lorinda S. (HATCH) 150
BUDLONG, Chloe 114
  Leander 100
BUEL, Angeline 122
  Eli 46, 64, 120
  Jenette P. 134
  Pamillia 122
  Phoebe (FREEMAN) 64
  Phoebe (LAMPHIRE) 120
BUELL, Ann C. 35, 37
  Chauncey 32
  Clinton C. 138
  Cora L. 191
  Eli 36, 132
  Elijah 19
  Esther 31
  F. M. 55
  Ira W. 31
  Irene B. 132
  Jennie A. 197
  John B. 200
  Joseph 63
  Lydia 31
  Mary A. (NILES) 138
  Mary E. 36
  Matilda A. 200
  Nettie J. 35
  P. C. 36
  Permelia 63
  Philander C. 35, 36, 37
  Rufus F. 36
  Samuel Warren 31
  Thomas 55
  Warren 63, 187
  Warren F. 197
  Warren J. 31
  William F. 63, 72
BUGBEE, Elle J. 205
  Martha A. (JONES) 144
  Rufus A. 144
BULLUS, Polly 129
BUMP, Roxana 82

BUMPUS, Isaac 112
  Matilda (OSGOOD) 112
BUNCE, J. W. 160
  Louisa (CLARK) 160
BUNO, Ellen R. (MELROY) 166
  Orson 142, 166
  Sarah F. (BENTLEY) 142
BURCHARD, --- (Rev.) 197
  Allie 40
  Anna 51
  Carrie 36, 188
  Cynthia S. 158
  Frank S. 40
  Freddie Lester 39
  Hannah (MILLER) 195
  Horace 75
  Horace S. 88
  Irene 36
  Irene (DUNHAM) 62
  Irene B. (DUNHAM) 137
  Jabez 10
  Louisa 152
  Louise 68
  Lydia Ann 128
  Mary 16
  P. H. 16
  S. B. 137, 188
  S. D. 152
  Seneca B. 36, 62, 195
  Sophia 17
  Sylvester 39, 40, 51, 68
  Theodore 17, 128
BURDEN, John (Mrs.) 88
BURDICK, Augusta S. (SMITH) 196
  Clara L. (SNOW) 162
  Clark 151, 213
  Clayton A. 207
  George M. 162
  George W. 207
  Helen M. 150
  Henry C. 136
  J. W. 126, 128
  James 145
  L. Lenora (CLARKE) 207
  Lucinda 151
  Lydia F. 138
  Marcelia B. (KEITH) 145
  Mary Jane (ROWLINGS) 145

BURDICK, Perrin 136
  Spencer S. 145
  Susan (DUTCHER) 136
  Violet A. 128
  William S. 196
BURDIN, George 157
  Seleria E. (SALISBURY) 147
BURDWIN, Rynaldo 43
BURGDOFF, Hattie 205
BURGESS, Alfred 150
  George F. 7
  Helen 7
  Sarah L. 33, 150
  William 110, 111
BURKE, Thomas 47
BURLINGAME, A. J. 126, 128
  Adelbert C. 163
  Dealton E. 184
  Ella 190
  Harriet F. (WITHAM) 126
  Harriet P. (WITHAM) 128
  Hattie (LAPHAM) 163
BURLINGHAM, Clara A. (LAMB) 184
BURLISON, Anna J. (DURKEE) 207
  Ashel M. 207
BURN, --- (Miss) 50
  G. F. (Mrs.) 50
  I. Irving 167
  Mary C. (RUSSELL) 167
BURNAP, Jennie 172
BURNHAM, Almira W. 47
  Elizabeth H. 145
  Lovisa W. 143
  Mathew K. 76
  S. 106, 198, 203, 204
  Samuel 33
BURNS, --- (Rev.) 168
  Florence A. 212
BURR, Benjamin J. 209
  Lizzie E. (CLUTE) 209
BURRITT, C. W. 64
  Sarah 64
BURROUGHS, Alvira S. (FIELDS) 127
  J. C. 127
BURROWS, J. L. 169
BURT, --- (Rev. Mr.) 115

BURT, Joseph 100
  Mary 100
BURTON, Amos 13
  Esther 104
  John E. 36
  Mary Lydia 23, 53
  Smith 49
  Thomas L. 53
BUSH, Calvin 99
  Henry C. 57
  Lillian M. 200
BUSHNELL, F. N. 39
BUTCHERS, Daniel 75, 143
  Phebe (KELLEY) 143
BUTLER, E. C. 107, 110
  Ernest 108
  Ernest C. 194
  George R. 149
  Lida 52
  Lois E. (FOSTER) 194
  Lucy 149
  Lydia 94
  Phebe 63
BUTTERFIELD, Anna 199
  Harriet (BABCOCK) 163
  Jane 168
  Leander 163
  Olvier 168
BUTTLER, Olive 119
BUTTLES, Gaylord A. 202
  Mary (LOOMIS) 202
BUTTON, Elias 2
  Eliza 77
  Lou 168
  Luther 77
BUYES, Charity E. (FORT) 219
  J. Franklin 219
BUYSBY, Sophia 115
BUZZELL, O. A. 198
BYER, R. Myra 173
  Sarah 114
BYINGTON, Dwight 144
  Emily Jane (EGGLESTON) 144
BYRD, Elizabeth (COOK) 172
  William 172
BYRNS, George 70
  Martha 70
CADWELL, Ashbel 114

CADWELL, Belinda 114
  Emma A. 192
  Maria (JEFFRIES) 114
  Mary 124
CADY, A. J. 42, 182
  Abbie H. 186
  Addie C. (KIMBALL) 201
  Adoniram J. 87
  Angie L. 31
  Arthur 188
  Belle R. 188
  Deette 167
  Elizabeth (POTTER) 182
  Emoline (BEECHER) 114
  James 195
  James E. 186
  Julia 156
  Nancy R. (TAYLOR) 195
  Nathan 114
  S. S. 152, 212
  Susannah 42
  Thomas H. 201
CALKING, Mary Ann (CARR) 137
  T. W. 137
CALKINS, Anna Maria (WILLIAMS) 142
  Celestia A. 122
  Cornelia S. 50
  Edmund L. 136
  Elizabeth (TOBY) 136
  F. W. 156
  Frank G. 72
  Harriet A. 132
  M. Irene (PIERCE) 156
  Mary Jane 136
  Melville K. 17
  Minerva A. 121
  O. F. 142
  Perces A. 125
CALLAHAN, H. 143
CAMP, Harrie 199
  Roxanna 124
CAMPBELL, --- (Mrs.) 152
  --- (Rev. Dr.) 165
  Amelia M. 42
  Amos 152, 153
  Archibald 28
  Archie 189
  Avis 40

CAMPBELL, Benjamin T. 33
  Charles 13, 30
  Daniel 40
  Elizabeth P. (THOMPKINS) 146
  Elizabeth R. 176
  Eusebia N. 162
  Ezra 13, 63
  Ezra B. 42
  Genevieve 181
  H. A. 144, 151, 162, 166
  Hannah 125
  Henry F. 13, 38
  Horace A. 117
  Horace W. 27
  Ida A. 166
  Jennie M. (ROSS) 189
  Lida O. 201
  Linus M. 34
  Lorain M. 153
  Lyman (Mrs.) 76
  M. N. 155
  Martha 116
  Mary 154
  Mary Ann 7
  Meroa 13
  Moses 7
  O. S. 38
  Otis S. 146
  P. Randolph 167
  Phila (ANDRUS) 117
  Phoebe 30
  Polly 39
  Robert A. 34
  Rosina 7
  S. M. 146
  Sarah J. (WITTER) 207
  Solomon A. 207
  Susan N. 32
  Theodocia 40
CANDEE, Julius 117
  Lucia M. (OSBORNE) 117
CARD, DeEste E. 149
  Fred L. 53
  Harriet 17
  Lettie I. 162
  William H. 145
CARDER, Sarah 33
CARET, Lawrence (Mrs.) 102
CAREY, Andrew M. 137

247

CAREY, Elizabeth A.
   (HOLLINGSWORTH) 137
  James 149
  Nancy B. 149
  Nancy B. (PERRY) 149
CARL, Ada 209
  Johnnie 57
CARMAN, Fran 98
  Frankie 98
CARPENTER, Adelia A. 164
  Ann E. 153
  Celesta A. (FOX) 146
  Frank L. 153
  Frankie 204
  Hattie (HOPKINS) 212
  Lettie M. (BRONSON) 153
  Louisa 156
  Nancy (WILLIAMS) 124
  Nelson 124
  Sarah 116
  Sarah E. 165
  U. G. 212
  Willis H. 146
CARR, Addie F. 153
  Mary Ann 137
CARRIER, Calvin S. 152
  J. N. 10
  Joel 10
  Maggie (BODY) 152
  Mary (BISHOP) 10
  Sophronia 10
CARRINGTON, M. Velona 186
CARRUTH, Carmi W. 215
  Levi 215
CARSWELL, Mary B. 63
CARTER, --- (Mrs.) 199
  Almina 219
  Almira 150
  Caroline 217
  Catherine E. (CHILDS) 136
  Chancey F. 189
  Charles D. V. 40, 155
  E. W. 157
  Guy 136
  John 65
  Libbie H. (SHORT) 157
  Mary A. 176
  Mary L. (PAYNE) 189
  Theresa 40
  Theresa (HOPSEGER) 155

CARVER, Esther C. 113
  George 164
  James 174
  Maryella (WHITMORE) 164
  Sarah C. (WENTWORTH) 174
CASE, Adria (KERN) 206
  Anna 72
  B. F. 49, 72, 197
  Benjamin F. 159
  Benjamin Franklin 41
  Burns 41
  Byron 41
  Caroline 41
  Dwight 41
  Frances M. 126
  Francis 41
  Grandley 57
  Grandly 41
  H. P. 85
  Hyman P. 41
  Isaac Newton 41
  John Quincy Adams 41
  Joshua 90
  Lafayette 41
  Lydia 125
  M. E. (PIERCE) 197
  Mary 210
  Myron 107
  Olive (BUTTLER) 119
  Phineas 119
  Ruhama (BONNEY) 41
  Will 206
CASEY, Eli S. 139
  John 105
  Mary K. (WALRATH) 139
  Michael J. 106
CASH, Coryden E. 161
  Corydon 69
  Ella M. (TALLCOTT) 204
  Frank 110
  Frank M. 204
  Sarah 69
  Sarah E. (HUGHES) 161
CASITY, Mary E. 207
CASLER, --- (Rev.) 194
  L. 178, 180
CASSELL, James M. 49
CASSLER, --- (Rev. Mr.) 145
  L. 146

CASTIDAY, George 110, 195
 Sarah D. (FISHER) 195
CASTIDY, George 108, 111
CATHALL, J. Everist 209
CATLIN, Richard 59
CAVERT, Joseph S. 217
 Mary E. (AMBROSE) 217
CAZEER, Matthias 116
CHADWICK, Isaac 44, 81
 Jane 81
CHAFEE, Ella (ARMOUR) 173
 William 173
CHAMBERLAIN, Amanda P. 143
 Ansel 143
 Isaac F. 17
 J. H. 130
CHAMBERLIN, W. R. 171
CHAMBERS, Amanda E. 87
CHAMPLIN, George 34
CHAMPNEY, Elmer 93
CHAPEL, Amanda J. 142
 Esther 2
CHAPELL, Martha 8
CHAPHE, Caroline M. 86
 Jenett 166
 Lizie M. 193
CHAPIN, --- (Rev.) 125
 Amelia 166
 Avaline Amelia 18
 Brooks 168
 Chester 11
 Hattie (MASON) 169
 I. D. 169
 James B. 139
 Sarah M. 168
 Sarah S. (REED) 139
CHAPMAN, Ann Vennette
  (WILBER) 136
 Anna 159
 B. Franklin 123
 Dorr C. 180
 Huldah (WILCOX) 123
 Jacob J. 136
 Rhoda 35
 Sally 95
 Sarah A. (THOMPSON) 180
 Stephen 95
 W. W. 216
CHAPPELL, Lewis 37
CHARGO, M. (Mrs.) 189

CHASE, Asa 37
 Edward 87
 Emerilla (HOPKINS) 72
 Freddie 79
 Loretta 161
 Luna 93
 Mattie S. 79
 S. S. 72, 79
 T. B. 199
CHATFIELD, Harriet L. 130
CHEESBRO, Abigail (ROWEO)
  152
 Adelbert 152
CHERITRE, Alice 196
CHESBRO, Alvin 182
 Hattie A. (HUNTLEY) 182
 Libbie 212
CHESEBORO, David D. 74
CHESEBRO, --- (Miss) 74
 Allie 213
 Clarissa (SAUNDERS) 138
 Eliza M. 136
 Herman D. 211
 Minnie F. (PALMER) 211
 Nathan H. 138
CHILCOTT, Julia A. 143
CHILDS, Catherine E. 136
 Ebenezer 64
 J. D. 160
 Susan 93
CHRISPELL, Ettie S.
  (FAGAN) 192
CHRISTIE, C. W. 175
 Margaretta 175
CHRISTMAN, Eaton 172
 Helen F. (HOLDREDGE) 172
CHUBBUCK, Ann M. 128
 Benjamin R. 14
 Catherine 13
 Charles 14, 21, 135
 E. C. 21
 Emily 135
 Julia Allin (TROWBRIDGE)
  142
 Levina R. 21
 Samuel 13
 Simeon 8, 21
 W. W. 142
CHURCH, --- (Rev.) 150
 --- (Squire) 200

CHURCH, A. M. 179, 200
  Betsey Ann (EVERETT) 117
  Birdie (BECKWITH) 178
  H. M. 197, 198, 200
  Louisa C. 131
  Mary 23, 141
  S. T. 141
  Sophia 19
  Thomas 82
  Uriah 19
  W. H. 199
  William 117
  William Lee 64, 178
CLARE, Tilda 207
CLARK, --- (Rev.) 145
  Abby Ann 51
  Albert A. 186
  Albert G. 32
  Almira 123
  Alna B. (TRIPP) 188
  Amy 18
  Andrew 50
  Andrew W. 188
  Anna 201
  Annette (FOOTE) 147
  Barbara M. 146
  Belle (STONE) 214
  C. 23
  Caleb 154
  Catherine 77
  Charles 144
  Charles (Mrs.) 101
  Charles M. 47
  Clarissa 18
  Cynthia D. 157
  David 50
  Davil 47
  DeEtta S. (HUDSON) 190
  Emily A. 38
  Enos 147
  Erastus D. 51
  Etta 209
  Experience M. 50
  G. L. 214
  George 190
  George C. 163
  Hattie E. 51
  Hattie Eliza 25
  Henry 85
  Hosea B. 146
  CLARK, J. 142, 146, 207
  J. L. 171
  J. P. 105
  James 23, 92
  Joel W. 115, 116
  Joseph 119
  Josiah W. 131
  Julia O. 120
  L. R. 191
  Lavina A. (HOPKINS) 179
  Leroy 77
  Louis L. 37
  Louisa 160
  Lucinda 151
  Luke 3
  Malvina (TERWILLIGER) 131
  Mary 51, 140
  Mary E. (FOLAND) 186
  Mary Jane 187
  Maxson 18
  Mercy 32, 38
  Milo 58
  Myra 93
  Myra A. 151
  Nancy A. (BRUCE) 85
  Nettie A. 163
  Pardon 59, 220
  Phebe L. 152
  Polly (WESTCOTT) 144
  S. T. 192
  Samuel 32, 38, 187
  Sarah 50
  Silas S. 179
  Simeon B. 32
  Sophronia (IDE) 119
  Thomas 10
  W. 169
  William 144
  Willie 43
CLARKE, H. Adella 198
  L. Lenora 207
  Rhoda 194
  Wait 213
CLARKSON, Charlton 1
CLEAVELAND, Erastus 122
  Julia M. 122
CLEVELAND, --- (Rev. Mr.) 184
  Ella (HOGAN) 201
  Sally 1

CLEVELAND, W. F. 201
CLOSE, Charles H. 194
  James 69
  Lyda A. (STEWART) 194
  Mary 206
  Polly 93
CLOUGH, E. D. 189
CLOWES, --- (Rev.) 123
CLOYES, Hiram D. 50
  Josiah 28
CLUTE, Katie F. 207
  Lizzie E. 209
COAN, Abbie J. 56
  Ambrose 143
  Elmora M. 190
  Henry 47, 107
  Isadore 158
  Julius 56
  Lovisa W. (BURNHAM) 143
  Mary 47
COATES, Diadama 128
COATS, Caroline D.
  (ROWELL) 134
  F. B. 134
COBB, --- (Rev. Mr.) 201
  Cornelia M. 129
  Josephine (BARRON) 144
  Josephine A. 51
  Louisa M. (NICHOLS) 170
  S. James 144
  W. R. 218
  William 170
  William H. 159
COBBIN, George H. 194
  Ruth G. (SLAYTON) 194
COCHRAN, A. 98, 207, 209
COCHRANE, --- (Rev. Mr.)
  161
COE, Abigail (FISHER) 141
  Abigail J. 164
  Charlotte 26
  Comfort S. 49
  Cora L. (BUELL) 191
  Helen (WEST) 123
  Huldah 82
  Isaac R. 84
  James 123
  Lewis 82
  Loretta 124
  Mary 53

COE, Melissa 82
  Ruth 82
  Sarah 53
  William 82, 141
  William C. 191
COLBORN, Helen Ada 54
COLBURN, --- (Rev. Mr.)
  119
  Harriet C. 217
  Johnson 217
COLE, --- (Mrs.) 102
  Albert J. 69
  Alvah 110
  Cena 115
  Charlotte A. 132
  DeEtte (PALMER) 169
  DeEtte O. 88
  James 15
  Jennie R. 194
  Lamott 169
  Marcia 133
  Martha A. 150
  Nellie A. (WALKER) 164
  O. W. 164
  Rose 196
  Sidney 102
COLEGROVE, F. W. 205
  Mabel (DART) 205
COLEMAN, Austin 131
  Eliza M. 205
  Lydia C. (BRATLEY) 131
  N. A. 209
COLEY, Eva E. (FAIRCHILD)
  161
  John G. 56
  John J. 161
COLGATE, Frances L.
  (GRIGGS) 138
  John H. 138
COLLESTER, Caroline 67
  Samuel 13
COLLINS, Albert 25
  Electa J. 82
  Elizabeth L. 148
  Ella 179
  Henry M. 186
  Jane R. 193
  Levi 218
  M. Velona (CARRINGTON)
  186

COLLINS, Maria 70
  Mary A. 161
  Mary C. 6
  Mehlon D. 82
  Patrick 102
  Rowland R. 6
  Sheffield 2
  Thomas E. 82
  Timothy 102
  William S. 128
COLLISTER, Cornelia J. 45
  Delos 80
  Emma (JEFFS) 186
  Frances Degrass 132
  Fred S. 206
  Isaac 45, 87
  James 108
  James D. 186
  John 20
  Mae E. 86
  Nellie M. (ALLEN) 206
  Samuel 132
COLSON, Brackley 85
  Caroline (SEYMOUR) 145
  Caroline M. 138
  Charles 53
  Cynthia 96
  Edwin M. 145
  Emer S. (HUNT) 139
  Herbie W. 81
  Ida (COREY) 211
  Josephine C. 140
  Lucy (CRANE) 114
  Lyman 114
  Martin R. 139, 211
  Minerva 113
  Rollin 91
  William 53
COLTON, Benjamin 125
  Hannah (CAMPBELL) 125
COLVIN, Mary 196
  Nancy E. (SPOONER) 195
  William G. 195
COLWELL, Daniel Smith 15
  Joseph 3
COMAN, Ellis 13
  Louise B. 38
  Lucian Mason 13
  Nellie D. 194
  Sophronia 13

COMBS, Betsey (GILBERT) 121
  Edmund R. 120
  Edward 121
  Elizabeth (GILBERT) 120
COMES, James R. 77
  Mary (LYNCH) 138
  Russell E. 138
COMFORT, --- (Rev.) 138
COMPTON, Armena Mary 18
  Caroline M. 8, 9
  Caroline M. (SMITH) 122
  David 21
  Henry 8, 9, 11, 122
  Henry A. 18
  John R. 18
  Sarah A. 18
COMSTOCK, Adelle (BANNING) 186
  Carrie A. 204
  Fannie 63
  G. S. 185
  Julia A. 154
  Lydia 38
  S. L. 63
CONANT, Mary 36
CONDIT, R. W. 124
CONE, Andrew 39
  B. F. (Mrs.) 99
  Belinda S. (MORSE) 39
  Leta 210
CONGER, Abel 142
  Elijah 90
  Harriet 142
  Sarah 90
CONICK, Margaret 123
  Robert 5
CONKEY, Bathsheba 17
CONSIDINE, Helen (PLUMBLY) 139
  J. W. 139
CONY, George R. 175
  Margaretta (CHRISTIE) 175
COOK, A. E. (Mrs.) 45
  Edward M. 194
  Elizabeth 172
  H. Geraldine 139
  Harriet M. 144
  Jennie R. 194
  Lottie A. 164

COOK, M. 208
  T. D. 170
  Viola E. 202
  William F. 93
  Z. 129
COOLIDGE, Frank 28
  Georgie S. 28
  James D. 11
  Mary A. 70
COON, A. W. 148
  Abram 47
  Amy 47
  Charles 95
  D. 113
  DeWitt C. 174
  Eulie 174
  Fannie A. (PALMITER) 170
  Mary D. 84
  Mary D. (BLUNT) 160
  Maudie 95
  Nathan M. 160
  Sarah J. 45
  Stephen 170
COONZER, Hattie (GORTON) 209
  J. 209
COOPER, James 86
  Nora 86
  T. 159, 160
  Theron 161, 162, 164, 165
COOTE, James 107, 108, 193, 194, 195, 196, 199
COPELAND, --- (Rev. Mr.) 132
CORBIN, Cordelia E. 149
  John 23
COREY, A. M. 137
  Amos 16
  D. 192
  D. G. 161
  Edwin 80
  Eli S. 139
  Eliza 80
  Ida 211
  Inez 199
  Mary A. 134
  Mary K. (WALRATH) 139
  May 203
  Winnie 80
CORNELL, Alfred 26

CORNELL, Amanda 26
CORNEY, Alice (MAHANEY) 208
  George E. 208
CORNICE, --- (Mrs.) 104
CORNICK, Florence 204
CORWIN, Daborah C. (ORTON) 114
  Eugene L. 44
  Jason 114
CORY, Roxana 144
COSMER, Libbie E.(HARTSHORN) 161
  Samuel D. 161
COSTELLO, Albert 195
  Ida S. (STEVENS) 195
  Jane Elizabeth 173
COTTON, C. L. 156
  Louisa L. (FELT) 156
COTTRELL, Elizabeth 142
  Roseanna (NEFF) 87
COULTIS, Alexander 168
  Jane (BUTTERFIELD) 168
COULTS, Jennie (HANLEY) 139
  W. H. 139
COVEY, Alexander M. 21
  Electa (BONNEY) 132
  Fannie P. 174
  S. H. 173
  Solomon 19, 132
  Theresa 173
COVINGTON, Sara A. 82
COWAN, William 65
COWDEN, Rosannah 116
COWIN, Julia (NYE) 114
  Warren 114
COX, --- (Mrs.) 4
  Martha 115
  T. 115
  Thomas 4
COY, Sally 115
COZZENS, --- (Mr.) 3
  Matthew 3
  Sophia 3
  William 3
CRAIG, Julia Ann 134
CRAIN, --- (Rev. Mr.) 164, 166
  Chauncey 97

CRAIN, Ebenezer 31, 42
  Fannie 31
  Ira 66
  Philip 13
CRAINE, Lizzie L. 203
CRAMPHIN, --- (Mrs.) 7
  Florence A. (BALLARD) 191
  Hannah 130
  J. T. 191
  Marietta 132
  Thomas 132
CRANDALL, --- (Rev. Mr.) 133
  Ada 194
  Adeline (CUTLER) 133
  Albert R. 129
  Amos F. 128
  Ann Eliza (BEACH) 182
  B. H. 181
  Betsey 40
  Charles 145
  Edgar W. 193
  Frances (DENNISON) 145
  Freeman P. 133
  Ira B. 39
  Jasper 10
  Jerome 94
  John T. 176
  Lizzie 207
  Lucy (REYNOLDS) 193
  Mary E. 94, 143
  Ruth 176
  Sanford W. 186
  Sarah A. 137
  Sarah E. (BEEBE) 129
  Sarah J. (MELVIN) 186
  Violet A. (BURDICK) 128
CRANE, Betsey (FARR) 117
  Charles 3
  Frances D. 139
  Harvey 144
  Joshua 218
  Lucus 117
  Lucy 114
  Roxana (CORY) 144
CRANSTON, Arnold 165
  Marinda 21
  Phebe (SKINNER) 165
  Phineas 21
CRAWE, David 10

CRAWFORD, Benjamin 142
  Philena 142
CRESSON, Solomon 90
CRIM, Italia T. 207
CRITCHEL, Libbie 203
CRITCHLEY, Mary 218
CRITTENDEN, O. L. 76
CROCKER, Alathea 101
  Amos 24, 101, 124
  Asa 41
  Cornelia M. 124
  Emily Maria 142
  Mary 121
CROCKETT, D. Z. 89
  Elizabeth 89
CROEL, Diadama (COATES) 128
  Nancy (KENYON) 128
  Ransford 128
  Solomon 128
CROMMIE, Nettie E. 174
CRONIN, H. C. 198, 199, 200, 201, 204, 211
  Henry 204
  Henry C. 200, 202
CROSS, Berdett 42
  Betsey 40
  Betsey C. 143
  Calvin 43
  Charles Finney 68
  Dora 42
  Dwight 26
  Elizabeth L. 155
  Fannie 197
  J. E. 80
  L. W. 127
  Lydia 42
  Maria (WAGER) 26
  R. T. 68, 183, 184, 185, 186, 187, 188
  Sarah Jane (WATERHOUSE) 127
  Theodore Bridgeman 65
CROSSMAN, Mary H. 200
CROWELL, Adelbert E. 172
  Alexander 99
  Cynthia M. (TUTTLE) 168
  Deette (WILLIAMS) 172
  Etta D. 204
  Harriet (HOWARD) 148

CROWELL, James D. 148
  Luther D. 168
CRUMB, Alanson S. 121
  Andrew V. 188
  Ann Eliza 54
  Annie E. (GREEN) 189
  Daniel T. 189
  David 63
  Finnett (PROBERT) 121
  Hattie E. (HIBBARD) 188
  Hoxie T. 187
  Irena S. (DUTCHER) 187
  Jane E. 192
  Lena 63
  Silas 121
CUBBERLY, James A. 197
  Viola G. (BROWN) 197
CULVER, Charles Beebe 89
  Dena J. (BEEBE) 200
  Frank 89, 109
  Frank L. 200
  Mina 89
CUMMINGS, --- (Rev.) 158
  --- (Rev. Mr.) 117
  William D. 51
CUMMINS, Frank E. 196
  Myrta (SINTON) 196
CUPPERNULL, Frances 36
CURREY, E. 21, 37
  Hannah 19
  Miranda 37
CURRIER, Mary 116
  Richard 217
  Samuel 116
CURRY, Clark D. 56
  E. 56
  Eben 182
  Julia A. (PIERCE) 182
CURTIS, Abel 49
  Addie (GREEN) 196
  Alethan 71
  Alonzo 39, 166
  Annie M. 47
  Annie M. (VAN DUSEN) 166
  Anson 81
  C. A. (Mrs.) 42
  Charles H. 58, 190
  Charles Henry 17
  Charles T. 15

CURTIS, E. 163
  E. (Mrs.) 37
  Edward S. 206
  Emogene 47
  Fedora M. 165
  Frances (HOLMES) 58
  Frances A. (MORSE) 149, 219
  George W. 91
  Gertrude 39
  Gertrude (JOHNSON) 206
  Hattie A. 201
  Helen 17
  Helen (OWEN) 145
  Jay D. 196
  Jerusha 49
  Joseph 145, 151
  L. W. 42
  L. Walker 47, 166
  Laura J. 151
  Louisa 47, 166
  Lucinda 22
  M. V. B. 149, 219
  Mary 202
  May L. 81
  Mehitable 38
  Rosetta (HARVEY) 149
  Samuel W. 47
  Seymour 149
  Sophie (BAKER) 190
  Susan 133
  W. H. 219
  Walker 201
  William 17
CURTISS, Ann 154
  Clarissa 96
CUSHMAN, Abram 81
  Addison J. 147
  Carrie E. 156
  Frances K. 168
  Frankie (ROOT) 147
  L. Melissa (BEACH) 133
  Lettie J. 182
  Louisa C. 27
  Mason 133
CUTLER, Adeline 133
  Fannie 167
  Joel 219
  Mary 186

CUTLER, Wealthy A.
 (SPAULDING) 219
DABOLL, George W. 72
DAGGETT, G. O. 181
 Harriet E. 171
 Helen L. (RICHMOND) 181
DAHM, Minnie M. 194
DAHN, Anna E. 213
DAILEY, Mary A. 181
DAINS, D. G. 202
 G. G. 203, 204
 G. T. 203
 George G. 86
DALEY, Mary E. 191
DALNES, G. G. 202
DALRYMPLE, Dewey 129
 Susan (PALMITER) 129
DALTON, M. L. 206
DAMON, Christine (ROBERTS) 202
 David 202
DANFORTH, Julia A. 165
 Matilda 74
 N. Jennie (STEWART) 150
 Silas L. 150
 Susan M. 142
DANIELS, Caroline 97
 H. Maria 154
 Lyman O. 11
DARBY, C. 129
DARLING, Alpheus 21
 Lois 21
DARROW, Caroline 6
 Charles Wesley 6
 Emily (DICCINSON) 86
 Franklin 89
 Frederick 86
 George W. 6
 J. J. 80
 John J. 77
 Joseph E. 92
 Marcia V. 77
 Phebe 92
 Thankful 80
DART, J. S. (Mrs.) 75
 Mabel 205
DAVIS, --- (Rev. Mr.) 173
 Angeline E. (PARMELEE) 124
 Anna 211

DAVIS, Charlotte E. 121
 E. S. 124, 163
 Ernest 209
 Etta D. (CROWELL) 204
 Frankie 148
 Frankie (DAVIS) 148
 Gates 115
 H. H. 201
 Harriet (JONES) 115
 Isaac 14
 John Landon 33
 Judson 173, 174, 175,
  176, 177, 178, 179, 180,
  181, 182, 183, 184, 185,
  186, 187, 188, 189, 190,
  191, 192, 193, 195, 200,
  202, 203, 204, 205, 212
 Kate L. 33
 L. W. 89
 Libbie E. 186
 M. Francelia 191
 Mary 133, 176
 Mary Eliza 133
 Millard 148
 Nellie (MC CARTHY) 209
 S. D. 112
 Stanton 204
 Thomas 121
 W. S. 164
 William Henry 33
DAWLEY, Clark 125, 126
 Harriet (WOODMAN) 125, 126
DAWLNIE, Fannie (MINTIE) 182
 Wesley 182
DAWSON, T. M. 157
DAY, --- (Rev. Mr.) 125, 127
 --- (Rev.) 154
 Betty F. 155
 Betty F. (DAY) 155
 Charles P. 151
 Jerusha D. 32
 L. P. 155
 Myra A. (CLARK) 151
 Robert 124
 S. A. 133
DE FOREST, Louia M. 152
DE GROAT, A. B. 160

DE LANCEY, John M. 137
  Mary Ann (LARKIN) 137
DE LONG, Abram 21
  Clara H. 87
  Henry 20
  Jennie A. 190
DE MILLS, J. H. 103
DE WITT, Deette L. 55
  J. Albert 90
  J. V. 131
  Louisa C. (CHURCH) 131
DE WOLF, Maria 124
DEAN, Benajah 3
  Hannah 5, 14
  Henry 52
  Henry S. 52
  Kittie 147
  Lyman G. 95
  Mary J. 95
DEANE, Nora A. 180
DECKER, Marion 190
DEEBE, Darius 54
DEITZ, Irving W. 161
  Mary A. (COLLINS) 161
DELANCEY, Henry 14
  John 14
  Sarah M. 125
DELINE, Cynthia L. (EDDY) 149, 219
  Levi 149, 219
  William 21
DEMMON, Emma W. (TAYNTOR) 23
  Maria 160
DENISON, J. D. 142
  Miranda J. (ATKINS) 142
DENNEY, Hattie 212
DENNIS, Elizabeth 218
DENNISON, Abigail R. (LOVE) 132
  Frances 145
  Henry C. 207
  Italia T. (CRIM) 207
  John Delos 132
  Lavilla 89
DEPRAY, Cola 108
DERRICK, James 49, 104, 106, 109
  James A. 71, 81
  Mary E. 71

DERRICK, Nancy 49, 104
  Nancy A. 71
  W. Frankie 49
DEWEY, --- (Mr.) 167
  A. Jane 35
  Ebenezer 6, 35, 48
  Frances A. 172
  James 6
  L. 215
  Lucy 35
  Orren 6
  William Pitt 172
DEWY, Laura 116
DIABEL, Viola 158
DIBBLE, J. Orlando 131
  Jerusha 7
  Rebecca T. (AYERS) 131
  Thomas 7, 11
  Thomas W. 11
DICCINSON, Emily 86
DICK, Abbie 47
  D. 47
  Eliza 19
  Levi 49
  Mariette 33
DICKASON, Viola J. 192
DICKENSON, E. H. 208, 209
DICKERSON, Myra 82
DICKINSON, Addie F. (CARR) 153
  Charlotte (HARVEY) 135
  Justus 153
  Manco Capac 135
DICKS, Elihu 117
  Miranda (BILL) 117
DIKE, Ada A. (SHELDON) 201
  H. C. 201
  Otis A. 201
DITCH, John A. 211
  Julia (PENDOCK) 211
DIVER, David 93
  M. Rose 93
DIX, John 17
  Oliver 125
  Zephaniah 53
DIXON, --- (Mr.) 40
  Phila (FILLMORE) 40
DODD, H. G. 182
  H. M. 208
  Ida M. (SEELEY) 182

DODGE, --- (Rev. Dr.) 185
  Bert J. 207
  Cora L. (BEECHER) 207
  D. 188
  E. 211, 213
  Helen D. E. 209
  Mehitable 218
  S. M. 194, 195, 196, 197, 199
  Sarah 207
  Seward M. 194, 198
  Stephen 218
DOLAN, Mary A. 98
DONALDSON, Eli 124
  Mary E. 124
DONNELLY, J. 152, 153
DONNER, Charles E. 202
  Nellie (ALLEN) 202
DOOLITTLE, --- (Rev.) 116
  Isaac P. 14
DORMAN, Christiana (FULKERSON) 160
  Electa 13
  Sally 13
  Thomas E. 13, 51
  William R. 160
DORN, Lydia 55
DORRANCE, Louisa 90
DOTY, Betsey 115
  Hylon 138
  Louisa (LIPPITT) 138
  Moses 2
DOUBLEDAY, Eliza S. 21, 130
  J. 21
  John 130
DOUGLAS, Charles A. 207
  Daniel C. 133
  Frances A. 133
DOUGLASS, A. S. 71
  Carrie D. (WHITE) 207
  Emily M. 91
  Esther L. (HEWITT) 217
  J. S. 73
  Srthur P. 217
DOW, Dorothy 118
  Eliza 115
DOWELL, D. M. 179
  John 143
  Lena 73

DOWELL, M. Matilda (WICKWIRE) 179
  Mary A. (SAWDY) 143
DOWNE, James 212
DOWNER, Lucinda (LOOK) 126
  W. B. 145
  William H. 126
DRAKE, Alfred 54
  Charles L. 175
  Chloe (FORD) 115
  Josephine (RISLEY) 175
  Mary (HUNT) 219
  Thomas 115
  W. F. 219
DRYER, Esther 43
  John 43
DUDLEY, H. 164
  H. F. 167
DUELL, Viola M. 204
DUNAHM, M. Louise (PECKHAM) 155
DUNBAR, --- (Capt.) 26
  Anna E. 72
  Asa 116
  Calphurnia 65
  Clara A. 140
  David 39
  Frederick 168
  Georgia 65
  James H. 49
  Martha (CAMPBELL) 116
  Mary (EDBERT) 168
  Rhoda 39
DUNCANSON, J. C. 207, 209
DUNHAM, A. L. 182
  Abbie 38
  Alexander L. 147
  Alpha 38, 60
  D. Theresa 219
  David 219
  E. L. 27
  E. M. 160
  Elizabeth 116
  Esther L. (NASH) 147
  Fidelia 23
  Fred 196
  Freelove 60
  George W. 29
  Helen A. 170
  Hiram A. 155

DUNHAM, Irene 62
  Irene B. 137
  J. C. 23
  Lottie M. (NASH) 182
  Nellie (BANNING) 196
  Rufus 62, 85
  Susan E. 79
DUNIGAN, John 59
DUNN, Margaret 101
DUNTON, Cornelia J. 178
  Rosa (MCDONALD) 140
  S. S. 167
  Samuel 140
DURANT, Louisa 178
DURFEE, Alice (PETTER) 213
  Amanda 82
  Amanda P. (SIMMONS) 146
  Benjamin 83
  Burrington 83
  Cornelius L. 146
  Cornelius S. 83
  Elizabeth B. 82
  Francis M. 135
  Franklin 147
  Goodwin 81, 83
  Harriet 83
  John 83
  Judith 83
  Kittie (DEAN) 147
  Lewis 58
  Malissa 83
  Samuel 83
  Stephen 82, 83
  Willard 213
  Willis B. 83
DURKEE, Anna J. 207
DURYEA, R. 190
DUTCHER, Alonzo 145
  Caroline E. (SAMPSON) 145
  Elizabeth 57
  Irena S. 187
  Susan 136
DUTTON, Annette 164
  N. F. 164
DWINNELL, Stephen 5
DYE, Carrie E. 98
  Harrie 199
  John 199
  Mattie E. 183
  Simeon 98

EAGER, C. Edward 209
  Marion (HARVEY) 209
EARL, Amanda E. (CHAMBERS) 87
  Moses 87
EASTMAN, --- (Mr.) 67
  Albert 144
  Frances A. (DEWEY) 172
  Harriet M. (COOK) 144
  William W. 172
EATON, --- (Rev. Dr.) 132, 154, 173
  C. Olivia (WOOD) 165
  Calista M. 123
  Calvin 49
  Elizabeth B. 48
  G. W. 127, 128, 133, 135
  George W. 55, 125, 136, 138, 142, 176, 193
  H. E. 165
  Hattie 202
  J. R. 70, 176
  John H. 147
  Lewright Boardman 70
  Lucy F. 78
  M. L. 70
  Margaret 147
  Mary H. 193
  Mattie E. (LEWRIGHT) 176
  Miranda 24
  N. P. 48
  Nathan 24
  Stillman 78
  W. F. 110
  W. G. 141
  W. S. 172
  Will 107
  William T. 42
EBBERT, W. H. 105
EDBERT, Mary 168
EDDY, Adelia F. 56
  Belle 150
  Cornelia 140
  Cynthia L. 149, 219
  D. B. 180
  Ebenezer 58, 62
  H. J. 135
  Hattie (LONT) 165
  Ida 58
  J. D. 165

EDDY, L. A. 209, 210
  Polly 11
  Sarah J. 159
  Saville 58
  Warren 48
EDGAR, Eliza (STEVENS) 114
  John 114
EDGARTON, Cornelia A. 148
  J. J. 148
  John 11
  Maria 43
  William W. 43
EDGERLY, John (Mrs.) 96
EDGERTON, Angela E. 27
  C. F. 27
  Lelia A. 27
EDGREEN, Anna (CHAPMAN) 159
  John A. 159
EDMONDS, Cordelia S. 9
  J. 9
EDMUNDS, C. S. (Mrs.) 8
  J. 8
  J. O. 8
EDSON, --- (Rev. Mr.) 131, 133
  S. 128
EDWARDS, C. A. 26
  Jemima (OSBORN) 146
  Mary 193
  Oscar T. 146
EGBERT, Liza 173
EGGLESON, S. A. 193
EGGLESTON, Emily Jane 144
  Levi 144
  Sarah M. 163
EHLE, George 16
ELDRED, Carrie S. 180
  John 136
  Mary (FRINK) 136
  Mary J. 169
ELDREDGE, Caroline 132
  Ede Maria (RANDALL) 56
  Eliza 9
  Emily E. 119
  G. S. 145
  James B. 2, 9, 116, 120, 132
  James E. 4
  Maria (MOSELY) 145

ELDREDGE, Nancy 2
  Sally 4
  Sarah (CARPENTER) 116
  Woodworth 56
ELDRIDGE, Alice E. (SNELL) 195
  J. Harvey 88
  William B. 195
ELLENWOOD, Mary J. (WILCOX) 68
  T. J. 68
ELLINGWOOD, Mary J. (WILCOX) 171
  Truman J. 171
ELLIOT, --- (Rev.) 141
ELLIOTT, D. T. 141, 142, 148
  Frank C. 197
  Lizzie (STOWE) 197
ELLIS, Charles W. 201
  Daniel 115
  Diana 162
  Elnathan 162
  Esther 137
  Louisa J. 217
  Nettie (WADSWORTH) 201
  Palmer 137
  Sally (COY) 115
  William 104
ELMER, Abram S. 175
  Anet R. (ORVIS) 175
  Sarah 23, 53
ELMORE, Jennie 93
  Madison 93
  Mary 132
ELPHIC, Frankie (JOHNSON) 179
  Wallace 179
ELPHICK, Addie R. 180
ELSBRE, Lavina 141
ELWELL, Jane Jenette 166
  Nellie 209
  W. D. 193
EMERY, G. F. 220
  Lizzie F. 220
  Merebah (WOODMAN) 151
  Samuel C. 151
EMMS, Walter 66
ENOS, Allen 78
  Allen E. 170

ENOS, Allen N. 206
  Benjamin 17
  Cordelia 118
  D. C. 71
  David 79
  Elsie Jane 13
  Emilus J. 13
  Eneas E. 103
  Hettie 78
  Lucy Ann 13
  Mabbett J. 108
  Mary E. 78
  Mary E. (THOMPSON) 170
  Polly 79
  Rose D. (THOMPSON) 206
  Samuel Dotty 17
ENQUEST, Mary Newell 213
ENSON, Minnie 67
ERSKINE, Rosaleia 190
ERWIN, --- (Rev. Mr.) 205
ESSLESTYN, Harriet 81
ETSON, Emmet O. 80
  Susan L. 56
EVANS, Albert W. 183
  Charles B. 11
  Diana 162
  Edward J. 59
  Ella A. (RICE) 183
  Ellen 207
  John J. 11
  Margaret 35
  William 34
  Winnie 205
EVARTS, Lyman 65
EVERETS, Martha 20
EVERETT, Betsey Ann 117
EVERTS, Frank L. 187
  Hattie M. 36
  N. R. 190
  Rosa C. (KEIM) 187
  W. W. 121
FAGAN, Albert 187
  Elbert 110
  Ettie S. 192
  Libbie D. (BIDWELL) 187
FAIRBANKS, Alice (WOOD) 212
  Eugene 212
FAIRCHILD, Anna (MAFFET) 121

FAIRCHILD, Carrie H. (HARRIS) 158
  Daniel 96
  Della (SMITH) 199
  Eva E. 161
  Janette 26
  LeRoy 199
  Lena 156
  N. J. 158
  Nelson 26
  William 56, 121, 161
FAIRCHILDS, Sidney D. 36
FANCHER, Winnie 207
FARGHER, Sophia (JACKSON) 149, 219
  Thomas 149, 219
FARGO, --- (Rev. Mr.) 152
  A. G. 163, 192
  A. P. 164
  F. A. 109
FARGOF, A. 110
FARLEY, E. J. 110
FARNAM, Sarah L. 210
  Stephen H. 210
FARNIUM, Hannah D. 182
FARR, Betsey 117
FARRER, Emily 212
FARRINGTON, C. 202
FAULKNER, Edward 165
  Sarah E. (CARPENTER) 165
FAY, Almira A. 20
  Clinton E. 20
  Clinton S. 20
  Franklin L. 128
  Hannah (BLACKWOOD) 126, 128
  James L. 41
  James R. 26
  Marila 26
  Mary E. (SEARS) 144, 155
  Orson C. 144
  Orson D. 155
FAYE, James L. 31
  Maria O. 31
  Willie Pearl 31
FELLOWS, Albert 208
  Arminda (JOHNSON) 115
  Henrietta (HAYWARD) 208
  Leonard 115

FELT, Blanche L. (HART) 204
 Carrie 189
 Cynthia A. 21
 E. 80
 Elias 144
 Ella L. 102, 176
 Florence 195
 Francella 164
 Harry 33
 Hattie (HALL) 168
 Jay M. 168
 Jay Morgan 80
 Louisa L. 156
 Phebe A. (PHELPS) 151
 Rosa 80
 Viola 185
 Walter W. 204
 Warren 21, 52
 William 38, 151
FENTON, Amariah 123, 132
 Eleanora G. 132
 Elizabeth Thompson 123
 Maggie 206
 Mary A. 103
 Milo B. 103
FERGUSON, Allen 166
 Jenett 166
 M. A. (Miss) 24
 R. G. W. 24
FERREL, Emma V. 158
FERRIS, --- (Rev.) 116
 Elizabeth 50
 I. B. 50
FERRY, Richard 91
FIELD, --- 58
 --- (Rev.) 118
 Anna J. 81
 E. B. 81
 Joshua 70
 Laura 81
 Lida 89
 P. 118, 176
 P. E. 156
 Pindar 118
FIELDS, Alvira S. 127
 Mary 89
 Pinder 134
FILLMORE, --- (Mr.) 40
 Phila 40

FINCH, Frances M. (CASE) 126
 Hannah 41
 Joshua 41
 Llias 126
 Sarah A. 138
FINNEY, Myra 180
 Sylvester 35
FIRMAN, Betsy (BARNES) 139
 W. H. 139
FIRTH, Adelaide S. (POST) 72
 George W. 72
FISH, Avery 149
 Lois J. (TAYLOR) 149
FISHER, Abigail 141
 Anna E. 170
 Clarissa 54
 Denos 76
 Esther 76
 Hattie 48
 John 54
 Johnny 70
 Lucina 140
 Mary 48
 Nathan 60
 Rhodie 142
 Sarah D. 195
 T. 210
 Thomas 94
 W. B. (Mrs.) 73
 William 48
FISK, --- (Rev. Dr.) 172
 Babcy R. 63
 Carrie 31
 Ephraim 63
 John 31, 36
 Nettie A. 31
 Olive 175
 S. M. 186, 187
FISKE, Eliza (OLCOTT) 114
 William E. 114
FITCH, Benjamin H. 53
 Catherine 62
 Eliza 1
 Helen Cornelia 17
 James H. 62
 Lucy A. 122
 Sarah 62
 Sarah B. 17

FITCH, Sheldon 17
  Stephen 1
FITCHER, J. J. (Mrs.) 94
FITZ RANDOLPH, Laura 192
FITZGERALD, Michael 90
FITZPATRICK, --- (Mr.) 108
  --- (Mrs.) 108
FLAHERTY, Barbary 37
  Michael 98
FLEMING, Altie (GREENE)
    203
  Ceriza W. (PALMER) 130
  Cora E. 178
  Edwin 110, 203
  Ira H. 130
  Richard 97
  Thomas 104
FLETCHER, Amelia A. 125,
    127
  E. T. 198
  George 139
  Ida 90
  Ida M. (USHER) 177
  John F. 177
  L. 122, 123, 124, 125
  Laura T. (WILBUR) 198
  Leonard 125, 127
  Louise (BAKER) 139
  Miranda 122
FLINT, Albert F. 203
  Lizzie (BRADY) 203
  R. 206, 208, 209
FOGUS, Carrie 180
FOLAND, Mary E. 186
FOLLETT, Judson L. 162
  Mertia 144
  Otis 144
  Viola (WICKWIRE) 162
FOLTS, Catherine 169
FOOT, --- (Miss) 114
  John 118
FOOTE, Adeline 29
  Almeda A. 134
  Almira H. 127
  Amasa 48
  Asa 127, 134
  Betsey 129
  Caroline D. 124
  Celett T. (HARVEY) 148
  David Y. 39

FOOTE, E. W. 29
  Esther Jane 20
  Frederick W. 20
  Genny (BAKER) 170
  George F. 170
  George N. 148
  Helen (GARVIN) 163
  Isaac 4, 48
  J. Crocker 163
  John 4, 86, 124
  John J. 121, 147
  Lyra 211
  Mary (CROCKER) 121
  Mary K. 4, 134
  Noah 124
  Noah B. 9, 12, 39, 129
  Sarah (KELLOGG) 48
  Sarah K. 74
  Sophia 9
FORBES, --- (Miss) 48
  --- (Mrs.) 48
  Andrew J. 48
FORCE, Jonathan 132
  Louisa (WAY) 132
FORD, Alfred H. 119
  Chloe 115
  Elizabeth (RICH) 119
  Isaac S. 151
  J. W. 105, 108, 111
  James W. 188
  Joseph 116
  Katie E. (JONES) 188
  Olive (LINSEY) 116
  S. T. 107, 196
FORT, Avery 104
  Charity E. 219
FORWARD, DeWitt D. 211
  Elizabeth W. 42
  Eugene 42
  Grace A. (HARVEY) 211
  Joseph 42
FOSTER, Adella 165
  D. N. 192
  Elias 47
  George 152
  H. J. 179
  Harleigh I. 71
  Harleigh J. 134
  Hattie M. 174
  Helen 47

FOSTER, John N. 89
 Joseph 49
 L. B. 57, 165, 174
 Lois E. 194
 Mary A. (COREY) 134
 Mary A. (WINCHESTER) 179
 Sarah 203
 Sarah (PYNE) 192
 William 28
FOTTE, Mary Annette 147
FOWLER, Ann 114
 F. S. 205
 Frank W. 66
 Harriet W. (WHITE) 143
 Lulu (ROOT) 205
 Lyman 143
 Nelson 95
FOX, C. P. P. 200
 Carrie 184
 Carrie (WALDRON) 30
 Celesta A. 146
 Charles P. 189
 Coralinn E. 30
 Ehle 210
 Frederick 118
 H. 181
 Hannah (ORMSBY) 118
 Luca A. (PADDOCK) 210
 Margaret 127
 Minette 30
 Nellie P. (SPENCER) 189
 Wesley 126
 Wilson 30
FRANCIS, Eliza (OTIS) 136
 J. D. 136
FRANKLIN, Joseph 193
 Mary 97, 193
FREAR, James H. 90
FREEBURN, Emily I. 136
FREEMAN, James W. 74
 Phoebe 64
FRENCH, Henry J. 51
 J. W. 50
 John O. 96
 Nancy R. 96
 Phebe 91
FREVUA, Frederick 1
FRINK, Asah 17
 Emeline 183
 Fannie 53

FRINK, Fanny 17
 Mary 136
FRISBIE, Elijah 98
 Eliza 34
 H. T. 37
 Louise 37
 Lyman 34
 Mary L. 37
 Rosie May 34
FROTHINGHAM, Arthur 192
 Laura (FITZ RANDOLPH) 192
FRY, Asa 55
 Charles E. 168
 Hattie 42
 Maggie (MC DONALD) 168
 Rebecca 55
FRYER, Clara M. 141
FRYOVER, Addie 176
 Catherine 57
FUESS, Lizzie (JENKINS) 213
 Louis 213
FULFORD, Elizabeth (WADDELL) 140
 Lucien 140
FULKERSON, Christiana 160
 Rebecca (RANSOM) 162
 Sarah J. 193
 William 162
FULLER, Arthur L. 86
 Celinda 38
 Deborah S. 143
 Fannie 192
 Fannie W. (HAYDEN) 204
 Gertie (PUTNAM) 196
 Granger E. 204
 Harriet 61
 Harriet (ACKLEY) 112
 Helen 140
 Herbert E. 196
 J. H. 181
 Josiah E. 153
 Lambert 38
 Loomis 61, 112
 Louisa (YEOMAN) 119
 Martha 86
 Mary A. (SAUNDERS) 153
 Nuell 119
 Sophia 192
FULLERSON, Frank W. 192

FULLERSON, Viola J.
  (DICKASON) 192
FURNISS, Dorothy (DOW) 118
  H. B. 118
GAGE, Allen L. (Mrs.) 47
  Arza 135
  Clinton 116
  L. Caroline 135
  Lucy A. 163
  Rosannah (COWDEN) 116
  Vine W. 47
GAGER, Clarissa (HUNT) 112
  Marvin 112
GALE, Almeda A. 134
  Charles 150
  Emma S. (LAY) 150
GALLAGHER, Elizabeth 76
GALLOP, Everett E. 82
  Youngs A. 82
GALLOWAY, W. T. 201
GALLUP, --- (Prof.) 144
  E. S. 140, 164, 168
GALPIN, Clinton S. 157
  Martha A. (YOUNG) 157
GANSEVOORT, --- (Col.) 215
GARDINER, Calista R.
  (HEAD) 189
  Hopey 16
  Hull S. 189
  Isaac W. 7
  Thomas 45
GARDNER, A. B. 164
  Adelia A. (CARPENTER) 164
  Benjamin 120
  D. S. 106
  E. S. 107
  H. A. 121
  H. S. 105
  Isaac 9
  Libbie C. (WHEELER) 151
  Lucinda 208
  Minerva A. (CALKINS) 121
  Miranda C. 149
  Nelson 149
  William 119
  William C. 151
GARNER, Taylor 75
GARRATT, Mary (DAVIS) 133
  Mary Eliza (DAVIS) 133
  William B. 133

GARRETT, Calphurnia 140
GARRISON, Carrie A.
  (BRATIHWAITE) 198
  Ira M. 198
GARTSOUGH, L. 140
GARVER, Mary L. 137
GARVIN, Helen 163
  Samuel B. 163
GASKILL, Edward B. 167
  Elizabeth R. (O'BANNON)
    167
GASTON, A. H. 138
GATES, Allison 205
  Carrie 81
  Carrie C. (SEELEY) 205
  Cynthia L. 17
  Eli 17
  Emma L. (THURSTON) 75
  Ezra 39
  Hiram D. 159
  Lida H. 205
  Lydia G. (ROGERS) 159
  Mary 17
  Mary A. 137
  Minerva 119
  Polly (CAMPBELL) 39
  Silas N. 33
  Solomon 81
GAUT, William 99
GAVIN, John 84
GAYLORD, Frederick S. 169
  Harriet E. (UPHAM) 169
GEE, Hiram 170
GEER, A. L. 180
  Allie J. (HUNT) 180
  Amos 32
  Amos T. 120, 121
  Asa B. 32
  Betsey 32
  Eunice H. 62
  Nettie E. 161
  R. H. (Mrs.) 104
  Sabrina Amelia (PARKER)
    120, 121
  William R. 62
GENUNG, G. F. 188
GEORGIA, Annie L. 192
GEWYE, Pamela 170
GIBBS, Benjamin F. 131

265

GIBSON, Ellen L. (SMITH) 141
Robert T. 141
GIFFORD, --- (Elder) 131
Anna (WILLIAMS) 75
Asa 113
Cainan 4
J. O. 170, 182, 183, 184
James O. 172
Louisa 91
Lucy (ALBERT) 113
GILBERT, Agur 121
Betsey 121
Charles 142
Elizabeth 120
Emeline 44
Hannah 116
Helen 160
Jenette (BRIGGS) 142
John 116
Katie J. 208
Lucy 58
Mary E. 208
O. B. 148
Robert 44
Salina E. 47
Sarah F. 50
Susan (BROWN) 116
Vine B. 116
GILLESPIE, Hugh 141
Lovina (TEMPLE) 141
GILLETTE, Morgan 121
GILMAN, Augusta 115
Julia A. (DANFORTH) 165
Sylvester 165
GILMORE, Aruna 22
George H. 84
Mary 117
Samuel 117
GIPSON, --- (Mr. & Mrs.) 202
GLADDING, Frances E. 142
GLANVILLE, John 125
Sarah A. (WILBER) 125
GLAZIER, George 197
Ida (MANN) 197
GLEASON, Clarissa K. (BOYCE) 13
James H. 13
John 6

GLEASON, Mary 34
GLIDDEN, Margaret H. (MANUEL) 126
P. N. 126
GLOVER, D. L. 135
L. Caroline (GAGE) 135
GODFREY, Charles 171
Emma (LAMB) 171
Frank 209
Kate (MURPHY) 209
GOLDEN, L. 207
GOODALE, Melinda 113
Samuel 154
GOODELL, Bell F. 63
Lydia 113
William L. 63
GOODENOUGH, --- (Prof.) 44
Mary Pauline 44
GOODING, Adeline 144
GOODRICH, A. B. 210, 213
Adelbert 108
GOODSELL, Vincent 40
GOODWIN, --- (Rev.) 114
Augustus H. 184
M. Nellie (BEEBE) 184
GORHAM, Alonzo 102
Alonzo D. 102
Matilda L. 157
GORMAN, Charles Downing 31
S. 31
GORTON, Benjamin 134
Catherine (YORK) 134
Emily J. 63
Hattie 209
Helen M. (BURDICK) 150
James L. 95
O. M. 150
Sophronia F. 95
Thomas R. 92, 178
GOSLEY, Delia (KELLY) 188
Henry 188
GOSS, Elizabeth Mills 135
James 135
GOULD, J. L. 184
Sophia J. (BLAIR) 184
GOULDING, --- (Mrs.) 72
Sarah W. 72
GOVE, Betsey (TERRY) 115
James 37, 115
GOWDY, Eugene 90

GOWDY, Laura Zoe 90
  Sarah 90
GRAHAM, --- (Mr.) 56
GRAIN, C. S. 165
GRANGER, Elizabeth L. 155
  Harriet 82
  Otis P. 155
GRANNIS, --- (Rev. Mr.) 163
  Harriet (GREEN) 160
  W. H. D. 160
  W. H. DeLancey 160
  William 158
GRAVES, Almira H. 122
  Lewis 68
GRAY, Alice 200
  Celia 169, 220
  Chauncey 116
  Cooley C. 79
  David 6
  Ebenezer 19
  Harriet A. (BARNETT) 142
  Hiram 6
  J. M. 142
  Lucy 114
  Melinda (SKINNER) 116
  S. P. 169, 220
GREEN, Addie 196
  Amelia (SANDERSON) 149
  Amellia 54
  Annie D. (REESE) 195
  Annie E. 189
  Charles 172
  Dora 197
  Elbro L. 54
  Enos 26
  Eva E. 208
  Evanna 137
  Floyd 26
  Geneva 172
  H. H. 131
  Hannah 46
  Harriet 160
  Horace 160
  Jeremiah 46, 56
  John 195
  John D. 18
  Jonathan 70
  Julia A. S. 135
  Lauriston B. 171
  GREEN, Lillie (HOOPER) 190
  Mahrion 129
  Margaret 113
  Mary 19
  Nancy 26
  Sabrina (MILLER) 131
  Sally 34
  Sarah G. 175
  Stafford 131
  Thomas 74, 149
  Viola 160
  William 196
GREEN(E), Carlton D. 168
  Flora M. 168
GREENE, Altie 203
  Chloe 68
  E. H. 68
  Jonathan 70
  Mamie E. 203
  Robert 1
  S. H. 188
  Wilmer F. 51
GREENLEY, Augusta S. (WAIT) 183
  Fred 183
  Lucy 56
  T. H. 56
  T. H. (Mrs.) 27
GREENLY, --- (Dr.) 7
  Elizabeth (HIGGINS) 120
  Frederick T. 120
  T. H. 154
  Thirza 1
  Thomas 1
GREENMAN, Emma 148
GREENWOOD, Altie M. 91
GREER, --- (Rev. Dr.) 160
  Osmond W. 64
GREGGS, John 65
GREGORY, Eli 119
  Thankful (REYNOLDS) 119
GREY, Abbie D. 159
  Lucy 159
GRIDLEY, Philo 117
  Susan (WILLIAMS) 117
GRIFFIN, Ann E. (CARPENTER) 153
  Charles B. 153
  Hannah 90
  Lucy A. (GAGE) 163

GRIFFIN, Otis 90
  Richard 77
  Sarah 77
  Sophronia 77
  Virmilye 163
GRIFFIS, Ellen (EVANS) 207
  John A. 207
GRIFFITH, David P. 90
GRIGGS, Caroline E. 128
  Florence D. 181
  Frances L. 138
  Ichabod 128
  Mary C. (WALKER) 18
  Mary L. (GARVER) 137
  Orlando 137
GRIMSHAW, Amy Y. 35
  John 22
GRISWOLD, --- (Mrs. Dr.) 48
GROSE, Silas E. 38
GROSH, A. B. 122
GROSS, Polly 50
  R. T. 183
GROSVENOR, Evaleen M. 162
  George G. 178
  Olive M. 187
  Sarah (MACKIN) 178
GROVE, Caroline L. (PRATT) 133
  DeWitt C. 133
  Dwight C. 85
GROVES, Henry H. 159
  Sarah A. (HYDE) 159
  Serepta 58
GROW, Charles Milas 147
  Lucinda E. (HILL) 147
GUERNSEY, J. 135
  Pheba Jane 135
GUION, Alvah 138
GULFORD, Martha A. 82
GUSTIN, --- (Mr.) 119
  B. N. 20
  Emiline M. 20
  Hiram E. 138
  Laura Jane (JACKSON) 139
  Luman 139
  Maria (LYON) 138
GUTHRIE, Albertus J. 149
  DeEste E. (CARD) 149
  Frances Jane 128

GUTHRIE, Mary A. 151
HADCOCK, Mary J. 150
HADCOCKS, Daniel 215
HADDEN, Emily 220
  Lyman 220
HADNETT, Jane S. 148
HAGGERT, Catherine 137
HAHN, Charles F. 198
  Hattie A. (HOWE) 198
HAIGHT, Clarissa T. 144
  Marian E. (LIVERMORE) 164
  W. H. 164
HALBERT, Polly 90
HALE, Catherine 104
  George 104
HALEY, Richard 110
HALL, Albert G. 22
  Alfred 133
  Anson B. 82
  C. S. 49
  Chauncey S. 33
  Clarissa T. (HAIGHT) 144
  Clarkson A. 83
  Earl 82
  Electa (ROBBINS) 133
  Ellen 49
  Emma G. 197
  Finetta 33
  George 20
  George K. 199
  Georgie 199
  Harriet L. 148
  Hattie 168
  Helen (GILBERT) 160
  Helen M. 89
  James E. C. 83
  Janette (SIMMONS) 199
  Jeremand D. 82
  John W. 17
  Lena M. 49
  Lucius S. 82
  Mary D. 82
  Murray 144
  Nancy E. 124
  O. S. 89
  Orville 160
  Reuben S. 33
  S. S. 148
  Samuel G. 82
  Solomon 158

HALL, Susan C. 158
  Timothy 82
  William 17, 83
HALLOCK, Harriet 114
HALLSTEAD, --- (Rev. Mr.)
  174
HALSEY, Carrie (FOGUS) 180
  Theodore 180
HALSTEAD, Elmer E. 196
  Etta C. (HOWE) 196
  T. P. 152, 153, 156
  T. T. 219
HALSTED, T. P. 150, 156
HAMBLET, Phineas 24
HAMILTON, Abbie 150
  C. E. 213
  Charles 12, 68
  Eliza 68
  Roxanna 50
HAMLIN, George (Mrs.) 95
  Julia M. 152
HAMMOND, --- (Rev.) 168
  Alfarettie Alzina 31
  Amos 31, 93, 94
  Andrew N. 31
  Betsey 137
  Ella May 43
  H. L. 128
  Humphrey 153
  J. W. 205
  Jane 43, 131
  Jane (MEAD) 128
  L. M. (Mrs.) 94
  Lovian 36
  Luna 31
  Luna (CHASE) 93
  Nathan 94
  Orrin 43
  Sarah E. (BRIGGS) 153
  Solomon 36
  W. A. 93
HAMON, Mary P. 176
HAND, Eliza (HURLEY) 183
  Peter 110, 183
  T. F. 210
HANDY, Polly 157
  W. R. 157
HANLEY, Jennie 139
  Thomas (Mrs.) 104

HANMON, Melinda (GOODALE)
  113
  Stephen 113
HANNA, --- (Mrs.) 195
  Nellie E. 165
  William 165, 195
HANNET, --- (Rev. Father)
  201
HANNETT, --- (Rev. Father)
  200, 206, 211
HANSEN, Honora 196
HANSHAW, E. F. 72
HANSON, Hortense H. 72
  Mandane (LARKIN) 181
  Samuel P. 71
  Smith M. 181
HARDACRE, --- (Mrs.) 195
HARDER, James 136
  Maria (HOLBROOK) 136
HARDEY, --- (Rev. Mr.) 185
HARDIN, D. 123
HARDY, G. M. 202
  George L. 187
  Jane A. 95
HARKNESS, --- (Mrs.) 112
  --- (Prof.) 112
  A. G. 205
  Katherine Margaret
    (BEEBEE) 205
HARMON, John 106, 187
  Olive M. (GROSVENOR) 187
  R. Howard 50
  Ransom H. 20
HARP, Alzina 143
  Lucy (SKELLENGER) 166
  Nicholas 166
HARPER, --- (Rev. Dr.) 69
HARRIMAN, Nettie A. 170
HARRINGTON, --- (Rev. Mr.)
  134
  Allie H. 219
  Leunetta 77
  M. 139
HARRIS, Carrie H. 158
  Daniel 1
  Electa 114
  George W. 160
  Henry H. 181
  Irvin I. 174
  Millie R. (BERKIN) 174

HARRIS, N. 109
  Nellie G. (BRIGGS) 181
  Norman 85
  Olive C. (BEEBE) 163
  Sarah M. 131
  Spencer 163
  Viola (GREEN) 160
HARRISON, Harriet L. 100
HARS, William P. 43
HART, Almeda (HOUSE) 170
  Blanche L. 204
  Elias K. 26
  Elizabeth L. (COLLINS) 148
  Emily C. 26
  Hubbard 148
  Jay 95
  John 95
  Minnie 167
  Solomon 220
  W. M. 170
HARTSHORN, --- (Elder) 154
  A. Minerva 56
  Arthur A. 212
  Asa 35
  C. D. (Mrs.) 88
  Charlotte 58
  Cordelia Ann 123
  Emalissa 15
  H. P. 59, 194
  Hannah 198
  Herbert 54
  Horace P. 56
  Jacob 123
  Laura J. 133
  Libbie E. 161
  Lydia B. (UTTER) 212
  Lynn Julian 70
  Mariar/Marian 30
  Mary C. 194
  Oliver 15
  Orvilla 70
  William B. 70
  William M. 70, 172
HARTSOUGH, L. 146
HARTWELL, --- (Rev.) 124
  J. 130
  Joseph 124

HARVEY, --- (Rev. Dr.)
  168, 175, 177, 181, 188, 189, 194
  --- (Rev. Mr.) 178
  Aurel (LYMAN) 116
  C. H. 129, 130
  Celett T. 148
  Charlotte 135
  Grace A. 211
  H. 174, 175, 179, 197, 211
  Marion 209
  Martha A. 177
  Nathan 116
  Rosetta 149
  Seymour 209
HARWOOD, Inez S. (BILLINGS) 167
  William H. 167
HASCALL, --- (Prof.) 115
  --- (Rev.) 115
  Daniel 114, 115, 117, 118, 119
  Delia (WALDO) 180
  J. R. 158
  James S. 180
  Ralph 2
HASH, Emogene C. (SAWDEY) 152
  James R. 152
HASKINS, J. R. 160
HASTINGS, Thomas S. 163
HASWELL, Eddie 96
HATCH, Anna 211
  Cassadan M. 155
  Charles M. 152
  Denison 133
  E. T. 18
  Elsie A. 211
  Erastus T. 124
  Frank F. 211
  Harriet (BICKNELL) 215
  John P. 44
  Julius W. 215
  Laura 114
  Lorinda S. 150
  Louia M. (DE FOREST) 152
  Lucy Ann (ALLEN) 133
  Lydia Lurancy 11
  Mary 11, 115

HATCH, Roxanna (CAMP) 124
 Stephen 11
HATHAWAY, Charles E. 211
 Cynthia M. (MOWERS) 211
HAUGHTON, Amelia B.
  (TAINTOR) 150
 Augustus 15
 Charles B. 150
 Jay Leroy 15
 Lucetta 134
 Maribee C. 15
 William 14
HAVENS, Catharine A. 130
 Clarinda J. (WELTON) 130
 Esther C. 113
 George F. 130
 Hannah 114
 Hiram 113
 Joseph 130
 Lyra (FOOTE) 211
 Marchia D. S. 120
 Marcia D. S. 121
 P. B. 121, 211
HAWES, Julia 216
HAWKS, Hiram 69
 Horace 25
 Zadoc 25
HAWLEY, C. M. 124
 Cornelia M. (CROCKER) 124
 Frank (PERKINS) 190
 Robert 190
HAY, Arthur 209
 Helen D. E. (DODGE) 209
 Mertia 144
HAYDEN, Fannie W. 204
HAYES, Bridget 104
 Charles Wells 142
 Frances E. (GLADDING) 142
HAYNES, Florence (FELT)
  195
 Hirtam 7
 Jerusha (DIBBLE) 7
 Myron W. 195
HAYS, Anna (LEONARD) 122
 Jacob S. 155
 Newton 122
 Sarah J. (SHAW) 155
HAYWARD, Allen 37
 Benjamin B. 28
 Chloe A. 30

HAYWARD, H. S. 30
 Harriet A. 213
 Henrietta 208
 J. 74
 Josephine L. 190
 M. Jenette 196
 Philura 37
 Samuel 2
HAYWOOD, C. R. 86
 Huldah 86
 J. 86
HAZSEN, H. A. 198
HEAD, Addison W. 195
 Alida S. (BENEDICT) 195
 Anna 74, 211
 Benjamin F. 206
 Calista R. 189
 Eveline 150
 Harriet S. 24
 J. A. 189
 Jerusha 174
 Julie E. 164
 Malvina W. (SMITH) 206
 Sanford 74
HEALY, Eliza Ann (SLOCUM)
  131
 William 131
HEATH, --- (Rev.) 114
HEBBARD, C. M. 213
 Sarah A. (SAWYER) 213
HECOX, Jacob 162
 Louisa 162
HEFFRON, Ann (CURTISS) 154
 John 154
HEMINGWAY, Eliza (DOW) 115
 Newell 115
HENDEE, Fred. O. 210
 Zella E. (WALL) 210
HENDERSON, Ada 93
 Andrew J. 152
 Carrie Jane 33
 Elizabeth M. (SMITH) 152
 Emma Belle 56
HENRY, Annie L. (SWIFT)
  179
 Eugenia 33
 H. M. 177
 Joie 182
 Mary E. 190
 Mattie E. 62

HENRY, Myron 33
　Myrtie I. 33
　R. L. 97
　Robert 116
　W. T. 209
　William D. 179
HENSHAW, Margareta H. 139
HERKIMER, --- (Gen.) 215
HERRICK, --- (Mrs.) 161
　Aldebert E. 192
　Elisha 1
　Josephine A. (STREETER) 192
HERRINGTON, Helen 212
HESS, Bradford 158
　Kate (JOHNSON) 158
　Sophia 178
HEWES, C. E. 143, 157, 159
　Florence A. 159
　James T. 37
　John H. 50
　Mary C. (PALMER) 171
　S. Brownie 171
　Sarah 161
HEWITT, Ella C. (TOMLINSON) 191
　Esther L. 217
　James H. 191
HEWS, Mary G. 6
　Moses 6
　Susan Ann 121
HIBBARD, Adella F. (SPENCER) 174
　Augusta L. (JOY) 135
　Chauncey R. 97
　Dan 135
　Francis H. 135
　Hattie E. 188
　R. Y. 174
HICKOCK, Henry 218
HICKS, Benjamin F. 91
　Sarah E. 91
HICOK, H. B. 106
HICTHCOCK, George E. 200
HIGGINS, --- (Mr.) 27
　Elizabeth 120
　Francis D. 154
　Justin 3
HILDRETH, Mary (HUBBELL) 154

HILDRETH, Truman 154
HILL, Amanda J. (ODELL) 174
　D. P. 91
　Daniel P. 8, 9
　Emma P. (LAY) 164
　Esther 91, 92
　H. 163
　H. H. 105, 106
　Hannah 55
　Harriet 10
　Heman 133
　Henry G. 8, 9
　Henry H. 164
　Ira R. 161
　John 174
　Lucinda E. 147
　Maria (HINKLY) 133
　Maria H. (HITCHCOCK) 161
　Mary (WILCOX) 157
　Mattie A. 167
　Samuel 10
　Sarah M. 8, 9, 91
　Smith 157
HILLS, Alfred C. 138
　Amasa 89
　Elsie S. (WOODMAN) 189
　H. I. 112, 189
　H. L. 112
　Lucy M. 145
　Ray Randall 103
　Sarah A. (MERRITT) 138
HINDS, H. M. 103
　Libbie E. (DAVIS) 186
　Maude 103
　T. C. 186
HINKLY, Maria 133
HISCOX, E. T. 172
HITCHCOCK, Ann (SMITHERS) 200
　Antrace 14
　Cordelia P. 14
　Eben 99
　Fallie C. 200
　Hannah W. 131
　Hiram 200
　Isaac 14
　J. C. 163
　Libbie L. (BOYD) 200
　Maria H. 161

HITCHCOCK, Phoebe T. 184
  Ruth 102
  Samuel 22, 54
  Seth 102
  Simon C. 22
HITCHMAN, J. 176
HOADLY, Elizabeth (DUNHAM) 116
  Leonard 116
HOAG, --- (Rev. Mr.) 134
  D. G. 219
  E. A. 184
HOBBS, B. 31
  Lora C. 147
  T. 31
  Thomas 49
  Willie H. 31
HOGAN, Ann Margaret (MASTERS) 126, 127
  Ella 201
  John 126, 127
HOGLE, Alice A. (HOLCOMB) 207
  John N. 207
HOLBROOK, Maria 136
  Rufus 77
HOLCOMB, Alice A. 207
  Almond 132
  Chester 29, 123
  E. H. (Mrs.) 132
  J. 106
  Lucy (TOMPKINS) 29, 123
HOLDREDGE, Helen F. 172
  John M. 50
  Wealthy 50
HOLDRIDE, J. H. 189
  M. (Mrs.) 189
HOLLAND, Edward (Mrs.) 102
  Elizabeth 61
HOLLENBECK, Casper 96
  Harriet 96
HOLLINGSWORTH, Elizabeth A. 137
  John 25
HOLLISTER, Harriet (HALLOCK) 114
  Henry 114
HOLMAN, Barbara M. (CLARK) 146
  George W. 146

HOLMAN, Mary 186
HOLMES, --- (Rev.) 123, 142
  Albert J. 32
  Alonzo 88
  Althea M. (MEAD) 151
  Amasa J. 205
  Ann 83
  Annette (DUTTON) 164
  Betsy 218
  Daniel 218
  Fannie C. 33
  Fannie L. 194
  Frances 58
  Grace 180
  Hattie E. 153
  Ira 165
  J. 153
  Jabez 32
  Jane E. 165
  John N. 151
  Lisle 33
  Nancy M. 158
  Sophronia (BLOWERS) 205
  Wilbur 164
  Willie R. 33
HOLROYD, E. 198
HOLT, Adell R. (PIERCE) 177
  Charles E. 205
  Curtis 26
  Ellen 205
  Eugenia S. 183
  May (ANDERSON) 205
  William E. 177
HOLZMAN, Mary 186
HOOKER, Betsy 16
  John T. 16
HOOPER, Lillie 190
HOPKINS, --- (Mrs.) 98, 100
  --- (Rev. Mr.) 117
  A. A. 164
  Adell R. (ALLEN) 164
  Alvah 40
  Anthony 74
  Bartley 107
  Bridget 57
  Bridget (LYON) 172
  Edward 100

HOPKINS, Edwin L. 76
 Ella 100
 Emerilla 72
 F. V. 69
 Gerry L. 69
 H. L. 69
 Harlow 129
 Hattie 212
 Isaac C. 151
 Isaac G. 77
 James 57, 172
 Jane Agnes 216
 Jay D. 98
 Josephine B. 98
 L. 179
 Lavina A. 179
 Lucinda F. (BEDELL) 151
 M. D. 183
 Margaret Louisa 57
 Mary A. 40
 Miranda (FLETCHER) 122
 Palmer 122
 Sarah Jane (TACKABERRY) 129
 Susan J. (BLAIR) 183
 T. R. 216
 W. H. 190
 William J. 3
HOPPIN, Curtis 45
 F. B. 34
 Sophia M. 49
HOPSEGER, Theresa 155
HORSTKOTTER, Anna 67
 Catherine 67
 Edward 67
HORTON, James 104
HOSEA, Lucy (KLINCK) 189
 Robert 189
HOSKOTTER, --- (Mr.) 110
HOSTLER, Alice M. 98
HOTCHKIN, Emeline J. (WARNER) 171
 Heman 171
 Henry F. 18
 Herman 46
 Mary 46
HOTCHKISS, Cyrus 9
 Sophronia 9
HOUGHTON, Augustus 35
 Caroline E. 27

HOUGHTON, Frank W. 27
 John 27
 John W. 158
 Samantha L. (ADAMS) 158
HOUSE, Almeda 170
HOUSTON, Carrie 188
HOVEY, Frank 93
 W. H. 165
HOWARD, --- (Rev. Mr.) 127
 --- (Rev.) 119
 Adin 25
 Almina (CARTER) 219
 Almira (CARTER) 150
 Ansel 150
 Emily 212
 Hannah 56
 Harriet 148
 Jackson L. 151
 James 54
 John M. 35
 L. 125, 126
 Lida O. 201
 M. A. 79
 Martha J. 152
 Mary 21
 Mary E. (RAMSDELL) 151
 Matilda 138
 Orris 212
 Preston C. 150, 219
 Sarah E. (RICHARDS) 150
 Sylvia E. 130
 V. R. 79
 Vinson R. 201
HOWE, Anna (LAWRENCE) 202
 C. H. 180
 Charles 202
 Etta C. 196
 H. C. 196
 Harry 44
 Hattie A. 198
 Jennie E. (RICHARDSON) 180
 Leonard 58
 Mary 44
 Otis B. 73
 R. H. 44
HOWES, Abigail 83
 Ella V. 182
 Fidelia S. 182
 Heman 52, 83

HOWES, Jacob S. (Mrs.) 56
  L. (Mrs.) (BRIGHAM) 66
  Mae 198
  Mathilda M. 16
  O. 198
HOXIE, Annie C. (WAGNER) 194
  George T. 194
  Maria (DEMMON) 160
  Mary Ann 45
  Stephen 5
  William 160
HOXWORTH, Sarah G. 211
HOYT, --- (Rev. Mr.) 128
  H. B. 154
  Wayland 193
HUBBARD, --- (Mr.) 86
  --- (Rev. Mr.) 196
  Albertis L. 59
  Bertrand 89
  Betsey C. (CROSS) 143
  Calvin 28
  Delevan 219
  Ellen A. 169
  Eunice 141
  George 30
  H. L. 197
  Harriet C. 82
  Ira 1
  Lyman 1
  M. W. 143
  Mary (WILBUR) 162
  Nellie 219
  Oliver 7, 9
  Rebecca 92
  Sarah A. 219
  Sophia Abbe 30
  Susan 28
  T. J. 16
  W. C. 144
  Wealthy 16
  William R. 30
  Wolcott 162
HUBBELL, Mary 154
HUDSON, DeEtta S. 190
  Sophia 208
  T. B. 195
HUFF, Elmer A. 203
  Jennie M. (TOOKER) 203
HUGHES, Carrie A. 199

HUGHES, Clara H. 184
  Edward 178
  Elizabeth 102
  Evan D. 102
  Louisa (DURANT) 178
  Lucy 121
  Nancy (MC COMBER) 121
  Peter D. 185
  Sarah C. (JONES) 185
  Sarah E. 161
  Truman J. 121
HUGHSTON, P. T. 160, 161, 166
HULBERT, E. B. 164
  E. M. 152
HULETT, Dwight 205
  Flora (PARLER) 205
HULL, Ann Elizabeth 123
  C. W. 123
  Charles F. 169
  Henry 12
  Martha (BOYD) 169
  Minerva 85
HUMPHREY, Dewitt 166
  Flora A. (LASSELL) 166
  Norman G. 26
  Willis 26
HUNGERFORD, Amzi S. 92
  Helen M. (OSGOOD) 132
  R. E. 132
HUNT, Albinus 34, 40
  Allen W. 57
  Allie J. 180
  Annie (SMITH) 205
  Caroline E. 22
  Caroline Elizabeth 131
  Celia G. 164
  Charles 22, 42
  Clarissa 112
  Cynthia 99
  Deborah 22
  Dorleska (TUTTLE) 163
  Edward W. 205
  Eliza Ann 92
  Emer S. 139
  Emily A. 157
  Ervilla 95
  George H. 163
  Gertrude E. 99
  Jerusha C. 124

HUNT, Mary 219
  Mordecai 95
  Nancy E. S. 141
  Samuel 141
  Sherebiah 131
HUNTER, Ann 133
  Emma B. (TEEPLE) 178
  J. W. 178
HUNTINGTON, Ann 2
  Eusebia N. (CAMPBELL) 162
  G. 139
  Harvey S. 162
  Henry 2
  Nehemiah 21
HUNTLEY, Hattie A. 182
HURD, Ann 122
  Benjamin 38
HURLBURT, Eunice 103
HURLEY, Eliza 183
HURN, Hattie Evelyn
   (WICKWIRE) 186
  J. W. 106
  James Whittier 186
HUTCHINS, Angeline (BUEL) 122
  Ormel 122
HUTCHINSON, George 124
  J. M. 213
  Loretta (COE) 124
HYATT, Aaron S. 219
  Elizabeth 193
  Francis A. 193
  Lydia 219
HYDE, Addie 153
  Asa P. 208
  Belle E. 174
  Charlotte 125
  Cornelia Eleanor 48
  Eliza M. (CHESEBRO) 136
  Ella L. 199
  G. 169
  Gurdon 88, 174
  Maria 218
  Mary F. (JACOBS) 208
  Newel 153
  Newell 136
  Philander 218
  Sarah A. 159
HYLAND, Frederick 208
  John 207

HYLAND, Minnie M. (MORGAN) 208
  Nellie (TEW) 207
IDE, Catherine (WARRINER) 181
  Oliver 181
  Patty 126, 127
  Sophronia 119
IGER, --- (Rev) 193
INGALLS, Amarintha 145
  Angie (BENEDICT) 206
  D. W. 162, 181
  DeWitt 145
  F. H. 173
  John W. 60, 156
  Mary A. 60
  Mary A. (WILCOX) 156
  Roxie L. 60
  Walter R. 206
INGERSOLL, J. M. (Mrs.) 72
INGRAHAM, Ashael 102
INGRAM, Benjamin 117
IRISH, George C. 41
IRVING, Elizabeth Ann
   (MCMASTER) 139
  James 139
ISBELL, Betsey E. 16
  Nettie 160
ISHAM, --- (Mrs.) 61
  Chancy 61
ISMOND, --- (Rev.) 158,
   162, 163
  Annie E. (NASH) 159
  L. V. 157, 158, 159, 161,
   162, 163
IVES, Jerusha 65
JACKSON, Angeline 156
  James C. 216
  L. W. 206, 209, 212, 213
  Laura Jane 139
  Maria 40
  Masas 40
  Sophia 149, 219
JACOBS, Mary F. 208
JACOBY, Nancy 37
JAMES, Almon 49
  Emily I. (FREEBURN) 136
  Thomas L. 136
JAQUAY, Hattie J. 195
JARVIS, Elsie 25

JARVIS, Per Lee 25
  Samuel 25
JEFF, Richard 25
JEFFRIES, Belinda
    (CADWELL) 114
  George 114
  Maria 114
JEFFS, Emma 186
JENKINS, Harriet L. 105
  Lizzie 213
  Thomas 213
  Timothy 105
JENKS, Albertus 155
  Benjamin R. 158
  Caroline (POWERS) 98
  Caroline Powers 97
  David 167
  Delancey W. 158
  Fannie (CUTLER) 167
  George S. 152
  Helen (STEINBERG) 158
  Maria (PALMER) 155
  Polly (MARVIN) 158
  Stephen B. 43
JENNESS, Abbie H. 186
JERIL, --- (Elder) 115
  Thomas 115
JEROME, Walter 138, 140,
    146
JERVIS, Cynthia (BRAYTON)
    119
  John B. 119
JESSUP, Samuel 209, 210
JEWEL, --- (Rev. Mr.) 144
JIPSON, Orin W. 62
  S. R. 62
JOHNSON, --- (Mrs.) 39
  Abbie D. (GREY) 159
  Abbie DeG. 48
  Arminda 115
  Beulah (BUCKINGHAM) 113
  C. M. 198
  C. T. 199
  Caroline 205
  Carrie E. (VAN AMAN) 209
  Catherine (FOLTS) 169
  Charles 78, 145
  Charles J. 48, 106, 159
  Corey 174
  Elias 113

JOHNSON, Elijah 134
  Ella L. (HYDE) 199
  Frankie 179
  George E. 209
  George W. 83
  Gertrude 206
  Hannah 115
  Harriet (HILL) 10
  Henry A. 49, 81
  Irene B. 146
  J. A. 193
  Jake 42
  James B. 169
  Jane (TITUS) 145
  Jane A. 132
  John B. 214
  Julia DeG. 48
  Kate 158
  Lydia 137
  Martha C. 203
  Mary 61, 78, 169
  Mary J. 159
  Mary Jane (MARSHALL) 163
  Mary M. 186
  Minnie 83
  Moses 10
  Nettie (AUSTON) 174
  R. M. 177
  Sarah L. 90
  Sophia M. (POWERS) 134
  Susan R. 171
  Timothy 132
  Tryphena (STARK) 177
  William 203
  William H. 163
  William J. 199
  William L. 111
  Z. M. (Mrs.) 81
JONES, --- (Rev.) 210
  Alvin 92
  C. M. 200, 201
  D. 214
  David M. 94
  Delia A. 128
  E. 59
  E. W. 73, 189, 190, 191,
    192, 193
  Elisha 48
  Elsie 58
  Emogene 48

JONES, Etta B. 183
  Frank 91
  Gilbert F. (Mrs.) 3
  H. W. 161, 162
  Harriet 115
  Harry W. 158
  Hugh 79
  Ida A. 63
  Ida A. (CAMPBELL) 166
  Isadore (COAN) 158
  J. H. 63
  J. R. (TIFFANY) 181
  James 193
  Jennie (VAN DUSEN) 193
  Jennie A. 73
  John 21, 181, 213
  John B. 91
  Katie E. 188
  Maggie E. 177
  Maria L. (RICHARDSON) 136
  Martha A. 144
  Mary (SQUIRES) 215
  Mary A. 168, 183
  Mary A. (JONES) 183
  Mary P. (LUCAS) 185
  Morah M. 136
  N. S. 183
  P. F. 137
  Pomroy 128
  R. T. 185
  Rosagene 48
  S. L. 211
  Sarah 70
  Sarah C. 185
  T. R. 183
  W. H. 63
  William H. 166
  Willie 36
  Wilmer E. 71
JOSLIN, Charles 17
  Etta A. 176
  Kezia 58
  Lester 60
  Lettie A. 191
  Mary (LAPHAM) 60
  Percs A. (CALKINS) 125
  W. C. 79
  W. C. (Mrs.) 77
  Willard 125
JOY, Augusta L. 135

JOY, Lewis 135
JOYCE, Anna S. (STEBBINS) 209
  J. Laister 209
JUDD, --- (Mrs.) 1
  Heman 1
  Sophia 79
JUDSON, A. 125, 127, 134
  Ard. 95
  E. C. (CHUBBUCK) 21
  Emily (CHUBBUCK) 135
  Emily S. (NORTON) 125, 127
  Jennie M. 95
JULIAND, Charlotte (HYDE) 125
  George 125
KEATING, Mary A. 194
KEECH, Francelia E. (ACKLEY) 158
  Willard 158
KEELER, --- (Rev.) 147
  Nathaniel 17
KEIM, Rosa C. 187
KEITH, Betsey 90
  C. A. 87
  Charles A. 86
  David 66, 78
  Elizabeth 16
  Fanny W. 66
  H. H. 197
  Henry 16
  Homer H. 171
  Julia C. 185
  Lewis 90
  Louise B. 86
  Marcelia B. 145
  Mary (SPEAR) 171
  Mary Elizabeth 16
  Nellie L. 87
KELLEY, Cora 202
  Hattie (TUCKER) 202
  Henry 193
  James 202
  Mary E. (SMITH) 193
  Pat 108
  Patrick B. 81
  Phebe 143
KELLOGG, Amanda 114
  Amelia 115

KELLOGG, Jacob 114
  Sarah 48
KELLOWAY, Emma M. 203
  Eunice Melvina 95
  Frank J. 192
  George 95, 111
  Hattie M. (FOSTER) 174
  Isaac 81
  Mary A. (WELLS) 192
  William 174
KELLY, Delia 188
  Thomas H. 61
KELSEY, A. M. (WOOD) 144
  Cornelia A. 32
  Cornelia A. (MEAD) 155
  D. A. 32
  D. W. 144
  Dennison A. 155
  Julius 32
  M. Gertrude 155
KEMPTON, George 123
  Sarah E. (MOTT) 123
KENDALL, David 48
  Elizabeth (OSGOOD) 123
  Henry D. 120, 121
  Hiram 123
  Louisa M. (READ) 170
  Louise M. (REED) 81
  Luther O. 170
  Marchia D. S. (HAVENS) 120
  Marcia D. S. (HAVENS) 121
KENDRICK, --- (Dr.) 115
  --- (Rev. Dr.) 117, 135
  --- (Rev.) 114, 115
  A. C. 121, 126, 128
  Cordelia C. 135
  N. 134
  Nath'l. 113
  Nathaniel 117
KENNEDY, Alexander 158
  Carrie R. (BROGAN) 199
  James K. 199
  John 105
  Mary (GILMORE) 117
  Napolean Bonaparte 117
KENT, Helen M. (LEWIS) 134
  Luther M. 134
  Marinda 4
KENYON, --- (Elder) 123

KENYON, --- (Rev. Mr.) 128
  H. 123
  James 190
  Joel 113
  Lavina (MAXON) 113
  Marion (DECKER) 190
  Mary Libbie 193
  Nancy 128
  Sarah S. 173
KERN, A. P. 172
  Adria 206
  Cornelia (EDDY) 140
  David C. 26
  Delia A. (TOWNSLEY) 150
  George 73, 107
  George C. 150
  John 70, 163
  Malvina S. 70
  Peter V. 140
KERSHAW, Elizabeth 170
  Marsden 89, 170
  Rebecca 89
KEYES, Bethsheba 44
  Helen 134
  Sarah A. 173
KIBBE, J. S. 141
  Joel 115
  Sophia (BUYSBY) 115
KILMER, Ebenezer 54
KILTS, Abram 147
  Addie (WELLS) 147
  Christopher 92
KIMBALL, Addie C. 201
  Elle J. (BUGBEE) 205
  Elvina 170
  Emma 95
  J. Jay 205
KIMBERLEY, Hattie M. (POTTER) 177
  Henry 84
  J. S. 177
KIMBERLY, Andalusia 84
  Eli T. 10
  Frank 85
  Henry 85
  Phebe 10
  Phebe (THOMPSON) 85
  Sherman 10, 85
KINDRICK, --- (Elder) 113
KING, A. C. (Mrs.) 99

KING, C. M. 198
  J. M. 198
  J. W. 27
  Mary 127
  Nathaniel 6, 65
  Ottillia 65
  Thomson 6
  W. H. 142
KINGSBURY, Edward 203
  Frank 185
  Ida (BRADSHAW) 185
  Lydia (GOODELL) 113
  Mary 157
  Pierce 113
  Sarah (FOSTER) 203
KINGSLEY, --- (Rev.) 113, 115
  A. 118
  A. K. 149
  A. Z. 50, 60, 125, 151, 179, 212
  Alice C. 60, 178
  Amos 113
  Avery 19
  Avery Z. 124
  Charlotte E. 44
  Delight (BEEBE) 172
  Helen T. 212
  K. W. 172
  Lucy M. 19
  Mary E. 151, 179
  Mary E. (LEWIS) 149
  Polly 50
  William 212
KINNEY, --- (Rev. Mr.) 133
  Calvin T. 187
  Charles B. 71
  Eliza E. 211
  Ida L. (SCOTT) 187
  Mary Ann 157
  W. H. 164
KINS, Amanda J. (CHAPEL) 142
KINSBURY, E. 112
KIRBY, Gurdon 1
KLINCH, Lucy 71
KLINCK, George 71
  Lucy 189
  Margaret C. 148
  O. K. 146

KLINCK, Owen 90
  Sophia J. (ROZELL) 146
KNAPP, Electa (PAYNE) 115
  F. L. 105
  Isaac 113
  Jacob 14, 115, 117
  Jemima 21
  John 39
  Lydia 131
  Mary (NORTON) 113
  Sally 39
KNIGHT, Eliza A. 17
KNOWLES, William 53
KNOWLTON, Asa 209
  Charles W. 211
  Eliza E. (KINNEY) 211
  Hattie 209
KNOX, Bethia 91
  Charles H. 53
  Orville L. 96
  W. 162
KOLB, Harriet (ROGERS) 188
  William L. 188
KRAMER, Avaline Amelia (CHAPIN) 18
  William 18
KRETZ, Frank J. 208
  Katie J. (GILBERT) 208
LA MUNION, A. J. 104
  Andrew 74
  Eliza (ALLEN) 184
  Lavina C. (BONNEY) 74
  Mary 38
  Mittie L. 160
  Seymour 184
  Sibyl 104
LA SELLE, A. Alymer 161
  Roxana 161
LADD, Frances E. 129
  Frances Elizabeth 84
  Jessie T. 45
  John B. 84, 129
  L. W. 26
  Lydia 84
  Orson T. 36
LAINING, Hannah 112
  Olive 113
LAKE, A. M. 158, 165
LALOR, Richard 23
LAMB, Ada 207

LAMB, Amos 74, 83, 84
  Clara A. 184
  Ed. 111
  Ella (BURLINGAME) 190
  Emma 171
  Eveleen 203
  George W. 207
  Gertrude 192
  John (Mrs.) 103
  Joseph 208
  Lucy 207
  Luva E. 213
  Mary 175
  Perlina 84
  Rhoda Ann (TUTTLE) 133
  Silas 133
  Tilda (CLARE) 207
  William E. 190
LAMPHERE, Alita 44
  Emma J. 175
  Francis M. (DURFEE) 135
  Phebe 173
  Vaulkert 135
LAMPHIRE, Phoebe 120
LANCKTON, C. M. 31
  Cordelia 31
  E. W. 31
LANDON, John 60
  M. D. 60
LANE, --- (Rev.) 116
  C. A. 200
  George 26
  Keziah 146
  L. 200
LANGWORTHY, Betsey W. 16
  Charles B. 16
  Harrie J. 199
LANPHERE, Daniel 66
  Philena 55
  Ransom 61
LANSING, Peter 11
LAPHAM, --- (Deacon) 113
  Amanda 47
  Deborah 113
  Duty 13
  Hattie 163
  Mary 60
LARKIN, James K. 137
  Mandane 181
  Mary Ann 137

LASELL, Dorcas 36
  Flora A. 166
LASELLE, Florence D.
  (WEDGE) 177
  George S. 177
  Josiah 34
  Mary E. 150
  Mason 62
  Roxana 63
LASHER, George Eaton 57
LATHAM, --- (Rev. Mr.) 116
  --- (Rev.) 113, 118
LATHROP, Mary B. 21
LATTIMER, George 200
  Mary (NIEDICK) 200
LATTIN, Lucy W. 5
  Wesley 5
LATTINA, Harriet 57
LAUDERBACK, M. 156
LAW, Mary A. 194
LAWLOR, Kate 89
LAWRENCE, A. F. 178
  Alvira 28
  Ann Eliza 15
  Anna 202
  Belle E. (HYDE) 174
  David 15
  Hattie B. 28
  Phila (FILLMORE) 40
  Pitt 40
  S. W. 202
  Sophia (HESS) 178
  W. M. 205
  W. W. 28
  William M. 174
LAWTON, Giles 18
  Lewis 158
LAWYER, J. D. 217
LAY, Caroline 54
  Emma P. 164
  Emma S. 150
  George C. 89
  Sarah C. 156
LE ROY, A. 182
LEACH, --- (Rev.) 124
  Abigail 125
  Addie 57
  Alice 198
  Allen N. 185
  B. M. 124

LEACH, B. N. 125, 128
  Backus I. 185
  Charles B. 204
  Clement 114
  D. 53
  Estelle 197
  Etta A. 185
  Hattie M. (SQUIRE) 185
  Henry 72
  Ida M. 192
  Laura (HATCH) 114
  Luna 62
  Mina V. (ROACHE) 204
  Nikles 109
LEAL, Robert A. 10
LEAVENWORTH, Almira G.
  (STREW) 130
  D. B. 130
LEE, Franc A. (SMITH) 177
  H. W. 139, 141
  Jennie E. (WALKER) 187
  Jerome E. 187
  Sophronia M. 157
  Welk M. 177
LEETS, George 104
LEGATE, O. M. 144, 155
LEIPSNER, B. F. 185
  Viola (FELT) 185
LELAND, Amasa 10
  Dwight 198
LEONARD, Alfred W. 14
  Anna 122
  Arah 14
  Henry B. 108
  Jannie (BROWN) 176
  Jefferson 176
  John S. 209
  Lizzie May (LOOMIS) 209
  T. 203
  Will 77
LESTER, Jason 2
LETCHWORTH, --- (Mr.) 33
LEVI, Bessie 63
LEWIS, --- (Mr.) 59
  --- (Prof.) 87
  A. E. 160
  Alcesta 171
  Alethan (CURTIS) 71
  Andrew R. 156
  B. 16

LEWIS, Bell 32
  Benjamin 212
  Birdsey 69
  Calvin B. 58
  Carrie E. (CUSHMAN) 156
  Charles 11, 71, 171
  Conway 14
  Cornelia 11
  E. (Mrs.) 20
  E. Lawrence 156
  Edward 35
  Ellen D. 49
  Elnora (SHAPLEY) 135
  Esther 35
  Franklin Merselon 11
  Glicera L. (SHERMAN) 156
  Helen 212
  Helen M. 134
  Henry 199
  Hiram 20
  J. J. 185, 191
  Janet (RUNDELL) 171
  John James 189
  John R. 103
  Judson 216
  Julia (HAWES) 216
  Lafayette 135
  Lillian E. 75
  Lydia 114
  Lywellyn H. 175
  M. S. (POTTER) 160
  Mary A. 18
  Mary E. 149
  Otis 18
  Sarah G. (GREEN) 175
  Virginia (POST) 177
  William 24, 46
  William A. 177
LEWORTHY, Elizabeth 60
LEWRIGHT, Mattie E. 176
  W. P. 176
LILLIBRIDGE, Ira J. 8
  James 8
  Mahlon 8
LILLIE, Anna M. 151
  H. S. 112, 159
  Henry 109
  Lucy 141
  Lucy B. (TOMPKINS) 159
LILLY, F. 129

LILLYBRIDGE, C. H. 135
  Freeman 135
  L. M. (OSGOOD) 135
  Mary (BRYANT) 135
LINCOLN, Abraham 2
  Fannie M. 95
  Joshua H. 57
LINSEY, Olive 116
LIPPITT, --- (Mr.) 52
  J. W. 166
  Louisa 138
LIVERMORE, Alpha 99
  Betsey ANne 77
  J. M. 32
  L. S. 147
  Marian E. 164
  Nancy 37
  Susan 114
LIVINGSTON, Hannah 31
  Jane E. 123
LLOYD, --- (Rev. Dr.) 214
  Mary 87
  Mary E. (BENNETT) 199
  Robert 199
LOCKHEART, Belle R. 188
LOCKMAN, Phebe 15
LOCKWOOD, Elmima O.
  (MERCHANT) 130
  George G. 130
  Henry 118
  Sophia S. (PECK) 118
LOGAN, Chloe (RALPH) 192
  Libbie 95
  Will 107
  William F. 192
LONG, Irene B. (JOHNSON)
  146
  Joseph 33
  Lydia B. 120
LONGLEY, Annie E. 210
LONIS, Fanny 213
LONT, Ada E. 184
  Beulah (OSTROM) 12
  C. B. 49
  Cephus 218
  Elbecca 134
  Elijah 123
  Florence S. 83
  Harriet 49
  Harriet (PECKHAM) 218

LONT, Hattie 165
  John 134
  John F. 12
  Margaret (CONICK) 123
  Matthias 146
LOOK, Lucinda 126
LOOMIS, Adaline 73
  Alfred 212
  Calvin 73
  Charles 189
  David 70
  Elizabeth Thompson
    (FENTON) 123
  Ella 191
  Ellen (RAMSDELL) 189
  Emily A. 92
  Emma E. 183
  F. H. 113
  George 212
  Hattie 54
  Henry M. 165
  J. J. (Mrs.) 98
  John B. 123
  John J. 209
  Lizzie May 209
  Mary 202
  Mary A. (WILLIAMSON) 165
  Nannie D. 212
  Olive (LAINING) 113
  Orlando 100
LORD, --- (Rev. Mr.) 206
  Ada Miranda 146
  Adeline M. 52
  Amasa 52, 146, 182
  Caroline 37
  DeForest 36
  E. B. 157
  Emma 176
  Hannah 36
  John 214
  Lulu 36
  Mary E. 182
  O. B. 36, 68, 153, 155,
    193
  Palmyra A. 68
  S. A. 193
  Sarah 214
  William 22
LOTTRIDGE, Delia 82
LOUDERBACK, A. 151, 152

LOVE, Abigail R. 132
  Anna 116
LOVEJOY, Benjamin 138
  John 157
  Mary (SWIFT) 157
LOVELAND, E. W. 167
  Emma J. (RICE) 167
  Joel 10
  Matilda 144
LOVERIDGE, D. H. 184
LOWDEN, Helen (WHEELER) 168
  J. 168
LOWE, Eliza 167
  Sarah E. 153
LUCAS, Fannie L. (TABER) 176
  Fanny (TABOR) 147
  Henry 147
  Henry V. 176
  John S. 74
  Mary 89
  Mary E. (DALEY) 191
  Mary P. 185
  Willey 110
  William 191
  Wilson 89
LUDDE, A. P. 57
LUDDEN, --- (Father) 61
  --- (Rev. Fr.) 183
  A. P. 172, 187, 191
  Anthony 57
  Honora 57
  James 57
  John 57
LUMBARD, Augustus 23, 54
LYLE, Albert F. 187
LYMAN, --- (Rev.) 116
  Aurel 116
  Isaac 5, 14
  Mary 5, 14
LYNCH, Mary 138
LYNDON, Kate 174
LYON, Bridget 172
  Hannah (JOHNSON) 115
  Janette M. 218
  Maria 138
  Minerva 115
  Nathaniel 115

LYON, Nettie E. (RICHARDSON) 175
  William W. 175
LYONS, James 92
LYPE, Ambrose 99
LYTLE, George I. 147
  Mary (SMITH) 147
MABIN, Luther 115
  Mary (PIERCE) 115
MAC MURRAY, Martha 214
  W. J. 214
MACK, Charles 69
  Clark A. 170
  Frankie (SOULE) 165
  William 165
MACKEY, Emeline 86
MACKIN, Sarah 178
MACOMBER, A. S. 58, 74
  Charles 75
  Cynthia D. 71
  Frank D. 58
  Joseph 19
  Malinda 75
  Margaret 19
  Mary E. 58, 74
  Miles R. 104
MACUMBER, --- 33
  Charles S. 33
  Joseph 48
MADISON, James 82
MAFFET, Anna 121
MAGIE, George A. 175
MAGINNIS, --- (Prof.) 122, 134
  --- (Rev. Prof.) 135
  --- (Rev.) 123
  J. S. 125, 126, 127
  John 5
MAHAN, Clara S. (TAFT) 191
  Eugen 191
MAHANEY, Alice 208
MAIN, Charles A. 151
  Ellen J. (ALDRICH) 151
MAINE, David 124
  Deloss 92
  Lodema 124
  Mary 92
MALLORY, N. C. 153
MALTBY, Agnes M. (WILKINSON) 187

MALTBY, James M. 187
MANCHESTER, Calista D. 44
  Daniel 94
  E. 132
  E. D. 162
  E. W. 13
  Edward 15, 134
  Eliza 94
  Emma A. (BARRETT) 200
  Emogene 103
  Enrestine M. (BETHKE) 196
  F. H. 197
  Fannie (WHITNEY) 162
  Fluvius J. 44
  George B. 13
  Hannah C. 82
  J. E. 103
  James D. 99
  Jennie Rose 204
  Julia 123
  L. Beach 85
  Lucetta (HAUGHTON) 134
  Lydia H. 13
  Mary 161
  Mary M. 13
  Orinda P. 103
  Orson P. 196
  William H. 200
MANN, Ida 197
MANNERING, Alfred G. 6
  David 124
  Maria (DE WOLF) 124
MANUEL, Margaret H. 126
MARCHISI, Emily (MERRILL) 154
  Henry N. 154
MARICLE, Cordelia 143
MARIKLE, Nettie E. 147
MARKHAM, Bradford P. 191
  Flora (Mrs.) 104
  Flora Lillian (WHITEMORE) 73
  Lilly F. (WHITMORE) 191
  T. B. 73
MARSH, Abbie (PIERCE) 169
  Daniel (Mrs.) 99
  David 2
  Frankie Clarence 219
  Isaac B. 196
  Jay A. 219

MARSH, Joseph G. 219
  Mary (COLVIN) 196
  Samuel 169
  Silas 33
  Smith D. 166
  Tacy A. (MOORE) 166
MARSHALL, --- (Rev. Mr.) 166
  --- (Rev.) 168
  A. H. 100, 194, 202
  A. W. 203
  Albert 202
  H. A. 164
  Harrington 100
  Mary Jane 163
  Thomas 70
MARSTON, John 93
MARTIN, --- (Mrs.) 97
  Darius 45
  George F. 147
  Louisa J. (ELLIS) 217
  Nettie E. (MARIKLE) 147
  Peter 217
MARTINIS, M. Gertrude (KELSEY) 155
  Nathan 155
MARVIN, Betsey 81
  Daniel J. 191
  Erastus 96
  Jane 96
  Mary E. (STRAUBE) 191
  Polly 158
MASON, Ashbel 9
  B. W. 130
  Charles 8, 9, 160, 169
  Christopher C. 137
  Cornelia Ann 8, 9
  Edward 90
  Ella M. 160
  Fanny H. (BOOTH) 144
  Fidelia S. (HOWES) 182
  G. S. 165
  Hannah (CRAMPHIN) 130
  Hattie 169
  Hattie E. 209
  Joseph C. 144
  Julia 90
  L. M. 164
  Lydia (JOHNSON) 137
  Marcus E. 182

MASON, Rachel R. 94
MASTERS, --- (Judge) 126, 127
  Ann Margaret 126, 127
  Frances Mary Upton (MORRIS) 129
  Justus S. 22
  Justus Smith 129
MATHER, Mary (KINGSBURY) 157
  Selden 157
MATHESON, Hattie (EATON) 202
  W. H. 202
MATHEWS, Blendena 36
MATHEWSON, A. E. (Mrs.) 37
  Phillip 5
MATHISON, W. H. 110
MATTESON, B. F. 138
  Matilda (HOWARD) 138
  S. J. 184
MATTHEWSON, Bethiah 15
  Sylvenus 15
MAXEY, E. W. 191
MAXON, DeEtte 168
  Lavina 113
MAXSON, Charles H. 143, 144
  Cordelia Ann (HARTSHORN) 123
  Harmon C. 85
  Joshua 139
  Lee 104
  Luke G. 123
  Phoebe C. 139
MAXSTED, Mary J. 208
MAXWELL, J. Allen 200
MAY, Rufus 92
  Samuel J. 161
MAYDOLE, A. D. 141
  Clara M. (FRYER) 141
  Myra M. 76
MAYNARD, --- (Rev.) 80, 209
  Arba K. 119
  Gertrude 80
  Henry J. 171
  Minerva (GATES) 119
  Moses 16
  Susan R. (JOHNSON) 171

MAYNARD, W. A. 181
  W. H. 194, 197, 205
MC CANN, Bethina 126
MC CARDY, Henry 125, 127
  Jane (PRENTISS) 125
  Margaret (PRENTISS) 127
MC CARM, Bethia 127
MC CARTHY, James H. 199
  Mary Ella (RICHARDS) 199
  Nellie 209
MC CLENTHAN, John 67
MC COMBER, Cynthia D. (CLARK) 157
  Miles 157
  Nancy 121
MC CREDY, Della C. (RHODES) 182
  W. H. 182
MC DANIELS, Florence A. (HEWES) 159
  John A. 159
MC DONALD, Alexander 140
  Helen (FULLER) 140
  John 61
  Lyman G. 210
  Maggie 168
  Martin 200
  Nora (MORAN) 200
  Rosa 140
  W. W. 210
MC DOUGALL, M. D. 210
  Mary E. 210
MC GAHEN, Emma E. (LOOMIS) 183
  Emory B. 183
  Florence D. (GRIGGS) 181
  J. H. 176, 177, 180, 181, 183, 188
  James H. 177
MC GLEW, Kate M. 84
MC GOHEN, J. H. 147
MC GRAW, Helen 158
MC GREGOR, John 3
  Rebecca (PALMER) 3
MC GUIRE, W. D. 218
MC HARG, --- (Rev.) 168
MC LEAN, Charles N. 94
  Ella (COLLINS) 179
  William 179
MC LOUGHLIN, Cornelius 216

MC LOUGHLIN, Mary Ann
  (WHITE) 216
MC MASTER, Elizabeth Ann
  139
MC MICHAEL, --- (Widow)
  114
MC MURPHY, A. T. 146
MC QUADE, Anna 172
  James 88
  Peter 20
MC QUIEN, Sarah 63
MC WHORTER, David 130
  Sarah J. (MURDOCK) 130
MEAD, A. H. 183
  Althea M. 151
  C. S. 136, 155
  Cornelia A. 155
  Eliza 118
  Jane 128
  Jennie E. 88
  N. B. 32
  Theodore 105
MEDBURY, A. 163
  Alfred 38, 135
  Emily 79
  J. Milton 46
  Joseph Edgar 62
MELROY, Ellen R. 166
MELTON, Jesse 67
MELVIN, Sarah J. 186
MENZA, Esther 159
  George 159
MERCER, Anna Lewis 42
  Lizzie M. 42
  William E. 42
MERCHANT, Cecelia 218
  Elmima O. 130
  William 218
MERRELL, J. D. 211
MERRIFIELD, Alanson 7, 9
  E. H. (Mrs.) 132
  Emma 54
MERRILL, D. Jerome 96
  Elijah B. 154
  Emily 154
  Gertrude E. (NASH) 204
  M. 208
  Will Foster 204
MERRIMAN, Elizabeth Mills
  (GOSS) 135

MERRIMAN, James 135
MERRITT, Adda L. 152
  E. 152
  Ira D. 210
  L. Jane 143
  Louisa 143
  Nehemiah 138
  Sarah A. 138
  Sophronia A. (WILLIAMS)
    210
MESSENGER, I. N. 220
  John M. 22
  John N. 220
  Phebe Gage 220
METCALF, Hattie A. 160
METTLER, Kate 206
MEVIS, S. W. 212
MEYER, Mary Jane
  (ROWLANDS) 83
  Van Cortland 83
MIDDLEBROOK, E. R. 151
  Emily S. (PAYNE) 151
MIKELS, Lydia A. (ALLEN)
  132
  W. S. 132
MILES, Abigail 33
  Alansing 27
  Landon 99
MILLARD, Fidella Valmette
  (SUMNER) 42
  Harry E. 42
  Thankful 135
MILLEN, Electa 50
MILLER, --- (Esq.) 126,
  128
  --- (Mrs.) 100
  Albert C. 213
  Amarantha 128
  Amarintha 126
  Celia (GRAY) 169, 220
  Charles Morton 25
  Clarissa 127
  Clarissa Fidelia 217
  Claude 100
  Cynthia (BACON) 117
  David S. 148
  Eunice (STEBBINS) 154
  Eunice L. (STEBBINS) 127
  George 117
  H. Maria (DANIELS) 154

MILLER, H. P. 169, 220
  Hannah 195
  Harriet (SHEPARD) 130
  Harriet L. (HALL) 148
  Henry A. 188
  Henry Onslow 25
  I. A. 78
  Ida Belle (WALDRON) 188
  J. 205
  Jacob R. 194
  John 217
  John T. 127, 154
  L. H. 154
  Linus H. 25
  Lucy 19
  Luva E. (LAMB) 213
  Maria D. 25
  Mason 130
  Morris S. 3
  Mott 100
  Nancy 117
  Orcelia 159
  Rebecca (REESE) 194
  S. 168
  Sabrina 131
  Samuel 157, 165, 178
  Stewart 23
  Thomas 92
  William G. 117
MILLS, Emory 91
  Helen A. 193
  John 206
  Mary (CLOSE) 206
MINER, Celia E. 47
  D. M. 110
  D. Marcello 106
  Elvira C. 196
  H. C. 47
  Harriet 142
  Herbert S. 211
  Jonathan 137
  Lizzie E. 182
  Lucretia (BLINN) 125
  Mary 188
  Mary A. (ARMSTRONG) 211
  Paul R. 182
  Roxey (PENDOCK) 137
  Seth 125
  William 105
MINOR, Jesse 114

MINTIE, Fannie 182
MITCHELL, Caroline D.
  (FOOTE) 124
  David J. 60
  G. W. 163
  Hugh 216
  Isabella 216
  John 124
  Oliver 56
MIZE, Sylvia E. (HOWARD)
  130
  William H. 130
MONROE, Almeda 3
  Charles L. 208
  Mary (ARNOLD) 208
MONTANA, Viola M. (DUELL)
  204
  Willis E. 204
MONTENA, --- (Mrs.) 104
  Ervin 37
MONTGOMERY, Charles E. 186
  Julia A. (BIXBY) 186
  Mary Newell (ENQUEST) 213
  William 55
  William Elmer 213
MONTROSS, Fanny M. 9
  Jacob 8
MOON, Nicholas 94
MOONEY, Michael 105
MOOR, Katie (SEVERANCE)
  196
  Otto P. 196
MOORE, Betsey Hills 22
  D. 167
  David H. 152
  Gordon 182, 183, 184,
    185, 186, 187
  Lois 168
  Mary Ann (BATEMAN) 152
  Tacy A. 166
  W. H. 22
  William 107
MORAN, Nora 200
MORE, Charles 25
MOREY, A. G. 25
  Alanson C. 184
  Celia 59
  Clara H. (HUGHES) 184
  Margaret 25
  Sally 78

MOREY, W. M. 162
MORGAN, Alice (TALCOTT) 167
  Anna H. 208
  Charles O. 193
  Charlotte (BEAR) 115
  Clara E. 51
  Delia 142
  Emory 167
  Frances A. 37
  Grace 41
  Harry 84
  John 161
  Lizzie M. (CHAPHE) 193
  Lucas 115
  Minnie M. 208
  Minnie S. 200
  Susie 84
  William 79
MORGEN, A. Daniel 41
MORRIS, --- (Gen.) 129
  Adon 21
  Aner 6
  Frances D. (CRANE) 139
  Frances Mary Upton 129
  Jonathan 139
  Mary E. 119
  Pardon 6, 21
  Richard 129
  Robert J. 119
  Sarah 21
  Sarah L. (STAFFORD) 129
  William 15, 21
  William W. 129
MORRISON, --- (Rev. Dr.) 175
  George R. 149
  Miranda C. (GARDNER) 149
MORSE, --- (Prof.) 76
  --- (Rev. Mr.) 116
  Addison 187
  Alpheus 132
  Andrew B. 39
  Anna (REYNOLDS) 187
  Asa 19
  Belinda S. 39
  Calvin 39
  Caroline 36
  Cemantha J. (PARMELY) 116
  Cornelia 179
  Cornelia (SCRANTON) 124
  Cyrus M. 144, 155
  Dennis 72
  Edward B. 145
  Frances A. 149, 219
  Hannah (SEYMOUR) 144, 155
  Henry Bagg 60
  Jabez 17
  Julia 71
  Marietta (CRAMPHIN) 132
  Mary A. (ARMSTRONG) 145
  Mary C. 39
  Mary Loree 39
  Mary Selina 76
  Moses S. 124
  Nettie G. (BAKER) 188
  Sally (SHAW) 113
  Sarah W. (GOULDING) 72
  William 113
  William C. 188
  Zenas 116
MORSON, --- (Mrs.) 39
  Reuben 39
MORTON, A. D. 191
  Adell (RICHARDSON) 195
  George H. 195
  M. Francelia (DAVIS) 191
  Mary (WHEELER) 163
  Reuben 163
MORY, Hattie 177
MOSELEY, Ada 173
  Addie A. (BEACH) 158
  Ambrose 14, 25
  Araunah 32
  E. L. 158
  George Murray 21
  Kate (LYNDON) 174
  Lille A. 191
  Mary 160
  Mattie L. 58
  Oscar 29
  Sarah M. 168
  Vashti 14
  Z. J. 160
MOSELY, Amrylis T. (ROGERS) 159
  Harvey 58
  Maria 145
  Mary 58

MOSELY, Oscar J. 159
MOSES, Delia (MORGAN) 142
　Lewis 142
MOSHER, Alonzo 20
　Eugene 18
　Horace 20
　Horace M. 133
　Jennie I. 20
　Susan 20
　Susan (CURTIS) 133
MOTT, Belle (EDDY) 150
　C. M. 150
　Edward B. 156
　Ezra D. 143
　George C. 93
　George S. 87
　Grace (BEADSLEY) 209
　James 209
　John G. 63
　Joseph 2, 35
　Joseph Addison 81
　Lena (FAIRCHILD) 156
　Louise (MERRITT) 143
　Lucinda 152
　Mary A. 150
　Mary C. 213
　Nettie C. 87
　Nettie C. (PECKHAM) 198
　Prudence O. (BLISH) 40
　S. R. 87
　Samuel R., Jr. 198
　Sarah E. 123
　Smith 40, 64, 152
　Susan 35
MOUNT, Arthur S. 82
　Francis 82
MOWERS, Cynthia M. 211
MULONEY, Mary 80
MUMFORD, --- (Rev. Mr.)
　139
　S. B. 218
MUNGER, Franklin J. 119
MUNROE, Almeda (SKEELS)
　113
　James 3, 113
MUNSON, Chancey 78
　Hilda (BEECHER) 78
　Joseph 117
MURDOCK, A. T. 39
　Alexander 100

MURDOCK, Cornelia J. 28
　J. 133
　John 101
　Nelson E. 28
　Sarah J. 130
　Tryphosa 39
MURPHY, Alice 206
　Caroline (JOHNSON) 205
　Howard 205
　Johanna 211
　Kate 209
MURRAY, --- (Rev. Dr.)
　200, 202
　J. B. 201
MYERS, A. 122
　John T. 153
　Mary 153
MYRIC, Luther 216
MYRICK, Hannah B.
　(SPRAGUE) 124
　Luther 215
　Minnie A. 195
　Thomas S. 124
NAISMITH, J. E. 194
NASH, A. T. 65
　Abner W. 130
　Andrew B. 34
　Annie E. 159
　Bertha 44
　Bertha M. 207
　Chloe 44
　Corriden E. 161
　Corydon 134
　Corydon B. 166
　Daniel P. 19
　David E. 44
　Elijah 70
　Emma A. 34
　Esther L. 147
　Fannie M. 34
　George E. 84
　Georgia (DUNBAR) 65
　Gertrude E. 204
　Harriet 35
　Hiram 124
　Horace 16
　J. LeRoy 162
　Lauraine F. 156
　Lottie M. 182
　Louisa (HECOX) 162

NASH, Louisa (STOCKING) 134
Lucinda 70
Lucy Ann (TORREY) 130
Mary (CADWELL) 124
Mary E. 166
Nettie 84
Norton 46
Sarah (HEWES) 161
Sophia (CHURCH) 19
Willard 147
Zenas 35
NASON, J. H. 159
NEAL, Delia (PATRIDGE) 178
John 178
NECOMBER, Charles S. 167
Minnie (HART) 167
NEFF, D. A. 63
Daniel 40, 87
Hannah 87
Roseanna 87
NEGUS, Flora B. 210
Frank 106
Milton F. 200
NELLIS, Caroline (SPRIGGS) 216
James W. 216
John 215
John I. D. 215
NELSON, David 175
E. E. (Mrs.) 73
H. 209
Mary (LAMB) 175
NEWCOMB, E. 103
Orinda P. (MANCHESTER) 103
NEWELL, Cornelia J. (DUNTON) 178
Henry G. 178
Lucy 189
NEWKIRK, Maryett P. 86
Sarah L. 210
NEWMAN, Eugenia S. (HOLT) 183
George W. 183
Jerusha (HEAD) 174
Thomas 174
NEWTON, Artemas L. 56
Artimas 50
Bert J. 203

NEWTON, Cynthia L. (PIERCE) 181
F. B. 189
Frank H. 178
George G. 49
Gertie M. (SHEPARDSON) 203
Isaac 104
Lewis D. 181
Lurensa 126
Marlitta 104
Mary 50
Palmer 158
Sarah H. (AVERY) 158
NEY, James 12
NICHOLS, A. S. 126, 127
Alfred 30
Bethia (MC CARM) 127
Bethina (MC CARM) 126
Byron O. 36
C. A. 109, 111, 192
Clarissa A. 27
E. (Mrs.) 170
Ellen J. 92
Eunice B. 198
Hanford 27
Helen F. 22
James J. 147
Jennie 109
Jennie E. 174
Jennie N. 27
Jennie S. (ROOT) 192
John 24
L. L. 22
L. W. 166
Lora C. (HOBBS) 147
Louisa M. 170
Mary Ellen 166
Nettie E. 192
Sabria 114
Sally 113
William F. 202
NICHOLSON, Fred 208
Nellie (RUNDELL) 208
Nettie 88, 201
NICKHAM, Nord D. 202
NIEDICK, Mary 200
NIEDOCK, Kittie 169
NIFF, Henry T. 71
NILES, A. H. 124

NILES, Abby Eliza (BOOTH) 137
  Achsa M. 126, 128
  Achsah 173
  Alanson 10
  Alanson Eugene 10
  Allen 80
  Daniel W. 137
  Elizabeth R. 176
  Ella 184
  Eugene 197
  John 138
  Lillian (BAKER) 197
  Lydia (BROWN) 10
  Lyman 78
  Marshall 176
  Mary A. 138
  Mary E. (DONALDSON) 124
  Mary E. (KINGSLEY) 151
  Mary N. 97
  Nahum 3
  R. Olmstead 151
NOBLE, Eliza 12
  L. L. 175
  William H. 12
NORRIS, Mary 135
  Robert J. 135
NORTH, Harlow 13
NORTHRUP, --- (Rev. Mr.) 178
  Ann (FOWLER) 114
  Harti H. 184
  Ira 4
  Jennie M. (PARKER) 184
  Lettie A. (JOSLIN) 191
  R. H. 182
  S. A. 191
  W. 165
  Whitefirld 114
NORTON, Abbey (SHERWOOD) 127
  Addie 153
  Addie (FRYOVER) 176
  Davis 163
  Elizabeth H. (BURNHAM) 145
  Emily S. 125, 127
  J. G. 163
  James 145, 215
  Joseph A. 34, 134

NORTON, Mary 113, 163
  Miles 127
  Polly 85
  R. R. 176
  S. H. 137
NOURSE, I. J. 207
  Joel 91
  Naomi 91
NUZUM, Eliza 30
  Kitty 30
  William 30
NYE, Ada Miranda 146
  Caroline M. (COLSON) 138
  James 10
  Joel 114
  Julia 114
  Mary Ann 129
  Sarah A. 165
  Susan (LIVERMORE) 114
  Thankful 10
  Theron 138
  Thomas C. 52
O'BANNON, Elizabeth R. 167
  Nellie 177
  P. H. 167
  P. N. 177
O'CONNELL, Daniel 89
  James 89
O'NEIL, Allie (WARNER) 209
  John 209
OAKE, Alice 210
OATMAN, Aletta J. (ARNESON) 159
  Amanda 31
  David G. 159
  E. G. 31
OBERT, Anna Louise (WILLARD) 167
  Frederick J. 167
ODELL, Amanda J. 174
  Jacob 157
  Johnathan 181
  Mary (SHATTUCK) 181
  Mary Ann (KINNEY) 157
OGDEN, D. L. 216
  Nellie 166
OGILVIE, Frank 200
  Lillian M. (BUSH) 200
OLCOTT, Darwin N. 194
  Eliza 114

OLCOTT, J. S. 189
  Mary A. (LAW) 194
OLDS, --- (Rev.) 113, 114
OLENDORF, Caroline 128
  Charles W. 154
  Justine (PELLET) 154
OLIVER, Henry 99
OLMSTEAD, D. C. 198
  Freedom (Mrs.) 2
OLMSTED, Mary H. 34
OMANS, Elizabeth 129
  Merrill 100
  Sophia 208
  W. P. 208
OMENS, Jamesie Gates 52
OMSBY, Charles S. 178
  Fannie S. (BARDIN) 178
ONDERDONK, Andrew 53
  James 31
  Margaret 53
ORIDLEY, Wayne 132
ORMSBY, --- (Mrs.) 163
  Anna R. 118
  Byron J. 64, 167
  D. R. 198
  Daniel 12
  Hannah 12, 118
  James B. 64
  Jonathan 127
  Margaret (FOX) 127
  Mary L. 64
  Mary L. (ANTHONY) 167
  Tillie M. (BOYLER) 198
ORR, Alpha F. 208
  Eva E. (GREEN) 208
  Nellie 180
ORTON, Beulah 13
  Daborah C. 114
  J. R. 8, 9
  Julia M. (CLEAVELAND) 122
  Lyman P. 122
  Philo A. 55
  Sophronia 8
  Sophronia (HOTCHKISS) 9
  Thomas 13
ORVIS, Anet R. 175
  S. M. 69
  Timothy 69
OSBORN, --- (Dr.) 195, 201
  Amos O. 129

OSBORN, Charles L. 199
  DeWitt 184
  J. Wheeler 129
  Jemima 146
  Julia J. (BATES) 184
  Kittie A. 180
  L. M. 180, 181, 199
  Malintha Sophia (SHORT) 129
  Martha E. (SHEFFIELD) 199
  Minnie 201
  White 10
OSBORNE, Harvey 66
  Lucia M. 117
OSGOOD, Cornelia E. 127
  David 119, 176
  David (Mrs.) 46
  Edward N. 16
  Elizabeth 123
  Elmer H. 11
  Hawley 50
  Helen M. 132
  John Pierce 27
  Kittie 176
  L. M. 135
  Lucian H. 179
  Lucy (PRESTON) 119
  Lyman C. 8, 9
  Matilad 112
OSTERHOUT, Annie E. (BEMAN) 172
  J. V. 172
OSTROM, J. 32
  John 32
  Lydia (PADDLEFORD) 113
  Sarah Ann 32
  Stepehn 113
  Stephen 12
  W. A. 32
OTCOTT, Israel 113
  Loe (ADAMS) 113
OTIS, C. G. 118
  Charles G. 136
  Eliza 136
OTTAWAY, Caroline (CARTER) 217
  T. P. 217
OVERHISER, Mary (KING) 127
  Warren T. 127
OWEN, Abigail (LEACH) 125

OWEN, Betsey (DOTY) 115
 Charles F. 121
 Elijah 115
 Helen 145
 Ira C. 134
 J. R. 98
 Jason 125
 Jenette P. (BUEL) 134
 Mary (SQUIRES) 118
 Mary Ann W. 98
 Mary L. 132
 Sarah M. 154
 Stephen 118
 Susan Ann (HEWS) 121
OWENS, J. P. 157
 Sophronia M. (LEE) 157
PACKARD, Lysander 21
PACKER, Harriet L.
  (PUTNAM) 124
 William S. 124
PADDLEFORD, Lydia 113
PADDOCK, --- (Rev.) 116
 B. G. 120, 121, 122
 Eunice K. 92
 Hiram C. 92
 Lizzie L. (CRAINE) 203
 Lucy A. 210
 Mary 174
 William L. 203
PAGE, Caleb S. 162
 Katie (POTTER) 162
 Mary M. 77
PAINE, --- (Deacon) 70
 Amanda (KELLOGG) 114
 Elisha 1
 Ellen P. Barnett 70
 John A. 114
PALMER, --- (Mrs. Dr.) 103
 Addie R. (ELPHICK) 180
 Alice V. 57
 Almira 89
 Amanda 113
 B. 153
 Bela 53, 151
 Ceriza W. 130
 Charles W. 155
 DeEtte 169
 Devillo 183
 Hannah 2
 Hannah R. 82

PALMER, Harriet 36
 Harvey R. 91
 Henry S. 142
 Joseph 2
 Julius D. 52
 Kate (PUGH) 155
 Lilla (BATES) 183
 Lodema 124
 Lydia 2
 Margaret (GREEN) 113
 Maria 155
 Mary 123
 Mary C. 171
 Minnie F. 211
 Nathan 155
 Polly 113
 Rebecca 3
 Sanford D. 180
 Sarah P. (STILLMAN) 155
 Sheffield 113
 Susan M. (DANFORTH) 142
 Theresa 168
 W. L. 139
PALMETER, Phoebe C.
  (MAXSON) 139
 William M. 139
PALMITER, C. R. 74, 178
 D. S. 74
 Edna B. (BUCKLEY) 208
 Emily A. (CLARK) 38
 Etta C. 178
 Fannie A. 170
 George E. 38
 Harley 208
 Meck V. 74
 Nora A. 213
 Susan 129
PARDEE, Belle 92
 Isaac 76
PARKE, James 157
 Susie C. 77
PARKER, Charles 22
 Denas 74
 Eliab 217
 Genevieve H. (WHEELER)
  163
 George 66
 I. 156
 Jennie M. 184
 Jesse 24

PARKER, L. May 210
 Lois 4
 Louise 201
 Marcella W. 34
 Mary 24
 N. Wilson 163
 Rachel 215
 Sabrina Amelia 120, 121
 Sarah M. 154
 William L. 79
PARKHURST, George F. 100
 Wealthy A. 100
PARKS, --- (Rev. Mr.) 134
 Barney 96
 Eustice L. 171
 Henry 60
 Isaac 136
 Nancy 96
 Orrin 113
 Polly (PALMER) 113
 Smith 6
PARLER, Flora 205
PARLIN, Benjamin 13
 Evaline 13
 Merville H. 13
PARMALEE, James G. 18
PARMELE, J. B. (Mrs.) 89
PARMELEE, Angeline E. 124
 Helen M. 138
PARMELY, Cemantha J. 116
 Jared 1
PARR, --- (Rev. Mr.) 135
PARRY, John J. 28
 Sarah M. (WILBER) 28
PARSONS, Charlotte 140
 Delia A. 160
 John R. 202
 Viola E. (COOK) 202
PARTRIDGE, --- (Deacon) 61
 A. J. 112
 Arthur J. 184
 Charles A. 78
 Clara J. (QUAIL) 194
 Clarissa R. 61
 DeEtte O. 153
 Ella (NILES) 184
 Elmer J. 166
 George H. 194
 Harriet A. 213
 Mary (PIERCE) 166

PARTRIDGE, Orrin D. 213
PATRAGE, C. C. 177
 Hattie (MORY) 177
PATRICK, Lydia 134
PATRIDGE, Delia 178
PATTERSON, Adella 165
 C. V. 111
 C. Venton 186, 187
 C. Vinton 190
 C. Winton 107, 206
 Ella S. (TRACY) 206
 Ernestine R. (RICHMOND)
  197
 John G. 206
 W. H. 197
PAUL, Rudolphus 94
PAWLETT, Henry 120
 Julia O. (CLARK) 120
PAYNE, --- 42
 --- (Rev. Mr.) 174
 Augusta F. 185
 C. C. 64
 Charles C. 63
 Charles R. 77
 Electa 115
 Elisha 7, 9, 42
 Emily S. 151
 Esther 17
 John C. 5, 14
 Lizzie M. (BAYLISS) 209
 Mary E. 63
 Mary L. 189
 Philena M. 117
 S. 189
 Sophronia 96
 Stillman 76
 Willis 209
PAYSON, David F. 122
 E. H. 182
 Lucy 157
 Lucy A. (FITCH) 122
 Lutie 200
 Mary E. 13
 Ruth 27
 S. H. 200
PEARCE, Charles A. 18
PEARL, --- (Rev. Mr.) 125
 Charlotte 167
 Clara 33
 E. C. 22

PEARL, Erastus 33
  Hattie 33
  Marsha C. 65
PEARNE, T. H. 135
  W. H. 126, 127
PEASE, --- (Mr.) 1, 9
PEASLEE, I. D. 173, 174,
  175, 176, 177, 179, 181,
  198
PEASLEY, I. D. 198, 199,
  200, 201
  J. D. 170, 171
PEBBLES, Fedora M.
  (CURTIS) 165
  Henry 165
  Lucretia 92
PECK, A. 42
  Alonzo 80
  Andrew 124
  Cordelia C. (KENDRICK)
   135
  E. M. 182
  Elizabeth 42
  Josiah 16
  Linus M. 135
  Marcus C. 80
  Maria 5
  Nathan 5, 116
  Phebe (TOMPKINS) 116
  Sophia S. 118
  Sturges 3
PECKAM, Abbey 59
  Claud S. 54
  Eliza 54
  Job 1
  Samuel 59
  Sidney 54
PECKHAM, Abigail (BIGELOW)
   191
  Arowit 26
  Daniel S. 102
  David 128
  Della 70
  Fallie 71
  Frances Jane (GUTHRIE)
   128
  George 91
  George Washington 26
  Hamilton 87
  Hamistont 87

PECKHAM, Harriet 218
  Helen (MC GRAW) 158
  M. Louise 155
  Mary E. 157
  Millie A. 76
  Nettie C. 198
  O. 191
  Orson 70, 191
  Phebe A. 165
  Priscilla (SIMMONS) 129
  Roxana 161
  Samuel G. 158
  Sarah J. 26
  Spencer 129
PEDDIE, J. 160
PEEBLES, Annie E.
  (LONGLEY) 210
  Hubert J. 210
  N. M. 140
  Rebecca 34
PEET, E. 50
  H. I. 67
  Rosie 50
PEILTZ, Daniel 213
  Fanny (LONIS) 213
PELLET, H. N. 122
  Justine 154
  Malvina (BOWEN) 122
  Solander 157
PENCE, Ellen E. 176
PENDLETON, Benjamin F. 128
  Delia A. (JONES) 128
  William H. 172
PENDOCK, John 62
  Julia 211
  Roxey 137
PENNOCK, Eliza (BROWN) 206
  M. S. 206
PENNY, Giles A. 152
  Phebe L. (CLARK) 152
PERCIVAL, J. K. 96
  Mortimer W. 10
PERDY, Ella A. (WILCOX)
   174
  Heamon 174
PERKINS, --- (Rev. Mr.)
   139
  --- (Rev.) 139
  A. 137, 138, 140, 141,
   155

PERKINS, Alice C.
  (KINGSLEY) 60, 178
 Charles H. 60, 170
 Clara 214
 E. 159
 Eli 60
 Frank 190
 G. H. 174
 Harvey J. 80
 Leverett 84
 Leveritt 176
 Lewis 149
 Lydia (LEWIS) 114
 Mary (DAVIS) 176
 Polly 157
 Rispy P. 149
 Thomas 114
PERRIOR, --- (Mrs.) 44
PERRY, Achsah (NILES) 173
 David 92
 Emma L. (WAITE) 213
 Eugene A. 173
 George 214
 George P. 213
 Horace 40
 Josiah 214
 Lucinda 92
 Lyman 43
 Maria 43
 Myron 149
 Owen F. 213
PETERSON, Ada O. 70
 Charles A. 177
 Ella (BRIGGS) 177
PETLEY, William 19
PETRIE, Araminta 23
 Hiram A. 23
PETTEN, Mary 114
PETTER, Alice 213
PETTIS, Albert M. 137
 Sarah A. (CRANDALL) 137
PETTIT, Solander 159
PEVIE, Jane E. 165
PHELPS, George 93
 Isaac 62
 Jacob 217
 Marietta 217
 Phebe A. 151
PHERIS, Ellen E.
  (STARKWEATHER) 184

PHERIS, Joseph M. 184
PHILLIPS, --- (Rev. Dr.)
 119
 --- (Rev. Mr.) 145
 Alseba 166
 Ambrose 76, 145
 Eleanor 70
 Elisha 121
 Ella V. (HOWES) 182
 Ellen 91
 Ellis Smith 75
 George B. 93
 Hannah V. (TURTON) 119
 Harry S. 93
 Hattie E. (HOLMES) 153
 John H. 93
 K. G. 182
 Lucy (HUGHES) 121
 Lucy M. (BROWN) 145
 Marcus T. 153
 O. G. H. 207, 208, 213
 Reuben 1
PHILPOT, E. C. 111, 203
 Etta A. 184
 Libbie (CRITCHEL) 203
PHINEY, Sally 118
PHINNEY, Anna E. (DAHN)
 213
 Lewis M. 213
PIERCE, A. A. 152, 204
 Abbie 169
 Adell R. 177
 Albert 34, 81
 Alice R. (TUTTLE) 197
 Betsey 118
 Catherine 15
 Chloe (WILCOX) 134
 Clara A. (SMITH) 181
 Cornelia M. (COBB) 129
 Cynthia L. 181
 David R. 68
 Deyer E. 121
 Elizabeth B. 46
 Ella A. 180
 Fannie (CROSS) 197
 Francis T. 152
 Frank T. 68
 George D. 15
 H. N. 181
 Hannah 113

PIERCE, Horace 27, 121
 Ira 172
 J. O. 134
 J. Osgood 129
 J. S. 165
 J. Smith 88
 John H. 197
 Jonathan O. 12
 Joshua 15
 Julia A. 182
 Juline 74, 196
 Lamott L. 197
 Leonard 158
 Lewis 112
 Louisa (BURCHARD) 152
 Louise (BURCHARD) 68
 Lucinda 34
 Lucinda (MOTT) 152
 M. E. 197
 M. Irene 156
 Martha 12
 Mary 84, 115, 166
 Mary E. (PYNE) 175
 Mary J. (ACKET) 121
 Nancy (BARTON) 112
 Nathaniel 43
 Nellie E. (HANNA) 165
 Orren P. 175
 R. (Mrs. Dr.) 184
 Rachel Maria 172
 Rachel Maria (PIERCE) 172
 Richie 34
PIERSON, Charles E. 72
 Henry 72
PIKE, William 148
PINCKNEY, Charles 3
PINKERTON, Maria E. 141
PIPER, Mary 217
PLATT, --- (Rev. Mr.) 123, 129, 145
 --- (Rev.) 122
 Frances Degrass (COLLISTER) 132
 M. 124
 M. S. 131, 132, 135, 146, 147, 150, 151, 152, 153, 155, 156, 160
PLIMBLEY, Thomas 20
PLIMPTON, Mary (ELMORE) 132

PLIMPTON, Stephen H. 132
PLUM, William M. 150
PLUMB, Albert B. 202
 Lura (THAYER) 202
PLUMBLEY, Charles D. 156
 Sarah C. (LAY) 156
PLUMBLY, Helen 139
POGSON, Sarah 113
POLLARD, Hannah M. 82
POND, Alanson P. 34
 Ann (HURD) 122
 Eli 34, 77, 163
 George 122
 Margaret 205
 Thomas Hart 132
PONE, Eleanora G. (FENTON) 132
POOL, Abijah 1
 Horace 84
 Isaac 5
 Lydia Florilla 131
 Matilda 5
 Polly 48
 Thaxter 48
POOLE, B. H. (BOON) 118
 Frank E. 157
 Hartley 157
 James 118
 Joseph 88
 Sarah (WILLIAMSON) 157
 Thaxter 88
POOTE, William 4
POPE, --- (Rev. Dr.) 158
 Anna P. (RUNDELL) 204
 Dennis A. 204
 Jedediah 12
 Susannah 12
POPLETON, Estella M. 207
POPPLETON, Maude E. 213
PORTER, --- (Rev. Dr.) 189
 Daniel S. 192
 Emma A. (CADWELL) 192
 G. J. 197
 Harriet 220
 Leafy 54
 Leroy 54
 Orlando 54
POSSEE, Carrie A. (HUGHES) 199
 George S. 199

POST, Adelaide S. 72
  C. P. 142
  Charles B. 130
  Ira H. 72
  Mary Ann (SIMONS) 130
  Minerva 168
  Virginia 177
POTHICARY, Betsey (PIERCE) 118
  Thomas 118
POTTER, --- (Rev.) 112, 113
  Ann 93
  C. R. 30
  D. C. 105, 107
  David 214
  Elizabeth 182
  Frederick A. 100
  Hattie M. 177
  J. 154
  Job 136, 137, 138, 139, 148
  John 93
  Katie 162
  M. S. 160
  Mary 105
  Sarah 30
  Stephen 217
POTTS, Julia G. 201
POWELL, --- (Elder) 114
  Alice (OAKE) 210
  Cornelia 34
  Elias 210
  Mary 77
POWER, Theodosia 70
POWERS, Caroline 98
  Charles R. 107
  Diana 80
  Esther A. 105
  Eva A. (SAWYER) 175
  Gilbert 105
  H. Q. 86
  Harvey 80
  Henry 80, 86, 89, 157, 159
  Judson L. 175
  N. S. 80
  Nancy 89
  Silas 80
  Sophia M. 134

PRATT, --- (Rev. Mr.) 120
  Caroline L. 133
  Cornelia R. 148
  Emeline (FRINK) 183
  George 183
  Harriet 112
  Milo 16
  Rachel 16
  Sabrina 57
  Seva 57
PRENTICE, A. M. 67, 174, 182
  Genevieve W. 67
  Harriet A. 65
  Harriet A. (CALKINS) 132
  Jennie (WHITTEMORE) 183
  Jennie A. 163
  Lucy (NEWELL) 189
  R. R. 60, 65, 156, 163, 172, 176, 182, 189
  Roswell R. 132
  Sarah (YORK) 60
PRENTISS, Jane 125
  Margaret 127
PRESCOTT, A. 172
  Elizabeth C. (SMITH) 189
  Oliver B. 189
PRESTON, --- (Dr.) 94
  Arthur M. 203
  Elizabeth 94
  Harriet 61
  Irvin J. 174
  J. D. 168
  Lucy 119
  Nelson S. 54
  Nettie E. (CROMMIE) 174
  Nettie L. (BABCOCK) 203
  Theresa (PALMER) 168
  William 61
  Wilmina 54
PRICE, Cornelia (BAKER) 165
  Edward W. 165
  Richard 71
PRINCE, Jonathan 117
  Nancy (MILLER) 117
PRISER, A. H. 206
PRITCHETT, E. C. 216
PROAL, --- (Rev. Dr.) 126, 128

PROBERT, Finnett 121
  James 121
PROCTOR, Grace (HOLMES) 180
  William 180
PUDNEY, Nellie D. 103
PUGH, Kate 155
PULVER, George 171
  H. Adella 198
  Lucena C. (WELCH) 171
  Peter 198
PURRINGTON, --- (Rev. Mr.) 196
  W. F. 199
  W. S. 196
PUTNAM, --- (Elder) 137
  Benjamin 122, 124
  Daniel 50
  Elijah 22
  Gertie 196
  Harriet L. 124
  J. H. 189
  James 34, 141
  John 22
  Lucy (LILLIE) 141
  Phebe 22
PUTNEY, Celia M. 159
  Hannah L. 156
PYNE, --- (Rev. Mr.) 178, 179
  H. R. 177
  Lucy 89
  Mary E. 175
  Sarah 192
QUAIL, Clara J. 194
QUICK, Peter S. 41
QUINCEY, Ida E. 75
  W. J. 75
QUIVEY, Byron F. 78
RACE, Ruth 94
RAILEY, Lydia 178
RALPH, Chloe 192
  William 107
RAMPTON, Sarah 169
RAMSDELL, Ellen 189
  Mary E. 151
  Ransom 62
  Silas 151
RANDALL, Amelia B. 119
  Charles 56, 119, 136

RANDALL, D. A. 169
  Ede Maria 56
  Ida May 92
  Lurensa (NEWTON) 126
  Polly P. 77
  Roswell A. 126
  Sands H. 92
  W. H. 145
RANDOLPH, R. F. 57
RANGER, H. P. 46, 161
  John T. 46
  L. Maryette 161
RANKIN, D. M. 190
RANKINS, Aaron 120
  Sarah G. (SIMMONS) 120
RANNEY, Elmora M. 190
  Ores 190
RANSOM, --- (Rev.) 129
  D. 131
  David 21
  R. M. (Mrs.) 21
  Rebecca 162
  Rosina (TOWN) 131
RATNOUR, Larny 113
RAWSON, G. A. 194, 196
RAY, Anna 105
  Betsey 124
  Ella A. (PIERCE) 180
  Franklin L. 126
  George W. 180
  Louisa 35
  Louise M. (WHEELER) 206
  Mary H. 131
  Samuel 206
  William 105
RAYLOR, Rosall 164
RAYMOND, Eliakim 125
  Mary A. 125
  R. R. 125
READ, Daniel 44, 81, 170
  Harriet 186
  Louisa M. 170
  Mary E. 182
  Mary P. 55
  Nettie 44
RECTOR, Elizabeth (DENNIS) 218
  Ellen 218
REDFIELD, Emiline (SHAPLEY) 46

REDFIELD, H. A. 131
  H. S. 46, 166
REED, Catherine (WEAVER) 115
  Charlotte M. 176
  Conrad 115
  D. 81
  D. E. 176
  E. D. 133, 137, 165, 170, 178, 188, 199
  E. E. 197
  E. G. 173
  Louise M. 81
  Norton J. 91
  Sarah S. 139
REESE, Anna 65
  Annie D. 195
  Jacob G. 159
  Orcelia (MILLER) 159
  Otto 64
  Rebecca 194
REEVE, Tapping 2
REMINGTON, Cecelia (MERCHANT) 218
  George 218
  J. C. 85
REXFORD, --- (Rev.) 113
  Daniel A. 95
  Fannie M. (LINCOLN) 95
REYNOLDS, A. Edward 160
  Albert N. 196
  Anna 187
  Benjamin F. 143
  Byron H. 79
  Elivra C. 196
  Ella C. 175
  Emily E. (BENNETT) 157
  Ernest 207
  Franc M. (BANCROFT) 160
  Franklin B. 182
  Hannah D. (FARNIUM) 182
  James (Mrs.) 99
  John W. 36
  Lucetta (SHERMAN) 143
  Lucy 193
  Lucy (LAMB) 207
  Maggie (RICHMOND) 179
  Niles 179
  Thankful 119
  Wilson A. 157

RHODES, Anna F. (BOSWORTH) 201
  Benjamin F. 72
  Betsey 28
  C. A. (Mrs.) 39
  C. F. (Mrs.) 99
  Christina 37
  Clarence J. 44
  Columbus 89
  Columbus F. 38
  Della C. 182
  Ella 38
  Ellen 38
  Frances A. 17
  Frances Ann 32
  Frances Josephine 17
  Frances W. 32
  George M. 39, 182
  Hamilton 166
  J. P. 17, 32, 160
  Lewis 89
  Mary E. 167
  Mattie (BRONSON) 201
  Nellie (OGDEN) 166
  Orlando Lavell 39
  Sarah A. (WAKELEY) 160
  U. N. 145
  Uri 201
  Uri N. 138
  William 28
  William A. 201
RICE, A. B. 191
  A. C. 75, 106, 107
  Arthur C. 188
  Baxter 39
  Carlton 167
  Cora G. 37
  DeEtte (MAXON) 168
  DeWitt 206
  Ella (LOOMIS) 191
  Ella A. 183
  Ella L. (WILLIAMS) 188
  Emma J. 167, 182
  F. G. 168, 177
  Frank M. 151
  George W. 168
  Harmony (WIGHT) 39
  J. A. 191
  Lelia 206
  Lois (MOORE) 168

RICE, Nellie (O'BANNON) 177
W. H. 217
Warren 37
RICH, Alida M. (THROOP) 195
Charles W. 195
Elizabeth 119
Harvey B. 21
Mary (HOLMAN/HOLZMAN) 186
William 186
RICHARDS, --- (Rev. Mr.) 155
Daniel J. 46
Lucinda 187
Mary 46, 93
Mary Ella 199
Sarah E. 150
Sybil Smith 146
RICHARDSON, A. A. 160
A. C. 168
Adell 195
Almor 118
Benjamin (Mrs.) 95
Jennie E. 180
Lou (BUTTON) 168
Maria E. (PINKERTON) 141
Maria L. 136
Mary (TURNER) 118
Nettie (ISBELL) 160
Nettie E. 175
Polly 58
Thomas M. 141
William 161
RICHMOND, D. 139
Damon 18
David 69
E. A. (HOAG) 184
Edward 134
Elizabeth (BRAINARD) 134
Ernestine R. 197
Florence A. 162
Frankie L. 33
Helen L. 181
Joel C. 29
Julia A. 18
Julia Ann 69
Kezia 19
L. L. 97
Lewis L. 150

RICHMOND, M. I. B. 184
Maggie 179
Mary 55
Mary E. (LASELLE) 150
T. H. 54
RICKARD, Abram L. 208
Jennie M. (BROTLE) 208
RIDDLE, R. R. 195
RIDDLEBARGER, M. 138
Sarah A. (FINCH) 138
RIDER, George L. 28
RIGBY, Betsey (RAY) 124
David 124
RIGGAL, Adella (PATTERSON) 165
Thomas 165
RINGGE, Isaac H. 169
Kittie (NIEDOCK) 169
RINGLEKA, Cordelia 158
RIPLEY, Lucemia M. (SPENCER) 138
Merrill W. 138
RISLEY, --- (Mrs.) 98
Ada (CRANDALL) 194
Allen 37
Amelia 43
B. F. 98
Byron 106
C. F. (Mrs.) 52
Charles 37
Chester C. 38, 53
Clarence 203
Cyrus 9
Edwin H. 160
Elizabeth M. (WOODMAN) 196
Elizur 43
Evanna (GREEN) 137
Flora A. 156
G. F. 137
Hattie A. (METCALF) 160
Henry 110
Henry D. 196
Ida B. 195
Josephine 175
Julius 87, 125
Leonard L. 29
M. F. (Mrs.) 99
May (COREY) 203
Mercell D. 152

RISLEY, Nora H. 53
  Olive (DIX) 125
  Romaine 194
  Sarah 53
  Sherman 37
  Sylvester 34
ROACHE, Mina V. 204
ROANTREE, Carrie (FOX) 184
  J. 184
ROBBINS, Electa 133
  Simon 133
ROBERTS, Angeline
    (JACKSON) 156
  Christine 202
  Mary Jane 6
  Mary Libbie (KENYON) 193
  Nathan S. 6
  Robert W. 193
  William 156
ROBIE, G. W. 141
  Harry 71
ROBINSON, --- (Rev.) 112, 123
  Anna 26
  Clara E. 35
  Harriet Ann 129
  Jennie 198
  Sarah (POTTER) 30
  Theophilus 26
ROCKWELL, John 157
  Lucy (PAYSON) 157
ROGERS, --- (Rev. Mr.) 140
  Amanda 125
  Amrylis T. 159
  Caroline 46
  H. M. 179
  Hannah 78
  Harriet 123, 188
  Hattie (KNOWLTON) 209
  Horatio 188
  Josephine 45
  Josiah 14
  Julia G. 201
  L. C. 147
  Leander A. 209
  Lydia G. 159
  Lyman 46
  Medad 39, 70, 123
  Mulford 23, 53
  Mulford (Mrs.) 78

ROGERS, Orlo 201
  Rufus 11
  Theodosia (POWER) 70
  Timothy 14, 39
  W. G. 208, 209
ROLLER, Edith (BALLOU) 47
  W. 47
ROLLINS, Clara 63
  H. O. 191
  Hattie J. (JAQUAY) 195
  Helen (UNDERHILL) 191
  J. Byron 195
  Oriana 82
  W. R. 191
RONNEY, William 74
ROOF, Daniel 114
  Mary (PETTEN) 114
ROOT, A. F. 111
  A. R. 106
  Alfred E. 212
  Beatrice K. (WALRATH) 212
  C. M. (Mrs.) 86
  Clara 80
  Clara E. (SIMPSON) 185
  Cora 79
  Elmer 109
  F. J. 111
  F. W. 67, 77, 173
  Frank J. 80, 185
  Frankie 147
  J. Rollin 6
  James W. 86
  Jennie S. 192
  Joshua 205
  Louisa D. 77
  Lulu 205
  Lyman M. 12
  Lyman N. 101, 135
  Mary E. 173
  Pheba 12
  Pheba Jane (GUERNSEY) 135
  Solomon 12, 79
  Susanna 12
RORABACK, Alvah B. 206
  Kate (METTLER) 206
ROSE, A. T. 154
  Mary (CAMPBELL) 154
  Mary (NORRIS) 135
  Mary E. (MORRIS) 119
  O. J. 188

ROSE, Samuel 119
  Samuel L. 135
ROSS, George 111
  Jennie M. 189
  John S. 140
  Josephine C. (COLSON) 140
ROTH, William (Mrs.) 97
ROWAN, James 61
ROWE, Abigail 152
  Mary 100
  Stephen 8
ROWELL, Amasa 35, 134
  Caroline D. 134
  Catherine G. 134
  Eli 29
  John 40
  Olivia (WEST) 89
ROWLAND, Eliza 161
ROWLANDS, Lizzie 81
  Lizzie A. 189
  Mary 81, 83
  Mary Jane 83
  Matilda 78
  O. W. 83
  W. O. 81
  W. R. 108
ROWLEY, Fred 209
  Hattie E. (MASON) 209
ROWLINGON, Adaliza A.
  (BROWN) 140
ROWLINGS, Mary Jane 145
ROWLINSON, N. H. 140
ROZELL, David R. 146
  Sophia J. 146
RUDD, G. R. 146
RUGER, William 8
RUGG, Adelbert 188
  Lille A. (MOSELEY) 191
  Martin L. 191
  Mary (MINER) 188
RUGGLES, Henry E. 136
  Julia Ann (BIERCE) 136
RUNDELL, Abel 77, 171
  Anna P. 204
  Cyrus 90
  Janet 171
  Nellie 208
RUSHMER, Thomas 200
RUSS, Annette L. (BABCOCK) 153

RUSS, John W. 153
RUSSELL, --- (Rev. Mr.) 184
  A. M. 157
  Calista 50
  Catherine 137
  Charles S. 73
  Clarissa (BIRDSLEY) 122
  F. M. (Mrs.) 174
  Francella M. (FELT) 164
  G. W. 73
  Helen A. (MILLS) 193
  Henry 37
  J. Thomas 40
  James 71
  Jane M. 150
  Jennie 32
  Lewis 193
  M. L. 32
  Mary 135
  Mary C. 167
  Mary S. 10
  Milo 109, 110
  Polly 36
  Prudence L. 50
  S. M. 32
  Samuel P. 122, 193
  Wells C. 75
  William J. 164
RUTAN, Enos W. 209
  Nellie (ELWELL) 209
RYAN, Edward F. 153
  James 88
  Julis 88
  Sarah E. (LOWE) 153
SACKETT, Calphurnia
  (GARRETT) 140
  Liester 140
  Philo 51
  S. W. 51
SAGE, J. H. 212
  James H. 163, 166
SAGENDORF, Lulu A. 210
SAGER, Sybil 47
SALEY, Arthur Leon 60
  E. S. (Mrs.) 70
  Emma J. 61
  M. L. 61, 70
SALISBURY, Ann (MEDBURY) 38

SALISBURY, Franklin W. 38
  Mary (CURTIS) 202
  Seleria E. 157
  William 202
SAMPSON, Caroline E. 145
  Mary J. 82
SANDERS, Ellen A.
    (HUBBARD) 169
  Francis M. 169
SANDERSON, Amelia 149
  Luther 208
SANFORD, A. 77
  Abel 10
  Abram 21
  B. F. 180
  Beardsley 9
  Clara 77
  David L. 9
  Frank F. 212
  Harriet 17
  Harriet L. 141
  Harriet L. (CHATFIELD) 130
  Helen T. (KINGSLEY) 212
  James Fenner 37
  Joseph 7
  Joseph H. 161
  Judson 17, 130
  Libbie E. (BROWN) 180
  Martha A. 12
  Mary 21
  Mary E. 177
  Meroa C. (BRIGGS) 161
  Miles 142
  Patience 23, 53
  Sarah 76
SAULSBURY, --- (Pastor) 187
SAUNDERS, Clarissa 138
  Esther (ELLIS) 137
  Lida (SHERMAN) 200
  Lydia 91
  Mary 149
  Mary A. 153
  Peleg 137
  Phebe M. 131
  William P. 200
SAVAGE, Emma (GREENMAN) 148
  Enoch L. 69

SAVAGE, George E. 148
  Richard 106
SAWDEY, A. M. (SEELEY) 171
  Alburtus 171
  Andrew J. 27
  Betsey 46
  Calvin W. 46
  Charles W. 129
  Eldora E. 46
  Emily R. (BENEDICT) 129
  Emogene C. 152
  M. W. 62
  Sherman 152
SAWDY, B. W. 200
  Calvin W. 83
  Carrie 202
  Deborah S. (FULLER) 143
  Eli W. (Mrs.) 47
  J. C. 110
  Mary A. 143
  Orsemus 143
SAWYER, B. F. 175
  Eva A. 175
  Sarah A. 213
SAYES, S. (Mrs.) 176
SCARRITT, Almeda C.
    (TACKABERRY) 142
  James M. 142
SCHAFFER, Jacob 44
SCHEMERHORNE, James 154
  Sarah M. (PARKER) 154
SCHENCK, Hannah
    (HARTSHORN) 198
  Marcus P. 198
SCHERMERHORN, Francella A. 28
  Homer 28
  Mary 28
SCHOFIELD, --- (Rev. Mr.) 137
SCHRODER, Mary E. (HENRY) 190
  William H. 190
SCOFIELD, --- (Rev. Mr.) 125, 129
  --- (Rev.) 142
  A. 134, 155, 156
SCOTT, Alice May 208
  E. A. (Mrs.) 51
  G. D. 51

SCOTT, George 82, 107
  George Dorrance 176
  H. D. 164
  Ida L. 187
  Kittie (OSGOOD) 176
  L. M. (MASON) 164
SCOVAL, M. A. (THOMPSON)
  183
  M. D. 183
SCOVILLE, Elva M.
  (SEVERANCE) 88
  S. 156
  Samuel 173
  W. N. 88
SCRANTON, Cornelia 124
  S. E. 192
SCUDDER, --- (Rev. Dr.)
  162
SEABURY, George L. 70
SEARS, Hiram 137
  Mary A. (GATES) 137
  Mary E. 144, 155
SEATON, Maria (SHARTS) 153
  Nelson J. 153
SEBRING, E. N. 210
SEDGWICK, --- (Rev. Mr.)
  139
  A. 137, 139, 141
  H. 140
SEELEY, A. M. 171
  Carrie C. 205
  Ernest 79
  Ida M. 182
  Mattie S. (CHASE) 79
  Miriam C. 170
SEGAR, Charle 210
  Lulu A. (SAGENDORF) 210
SELFE, Rose 194
  Samuel 194
SERGANT, Jay D. 203
  Nettie (BLAIR) 203
SERGEANT, Alvin D. 149
  Cordelia E. (CORBIN) 149
SERVERANCE, Elva M. 88
SETON, Calista 40
  George R. 40
  Linn 40
SEVERANCE, James 88
  Katie 196
SEWELL, Cora E. (WOOD) 198

SEWELL, William D. 198
SEXTON, Pliny 1
SEYMOUR, Achsah
  (WELLINGTON) 53
  Addison 176
  Alfred 16, 34
  Caroline 145
  Edith M. 161
  Eleazer 29
  Elizur 53
  Ellen E. (PENCE) 176
  Freddie Lincoln 34
  Hannah 144, 155
  Melona 99
  Miranda 99
  Rhoda 16, 34
  Robert G. 198
  Silas 27
SHAFFER, Philip 41
SHANNON, Margaret 75
  William 75
SHAPLEY, Abigail C. 140
  Betsey (WHEELER) 119
  Chloe (BUDLONG) 114
  Daniel 114
  Daniel B. 135
  David 154
  David A. 127
  Dora C. (STEWART) 163
  Dunham 28
  Elnora 135
  Emiline 46
  H. B. 140
  Hannah 154
  Hannah (WILLARD) 127
  I. A. 17
  Johnson 119
  Julia H. 169
  Lewis 83
  Rebecca 76
  Sally (BELDEN) 28
  Spencer B. 163
SHARMAN, Daniel D. 191
  Lizzie G. (THOMPSON) 191
SHARP, Samuel T. 76
  Sarah A. 161
SHARTS, B. W. 150
  D. W. 153
  Hobart E. 35
  M. 52

SHARTS, Malachi 84
  Maria 153
  Sarah A. (WELTON) 52
SHATTUCK, Mary 181
SHAUL, Andrew J. 194
  May E. (BAKER) 194
SHAW, --- (Rev. Mr.) 186
  --- (Rev.) 113
  Cyrus 155
  Harriet 69
  L. Jane (MERRITT) 143
  Levi 141
  Lucina (WALDEN) 141
  Martin K. 143
  Mary E. (SPRAGUE) 146
  Sally 113
  Sarah J. 155
  William W. 146
SHEAD, Frances A.
   (WILLARD) 210
  Horace 210
SHEFFIELD, Joseph W. 145
  Marthe E. 199
  Sarah A. 145
SHELDON, --- (Rev. Mr.)
   132, 134
  --- (Rev.) 164
  A. N. 84
  Ada A. 201
  Albert N. 129
  Anna Maria (ALDRICH) 149
  C. P. 131, 132, 133, 143,
   144, 145, 146, 178, 179
  Charlotte A. (COLE) 132
  Clesson P. 131
  Frances E. (LADD) 129
  Frances Elizabeth (LADD)
   84
  Jennie C. 208
  Laura A. 120
  Lydia Ann (BURCHARD) 128
  O. M. 128
  William W. 149
SHELTON, Julia A. 201
SHEPARD, Aaron 122
  Caroline (OLENDORF) 128
  E. Ann 122
  Esther 52
  Harriet 130
  Harriet (READ) 186

SHEPARD, Juliaett A. 5
  Levi 44, 128
  Lyman G. 210
  Thomas 186
  Vincent 5
  William 44
SHEPARDSON, A. Coleson 186
  Gertie M. 203
  J. E. 174
  Jennie E. (NICHOLS) 174
  Mary (CUTLER) 186
  Nellie 186
SHEPPARD, Alonzo 99
  Cynthia (HUNT) 99
SHERILL, S. R. 59
SHERMAN, Alida 73
  Charles F. 194
  Elvina (KIMBALL) 170
  Fannie L. (HOLMES) 194
  George 170
  Glicera L. 156
  Hattie 73
  Henry L. 53
  John 73
  Lida 200
  Lucetta 143
  O. Sophia 143
  Palmer 72
  Samuel 12, 19
  William 43
SHERRILL, Achsa M. 98
  Achsa M. (NILES) 126, 128
  Alice Aletta 19
  Caroline E. 19
  Caroline E. (HUNT) 22
  Charles E. 126, 128
  David H. 19, 22
  Edwin B. 162
  Eliakim 119
  Emily E. (ELDREDGE) 119
  Florence A. (RICHMOND)
   162
  H. J. 59
  Nancy 35
  Rebecca (SHAPLEY) 76
  S. R. 35
  S. R. (Mrs.) 59
SHERWIN, John 218
  John F. 129
  Mahrion (GREEN) 129

SHERWIN, Susannah 218
SHERWOOD, Abbey 127
  Caroline (ELDREDGE) 132
  Elsie 11
  Francis S. 8, 9
  Isaac 217
  L. 8, 9
  Lorenzo 11, 132
  Sephen 217
SHIPMAN, E. D. 179
  Emergene (BEACH) 123
  Gussie A. (WALES) 179
  Ira 123
  L. (Mrs.) 92
SHIRLEY, Mittie L. (LA MUNION) 160
  William 160
SHIRSPELL, Walter 192
SHOLES, Betsey 83
  H. G. 66
  Horatio G. 83
  Ida May 83
  Mary 66
  Nelson F. 83
SHORES, Angeline 25
  Harriet Roselthia 25
  James W. 25
  Laura 62
  Mary 9
  Zepheniah 9
SHORT, Fred 180
  Harmon 73
  J. L. (Mrs.) 72
  Libbie H. 157
  Lucy 73
  Lucy A. 129
  Malintha Sophia 129
  Martha A. (COLE) 150
  Myra (FINNEY) 180
  N. H. 150
SHOTWELL, S. 129
  S. R. 125
  Samuel R. 125
SHUFFER, Idella 88
SHULTS, Edward S. 210
  Flora B. (NEGUS) 210
SIMMONS, Adda L. (MERRITT) 152
  Alfred 82
  Amanda 85, 137

SIMMONS, Amanda P. 146
  C. H. 109
  Calista 122
  Carrie (FELT) 189
  Charles 76
  Clara 76
  Cornelius 18, 122
  Emily Maria 142
  Emma 76
  Franklin A. 152
  George B. 194
  Gerrit S. 152
  Gideon D. 82
  Hannah 117, 129
  Isaac 56
  J. P. 135
  Janette 199
  Jennie L. (BROWNELL) 188
  Julia T. 56
  Lucinda H. 13
  Mary 144, 147
  Mercell D. (RISLEY) 152
  Olivia F. 209
  Otis 85, 88
  Otis T. 189
  Priscilla 129
  Rhoda 89
  Sarah G. 120
  Susan 82
  Walter 13
  William C. 187
  Zara 4, 89
  Zarah 117, 199
SIMON, Ellen M. (VAN DEUSEN) 156
  Richard 156
SIMONS, A. 168
  Augustus 142
  Benjamin 81
  Burdett J. 167
  Deette (CADY) 167
  E. C. 193
  Frances A. 169
  G. B. 194
  G. R. 106
  George 219
  George B. 195
  Mary Ann 130
  Otis 73
  Phebe 73

SIMONS, Rhoda 194
  Zarah 169, 194
SIMPSON, --- (Rev. Mr.)
  180
  Charles 185
  Clara E. 185
  Cora E. (FLEMING) 178
  Eliza C. 69
  Hattie T. 202
  John B. 34
  R. A. 178
  Sorannius 69
SINTON, Myrta 196
SISSON, Benjamin G. 212
  E. P. 109, 111
  Eugene P. 171, 197
  Jennie A. (BUELL) 197
  Mary A. 88
  Mary A. (WICKWIRE) 171
  Mary O. A. (WOODS) 212
SIZER, Asa B. 2
  Mae (HOWES) 198
  Samuel 2
  Wells B. 198
SKEELS, Almeda 113
SKELLENGER, Lucy 166
SKINNER, Amarantha
  (MILLER) 128
  Amarintha 144
  Amarintha (MILLER) 126
  Asahel 55
  B. F. 122
  D. W. 162, 165, 180, 181,
    186, 189
  Eliza C. (WOODMAN) 151
  Eliza G. (BLISH) 122
  George W. 151
  Giles 102
  H. F. 141
  Isaac 126, 128
  Jonathan 116
  Mary M. 162
  Melinda 116
  Orra S. (TORREY) 141
  Phebe 165
  Warren A. 126, 128
SLACK, George R. 202
  Sarah E. (WATERSON) 202
SLATER, Addie E. (WATERS)
  153

SLATER, Edwin R. 153
  Sarah B. 181
  Silas Seymour 27
SLAUGH, J. E. 194
  Nellie D. (COMAN) 194
SLAUGHT, --- (Dr.) 87
  J. E. 110
  Louisa C. 87
SLAWSON, A. L. 164
  Hattie (WALDRON) 164
SLAYTON, Ruth G. 194
SLOAN, Andrew S. 10
SLOANE, A. Scott 135
SLOCUM, Alfred 119
  Alfred G. 86
  Alfred W. 107, 187
  Amelia B. (RANDALL) 119
  Elijah 113
  Eliza Ann 131
  Eliza Ann (SMITH) 113
  H. E. 57
  Katie A. (THOMPSON) 187
  Olive (FISK) 175
  Othinal 33
  Peleg 95
  Philip C. 43
  Wilson 175
SLOSSON, Enoch 4
SMALLEY, Philena M.
  (PAYNE) 117
  Seth 117
SMATHEREST, Richard 61
SMITH, --- (Col.) 27
  --- (Rev. Mr.) 131
  A. C. 167, 173, 210
  A. J. 109
  A. W. (Mrs.) 80
  Adelaide G. (BROOKS) 179
  Adon 20, 52, 59, 91, 171,
    176, 220
  Adon N. 91, 106, 185
  Alcesta (LEWIS) 171
  Alexander 193
  Almira 118
  Alvin 90
  Anna 1
  Anna Norris 52
  Annie 205
  Augusta S. 196
  C. A. 90, 210

SMITH, C. C. 171
C. P. 147
C. W. 194
Caroline M. 122
Charles 3, 33, 121
Charles C. 102
Charles H. 101
Charlse H. 140
Chauncey D. 184
Chauncey S. 122
Christopher E. 137
Clara A. 181
Clarissa B. 36
Cora (WESTCOTT) 200
D. W. 126
Daniel 3
David M. 49
David N. 178
Della 199
Dwight 57
E. Caroline 7
E. L. (Mrs.) 38
E. P. 66, 181, 183
Ebenezer 123
Edwin 71
Edwin D. 20
Elijah 124
Eliza (LOWE) 167
Eliza Ann 113
Elizabeth C. 189
Elizabeth M. 152
Ella J. 91
Ella J. (TOMPKINS) 185
Ellen L. 141
Emily 49
Emily C. 134
Emma 167
Emma G. (HALL) 197
Emma I. 47
Emma J. 47
Estelle (LEACH) 197
Fanny 217
Franc A. 177
Frank 68
Frank H. 64
Frank L. 197
Freddie 52
George 146, 151, 200
George A. 187
George F. 123

SMITH, George W. 199
H. A. 38, 150, 171
Hannah 71
Harriet A. 146
Harvey 55
Hattie (SQUIRES) 184
Helen T. 171
Henry C. 72, 101
Homer L. 66
Howard 55
Hyleman 17
J. D. F. 68
J. Morgan 182
J. Moss 179
J. Sterling 151, 157
Jesse L. 204
John 36, 51, 110
John W. 58
Joseph A. 81
Joseph Sterling 74
Josephine E. (WAKELEE) 149
Judson 149
Julia Ann 136
Keturah 17
Leroy 36
Libbie M. 213
Louise 38
Louise J. (BAUMES) 140
Lucinda 3
Lucius 32
Lydia (RAILEY) 178
M. A. (Mrs.) 48
M. W. 16
Malvina W. 206
Marcella E. 137
Marcella E. (SMITH) 137
Margaret 90
Martha (EVERETS) 20
Mary 72, 117, 147, 181
Mary A. 123
Mary A. (SMITH) 123
Mary Ann 36, 121
Mary Ann (ALBEE) 122
Mary Ann (SMITH) 121
Mary C. (HARTSHORN) 194
Mary E. 156, 179, 193
Mary R. 199
Mercy 28
Miranda M. 53

SMITH, Nancy E. (HALL) 124
 Nathan 1
 Nehemiah 39
 Noah 123
 O. S. 217
 Orrin H. 51
 Orville 181
 Peter 113
 R. J. 200
 R. K. 200
 Rebecca (TOMLINSON) 204
 Robert (Mrs.) 81
 Ruth 68
 Samuel 131
 Samuel A. 66
 Sarah (POGSON) 113
 Sarah (STOCOUM) 146
 Sarah L. 131
 Sidney 100
 Sumner 47
 Truman 32
 W. A. 66, 158, 159, 161, 164, 165, 166, 190
 Waldo B. 167
 William 197
SMITHERS, Ann 200
SMITSER, John 64
SMITZER, John 115
 Mary (HATCH) 115
SNASHALL, Jebez 169
 Julia H. (SHAPLEY) 169
SNELL, Alice E. 195
 DeEtte O. (PARTRIDGE) 153
 Herman 153
SNIDER, Sarah J. 184
SNOW, Clara L. 162
 Flora A. (RISLEY) 156
 Melville 156
 R. V. W. 44
SNYDER, B. D. 213
 B. DeForest 213
 Samuel 91
SOLES, Carrie (GATES) 81
 Elmer 81
SOPER, George F. 205
SOULE, --- (Rev. Mr.) 136
 C. W. 187
 Emma (STONE) 187
 Frankie 165
SOUTHWORTH, Joel 93

SOUTHWORTH, Lena 71
SPAULDING, G. 207
 Wealthy A. 219
SPEAR, --- (Dr.) 169
 Frank 173
 John W. 169
 Mary 171
 P. B. 126, 128, 171, 173, 185
 Sarah (RAMPTON) 169
 Sarah S. (KENYON) 173
SPEISS, Jacob 96
 Julia A. 96
SPENCER, Addie Julia 25
 Adella F. 174
 David 210
 Dorr P. 207
 Estella M. (POPLETON) 207
 F. A. 216
 Israel S. 6
 Louisa 166
 Lucemia M. 138
 Mary E. 204
 Mary Jane (ROBERTS) 6
 Nellie P. 189
 Noah 166
 Sarah E. 25
 Theodore L. 25
 W. H. 216
SPENCER-COMSTOCK, Homer 204
 Mary E. (SPENCER) 204
SPERRY, Bert 112
 Burt P. 203
 Martha C. (JOHNSON) 203
SPOONER, Antionett (YORK) 140
 Bill 140
 Nancy E. 195
 Nelson 52
 Prince 12
SPRAGUE, Aneglina E. 146
 E. J. 209
 Hannah B. 124
 Mary E. 146
 Olivia F. (SIMMONS) 209
SPRAKER, David 193
 Fannie 193
SPRIGGS, Caroline 216
 John 216

SPURR, Huldah A. 34
SQUIER, Mary Chaney 11
  Socrates W. 11
SQUIRE, Hattie M. 185
SQUIRES, Ada L. (BENEDICT) 199
  Adelbert 106
  Annette 30
  C. S. 141
  David 22, 55
  E. D. 199
  Elizabeth J. (BENTON) 141
  Eva 185
  Harriet 95
  Hattie 184
  Henry 14
  Herlbert 30
  Joseph 126, 127
  Mary 118, 215
  Mary P. 22
  Melissa E. 22
  N. M. (PEEBLES) 140
  N. P. 140, 185
  Patty (IDE) 126, 127
  Rhoda 55
  William 30
STABBINS, Rosetta H. 195
STACEY, Nathaniel 114
STACKPOLE, H. 206
  H. S. 201
  S. H. 111, 205
  Stephen Henry 94
STACY, --- (Mr.) 112
  --- (Rev.) 116, 119
  Nathaniel 118
STAFFORD, Elizabeth (PRESTON) 94
  Joab 94
  Sarah L. 129
  Truman 3
STANBRO, Duane 104
  Etta C. (PALMITER) 178
  J. H. 164
  Maude E. (POPPLETON) 213
  William 104, 178
  William, Jr. 213
STANDISH, Amanda P. 143
STANFORD, Richard L. 21
  Sarah E. 21

STANLEY, Cornelia E. (OSGOOD) 127
  Fanny 11
  M. H. 127
STANTON, Hattie 162
  Nathaniel 122
  Peleg 72
  Samantha (TRACY) 122
  W. E. 157
STAPLES, Fidelia A. 213
  W. W. 193
STAPLETON, Etta (CLARK) 209
  Mary M. (SKINNER) 162
  Thomas 162
  Will 209
STARK, Mary A. 204
  Tryphena 177
STARKWEATHER, Ellen E. 184
STARR, Betsey 47
STEARNS, Carrie O. 67
  E. P. 81
  T. O. 81
  Willie L. 81
STEBBINS, Anna S. 209
  Cordelia (RINGLEKA) 158
  Delos 192
  Elisha W. 158
  Eunice L. 127, 154
  Hannah 117
  Ida M. (LEACH) 192
  Thomas Jefferson Simon Bolivar 12
STEDMAN, Albert Burdette 18
  Elisha 18
  Eliza (WING) 114
  Harriet 18
  Wells 114
STEELE, George H. 65
STEERE, Esek 14, 33
  Julia Ann (SMITH) 136
  Mary 33
  Samuel 136
STEINBERG, Helen 158
STERNBERG, Viola (DIABEL) 158
  William 158
STERNBERGH, Catharine 16

STETSON, Lucretia (TENNY) 115
  Orrin 115
STEVENS, --- (Mr.) 159
  A. M. 208
  Abigail 83
  Aliza M. 159
  Chauncey 21, 130
  Chester A. 132
  Cordelia (MARICLE) 143
  Eliza 114
  Eliza S. (DOUBLEDAY) 21, 130
  Ida S. 195
  Jane A. (JOHNSON) 132
  Judson T. 98
  Lester 143
  M. 176
  Mary A. (CARTER) 176
  Newton R. 98
  William 74
STEVENSON, Mary E. 173
  T. A. 209
STEWART, Adelia 41
  Almon 29
  Dora C. 163
  Elizabeth (OMANS) 129
  Frank 41
  Henry A. 165
  Honora (HANSEN) 196
  Lizzie 41
  Lyda A. 194
  Marvin 196
  Mary 82
  Moses 129
  N. Jennie 150
  O. Anna 26
  Sarah A. (NYE) 165
  Susan 43
  Thomas 15
STICKER, A. M. 96
STICKLAND, W. P. S. 203
STICKNEY, Harriet 175
  Washington 175
STIFLER, J. M. 187, 189, 190, 191, 192, 193, 194, 195
  James M. 191
STILES, Albert 34
  Lamon H. 218

STILES, Mary 163
  Sarah 34
  Whitford 34
STILLMAN, Amarilla 16
  Cornelia Adelaide 16
  F. W. 16, 146
  Libbie (CHESBRO) 212
  Mary A. 146
  Mattie A. 210
  Sarah P. 155
  William E. 212
STOCKING, --- (Rev. Mr.) 137
  Chauncey 112
  Harriet (PRATT) 112
  Louisa 134
STOCOUM, Sarah 146
STODDARD, C. (FARRINGTON) 202
  E. G. 202
  Elizabeth A. 143
  Emily C. (SMITH) 134
  Frank 109
  Thomas O. 143
  W. B. 134
STONE, A. C. 145
  A. E. 173
  Abigail (WEATHERLY) 115
  Belle 214
  David 68
  DeWitt 204
  Emma 187
  Frankie (CARPENTER) 204
  George H. 59, 220
  John 5
  Marcena 136
  Mary 153
  Mary A. (BABCOCK) 173
  May 211
  Samuel F. 24
  Thomas 115
STORES, Adella 170
STORRS, C. E. 195
  E. P. 182
  Edwin 56
  Joie (HENRY) 182
  Mary Ann 133
STOW, --- (Rev. Mr.) 174
STOWE, Lizzie 197
STOWEL, Nancy 126

STOWELL, Daniel 55
  Daniel T. 106
  Enoch 65
  Francena A. 198
  Hannah 65
  Harriet N. 97
  Lucina (FISHER) 140
  Nancy 127
  William 140
STOWER, Amelia (KELLOGG) 115
  Batharick 57
  Dennis P. 22
  Harriet 2
  John G. 2, 113, 115
  Martha M. 22
STRADLING, Agnes 86
  David Stewart 80
  Ellen (THOMPSON) 159
  Mehala 68
  O. H. 80, 86
  Sanford J. 86
  Thomas 159
STRAUBE, Mary E. 191
  Nellie 187
STREETER, Josephine A. 192
  S. W. 217
STREVER, Frank 172
STREW, Almira G. 130
STRINGER, John 135
  Rachel (TUKE) 135
  William H. 96
STUART, Hugh 55
  J. A. P. 73
  M. 104
  O. Anna 219
STURTEVANT, Abigail 58
  Artimecia 38
  Frances M. 138
  James F. 19
  James W. 19
  Oran 38
  Sarah 19
SULLIVAN, --- 4
SUMNER, Emma M. 164
  Fidella Valmette 42
  Harriet Ann (ROBINSON) 129
  John B. 129
  William O. 42

SUTTON, Cordelia A. 163
  Frances A. (SIMONS) 169
  Nelson 169
SWAN, Charlotte A. 13
  J. S. 119
  Lyman 13, 80, 92
  Malinda A. 80
  Malissa 13
  W. L. 214
SWANCOTT, Mary 96
  Philip 96
  Samuel 96
SWART, Isaac 130
SWEATMAN, Francis A. 194
  Mary A. (KEATING) 194
SWEET, Jonathan 44
  Lyman 14
  Susan 44
  Tryphosa 39
SWIFT, A. B. 72
  A. S. 179
  Annie L. 179
  Celia G. (HUNT) 164
  Charles L. 71
  David 164
  Lansing 55
  M. H. 190
  Mary 157, 179
  Mary A. 76
  Nellie 184
TABER, David P. 193
  Fannie L. 176
  Lillie (TOOGOOD) 193
  Loyal 156
  Mary E. (SMITH) 156
TABOR, Fanny 147
  George 90
TACKABERRY, Almeda C. 142
  Middleton 71
  Sarah Jane 129
TAFT, Clara S. 191
TAGGART, Lydia Florilla (POOL) 131
  William L. 131
TAINTER, Ann 37
TAINTOR, Amelia B. 150
  Joseph 150
  O. 150, 161, 163
TALCOTT, Alice 167
  Arthur C. 206

TALCOTT, Ella M. 204
 Maggie (FENTON) 206
 Nellie M. (BROWN) 191
 Samuel 59
 Sarah K. 82
 Warren J. 93, 191
 William 167
TALLET, Jennie 190
TALMAN, Anna (CLARK) 201
 Chauncey E. 201
TANNER, Anna (WOOD) 200
 Charles R. 200
TAYLOR, --- (Dr.) 165
 --- (Mrs.) 108
 --- (Prof.) 108
 --- (Rev. Dr.) 167
 Alfred 65, 176
 Alfred (Mrs.) 77
 Alice (CHERITRE) 196
 Almira R. 153
 Anna 96
 Anna M. 72
 Charles 58
 Charlotte E. (DAVIS) 121
 Corydon 59
 Darius 91
 E. D. 136
 E. E. L. 121
 Eliza A. 65
 Frank 102
 George W. 131
 Helen T. (SMITH) 171
 Helena A. 100
 Henry 42
 Huldah 91
 James H. 121
 James M. 174
 L. W. 196
 Leta (CONE) 210
 Lewie J. 96
 Lizzie H. 65
 Lois J. 149
 Marshall W. 210
 Mary 72
 Mary (PADDOCK) 174
 Mary E. 73
 Mary J. 42
 Minnie S. 86
 N. (Mrs.) 80
 Nancy R. 195

TAYLOR, Nelson 42, 72
 O. B. 172
 O. D. 195
 Phebe M. (SAUNDERS) 131
 Sarah A. (KEYES) 173
 Theodore F. 171
 W. C. 207
TAYNTOR, --- (Rev. Mr.)
 173
 Bell E. 173
 Emma W. 23
 Joseph 52, 168
 Minerva (POST) 168
 O. 164, 179
 O. Ads 23
TEEPLE, Emma B. 178
TEESDALE, Anna C. (BELL)
 212
 John F. 212
TEFFT, Charles A. 210
 Mattie A. (STILLMAN) 210
TELFER, John 213
 Mary C. (MOTT) 213
TELLER, D. W. 213
TEMPLE, Almon 28
 Lovina 141
 Solomon 90
TENNANT, Philena 142
TENNY, Lucretia 115
TERHUNE, Edith M.
 (SEYMOUR) 161
 Frederick W. 161
TERRETT, --- (Rev. Mr.)
 203
TERREY, Helen A. 49
 John C. 48
 Norman W. 49
TERRY, B. S. 111
 Benjamin S. 98
 Betsey 115
 C. 154
 Charles G. 20
 Isaac 85
 Leonard 20
TERWILLIGER, Malvina 131
TEW, Nellie 207
THACHER, W. 134
THATCHER, --- (Rev. Mr.)
 133, 146
 C. O. 209, 211, 212

THATCHER, W. 132, 133
  Washington 130
THAYER, Catharine 17
  Lura 202
THOMAS, Ann Janette 20
  Anna (DAVIS) 211
  Anthony 55
  Carrie A. (COMSTOCK) 204
  Elisha L. 19
  Elizabeth A. 143
  Ella E. 58
  George D. 204
  Henry 211
  James R. 204
  Nellie (STRAUBE) 187
  Samuel 19, 20
  Samuel K. 75
  Sarah 19, 20
THOMPKINS, Elizabeth P. 146
  John 146
THOMPSON, Alvira B. 164
  Arnold 67
  Benjamin L. 207
  Betsey 136
  Calvin 36
  Charles P. 42
  Cornelia A. (EDGARTON) 148
  Cyrus 82, 141
  E. J. 210
  E. Whitford 192
  Elihu 71
  Elijah 170
  Ella C. (REYNOLDS) 175
  Ellen 159
  Emily 80, 141
  Emma A. 162
  Fannie 164
  George 140
  Gertrude (LAMB) 192
  H. Geraldine (COOK) 139
  H. S. 170
  Helen A. (DUNHAM) 170
  Helen M. 67
  Henry C. 139
  Horace 144
  John 70
  Katie A. 187
  Lizzie G. 191

THOMPSON, Lucinda 72
  M. A. 183
  Mary (CLARK) 140
  Mary E. 170, 207
  Matilda 144
  Nina 83
  Peter M. S. 90
  Phebe 85
  R. J. 207, 213
  Ralph E. 175
  Rose D. 206
  Roswell 148
  Roswell P. 17
  Sally 70
  Samuel 11
  Sarah A. 180
  Theron 148
THORNE, Charles E. 160
  Ella M. (MASON) 160
THROOP, Alida M. 195
  C. D. 57
  Calphurnia (DUNBAR) 65
  Erastus 129
  Fanny L. 95
  Lucius D. 57
  Mary Ann (NYE) 129
  Mary M. 68, 180
  Sarah 95
  Sterry S. 95
  W. H. 57, 68
  William 65
  William H. 83
THURSTON, Elizabeth 52, 75
  Emma A. (BAKER) 178
  Emma L. 75
  Harriet M. 145
  Jonathan 22
  Thomas 75
  William C. 178
TIBBETS, --- (Mrs.) 52
  A. M. 52, 108
  Austin 77
  Daniel R. 52
TIBBETTS, Emora A. 201
  Emory 84, 110
  Fannie E. 179
  Julia A. (SHELTON) 201
  Leonard O. 63
TIBBITTS, A. M. 63
  Austin M. 157

TIBBITTS, Linn R. 63
  Matilda L. (GORHAM) 157
TICHENOR, Amos 193
TIDD, Ebenezer G. 45
  Elbridge G. 53
  Mary Y. 190
TIFFANY, J. R. 181
TILLINGHAST, --- (Mrs.) 16
  A. P. 102
  Bradley 16
  Jefferson 69
  John 97
  Julia 16
  Lizzie F. 220
  Mary Jane 97
  O. H. 220
TILLOTSON, Albert 97
  Frances 97
  Willie 97
TIMBERLAKE, J. 147
  Margaret 147
TINLOW, --- (Rev. Mr.) 134
TISDALE, Jennie M. 210
  W. 210
  W. L. 213
TITCHENER, Ann 58
  Libbie M. 66
TITCHNER, Amos 58
  Charles J. 58
TITUS, Jane 145
  Tryphenia 33
  W. S. 169, 170, 171, 172
TOBY, Betsey (THOMPSON) 136
  Elizabeth 136
  John 136
  Tabour 136
TODD, E. 151
  J. H. 207
  J. M. 151, 174, 186, 211, 213
  O. M. 194
TOMLINSON, Alice 96
  Ella C. 191
  Rebecca 204
TOMPKINS, Cynthia F. 149
  Cynthia F. (TOMPKINS) 149
  Eliza M. (COLEMAN) 205
  Ella J. 185
  Eunice B. 198

TOMPKINS, F. N. 195
  Frank 82
  Gilbert 123
  Hannah (SIMMONS) 129
  Harriet Eva (VAN HOUSEN) 177
  Harriet S. 60
  Herman W. 149
  Howard H. 205
  Iantha 56
  James 21
  Julia (MANCHESTER) 123
  Lucinda 187
  Lucy 29, 123
  Lucy B. 159
  Mary 11
  Melissa 58
  Minnie A. (MYRICK) 195
  Myron 105, 177
  Phebe 116
  Phillip 149
  Sidney 60, 159, 187, 198
  Sidney (Mrs.) 88
  W. R. 185
  William H. 129
TOOGOOD, Lillie 193
TOOKE, Clarence 76
  Emma M. (KELLOWAY) 203
  Emmett 111
  Emmett A. 203
  Michael 76
  Nathan 110
  Sarah A. 141
  Sedate 76
  W. F. 203
TOOKER, Jennie M. 203
TOPLIFF, Adeline M. 35
  E. C. 35
TORREY, Clara A. (DUNBAR) 140
  Dura 88
  Eliza A. 59
  H. R. 59
  Hattie 92
  Hattie A. 148
  Helen (BROOKS) 162
  John C. 140
  Lucy Ann 130
  Mary (SMITH) 181
  Mary J. 83

TORREY, N. W. 83
  Norman W. 162, 181
  Olive 50
  Orra S. 141
TORRY, --- (Widow) 119
  D. 113
  Lyman 1
  Sally (NICHOLS) 113
TOUSLEY, Dora (GREEN) 197
  Ellen M. (TUKE) 140
  Jesse 197
  W. E. 140
TOUSSAINT, Jane Elizabeth
  (COSTELLO) 173
  Peter 173
TOWER, N. H. 184
  Phoebe T. (HITCHCOCK) 184
TOWLE, --- (Mrs.) 108
  --- (Prof.) 108
  F. W. 106
TOWN, Rosina 131
TOWNE, Celestia A.
  (CALKINS) 122
  Joseph 122
TOWNSEND, --- (Rev. Mr.)
  173
  Dwight 76
  Mary G. 211
  Sarah 71
  T. R. 46
TOWNSLEY, Delia A. 150
TRACY, Andrew S. 213
  Ebenezer S. 118
  Eliza (MEAD) 118
  Ella S. 206
  Ephraim 218
  Harriet 218
  John 31, 72
  Mary 72
  Matilda N. 83
  Nora A. (PALMITER) 213
  Samantha 122
  Sibill 218
TRAVER, H. R. 167
  Mary E. (RHODES) 167
TRAVIS, G. J. 184, 187
  J. G. 193
TREADWAY, Ezekiel 13
TREMAIN, H. 126, 128
TRESCOTT, Annie L. 183

TRIPP, Alna B. 188
  Mary B. 143
TROWBRIDGE, George 142
  Julia Allin 142
TRUESDELL, Joseph 4
  Perly 4
TRUMAN, Ira 166
  Julia (BROWN) 166
TUBBS, A. 200
  Geneva M. (BROWN) 200
TUCKER, --- (Rev. Mr.) 140
  Adoniram J. 164
  Alvira B. (THOMPSON) 164
  Appleton 91
  Cora (KELLEY) 202
  Corydon 22
  Eber 115
  Ephraim S. 141
  Eunice (HUBBARD) 141
  Hattie 202
  Hiram H. 54, 192
  Jane E. (CRUMB) 192
  John 131
  Luzon 76
  Lydia (KNAPP) 131
  Martha (COX) 115
  Samuel 202
TUCKERMAN, Delia
  (BLACKMAN) 116
  Jacob 36, 116
TUE, --- (Mrs.) 42
  John 42
TUKE, --- (Rev. Mr.) 135
  Ellen M. 140
  M. M. 133
  Rachel 135
TURNER, Albert N. 160
  Allen 92
  Amanda 43
  Amanda (WHEELER) 115
  Benjamin 52
  Catharine A. (HAVENS) 130
  Delia A. (PARSONS) 160
  H. 43
  Howland 115
  James W. 166
  Martin 8, 9
  Mary 118
  Mary Ellen (NICHOLS) 166
  R. B. 130

TURPIN, Mary M. 175
TURTON, Hannah V. 119
  Joseph 119
TUTTLE, Alice R. 197
  Cynthia M. 168
  Dorleska 163
  E. 137
  E. A. 207
  Emma C. 81
  Julius 49
  O. E. 109
  Rhoda Ann 133
  Samuel 53
TWING, A. T. 150
TWIST, Delia Ann (WILBER) 148
  Delos 148
TYLER, --- (Rev. Dr.) 167, 168, 169, 170
  C. R. 38
  Celinda 55
  D. 112
  Frank D. 74
  George 144, 190
  Mary A. (WOOD) 144
  Noah 49, 52
  Sarah 49
  Thomas P. 162
TYNELL, Hattie E. 208
TYRON, Isaac C. 143
  Julia A. (CHILCOTT) 143
UNDERHILL, C. W. 77, 189
  Charles W. 173
  Helen 191
  Louise S. 80
  Mary E. (ROOT) 173
UPHAM, A. S. 6
  Ebenezer P. 7
  Elizabeth A. 44
  Elizabeth C. 6
  Harriet E. 169
  Joshua 22
  Joshua Chamberlain 6
  Rhodie (FISHER) 142
  Robert P. 142
UPHOLD, --- (Rev.) 118
UPSTON, Betsey Ann 133
UPTON, A. G. 208
USHER, --- (Mr.) 114
  Ida M. 177

USHER, William 52
UTTER, Claude W. 43
  Electa 43
  Lettie I. (CARD) 162
  Lydia 116
  Lydia B. 212
  S. S. 160, 171
  William C. 43, 162
VALE, Harry 2
  Melissa 2
VAN AMAN, Carrie E. 209
VAN CLEFT, A. 212
VAN DEUSEN, Ellen M. 156
VAN DOZEN, --- (Mr.) 47
VAN DUSEN, Annie M. 166
  Jennie 193
VAN DYKE, William 99
VAN EPS, Electa (HARRIS) 114
  Everitt 114
VAN FRADENBURGH, Edward 159
  Sarah J. (EDDY) 159
VAN HOESEN, Ella 36
VAN HORN, Lorenzo 92
  Sedanna 92
VAN HOSEN, John J. 78
VAN HOUSEN, Charle B. 111
  Charles 206
  Harriet Eva 177
  Louisa (YORKER) 206
VAN NORMEN, George 84
VAN SCOTT, R. W. 176
VAN SICE, Anna Maria 4
  Harriet 2
  J. P. 215
  John P. 4, 8
VAN SLYCK, Abi 78
  Abi (Mrs.) 78
  Clara 64
  DeWitt C. 64, 89
  E. D. 185
  Eleanor 64
  Emanuel 79
  Philip 34
VAN SLYKE, E. D. 100
VAN VALKENBURGH, Sarah A. 90
VAN VLECK, Carter 31
  Marsia L. 13

VAN VLECK, V. H. 13, 31
VAN WINKLE, John L. 18
VANDERPOOL, Allen 161, 192
  Cynthia M. (BOOTH) 161
  Nettie E. (NICHOLS) 192
VANESS, Charles 218
  Harriet (BARBER) 218
VAUGHAN, C. Egbert 182
  Emma J. (RICE) 182
VEDDER, Harriet E.
  (DAGGETT) 171
  Riley J. 171
VICKERY, Emily (THOMPSON)
  141
  John 141
VINING, --- (Elder) 214
VISSEL, Jennie C.
  (SHELDON) 208
  Theodore T. 208
VOGELL, H. C. 131
VOSBURG, Frank 183
  Matti E. (DYE) 183
WADDELL, Elizabeth 140
WADE, Deborah (LAPHAM) 113
  Jonathan 113
WADSWORTH, --- (Rev. Mr.)
  145, 157
  H. A. 201
  Nettie 201
WAGER, A. 26
  Maria 26
WAGNER, Annie C. 194
  Flora P. (AVERY) 209
  Herbert A. 209
  Levi P. 56
WAGONER, J. H. 104
WAIT, Augusta S. 183
  Charles B. 180
  George 78
  John 134
  M. C. 60
  M. Lavel 78
  Mary K. (FOOTE) 134
  Minnie 78
  Nellie (ORR) 180
  S. 183
WAITE, Emma L. 213
  George M. 194
  H. 211
  Hiram N. 102

WAITE, M. C. 213
  Minnie M. (DAHM) 194
WAKELEE, Josephine E. 149
WAKELEY, Sarah 160
WALDEN, Lucina 141
  Mary Jane 142
  Philo 142
WALDO, Delia 180
WALDRON, Carrie 30
  DeAlton 19
  Florence A. (BURNS) 212
  G. R. 19, 30, 188
  George W. 212
  Hattie 164
  Ida Belle 188
  Mary E. 19
WALES, Gussie A. 179
  M. D. V. 190
WALKER, Almira 12
  Almira (SMITH) 118
  Alvan 114
  Charles 18, 74
  Ervin E. 190
  Ferdinand 12, 118
  Frances Melvina 12
  G. C. 139
  Jennie (DE LONG) 190
  Jennie E. 187
  Lucy (GRAY) 114
  Mary C. 18
  Nellie A. 164
WALL, Sophie A. 210
  Zella E. 210
WALLACE, Lizzie (ROWLANDS)
  81
  Lizzie A. (ROWLANDS) 189
  Margaret M. 51
  Robert 81, 189
  William 51
WALRATH, --- (Rev. Mr.)
  203
  A. J. 205
  A. S. 208
  Beatrice K. 212
  Franklin W. 91
  Mary K. 139
WALTER, Allie (CHESEBRO)
  213
  William N. 213
WALTON, Frederick 26

WALWORTH, --- (Rev. Mr.) 202
A. J. 197
WAMPLE, Nellie A. 178
WANZER, Frances T. Lewis (BROWN) 165
George G. 165
WARD, Ann Elizabeth 23
Diana 76
Edger Pope 23
Jane S. (HADNETT) 148
John 147
John C. 18, 148
Lottie A. (COOK) 164
Lucy A. 18
Mary (CHURCH) 23
Mary Emma 23
Runyon R. 23
S. R. 216
Waulstean P. 164
WARING, Harriet M. 145
Solomon 145
WARNER, --- (Elder) 120
Addie M. 178
Allie 209
Charles W. 163
Cordelia A. (SUTTON) 163
Edgar L. 32
Elijah 47
Ella L. (FELT) 102, 176
Emeline J. 171
Emma A. (THOMPSON) 162
Hiram S. 162
Ira F. 102
Irwin 102
John 42
Katie F. (CLUTE) 207
Martha M. 172
Mary E. 166
Matilda 47
R. A. 173
S. J. 102
S. Judson 176
Samuel E. 57
Stephen H. 67
William 207
WARREN, --- (Gen.) 4
--- (Rev.) 133
Jared 14
Mary Caroline 78

WARREN, Sarah C. 14
William F. 49, 78
WARRINER, Catherine 181
E. J. 164
WARRINGER, Fannie (THOMPSON) 164
J. H. 123
Jane E. (LIVINGSTON) 123
WASHBURN, Cornelia J. (MURDOCK) 28
Frank 28
Sarah J. (SNIDER) 184
Sophia A. 71
Wright F. 184
WATERHOUSE, Sarah Jane 127
WATERS, Addie E. 153
Charles 34
Charles S. 218
Deette 175
Frank P. 204
Isaphine J. 206
Janette H. (LYON) 218
Mary A. (STARK) 204
Richard 34, 113
WATERSON, Sarah E. 202
WATKINS, Ira 138
Lydia F. 138
WATROUS, Betsey (HAMMOND) 137
Edwin 137
WATSON, Ada (BARDEEN) 191
C. H. 191
Charles H. 192
DeWitt C. 64
Jennie P. 64
Mary Lucina 64
WATTLES, Elizabeth 155
Lemuel 155
WATTS, Mary A. 201
WAY, Delavan B. 157
Louisa 132
Mary E. (PECKHAM) 157
S. P. 125
WEATHERLY, Abigail 115
WEAVER, Caroline Howe 76
Catherine 115
Charles 48
Delos 22
E. H. 129
Elias 73

WEAVER, Elizabeth 48
 Isaac 7
 Jehial 32
 Joshua 48
 Lucy (SHORT) 73
 Lucy A. (SHORT) 129
 Mary L. 121
 Stephen 32
 Zebulon 7, 121
WEBB, Ann Elizabeth (HULL) 123
 Anna E. 14
 Henry L. 14, 123
 Mary Otis 14
WEBBER, Benson H. 19
 Flora V. (WHEELER) 212
 Henry 12
 Mary 12, 14
 Mary Avaline 14
 Roxanny 10
 S. S. 19, 151, 160
 Samuel 10
 Sheppard 14
 Sophina B. 12
 Will T. 212
WEBER, W. 32
WEBSTER, D. E. 74, 107
 Edward D. 187
 Harriet 37
 J. G. 199
 James DeForest 74
 Jennie (WICKWIRE) 74
 Jennie L. (WICKWIRE) 187
WEDGE, Charley O. 210
 Evaleen M. (GROSVENOR) 162
 Fannie O. 71
 Florence D. 177
 Homer B. 172
 J. Eugene 162
 Lyman P. 57
 Marcin H. 131
 Martha M. (WARNER) 172
 Mary 29
 Mary E. (MC DOUGALL) 210
 Mary H. 131
 Merrit 29
 Merrit D. 76
 Orlando A. 161
 Oscar A. 26

WEDGE, Sarah A. (SHARP) 161
 Truman Z. 29
WEED, LaFayette L. 87
WEEDEN, Abigail J. (COE) 164
 Adelbert 186
 Anna M. (LILLIE) 151
 Jerry 151
 Mary M. (JOHNSON) 186
 Philip 164
 Philip D. 65
WEEKS, G. E. 185
 Julia C. (KEITH) 185
WEIR, Nancy 33
WELCH, A. L. 63
 Fred H. 193
 George W. 104
 Henry 3
 Horace 40, 124
 Jane R. (COLLINS) 193
 Jerusha C. (HUNT) 124
 Lucena C. 171
WELDER, Edgar 205
 Hattie (BURGDOFF) 205
WELLINGTON, Achsah 53
 David 103
 Erastus 74
 Mary Jane 142
 Matilda (DANFORTH) 74
WELLMAN, Cammilliad 217
 William 217
WELLS, Addie 147
 Alfred 6
 Clark (Mrs.) 197
 Daniel 30, 76
 Flora M. 168
 Frank L. 88
 Jonathan 42
 Joshua 29
 Joshua A. 197
 M. 208
 Mary 42
 Mary A. 192
 Oscar Eugene 6
 Solomon 89
WELTON, --- (Rev. Mr.) 120, 121
 Ada Fitch 58
 Alex (Mrs.) 27

WELTON, Alonzo 120, 121
  Annie L. (GEORGIA) 192
  Clarinda J. 130
  Edward E. 27, 124
  Emeline (BONNEY) 124
  Emma N. 27
  Henry C. 58, 62, 192
  Isaac 130
  J. E. 168
  Mary A. (JONES) 168
  Sarah (FITCH) 62
  Sarah A. 52
  Sarah C. 58
  Willard 38
WENTWORTH, Chester 154
  James 163
  Sarah C. 174
  Sarah M. (OWEN) 154
  William 111
WERNER, Brettie 102
WESCOTT, Norman 94
WEST, A. H. 50
  Addison (Mrs.) 76
  Addison J. 59
  Alice (GARY) 200
  Alonzo H. 36
  Electa 113
  Eliza 59
  Emily 99
  George W. 70
  Helen 123
  Helen F. 36
  Lena B. 59
  Mary F. 36
  Nathaniel 47, 99
  Olivia 89
  William M. 200
  William W. 50
WESTCOTT, Carrie A. 209
  Cora 200
  Edgar 199
  Ezekiel 52
  Georgie (HALL) 199
  Hiram 76
  Phebe 24
  Polly 144
  Rebecca 55
  S. N. 150, 164, 166, 167
WESTON, David 62
WHALEN, John 169

WHALEN, Margaret 98
  Mary (JOHNSON) 169
WHAN, Eliza A. 189
WHEAT, Charles H. 70
  Eliza P. 70
  H. 150
WHEATON, Emma (LORD) 176
  Frank 176
WHEDON, D. A. 141, 160
WHEELER, --- (Rev.) 118
  Aaron C. 92, 118
  Amanda 115
  Betsey 119
  E. D. 25
  Elizabeth A. (UPHAM) 44
  Emma G. 190
  Erastus 44, 163
  Erastus D. 27
  Erial C. 45
  Flora V. 212
  Genevieve H. 163
  H. C. 168
  Helen 168
  Henry O. 71
  Hiram 54, 86
  Janette 25
  Jerome 189
  Lewis E. 145
  Libbie C. 151
  Louise M. 206
  Malissa 93
  Mary 163
  Miranda (BEACH) 118
  Rebecca L. 54
  Sarah A. (SHEFFIELD) 145
WHEELOCK, Emma G.
  (WHEELER) 190
  Frank G. 190
  L. J. 210
WHIPPLE, --- (Col.) 151
  Eliza T. 151
  J. 112
WHITCHER, B. W. 135
WHITCOMB, Aurelia R. 126
  Julius 126
  Mary 141
WHITE, --- (Rev. Mr.) 123
  Alexander 218
  Alice (MURPHY) 206
  Almira H. (FOOTE) 127

WHITE, Amelia 105
  Amos K. 8, 122
  Ann (BROWN) 122
  Asa P. 179
  Augusta F. (PAYNE) 185
  Benjamin N. 25
  Bradshaw 90
  Bulah 20
  Carrie D. 207
  Charles A. 15
  David 90
  DeWitt 25
  Eilen J. 150
  Eli 28
  Elijah K. 8
  Eliza 100
  Emille B. 25
  F. J. 174
  F. M. (Mrs.) 174
  Fannie E. (TIBBETTS) 179
  Flavia 15
  George 51, 105, 145
  Harriet W. 143
  Isaac 54
  J. Antle 127
  J. W. 167
  Jacob LeRoy 185
  John 10, 206
  Larny (RATNOUR) 113
  Lucy M. (HILLS) 145
  Maricon C. 25
  Mary (POWELL) 77
  Mary Ann 216
  Noah 216
  P. G. 139, 144, 148
  Perry 138, 139, 140, 141, 143, 147, 154
  Perry G. 136, 137, 143, 154
  Polly (BULLUS) 129
  Samuel 15, 20, 28
  Sophronia E. 18
  Stillman M. 218
  Syrenus 129
  Thomas 77
  Walter 113
  Ward W. 25
WHITEMORE, Flora Lillian 73
  J. S. 73

WHITFORD, Carrie (SAWDY) 202
  Hamilton J. 202
WHITMORE, C. Erastus 161
  Cornelia Smith 69
  Dwight E. 149
  Frances Y. 104
  Francis 7
  Jane M. 54
  Joel 104
  L. Maryette (RANGER) 161
  Lilly F. 191
  M. Josie 54
  Marlitta (NEWTON) 104
  Mary (SAUNDERS) 149
  Maryella 164
  Newton H. 104
  Russell 54, 69
  Sanford 71
WHITNEY, --- (Rev. Mr.) 178
  D. Brainard 157
  Fannie 162
  Frank E. (POOLE) 157
  Isaac 78
  J. H. 197
  M. (Mrs.) 33
  Ruth 78
WHITON, Sybil Smith (RICHARDS) 146
  Wilson 146
WHITTEMORE, J. T. 146
  Jennie 183
  Mary A. (STILLMAN) 146
WHITTMORE, H. 136
  Mary Jane (CALKINS) 136
WICKWIRE, --- 46
  Abigail C. (SHAPLEY) 140
  Burr 46
  C. A. 200
  C. M. 110
  Charles 105, 201
  Frances K. (CUSHMAN) 168
  Frank 67
  Frank G. 104
  Frank S. 177
  George 131
  Hannah W. (HITCHCOCK) 131
  Hattie Evelyn 186
  J. 8

WICKWIRE, James 30, 75, 133
  Jarit 19
  Jennie 74
  Jennie L. 187
  Laura A. (SHELDON) 120
  Lewis 44, 120, 140
  Louise (PARKER) 201
  M. Matilda 179
  Mary 8
  Mary A. 171
  Mary E. 67
  Mary E. (SANFORD) 177
  Mary M. 19
  Mattie S. (WRIGHT) 202
  N. R. 105
  Newton 79
  Newton E. 165
  Newton R. 67, 202
  O. C. 168
  Phebe 79, 105
  Phebe A. (PECKHAM) 165
  Phoebe 67
  Rachel (ALDRICH) 133
  Rena 67
  Ruth 12
  Samuel 80
  Viola 162
WIGHT, Harmony 39
WIGHTMAN, A. O. 143
WILBER, Ann Vennette 136
  Benjamin 28, 74
  Delia Ann 148
  H. C. 133
  Malinda 28
  Marcia (COLE) 133
  Sarah A. 125
  Sarah M. 28
WILBUR, Ada 206
  Byron 65
  Eliza 40
  George 169
  Georgie 65
  Janette C. 90
  Jeremiah 90
  Laura T. 198
  Margaret 59
  Mary 162
  Nettie E. 173
  Sarah Ann 139

WILCOCKSON, Albert 178
  Nellie A. 178
WILCOX, A. 123
  A. J. 54, 108
  Abby 35
  Abigail 28
  Alfred M. 84
  Amey E. 54
  Asa J. 173
  C. 154
  Champlin 49, 84
  Charle 43
  Chloe 134
  Clark D. 107
  Corda Violet 35
  Elizabeth 94
  Ella A. 174
  Ellen 46
  Freddie H. 28
  G. I. 110
  George 31
  Gertie C. 46
  Gillette I. 203
  H. S. 141
  H. T. 139
  Helen M. 139
  Helen M. (WILCOX) 139
  Hiram T. 46
  Huldah 123
  Lavina (ELSBRE) 141
  Louisa 104
  Mamie E. (GREENE) 203
  Marvin W. 200
  Mary 157
  Mary A. 156
  Mary F. 175
  Mary H. (CORSSMAN) 200
  Mary J. 43, 68, 171
  Nelson 28, 35
  O. B. 150
  O. E. 33
  Oliver 87
  Phebe 54
  Phebe (LAMPHERE) 173
  Randall 154
  S. 197
  S. E. 197
  Sanford 14
  Sarah (BAKER) 197

WILCOX, Sarah L. (BURGESS) 33, 150
  Slymena 87
  Sophia 92
  Thomas 21
  William 92
WILCOXSON, Mary E. 177
WILD, Melvin 97
  Melvin F. 97
WILDRON, Frankie 49
  George G. 49
  Minnie A. 49
WILES, Adam F. 35
  Henry 35
  Julia A. 35
WILEY, Lauraine F. (NASH) 156
WILIS, Sophronia 146
WILKINS, Lewis M. 125
  Sarah M. (DELANCEY) 125
WILKINSON, Agnes M. 187
  Eva 207
  J. E. 111, 205
WILLARD, Anna Louise 167
  Clarissa (MILLER) 127
  Frances A. 210
  George P. 167
  Hannah 127, 154
  Joshua 38
  K. J. 210
  Laura 37
  Morris W. 79
  Sarah 30
  Susan 12
  W. W. 38
  William F. 127
WILLCOX, Abigail 19
  Clara E. 19
  Emily 141
  Nelson 19
WILLEY, Edward 45
  George A. 156
  Gilman D. 148
  Hattie (STANTON) 162
  Hattie A. (TORREY) 148
  Sereno 162
WILLIAMS, --- (Rev. Mr.) 199
  Albon C. 82
  Anna 75

WILLIAMS, Anna B. 82
  Anna Maria 142
  Arisstarchus 75
  Betty 75
  Charlotte (PEARL) 167
  D. 145, 161
  Deette 172
  Delight 118
  Delos H. 211
  Dwight 145, 146, 181, 184, 201
  Elizabeth (COTTRELL) 142
  Ella L. 188
  Elsie A. (HATCH) 211
  Erastus F. 135
  Ezra T. 151
  F. G. 26
  Fred H. 82
  George 109, 114, 167
  George A. 6
  George H. 138
  Humphrey 103
  James 5
  John A. 88
  John J. 220
  Julia (BARBER) 138
  Keziah (LANE) 146
  Liza (EGBERT) 173
  Lizzie 43
  Lois A. P. 100
  M. B. 132
  Mahlon J. 82
  Mamoris 46
  Martha 103
  Mary (RUSSELL) 135
  Mary I. 82
  Mary L. (OWEN) 132
  Morris 95
  Nancy 12, 124
  Nettie 201
  O. S. 76
  Richard R. 193
  Samuel R. 142
  Sarah (BYER) 114
  Sophronia A. 210
  Susan 117
  Susan E. (BOLAND) 195
  Thomas 173
  W. H. 195
  W. W. 204

WILLIAMS, William 209
WILLIAMSON, Addie M.
  (WARNER) 178
  Henry M. 178
  Herbert 161
  Loretta 161
  Mary A. 165
  Nannie D. (LOOMIS) 212
  Robert 212
  Sarah 157
  Thomas 157
WILLIS, Elisha G. 5
  Morris W. 10
  Riley 10
WILLOUGHBY, Ira 113
  Minerva (COLSON) 113
WILSE, A. M. 119
WILSON, --- (Mr.) 118
  --- (Rev. Dr.) 154
  A. E. 191
  Chauncey 16
  Cordelia (ENOS) 118
  J. J. W. 195
  J. W. 194, 196
  Julia Ann 16
  Libbie M. (SMITH) 213
  M. V. 150
  Marverick C. 16
  Thomas 195, 206
  Winfield S. 213
WINCHELL, Reuben 1
WINCHESTER, Mary A. 179
WING, Anna H. (MORGAN) 208
  Eliza 114
  Fred E. 208
WINKOOP, --- (Rev. Mr.)
  124
WINN, --- (Mrs.) 53
WINNIE, E. P. 209
  F. P. 208
WINSTON, Lucy M. 69
  Meriwether 69
WINTER, Florence Ella 88
  Frank W. 195
  Ida B. (RISLEY) 195
  Mary E. 88
  Merritt 88
WINTERS, James 214
  Martha (MAC MURRAY) 214
WIRES, Gilbert B. 156

WIRES, Louisa (CARPENTER)
  156
WITHAM, Harriet F. 126
  Harriet P. 128
WITTER, Sarah J. 207
WOLF, Daniel D. 114
WOOD, A. M. 144
  A. N. 165
  Alice 212
  Allan N. 123
  Allen 1
  Anna 200
  Arthur 204
  Bell E. (TAYNTOR) 173
  C. Olivia 165
  Calista M. (EATON) 123
  Charles T. 85
  Cora E. 198
  Danforth 102
  Elizabeth H. 102
  Erastus H. 190
  Henry 78
  Jennie Rose (MANCHESTER)
  204
  John 201
  Leroy 173
  M. H. 190
  Mary A. 144, 201
  N. B. 98
  Samuel 204
  Sarah F. (BELL) 204
  Stephen 144
WOODARD, F. A. 194
  Jedediah 12
  Jessie 190
  John 61
  Susannah (POPE) 12
WOODHEAD, Godfrey 175
  Mary M. (TURPIN) 175
WOODHULL, Anna
  (BUTTERFIELD) 199
  Dell 199
WOODMAN, Ada (LAMB) 207
  Alice 80
  Alice (LEACH) 198
  Amelia J. 13
  Anna 49
  Annie B. 159
  Brownell 49
  Catherine (RUSSELL) 137

WOODMAN, Charles 80
  Charles S. 198, 203
  E. B. 44
  Eliza C. 151
  Elizabeth M. 196
  Elsie S. 189
  Eveleen (LAMB) 203
  Francena A. (STOWELL) 198
  Franklin 131
  George 151
  George B. 144
  George V. 6
  Harriet 125, 126
  J. M. 109
  J. N. 198
  Jane 13
  Jane (HAMMOND) 131
  Jay 66
  John 6, 13, 79, 137, 173
  Lelia (RICE) 206
  Mary (SIMMONS) 144
  Melissa N. 44
  Merebah 151
  Milton 206
  R. Myra (BYER) 173
  Roxa S. 67
  Ruth H. 44
  W. D. 207
  Z. S. 111
WOODREDGE, Jane Jenette
  (ELWELL) 166
  William 166
WOODRUFF, H. W. 27
  J. D. 186, 187
WOODS, E. Arthur 158
  H. C. 193
  Mary (BLAIR) 158
  Mary H. (EATON) 193
  Mary O. A. 212
  Roxanna E. 50
  Wallace 50
WOODWARD, Jedediah 127,
  132
  N. 182
WOODWORTH, Daniel 91
  John R. 43
  Merwin B. 96
  Polly 43
WOOLEY, --- (Capt.) 123
  E. M. 134

WOOLEY, Mary (PALMER) 123
WOOLLEY, --- (Rev. Mr.)
  122
WOOSTER, Ephraim 100
WORDEN, S. A. 210
WRATTEN, Elizabeth 155
WRENCH, Lydia 169
WRIGHT, --- (Rev.) 127
  A. P. 146
  Calista (SIMMONS) 122
  Hiram 208
  J. T. 130
  John 102
  Julia A. S. (GREEN) 135
  L. 218
  Lucetta 146
  Lucinda (GARDNER) 208
  Lyman 132, 160
  Mary (MANCHESTER) 161
  Mary A. 102
  Mattie S. 202
  Oren 122
  Robert 161
  S. 123
  Thomas G. 135
WYATT, Hannah (GILBERT)
  116
  Tommy 116
WYLIE, Ann (HUNTER) 133
  Beriah W. 133
  Julia (ALLEN) 133
  Lucretia 24
  Thomas 31, 115, 117
  William 133
WYMAN, Levi 100
WYNN, Bryant 33
  Nancy R. 33
  Simeon 61
YALE, R. 166
YAP, Bert 207
  Lizzie (CRANDALL) 207
YARRINGTON, --- (Rev.) 123
YAW, Polly 99
YEOMAN, Louisa 119
YEOMANS, William 16
YOAR, Mary 35
YORK, A. L. 167, 168, 219
  Antionett 140
  Catherine 134
  Elizabeth 73

YORK, Lodowick Clark 132
  Mary Jane (CLARK) 187
  Otis 187
  Sarah 60
YORKER, Louisa 206
YOUMANS, Anna 103
YOUNG, --- (Mrs.) 99
  Abbey Odessa 99
  Deborah 55
  James 93, 180
  Lorance 212
  M. G. 99
  Martha A. 157

YOUNG, Miles (Mrs.) 88
  Miller 55
  Mirton 186
  Nellie (SHEPARDSON) 186
  Nettie J. (ANDERSON) 212
  Nora A. (DEANE) 180
  Ruth A. 27
YOUNGLOVE, Daniel 22
  Frederick 159
  J. Arthur 192
  Lucy (GREY) 159
  Sophia (FULLER) 192

Other Heritage Books by Mary K. Meyer and Joyce C. Scott:
Cemetery Inscriptions of Madison County, New York, Volume 1

Other Heritage Books by Mary K. Meyer:

A Directory of Cayuga County Residents Who Supported Publication of the History of Cayuga County, New York

Abstracts from Madison County, New York Newspapers in the Cazenovia Public Library

Baltimore City Birth Records, 1865-1894

Divorces and Names Changed in Maryland by Act of the Legislature, 1634-1867

Free Blacks in Harford, Somerset and Talbot Counties, Maryland 1832

Meyer's Directory of Genealogical Societies in the U.S.A. and Canada: 1998-2000, 12th Edition
Family of Mary K. Meyer

Westward of Fort Cumberland: Military Lots Set Off for Maryland's Revolutionary Soldiers

Who's Who in Genealogy and Heraldry 1990
Mary K. Meyer and P. William Filby

www.ingramcontent.com/pod-product-compliance
Lightning Source LLC
Chambersburg PA
CBHW060942230426
43665CB00015B/2028